עץ חיים

ETZ HAYIM

Study Companion

עץ חיים

ETZ HAYIM

STUDY COMPANION

Edited by JACOB BLUMENTHAL
and
JANET L. LISS

Foreword by DAVID WOLPE

THE RABBINICAL ASSEMBLY
THE UNITED SYNAGOGUE OF CONSERVATIVE JUDAISM

Produced by THE JEWISH PUBLICATION SOCIETY

The Rabbinical Assembly
3080 Broadway
New York, NY 10027

Composition by VARDA Graphics, Skokie, Illinois

Manufactured in the United States of America

05 06 07 08 09 10 10 9 8 7 6 5 4 3 2 1

CONTENTS

BIBLICAL FOUNDATIONS: LAW

BIBLICAL FOUNDATIONS: SOCIAL AND ETHICAL
RESPONSIBILITIES

BIBLICAL FOUNDATIONS: PRAYER AND RITUAL MITZVOT

THE CHALLENGE TO CONTINUE STUDY

FOREWORD

David Wolpe

For generations Jews regarded the Bible as a book with no history—all its stories were faithful to exactly what transpired, and its messages were those divinely wrapped up in an endlessly intricate tapestry. The brilliant commentary of the classical Rabbis was devoted to unfolding the mysteries and beauties of the text on its own terms.

Many things combined to complicate this picture. The advances of science gave us a deeper understanding of the natural world. New techniques of historical research and literary analysis were developed, casting the Bible's structure in a different light. Scriptural repetitions and contradictions, the different levels of the Hebrew (for Hebrew, like any language, developed over time), and parallels to other stories circulating in the Ancient Near East in biblical times gave us a more advanced understanding of the formation of our central sacred text.

One's reaction to these developments ranges from outrage to keen curiosity. Because if the Bible is (at least in part) a product of historical influences, how much can we learn by studying its history? Why does the book of Deuteronomy use such different rhetoric than the book of Genesis? Why are so many of the early stories in the Bible never mentioned again? How did the societies existing around the time of the ancient Israelites view themselves? And perhaps most intriguing, did God speak in one commanding moment alone, or can God also speak through the unfolding story of our people and our world?

Conservative Judaism might be called the Judaism that believes God's voice can be heard through human history. Conservative Judaism is dialogic Judaism: it understands the relationship between God and Israel as analogous to a friendship that has both a powerful history and a promise of development. The use of the word friendship does not imply equality, but rather the continuing, flourishing nature of the covenant. The dynamism of Judaism is the dynamism of the yet unspoken—all the things that are still to grow in the inexhaustibly rich soil of the past. We are a people balanced between history and prophecy, past and future. Both the ancient sage and the modern seeker have something indispensable to contribute to the dialogue between Israel and God.

We have never been just the Bible's readers; we have also and always been its interpreters. The answers to most questions Jews ask will not only be found in the pages of the Bible; they are also in the elaborations by the classical Rabbis, the medieval sages, and modern scholars. That is why the word "Torah" refers both to the Five Books of Moses and to the entirety of Jewish learning. The Bible has always been understood as the first word spoken—the indispensable "Word"—but never the last word. Building on the achievements of our ancestors we are able to shift the prism of the Bible's beauty to reflect ever new light. The essays in this study guide provide us with some ways to see the Bible anew.

One cannot really understand the Bible just by reading its words once. For all true reading is rereading. Each story yields its depths only upon renewed acquaintance, and each reader will discover how constant meditation on the messages of the Torah enables her or him to come to new understandings and often to find a kinship with the commentators of the past.

Each verse is a reservoir. Don't skim, not unless you intend to go back and read over and over in depth. A man once came to the rabbi and boasted that he had been through the Talmud three times. "My question," responded the rabbi, "is how much of the Talmud has been through you?"

As you read through the essays in this guide, remember that we are searching in our reading of the Bible for our history, to situate our own souls in this world, and to seek God. How does our reading change once we know the Near Eastern background of the text, the way Jewish law has developed from a given verse, or what modern theologians have to teach us? The essays herein will help deepen our study of the text by keeping these questions in our minds.

No matter how imprecise the details may be, the Bible is the family diary of our nation. It is as if, as a Jewish thinker once remarked, you were walking through your great-grandmother's house and found her journal under a creaky floorboard. This is our story—your story.

Our story in the Torah is deliberately incomplete. Although these five books point toward entering the land of Israel, when Deuteronomy ends, we are still in the wilderness. This may be the Torah's way of teaching us that we live in an unredeemed world, a wilderness, and we need community, tradition, a road map, and a guide. The road map is the Torah; the guide is God.

The essays that follow are products of the care, scholarship, and love characteristic of the Conservative movement's approach to Torah. For we believe that through the ancient cadences we can hear the voice that our ancestors knew at Sinai. We understand that some messages will change their emphasis with the ages, and some will remain constant. Israel brought the Torah to the world. The scholars in this guide will help bring it anew to each of us and to those who will follow.

INTRODUCTION

Jacob Blumenthal

The essays here were originally published in *Etz Hayim: Torah and Commentary,* designed for liturgical use in synagogues during worship services. Tucked in the back of the big book, they are often overlooked, since during religious services most people give their full attention to the weekly Torah readings. In this volume these wonderful essays come out of the shadows so that we may read them for all their richness and insights

In its embrace of modern methods of scholarship, the publication of *Etz Hayim* marked an important step in the history of Conservative Judaism. Though central to the intellectual and theological development of Conservative Judaism since its inception in the late 19th century, it took decades until a volume for synagogue use appeared that fully used these methods.

These modern methodologies are exhibited on every page of *Etz Hayim* in the *p'shat* commentary, the "straightforward" explanation of the text that appears immediately below the Hebrew text and English translation. However, they are also used in equally impressive fashion in the essays in that volume, which are republished here. The essays are written by many of Conservative Judaism's most prominent 20th-century scholars. Their work reflects the evolution and maturity of these modern forms of biblical scholarship and their centrality to the Conservative Movement. Such ways of looking at the biblical text stress a systematic historical, contextual, and literary examination of the Bible.

The essays are incredibly rich and full of new ways to read the biblical text, while the summaries and thought/discussion questions that bracket them are meant to guide you in your journey of study and enlightenment. They will help you focus on the structure of each essay, explore each essay's main ideas, investigate some points in greater depth, and ask questions about the implications of the scholarship for your own beliefs and practice.

The Structure of the Book

The essays here are presented in a different order than in *Etz Hayim*. Since this book is meant both for individual and group study, it is arranged with an eye toward a program of learning and is organized into various parts:

- The first unit deals with methods of Bible scholarship. The essay that is central to understanding the material in this book is "Modern Methods of Bible Study;" the essays that precede it describe more traditional forms of interpretation.

- The second unit focuses on the origins of the Bible. It is fascinating to see how the ideas in each essay correlate with the assumptions about study methods described in Unit 1. They will encourage you to think about your own theological ideas about the Bible and its origins and how these ideas can influence your reading of it.

- Units 3 through 6 emphasize the way the Bible remains the foundation of Jewish belief and practice and how rabbinic Judaism has evolved from those roots. As you read, consider how what you believe and do as a Jewish person is rooted in the biblical text and how ancient beliefs and practices have changed and evolved over time.

- The essays in Unit 7 encourage you to think about how we relate to the characters and leaders in the Bible and how their roles and character traits fit into our own society.

- Unit 8 contains essays that put the Bible in its historical context and raises in our minds questions such as: Is the Bible a book of history? Is it more or less meaningful to us if we understand it in the context of other ancient cultures?

- Finally, Units 9 and 10 show how Judaism keeps the Bible at the core of Jewish study and ritual.

Suggestions for Individual Study

As you read on your own, consider the following suggestions:

- Even though the questions are located after each essay, read them first. Then look at them again after you finish reading the essay and see which questions challenge you.

- Each section, and even each essay, is a self-contained study unit, not dependent upon any preceding material, so you can freely choose which essays to read and the order in which to read them.
- It's a good idea to keep a copy of the JPS TANAKH at hand as you read so that when an essay writer cites or quotes a passage, you can read it and evaluate it for yourself within the context of the other verses around it.

Specific Suggestions for Group Study

- Group facilitators may want to keep the following suggestions in mind in developing a curriculum: Studying Unit 1, and particularly the essay "Modern Methods of Bible Study," will give the background necessary to understand the methods used in the other essays in the book. However, the material in this unit is among the most complex in the book and is very theoretical in nature. An alternative approach is to select a different short unit or individual selected essays to read first, as an "appetizer." (Consider Gordon Freeman's "Israelite Society in Transition," Neil Gillman's "Eschatology," or Joel Roth's "*Shabbat* and the Holidays.") Discuss how these essays use an approach that places the material "in their original, historical, and cultural contexts," the first point of Scolnic's essay. Notice that these essays do not focus on the divinity of the text and how they assume the historical development of Jewish tradition. Then read the "Modern Methods" essay. Finally, read the first essays in the unit and see how these methods differ from traditional ways of reading the text.
- Unit 2 focuses on the question of the divine origins of the biblical text. In a group setting, set aside time for a preliminary discussion about participants' beliefs in the origins of the Torah before reading the essays. Then, after reading the essays, ask the group if their ideas have changed in any way. This unit can be linked with the first unit to encourage a discussion about how our assumptions about the origins of the Bible affect and are affected by our study methods. It may also be interesting to link the study of

this unit to Elliot Dorff's essay, "Medieval and Modern Halakhah," which focuses on how this central question influences decisions about modern Jewish law and practice.

- Units 3 through 7 cover a tremendous amount of a material. Individuals or a group might choose to focus on particular topics, or you might ask one or two participants to read and prepare a summary of one essay for the class and facilitate the discussion. This approach may be particularly relevant for Units 3, 5, and 6. It may also be interesting to draw attention to contrasting essays. A good example for this is the differing emphases in Judith Hauptman's "Women" and Debra Orenstein's "Matriarchs and Patriarchs." A focus on current events might invite an interesting reading of the last three essays of Unit 6 ("Land of Israel," "Dealing with Strangers," and "War and Peace"), leading to a lively discussion about how biblical ethics relate to the modern State of Israel.
- Unit 8 will challenge readers. Gordon Freeman's "Israelite Society in Transition" is a broad reading of the Bible using an historical lens that puts the Bible's own narrative perspective in stark relief. The succeeding essays show how the biblical material relates to physical and literary materials from its own time period.

Suggested Curriculum for a Six-Session Course

- **Week 1:** Unit 1, Torah Study, focusing especially on "Modern Methods of Bible Study." It will be very helpful to combine this with other selected essays, as described above.
- **Week 2:** Unit 2, Revelation. Focus on how these essays relate to those in Unit 1 and also to Elliot Dorff's "Medieval and Modern Halakhah."
- **Weeks 3 and 4:** A selection of material from Biblical Foundations, units 3 through 6, depending on student or facilitator interest. (The course can be extended to include more of this material.)
- **Week 5:** Unit 7, Biblical Models of Character and Leadership.
- **Week 6:** Unit 8, Understanding the Bible in Its Historical Context.

A Religious and Spiritual Journey

Conservative Judaism owes a great debt to the past 150 years of biblical scholarship, for it has helped us to see the Bible with new eyes. However, one of the challenges presented by these essays is to take these modes of reading and help them feel "holy" or "spiritual."

Judaism has always believed that study is in itself an act of prayer and connection with the Holy One. Conservative Judaism believes that all forms of study, whether using traditional methods of midrash or medieval exegesis, or the modern literary, historical, and scientific methods engaged by these essay writers, are sacred acts of religious significance. Make your learning experience an act of "mitzvah"—of spiritual connection. Consider beginning and ending each reading or discussion with the blessings and meditation provided in the appendix.

Ultimately, you will find that this is not just a book about the Bible or biblical interpretation. It is about how we live our Judaism. It not only shows us our roots, but demands that we see Judaism as a way of thinking and acting that evolves with us. The Bible has stood at the core of Judaism for millennia and our constant challenge is to make it the core of our being. As Moses said as he passed his leadership to the next generation, "*hazak v'ematz*"—be strong and always strive. May your study of these essays, and of the Bible, always challenge and inspire you.

Torah Study: Making the Bible Meaningful and Relevant in Every Age

A NOTE ON THE SPIRITUALITY OF TEXTS

Michael Fishbane

Summary

Judaism is a religion based on a number of classical texts. Those who read and interpret these texts can grow spiritually through the experience of study. Frequently, insights obtained from the texts provide the language and ideas through which the reader comes to understand and explain his or her life. In a reciprocal manner, readers bring new insights to the texts and "breathe new life" into ancient words.

Much of modern society and technology is oriented toward the rapid transmission of information. In this brief essay, Michael Fishbane argues that to create a religious and spiritual experience through reading the Bible, we must learn a different mode of reading and study. For the reading of texts to take on a spiritual quality, it must be slowed down enough to encourage a renewal of both the text and the life of the reader.

Judaism is a text culture that always has been nurtured by study and interpretation. The interpreter and the text interpenetrate in dynamic ways. The individual finds and realizes that the layers of his or her deepest self have been "textualized" by study, so that the sacred texts provide the language for ongoing life experience and inspiration. The text, on the other hand, reveals itself through the accumulated readings of its many seekers and learners. In a profound reciprocal way, every renewal of the self is simultaneously a renewal of the text, while every deadening of human sensibility is a simultaneous deadening of the life breath of the text. The biblical text is a shaping of the divine spirit by the human breath of Moses and the prophets; but it may speak now only through the spirit and breath of its interpreters.

Martin Buber once said that the task of the biblical translator is to overcome "the leprosy of fluency," a disease of the spirit that can lead us to imagine that we already know what we are reading, causing us blithely and triumphantly to read past the text. The effective translator must, therefore, reformulate the word or the words of the text to produce a new encounter with its language and thus facilitate a new hearing and a new understanding. The spiritual task of interpretation, likewise, is to affect or alter the pace of reading so that one's eye and ear can be addressed by the text's words and sounds—and thus reveal an expanded or new sense of life and its dynamics. The pace of technology and the patterns of modernity pervert this vital task. The rhythm of reading must, therefore, be restored to the rhythm of breathing, to the cadence of the cantillation marks of the sacred text. Only then will the individual absorb the texts with his or her life breath and begin to read liturgically, as a rite of passage to a different level of meaning. And only then may the contemporary idolization of technique and information be transformed, and the sacred text restored as a living teaching and instruction, for the constant renewal of the self.

Study Questions

1. What is a "text culture"? In what way does a canon—a defined set of texts regarded as authoritative—create a community?

2. The 20th century scholar Judah Goldin once observed, "Text and experience are reciprocally enlightening." How is this a good summary of what Fishbane is trying to say in his essay? Have you found this to be true of your own studies of Jewish texts?

3. What does Martin Buber's phrase, "The leprosy of fluency" mean? Have you had an experience where a translation was so smooth that you "already knew what you are reading?" What are some ways to avoid this problem?

4. Select a passage from *Etz Hayim* (for example, Gen. 1, Gen. 12:1–9, Exod. 40:17–38, or Deut. 10:12–22) and read it in comparison to other modern English translations such as those of Everett Fox, Richard Elliot Freidman and/or Robert Alter. How do the translations differ and reveal aspects of the text that are obscured by a single translation? Does a particular translation lend itself to a slower, more careful reading? What is it about the translation that makes that happen?

5. Do you find it more meaningful to study texts as an individual or in a group setting? What are the advantages or disadvantages of each in terms of a "spiritual" experience?

6. How might a slow-paced reading encourage self-reflection, deepen personal understanding, and create spiritual renewal? Is it related to the amount or quality of the content one absorbs, or to the experience of reading?

Study materials by *Baruch Frydman-Kohl*

MIDRASH

David Wolpe

Summary

According to David Wolpe, the Bible is at once powerful and cryptic, serious and playful. This is a good description of why the Bible is so compelling. It is a blueprint for living a life infused with holiness and purpose. The design, however, is not totally clear. For example, *Shabbat* is legislated but it is hard to know from reading the Torah exactly how to observe and celebrate *Shabbat* properly.

Midrash revels in the ambiguities of the text. It attempts to fill in the details and create an ongoing search for God's voice. This process reflects the original meaning of the word "*lidrosh*," to search out God's will in an oracular sense, as in this passage from Genesis: "Rebekah conceived. But the children struggled in her womb, and she said, 'If so, why do I exist?' She went to inquire [*lidrosh*] of the Lord" (25:22). The study and creation of *midrash* is a way to seek out what God wants us to "understand and do."

Wolpe provides a brief history of the major works of classical *midrashim.* Some are internal to the Bible itself, providing explanations and reconciliations of language or traditions, and others are the product of the Palestinian community from the 3rd century C.E. to the 9th century. Some seek to expand or clarify legal or ritual requirements, while others focus on filling out the narrative portions of the text. *Midrash* is based on the following assumptions: God authored the Torah, nothing within the biblical text is irrelevant or superfluous, and the narrative is not tied to linear time. *Midrash* can be imaginative and daring, such as when it describes God's motivations or feelings. In addition, *midrash* highlights the centrality of Hebrew by using single letters, words puns, and juxtapositions as invitations for further exposition. The technique of *midrashic* writing continues into the modern period, often overlapping with well-crafted sermons and Jewish literature. Over the generations it has become a beloved form of Hebrew literature, which continues to inspire today.

The Bible is at once powerful and cryptic. Characters are often sketched rather than elaborately described, and key concepts are not always spelled out. The Bible instructs us not to perform *"m'lakhah"* on *Shabbat,* but the word *m'lakhah* is never defined! The rabbinical tradition comes along to fill gaps, analyze implications, color in characters, spin tales, and derive laws—to take the biblical text as a starting point for building the structure of Jewish life.

The medium through which the Sages work is *midrash.* The word *midrash* comes from the root דרש—to search out. Use of this word can be confusing, because it refers both to a method and a body of work. There are books of collected *midrash* (plural: *midrashim*), the most well-known being *Midrash Rabbah* (literally: Great Midrash, Large Midrash). The body of *midrash* in the Talmud is referred to as *aggadah.* Yet one can also speak of "doing" *midrash,* of seeking out and explicating texts. *Midrash* is a type of investigation of a text, or a genre, not just a body of literature; and it is found in different measures in all the classical rabbinical literature.

Most classical *midrash* originated in ancient Palestine, among rabbis who lived from the end of the Roman Era (ca. 3rd century c. e.) to the beginning of the Islamic Era (the 8th or 9th century c. e.). Some *midrashim* were written and polished later than the 7th century, and the origins of *midrash* go back much further, not only to earlier sages (of the Tannaitic period, the first few centuries of the Common Era) but also back, in fact, to the Bible itself.

In Exod. 12:8, we are told that the paschal sacrifice must be eaten "roasted over the fire." Deut. 16:7 states: "You shall cook and eat it." The words for "cook" and "roast" denote different processes. In 2 Chron. 35:13, there is a reconciliation: "They roasted the passover sacrifice in fire, as prescribed, while the sacred offerings they cooked in pots." This simple illustration of the midrashic process at work in the Bible shows how problems of interpretation arise and are resolved from the very beginning of a system of law and lore.

In Jer. 25:11–12, 29:10, a prophecy reads: "And those nations shall serve the king of Babylon seventy years. When the seventy years are over, I will punish the king of Babylon and that nation. ... For thus said the LORD: When Babylon's seventy years are over, I will take note of you, and I will fulfill to you My promise of favor—to bring you back to this place." God apparently made a clear promise to the people through Jeremiah: In 70 years, they would be redeemed. But a few hundred years later, in the time of Daniel, it appeared to Daniel and his contemporaries that the prophecy had not been realized. They were still not free. So Daniel re-envisioned the prophecy: "Seventy weeks [of years, i.e., 70 x 7] have been decreed for your people and your holy city until the measure of transgression is filled and that of sin complete" (Dan. 9:24). Daniel has recast Jeremiah's prophecy to mean 490 years.

Both of these examples, although they come from the Bible itself, illustrate important principles about the Midrash as it flourished among the Sages. First, there is the fundamental underlying assumption that the Torah is entirely the word of God. Therefore, all of it is true and all of it is relevant. If something in the Torah seems to contradict experience, either the experience has been wrongly interpreted or the Torah has not been properly understood. Thus the text of Daniel has no qualms about understanding the Torah differently from what we might see as the "plain" sense of the text. For the Torah cannot get it wrong. It must be correct, and it must be all-inclusive. As Mishnah *Avot* (5:22) puts it: "Turn it [the Torah] over and over, for everything is in it."

Scholars divide *midrashim* differently. The oldest categorization is between legal and homiletical *midrashim*; from the Bible onward, there were *midrashim* whose aim was primarily legal (as in which way the paschal lamb should be cooked) and others that were primarily homiletical (sermonic, as in when redemption would arrive). The legal *midrashim* have been called *midrash halakhah* and the homiletic, *midrash aggadah*.

The legal *midrashim* deal with the whole range of Jewish law, which is as wide as human experience. Everything from dietary laws to sexual practices to civil codes rests on a network of interpretation that views the entire Torah as one seamless, interconnected web of the divine word. The homiletic *midrashim* gave the rabbinical imagination free rein: stories, counsel, pithy wisdom, and far-fetched fables all found their way into the *aggadah*.

The third lesson to be derived from these examples is that the Torah is not only all-inclusive but also does not wane or change with time. Because God has authored the text, the entire text is sacred and timelessly relevant. The midrashic sense of time is not entirely linear. In God's word, the past and future live in constant interaction. There is no anachronism, no sense that things are out of time sequence and therefore impossible.

Thus in elaborating the story of the Binding of Isaac (Gen. 22:1–19), medieval *midrash* has Abraham quoting a psalm that would not be written for some 1,000 years: "Abraham's eyes were fixed on Isaac's, while Isaac's eyes were fixed on the heavens. Tears flowed from Abraham as he cried out 'My son, may your Creator provide another sacrifice in your stead.' A piercing cry of agony rose from his lips; his eyes, pained and trembling, looked at the divine Presence as he raised his voice and said: 'I will lift my eyes to the mountains; from where shall my help come?'" (Ps. 121:1; Yalkut Sh. 101). Similarly, for Daniel the prophecy of Jeremiah is not time bound; it must be relevant to Daniel's own situation, for the word of God does not lapse or expire.

Law and lore are not the only way to divide up the Midrash. Other possible divisions exist, including distinguishing between literary forms, such as sermonic and expositional. A famous collection of sermonic *midrashim* is *P'sikta d'Rav Kahana*. Sermonic *midrashim* draw a moral point, usually by ranging far over Scripture and tradition. They generally use a verse as a jumping-off point to display textual and rhetorical virtuosity. For instance, the phrase "on the day that Moses finished setting up the tabernacle" (Num. 7:1) provides *P'sikta d'Rav Kahana* with an opportunity to begin a beautiful homily. The problem: Moses was not the architect—Bezalel ben Uri was responsible for construction; so why does the Torah credit Moses? The Midrash explains how in each generation evil people push the divine Presence away from the world, while *tzaddikim,* the righteous, bring it closer. Because God's Presence dwelt in the tabernacle, it was Moses' merit to have drawn that Presence down to earth. In the process of this explanation, the Midrash quotes numerous sources, makes wide connections over different parts of Scripture, and winds up by returning to the opening verse (the *p'tiḥta*) with which it began. By the end we have been taken on a theological tour of history, including times when God's presence seemed far away, and we are taught how the tabernacle and the merit of the righteous combined to bring God close.

Other *midrashim* form a sort of running expositional commentary on the Bible. They are explanatory, not sermonic, and follow the Bible verse by verse. A famous example cites the *Akedah,* the Binding of Isaac mentioned above. The Midrash follows the drama from the outset. Here is an example of continuous commentary:

> **Ber. R. 55:7.** *Take your son, your favored one* (lit.: your only one)*, whom you love, Isaac* (Gen. 22:1). [The Midrash now envisages a dialogue between God and Abraham that accounts for the apparent redundancy of that sentence.] "*Take your son,*" God said. "Which one?" asked Abraham. "*Your only son,*" replied God. "But each is an only son to his mother," answered Abraham. "*Whom you love,*" said God. "But I love both," answered Abraham. Finally, God said, "*Isaac.*"
>
> **55:8.** Rabbi Simeon bar Yoḥai said: "Both love and hate disturb the usual patterns of life. Thus it says: *So early next morning, Abraham saddled his ass* (Gen. 22:2). Surely he had many slaves [who could have done it for him]! But love changes the usual pattern. Conversely, it says: *When he arose in the morning, Balaam saddled his ass* (Num. 22:21). Surely he, too, had many slaves! But he did it himself because hate changes the usual pattern."

We see here that the Midrash explores Abraham's psychology through continuous comment. In the first place, it shows that Abraham, who in the biblical text seemingly raises no protest, tried to confuse the issue until God made clear He was asking for the sacrifice of Isaac. At the same time the Midrash exploits a redundancy in the text. In the second case, Abraham's saddling his own donkey is tied to a later instance when the pagan magician Balaam saddles his own donkey to curse Israel. The Midrash makes the acute psychological point that passion leads one to perform an action oneself; we do not trust others to take care of our beloved or to dispatch our enemies. At the same time, it reveals that Abraham's state of mind was ardent, not indifferent, as one could assume without the aid of the Sages' reading.

For the Sages, the biblical text is a springboard. But not all *midrashim*—even the non-legal *midrashim*—are concerned with interpreting the Bible. The Sages also tell tales of postbiblical personalities and events. There are tales of rabbinical figures, of kings, of pagans, and of princes. Still, the bulk of *aggadah* fills in the tales of characters or events in the Bible. *Midrash* advances our understanding of the biblical characters and fills in gaps in the text. What happened during the three days that Abraham and Isaac traveled to Mount Moriah for the *Akedah*? What exchanges took place between Moses and God at the end of the Torah as this greatest of prophets stood alone on the mountain preparing to die? The Sages, with their human insight and exhaustive familiarity with the biblical text and tradition, are ready with a story, a poignant observation, or a subtle interpretation that helps the text live anew.

No character is more often illumined than the character of God. The text that tells of God's destruction of the tower of Babel reads: "The LORD came down to look at the city and the tower" (Gen. 11:5). Surely God does not need to move down? The Sages could have engaged in abstract discussion about whether the text really intends to suggest that God moved. That would be the tack of the philosopher. Instead, they drew a lesson: Although God sees all, "came down" is written to teach us that one should not pronounce judgment on that which one has not personally examined (Tanḥ. B. Noaḥ 28).

Many of the *midrashim* about God compare Him to a king and contrast God's behavior with that of an earthly monarch. A *midrash* on Psalms (149:1) is typical: "While an earthly king has all sorts of attendants and lieutenants and viceroys who share in his tasks and his glory, it is not so with the King of kings: God bears the burdens alone, and God alone deserves our praise."

Midrash is both serious and playful. Although some of the fables stem from a religious inclination, many represent an artistic vehicle. Often the narratives of *midrash aggadah* appeal to our human imperative to tell and hear stories. As stated in the Midrash: "In olden days when people had means, they would want to hear words of Mishnah and Talmud. Now when people are impoverished, and suffering from the pangs of exile, they want to hear Bible—and the tales of *aggadah*" (PdRK 101).

Finally, the text itself impels *midrash*. The Bible demands *midrash* when there is some problem, inconsistency, or oddity. If a word is spelled peculiarly, if an unusual word is used, or if the sequence of words or

verses is strange, the Midrash leaps in to illuminate, explain, or speculate. At the end of the story of Joseph, his father, Jacob, has died. Joseph
is viceroy of Egypt. Joseph's brothers, afraid that he will now seek to
exact punishment for their early treatment of him, send a message to
Joseph. The brothers contend that their father, Jacob, before he died, left
a message asking Joseph to please forgive his brothers (Gen. 50:17). The
Sages, noting that the message contains the word "please" three times,
state: "One who has wronged another is obligated to seek forgiveness
at least three separate times" (BT Yoma 87a). From here later authorities derived the practice of asking for forgiveness three times before *Yom
Kippur* if we have wronged another (see S.A. O.Ḥ. 606). Not only have
the Sages called attention to the language of Joseph's brothers, thereby
giving us an insight into their state of mind, but they have drawn from
the verse an important moral lesson.

In exploring the biblical account of Creation, the Sages exhibit a
natural interest in the nature of humanity. That, allied to the deep interest in words we mentioned above, leads to the following *midrash*: "The
LORD God formed [וייצר; *va-yyitzer*] man" (Gen. 2:7). "Why does וייצר
have the letter *yod* twice [which is not necessary for proper spelling]? To
show that God created the human being with both a good inclination
and an evil inclination" (BT Ber. 61a). This *midrash* shows the Sages
using the text as an opportunity. Surely the rabbinical notion that human beings have two opposing natures battling in our breasts did not
arise because of the spelling of the word *va-yyitzer*! From experience and
learning, the Sages concluded this about humanity; the next step was to
find a biblical basis for this observed truth.

That is why even frivolous *midrash* is serious. *Midrash* is the tool by
which our ancestors unpacked the meaning of a text or even read their
own meaning into the text. *Midrash* is associative; a word that appears
in two entirely different contexts can be used to link them together.
Because everything is written by God, there can be no accidental juxtapositions.

By now we can understand why Hebrew is so vital to the midrashic
enterprise. Texts written in Hebrew, the holy tongue (*l'shon ha-kodesh*),
are in the original language. Many *midrashim* are based on puns and
other Hebrew allusions and cannot truly be appreciated without re-

course to Hebrew. Because there is nothing superfluous in the biblical text and Hebrew is the sacred language, the "trigger" for a *midrash* need not be a whole story. The trigger can be a verse, a word, or even a single letter—as we saw above in the case of *va-yyitzer.*

The Bible is not a text that can be emended. No verse can be added or cut out. The only way to get the Bible to yield different meanings that can accommodate new situations is to interpret.

Although classical *midrash* is time bound, the midrashic enterprise continues. In our own day, scholars, preachers, and interested readers develop their own interpretations and tales about the Bible. In each generation, different concerns and disciplines lead readers to new insights. From the beginning of Jewish tradition, pious Jews not only have received the text but also have helped shape it through their clarifications, expositions, additions, and interpretations—in short, through *midrash.* By *midrash* we make the text more vivid, and we make it our own.

Study Questions

1. Does it seem plausible that a book can contain an entire code for living? Does your appreciation of the Bible demand a belief in its infallibility and perfection? Would skepticism erode its holiness for you? How does a midrashic approach open up the possibilities of the book?

2. Aviva Zornberg has noted that the Midrash contains great psychological insight into the text. Wolpe uses the *Akedah* (Exod. 22:1), Joseph and his brothers (Exod. 50:17), and the Creation (Exod. 2:7) as good examples of *midrash.* Using Zornberg's description, what sorts of unconscious or psychological insights emerge from the *midrashim*? You may want to compare the original biblical text with the *midrashim* to find the linguistic hints that can lead to deeper questions. Do the ideas seem medieval or contemporary?

3. What can *midrash* teach us about what it means to read a text Jewishly? When reading the Bible, how helpful is it to be able to

understand it in Hebrew? How can comparing translations help a modern reader to appreciate midrashic style?

4. Many *midrashim* end with a hopeful note, describing a reinvigoration of the bond between God and Israel and relief from persecution. They tend to look backward into the language of the text to prove that God has not abandoned the Jewish people. How are these messages relevant in our own era?

Study materials by *Jane Sherwin Shapiro*

TRADITIONAL METHODS OF BIBLE STUDY

Benjamin Edidin Scolnic

Summary

Benjamin Edidin Scolnic presents two complementary essays on classical and contemporary approaches to the study of Bible. In the first essay he describes the guiding principles of all traditional commentary (*parshanut*), focusing on some of the most famous commentators *(m'forshim)*, including Rashi, Ibn Ezra, Rashbam, Ramban, Sforno, and Abravanel. For these writers, the Torah is the personal voice of the eternal and perfect God. The text is immutable and complex and requires human interaction and interpretation. As Scolnic notes: "Every utterance, every word, must be filled with meaning; it is the task of the commentator to discover the levels of meaning." He then describes a medieval mnemonic for these levels, *Pardes,* which means an "orchard" or "paradise." This concept suggests the deeper meanings that exist below the surface of the Torah text, as well as the necessity of rooting Jewish mystical experience in deep textual analysis. He provides examples of *p'shat, remez, d'rash*, and *sod* on several biblical passages.

These approaches are efforts to understand the Bible on a variety of levels: literal, moral, ideological, halakhic, allegorical, philosophical, and mystical. Dialogue among the different commentators appears on the printed page of the *Mikraot G'dolot*, the traditional edition of the Bible text. This multi-valence underscores the idea that the Torah, like God, is beyond time and space, eternal and without limit.

What we think the Torah is helps determine the way in which we read it. Traditional Jewish commentators believe that the words of the Torah were revealed by God to Moses. Therefore, when there seem to be contradictions or errors, the commentators set about to harmonize apparent inconsistencies into one true and consistent Torah text. They also try to explain any discrepancies between biblical concepts and the ideas and beliefs of their own time. Interpretation is thus a necessity for every generation.

Modern critical scholarship reads the Bible as a document of religious faith expressed within a specific culture, tied to a specific time, limited by the meaning of the authors. Every text of the Bible, in this view, is time bound. Traditional commentators in every age seek the timeless, eternal voice of God in the words of the Torah; their reading of the Bible is informed by a deep theological commitment to an eternal God whose very word is understood as being imbedded in the text.

Over the centuries, traditional commentators have used several different approaches to discover the layers of meaning in the Torah. A convenient way to think about these approaches or levels is through a Hebrew acronym that was created for this purpose: "PaRDeS." To illustrate what PaRDeS means, let us briefly examine two verses that tell of the journey of Abraham (then known as Abram) from Egypt to Canaan:

> And he proceeded by stages from the Negeb as far as Bethel,
> to the place where his tent had been formerly, between Bethel
> and Ai, the site of the altar that he had built there at first; and
> there Abram invoked the LORD by name (Gen. 13:3–4).

The commentators interpret the text using the following approaches:

- *P'shat:* the plain, literal sense of the verse in its context. Abraham returns to Canaan from Egypt "by stages"; he moves from one oasis to another.
- *Remez* (hint, symbol): the allegorical meaning of the verse. Each character or place in the text has a symbolic meaning. The word "Abram" is understood to be the soul; his travels trace its spiritual journey.
- *D'rash:* the homiletical meaning of the verse as viewed outside of its original context. Specific ideas and values are derived from the text, whether the text, in its literal meaning, could mean this or not. This approach reveals Abram's true intention: to visit many places where he could teach the word of God.
- *Sod:* the secret, mystical interpretation of the verse. This approach teaches that the land of Israel draws Abram from a purely nonphysical state of being to one of concrete physical reality.

PaRDeS has become a well-recognized framework for understanding traditional methods of Torah study. No single method of interpretation is considered to be the best, because the Torah is layered with meaning, is multifaceted. Although each verse means something in its specific context, it can mean many other things as well. This is demonstrated in *Mikra·ot G'dolot,* a traditional edition of the Bible in which each page contains a biblical verse or a passage in Hebrew, an ancient Aramaic translation of the text, and a number of medieval commentaries in Hebrew. Different interpretations are placed on the same page, presenting the message that there is no one definitive interpretation of any verse.

P'SHAT AND D'RASH

The most important traditional methods of study are *p'shat* and *d'rash*. *P'shat* is literal; it is "reading out" from the text (exegesis); *d'rash* is non-literal, it is "reading into" the text (eisegesis). Although it may seem that *p'shat* preceded *d'rash,* the historical fact is that *d'rash* was the primary Jewish method of study until the 11th and 12th centuries C. E.—the time of Rashi, Ibn Ezra, and Rashbam. *P'shat* is interested in the original meaning, though sometimes a *p'shat* is a reading out of context that has become authoritative and accepted.

D'rash implicitly states: "What these words may have meant originally in their context is not all that they mean. We of a later generation can understand these same words in a different manner." The sometimes imaginative daring of *d'rash* demonstrates its ability to transform meaning and its refusal to remain bound by the context of an earlier time.

To illustrate how *p'shat* and *d'rash* produce quite different interpretations, let us focus on Gen. 49:10, a verse that many call the most controversial in all of Genesis. Jacob, the third of the patriarchs after Abraham and Isaac, gives his last will and testament to his 12 sons, including these words to his son Judah:

> The scepter shall not depart from Judah,
> Nor the ruler's staff from between his feet;
> So that tribute shall come to him
> [lit.: "Until he comes to Shiloh"]
> And the homage of peoples be his.

Many explanations have been given for the word "Shiloh." Rashbam, a great *p'shat* commentator and the grandson of Rashi, states that this verse is a prediction of events that will happen centuries in the future. After the successful reigns of two kings from the tribe of Judah, David and Solomon (ca. 1000–920 B.C.E.), Solomon's son Rehoboam will be unable to hold the kingdom together. Rehoboam will come to the northern city of Shechem and antagonize the 10 northern tribes, who will then secede from the united kingdom. Rashbam explains that the scepter will not depart from Judah until Rehoboam comes to Shechem, because that is where the kingdoms will be divided. Shechem is next to Shiloh. In this interpretation of Gen. 49:10, Jacob predicts that Judah's privilege of sovereignty over his 11 brothers will last only until he (Judah's descendant) comes to (the city of) Shiloh.

This *p'shat* interpretation places the verse in a historical context. The verse is a reference to a one-time event that will be fulfilled. If this interpretation is correct, it makes the enigmatic verse from Jacob's prophecy into a prediction of an event of historical interest.

D'rash moves the discussion to a different level. In rabbinical interpretation, this verse becomes the primary source in the Torah for belief in the Messiah. Thus in this verse Jacob is blessing, and prophesying about, his son Judah, the ancestor of King David; Jacob's last words to Judah seem to be a logical place for a reference to the Messiah, who will be descended from Judah and that great king. The ancient Aramaic translation by Onkelos renders this verse as "until the Messiah, to whom the kingdom [Shiloh as *shelo,* or "his"] comes."

Rashbam accepted this interpretation and concluded that "the scepter" would never depart from Judah—because the Messiah, a descendent of the tribe of Judah, would reign forever. Christian interpretation, however, claimed that the verse pointed to Jesus, who came after the Hasmonean monarchy ("the scepter") had departed from the Jews, as the patriarchal blessing had foretold. To counter this claim, Baḥya ben Asher argued that the Messiah could not be divine as the Christians claimed, because "Shiloh" derived from *shilya* (placenta), proving that the Messiah would be a human being, naturally conceived and born to a woman.

It is instructive to see how *d'rash* has taken this verse from a specific historical reference to a verse of the greatest magnitude for Judaism and the future of humankind. But it is also ironic that only because the verse was interpreted midrashically to predict the Messiah did the Jews have to defend the text against Christian claims. Once this verse, or any other verse, is open to noncontextual exegesis, there are no objective standards for validity in interpretation. It is also important to note that *p'shat* is the best defense against the Christian suggestion that Shiloh is a prediction of Jesus. In referring us to the literal meaning of the verse in its historical context, *p'shat* presents a meaning that obviously has nothing to do with events 1,000 years after the time of King David.

Let us turn to a different example of how *p'shat* and *d'rash* work by examining another well-known verse: "And this shall serve you as a sign on your hand and as a reminder on your forehead" (Exod. 13:9). Rashbam comments: "It shall be for you a reminder as if they [the events of the Exodus] were written on your hand. They are to be taken [figuratively,] just as in 'set me as a seal upon your heart' [Song 8:6]." Rashbam carefully separates the *p'shat*, the literal, contextual explanation of the verse, from the traditional understanding of it with its halakhic (legal/ritual) implications. Rashbam does not need to make the *p'shat* and the *halakhah* one and the same. The Sages do interpret the text as mandating the putting on of *t'fillin*, and that is the *halakhah;* but it is not the *p'shat* of the text. The latter is a metaphor for always being mindful of God's commandments. Even the great *p'shat* interpreter Ibn Ezra did not go this far, agreeing that the verse had the halakhic ruling in mind. Like the Sages, he saw the need for unambiguously supporting the *halakhah* of donning *t'fillin* for the morning service with a biblical injunction.

This careful separation of the *p'shat* from *halakhah* seems natural to modern readers; the direct reading of the verse without *midrash* as an intermediary is closer to our way of reading. It would be more useful for religious transmission, however, if the verse did refer to *t'fillin*.

When considered out of context, both *p'shat* and *d'rash* are limited. In the case of Gen. 49:10, the *p'shat* is a specific historical reference, whereas the *d'rash* creates a difficult problem for Jews living in a Christian culture. In the case of Exod. 13:9, the *p'shat* is a valid reading of the verse but is much less halakhically relevant than the *d'rash*.

Traditional commentators often struggle with contextual interpretations based on *p'shat* and acontextual explanations of laws based on *d'rash.* But the struggle is a necessary one; it is an example of how the complexity of the Torah demands sophistication. We need both *p'shat* and *d'rash* to understand that God's word has been interpreted according to God's additional revelations. *P'shat* is the word of God, the verse itself; the additional revelations, manifested in the interpretations that created and reflect normative Judaism, are illuminated by the various methods of study.

REMEZ

The third element of the PaRDeS grid is *remez,* the allegorical or philosophical interpretation. The great period of this type of interpretation encompassed the 14th through 16th centuries when such luminaries as Ralbag, Arama, Sforno, and Abravanel wrote their commentaries. An example of *remez* can be found in Abravanel's philosophical understanding of the people's sin with the Tower of Babel (Gen. 11:1–9).

> Adam and Eve were expelled from the Garden of Eden because they made the tree of knowledge their ultimate aim and neglected the tree of life, the true purpose of humankind. In the same way, the people of Babel had all of life's necessities ... provided for them by God from heaven. They ... could have devoted themselves entirely to the attainment of perfection for their souls. ... They sought instead ... to build a city in which all kinds of work could take place. There would be a tower in that city. ... But arising out of this kind of life are the struggles for fame, titles, and power—for illusory honors and the accumulation of possessions. ... Since all of this is truly superfluous ... preventing men from attaining their true perfection, that of the soul, therefore these sinners against the soul were punished in that God confused their tongues and scattered them on the face of the earth.

Abravanel's message was for the city dwellers of his own time. He knew that people like himself would seek to rise in civilized society. Even so, they must not forget the true purpose of life—the fulfillment of the soul.

Another example of *remez* can be found in Lev. 14:33–53, a passage concerning a mold or fungoid blight (*tzara·at*) that produces discoloration in the plaster or mud used to cover building stones. The home-owner reports the condition to the priest, who either declares the house "pure" or orders its dismantling. For Arama (in *Akedat Yitzḥak*), the blemishes that afflict the house are symbolic of bad habits acquired through association with bad people.

> The house is representative of one's wider social contacts. ... Locking up of the house by the priests suggests to the owner that he must keep away from his usual social environment and get rid of the negative influences he has acquired through such associations. ... The very fact that the Talmud states such stringent criteria ... makes it practically impossible for these requirements to be fully met. This bears out the symbolic nature of this piece of Torah legislation.

Allegorical interpretation explains a text from within a cultural situation in which a literal interpretation would be incomprehensible. When encountering a literal reading that seemed irrelevant or inconsequential, traditional commentators learned how to find levels of meaning that were important for their own time.

In *remez,* a traditional commentary finds contemporary meaning in the biblical text. Instead of a house with fungus, we are confronted by a person's associations with evil people. A literal interpretation limited in scope is replaced with a symbolic explanation that is more edifying.

SOD

We turn now to mystical interpretation. One of Rashi's most important accomplishments was transmitting the important rabbinical *midrashim* on the biblical text. Later commentators, however, would often have difficulties with Rashi's presentation of these *midrashim* at face value. Mystical commentators gave these same *midrashim* deeper, secret meanings (*sod*). For example, Rashi cites a *midrash* that teaches that the ram's horn that sounded on Mount Sinai at the time of Revelation (Exod. 19:13) was the horn of the ram sacrificed by Abraham as a substitution for Isaac (Gen. 22:13). The Binding of Isaac, with all of its emotional power, with its great message of faith at all costs, is now connected with the binding of the Israelites to God at Mount Sinai. Ramban denies that this could be, recalling that the ram had been completely burnt as a whole offering, including its horns. Ramban goes on to teach a *sod* interpretation: The voice that was heard on Mount Sinai was the voice of what was known as "The Fear of Isaac." This is one of the 10 aspects (or emanations) of God (symbolizing *G'vurah*, "strength") in the kabbalistic system.

A longer example may more fully illustrate the mystical development of *midrashim*. In both the story of the Burning Bush (Exod. 3–4) and the Call of Moses in Egypt (Exod. 6–7), we have the same elements:

1. God tells Moses of His plan to save Israel and commands Moses to tell the people of the plan.
2. Moses learns God's sacred name, which had not been known before.
3. God commands Moses to go to Pharaoh.
4. Moses objects that he is of clumsy speech, and Aaron is therefore appointed as a spokesman.
5. Moses and Aaron confront Pharaoh and are rejected.

The exegetical challenge is to explain why God calls Moses a second time—and why all of these elements, especially the appointment of Aaron, are repeated.

The rabbis of the Midrash saw the challenge in finding two versions of one story in the Torah. Akiva's interpretation is as powerful for our generation as it must have been for his. He said that Moses argued:

> "I know that You will deliver the Israelites one day, but what about those who have been buried alive in the building?" Then did the divine attribute of justice seek to strike Moses, but after God saw that Moses argued in this way only because of Israel's suffering, He retracted and did not allow the attribute of justice to strike him, instead dealing with him according to the divine attribute of mercy.

Moses' question is very much like the question many modern Jews have asked: "It's wonderful and comforting that the State of Israel now exists, but where was God during the Holocaust while six million were being killed?" Here Moses says, "It's wonderful that You're going to save the

Israelites from slavery, but what about all of the Israelites who have been killed during their enslavement to these evil Egyptians?" The Sages saw God as having two attributes: the attribute of justice, which is represented by the divine name *Elohim* (or *Adonai*), and the attribute of mercy, which is represented by the divine name *YHVH*. The attribute of justice (*Elohim*) wants to kill Moses for his challenging question, but the attribute of mercy (*YHVH*) wants to save him, because it knows that Moses is asking only out of his anguish for those who have been killed.

The second call is, in this reading, part of a dramatic situation that needs a solution, an interesting challenge to God that needs an answer. Moses and God, at odds with each other, must be reconciled. To bring about this reconciliation, God needs to send forth a renewed call, full of reassurance for Moses, who needs to hear everything all over again. And that is why, according to this *midrash*, there was a second call so similar to the call at the Burning Bush.

However, the Zohar explains that different aspects of God, represented by the different names of God, are part of the dramatic dialogue between God and Moses. This *sod* interpretation then goes on to explain that two methods of communication—voice and utterance—are represented by the figures of Moses and Aaron. The Zohar then wonders how Moses can bring up the problem of speaking again, because it had already been dealt with at the Burning Bush. The apparent redundancy points to an inner meaning. Moses has voice but lacks utterance. Pharaoh can hear God's demands only if voice and utterance are one. God gives Aaron (utterance) to be at the side of Moses (voice). But it was only at Mount Sinai that voice was actually united with utterance. It was only then that Moses was healed of his impediment, when voice and utterance were united in him as their organ.

In modern literary terms, we can speak of the content of God's message, represented by Moses (voice), and the form, symbolized by Aaron (utterance). Traditional interpretation strives to unite the words of the Torah with the revelations of God. If the Torah is the word of God, then its words, its utterance, express the content of His revelations. Every utterance, every word, must be filled with meaning; it is the task of the commentator to discover the levels of meaning. Moses needs Aaron, content needs utterance, and the Torah needs commentary.

For the modern reader who believes that the Torah is the word of God, discovering the levels of meaning in the biblical text is a fundamental part of life. But what of the modern reader who does not believe that the Torah is the revelation of God, who thinks that traditional commentaries are inventing all meaning above the level of *p'shat?* For this reader, traditional Jewish commentary can be understood as a fascinating process, a dialogue between the sacred text and the generations of Jews who have kept it at the center of their lives. Commentary is not simply an attempt to know what the Torah is saying, but the intellectual foundation for the process by which Judaism has grown, adopting and adapting to new environments and cultural situations. The openness to new interpretation assumes the belief, or concept, that God's revelations are still unfolding.

There is something about the Torah that prevents all commentators, whether traditional or modern, from finding definitive solutions; the problems usually remain problems. The Torah remains open; no one can close it. Modern readers may think of themselves as strangers in PaRDeS, uncomfortable with anything but literal interpretation. But modern readers need to recognize that all language is figurative and thus must remain open to interpretation. Just as angels guard the way back to the Garden of Eden, the traditional commentators show the way back to the paradise of Jewish meaning.

Study Questions

1. When you look at a page of *Mikraot G'dolot,* the Torah is at the center, but there is no one definitive interpretation. Scolnic tells us that the Torah texts become clearer and "more true" in conversation with others. Is this like any other types of study you have done? Do you think that this method of study increases your understanding of the text? Is the medium of Bible study its message? Are there uniquely Jewish ways to read a text?

2. For you, is the Bible a "fixed" book of truth? When you think about the Bible as a book that demands flexibility and interpretation, does this change your relationship to the book? Does the Bible seem less authoritative?

3. Scolnic writes, "Once … [a] verse, or any other verse, is open to noncontextual exegesis, there are no objective standards for validity in interpretation." As an example he uses a reference with a messianic *d'rash* that has different implications for Jews and Christians. Some controversial texts that could be interpreted differently in our generation might include those that reflect upon the role of women, homosexuality, or relationships with gentiles. To what extent do historical or social circumstances determine what sort of *d'rash* is valid or acceptable? Historically, who determined what is "acceptable?" Who determines this today?

4. What does it mean to say that the bible is an "Eternal Book?" How does your study of the Bible help it live up to this expectation?

Study materials by *Jane Sherwin Shapiro*

MODERN METHODS OF BIBLE STUDY

Benjamin Edidin Scolnic

Summary

In this companion essay, Scolnic discusses how modern assumptions about the Bible differ radically from the traditional notions, and how they inform alternative ways to interpret the Bible from the *Pardes* method. Here, the Bible is considered to be a collection of documents written by humans between 1200 and 400 B.C.E. and not authored by God. There are no hidden levels of meaning embedded in the text. The text can be subjected to the same analysis and scrutiny as any good literary text and the role of scholars and students is to understand the text as part of the ancient historical context. If one learns more about ancient Near Eastern culture, one can have a better understanding of how the Bible is a product of the culture and from where the unique message of the Bible evolves. Scolnic identifies five methods of analysis used by contemporary readers to read the text.

- The first method, known as *textual criticism*, looks at the history of the text as it has been transmitted. Comparing and contrasting manuscript traditions or translations of the text can bring us closer to what it must have been originally. Discrepancies can be reconciled and unusual narratives confirmed. The scrolls found at Qumran near the Dead Sea have been extremely valuable because they have shown how reliable the ancient transmission of the text actually has been.

- *Source criticism* explains inconsistencies or redundancies in the text as traditions coming from different communities over a long period of time. At a later date, approximately 600 to 400 B.C.E., they were compiled and edited as a unified text. Source critics try to unravel these strands and identify the earlier sources of the book by their consistent use of one name of God or another, or by emphasis on one leading tribe or another.

- As a great book, the Bible can be subjected to the full battery of techniques known as *literary criticism.* Its richness emerges through close analysis of use of language, character development, dramatic tension, poetry, narrative, and style. Instead of looking at the smaller pieces of biblical text or its sources, literary critics read it as an edited and unified whole.

- Finally, the *structural* and *deconstructivist* modes look at the language of the Bible in a totally different way, noticing the cultural assumptions that we bring to the text as readers as well as the ambiguities that emerge by the selection of one word over another. Both modes have a surprising affinity to the traditional stance that the Bible has endless possibilities of meaning, which are progressively revealed to each generation. These approaches stress personal interpretation and understanding. These departures from the traditional method have opened up new possibilities and pathways into the Bible and broadened appreciation for its greatness among contemporary readers who have lacked experience in traditional modes of learning.

Modern biblical criticism is based on two assumptions: (a) Because the Bible is a collection of documents written in human language by human authors, it is subject to the same methods of historical and literary investigation as all other books and documents. Modern critical study rejects the idea of divine authorship and the concept of multiple levels of meaning that all emanate from God. (b) The biblical texts must be understood in their original, historical, and cultural contexts. Modern biblical criticism employs many methods of interpretation, the most important of which are textual criticism, source criticism, literary criticism, and structuralism and deconstructionism.

TEXTUAL CRITICISM

Textual criticism attempts to understand the words written by the human authors. The oldest complete forms of the books of the Torah extant today are in manuscript (handwritten) copies, none of which is earlier than the 10th century c. e. There is, therefore, a gap of as much as 2,000 years between the original writing of the document and the earliest complete copy to which we have access.

Of the several thousand manuscript copies and fragments of the various parts of the Bible that exist today, no two are identical. This is to be expected. How could any literary work that was handed down for many generations be free from error? And yet, the evidence of the Dead Sea Scrolls from Qumran, dating from 2,000 years ago (and thus 1,000 years earlier than the complete copies), confirms the general reliability of the basic textual tradition that has been transmitted.

Although average readers of the Bible will not concern themselves with the details of textual criticism, modern study of the Bible has benefited greatly from the diligent research of textual critics. This type of criticism is the basis for the translation of the Bible from its original Hebrew and Aramaic into the languages of the modern reader. In that every translation is an interpretation, the basis for translation must be studied carefully.

Many of us naively assume that the Torah we use today is an exact copy of one original text, but there are many versions of the text of the Torah. Most of the English translations of the Torah under Jewish auspices are based on what is called the Masoretic text, a text that has been passed down to us by a group of scholars and scribes called the Masoretes, who lived around 1,000 years ago. This text is the Torah as we know it. We have a Greek translation of the Hebrew Torah that is well over 1,000 years older than the Masoretic text. Of the manuscripts that we actually have, the Greek version, the Septuagint (sometimes referred to as the "LXX"), is much closer in time to the original Torah. If there is a difference between the Septuagint text and the Hebrew Masoretic text, the Greek is not necessarily more valid simply because it is older. However, when there are significant differences, the Greek version is given serious consideration.

In the Masoretic text, we read about Moses' parents in Exod. 6:20: "Amram took to wife his father's sister Jochebed, and she bore him Aaron and Moses." The Greek version of this verse reads: "Amram took to wife the daughter of his father's brother." Why would anyone present a different version of that verse? Probably because the Septuagint translators could not accept the idea that, by the standards of other parts of the Torah, Moses was born out of an incestuous union. Thus, for example, we read in Lev. 18:12: "Do not uncover the nakedness of your father's sister, she is your father's flesh." The Greek version has Amram marrying his cousin, but the Masoretic text states that Amram married his aunt.

Historically speaking, Amram could not have known the prohibitions expressed in Leviticus. But it is difficult to think of Moses as the product of a union that he himself will later call an abomination, especially for a religious person. So the Greek version subtly makes a dogmatic correction in its translation of the verse. This example shows how the slightest divergence in a reading can change a point or avoid difficulties in a text. Because of variant readings, it is a useful method of study to examine all early versions of the biblical text in our search for every possible meaning.

SOURCE CRITICISM

The Torah may seem to present a unified account of Israelite history and law during the patriarchal and Mosaic periods. Detailed study of the text, however, has led modern critical scholarship to theorize that the Torah is a compilation from several sources, different streams of literary traditions, that were composed and collected over the course of the biblical period (ca. 1200–ca. 400 B. C. E.). Because the Torah, in this perspective, is an amalgam of the works of different authors or schools, it contains an abundance of factual inconsistencies; contradictory regulations; and differences in style, vocabulary, and even theology.

The first period of Israelite history is that of the patriarchs, described in the Book of Genesis. Beginning with Exodus, the Torah describes events of the Mosaic period.

How did the religion of the patriarchs differ from that of Moses? The Torah makes it abundantly clear that most of the commandments and laws revealed to Moses are new. What about the faith of Moses as opposed to that of the patriarchs? The Torah presents the idea that Moses had a more intimate relationship with God than the patriarchs did: "God spoke to Moses and said to him, 'I am the LORD [*YHVH*]. I appeared to Abraham, Isaac, and Jacob as *El Shaddai*, but I did not make Myself known to them by My name *YHVH*" (Exod. 6:2–3). The patriarchs knew God as *El Shaddai*, but Moses will know God by His more sacred, more intimate name, *YHVH*.

The revelation of God's name is literally an epoch-making event. When Moses and the Israelites are informed of God's name, they become a special people with the destiny of having a sacred covenant with God. This new revelation of God's name raises two striking questions. First, this name of God was already used in the Book of Genesis. In Gen. 4:25–26 we read: "Adam knew his wife again, and she bore a son and named him Seth. … And to Seth … a son was born, and he named him Enosh. It was then that men began to invoke the LORD by name." Thus we learn that long before Moses, even long before Abraham, people used the name *YHVH*. How, then, can Exod. 6 tell us that the patriarchs used the name *El Shaddai* only? There are texts in Genesis that use the name *El Shaddai*, but there are even more texts that use the name *YHVH*. Moses' mother, Jochebed, bears a name compounded with *YHVH*. So how can the name *YHVH* be considered new to Moses?

Second, God had already revealed the name *YHVH* to Moses at the Burning Bush. "Moses said to God, 'When I come to the Israelites and say to them, "the God of your fathers has sent me to you," and they ask me, "What is His name?" what shall I say to them?' And God said to Moses, 'Ehyeh-Asher-Ehyeh'" (Exod. 3:13–14). *"Ehyeh-Asher-Ehyeh"* means "I will be what I will be," and *"YHVH"* means "He will be." God explains that: "This shall be My name forever, / This My appellation for all eternity" (3:15). If the name *YHVH* had already been revealed to Moses in Exod. 3, why is it given as if for the first time in Exod. 6?

To review, although the distinctively Israelite name of God is *YHVH*, various sources disagree as to when this name was first used. Two sources tell us that *YHVH* was a name not revealed to the Israelites until God revealed it to Moses at the Burning Bush (3:13–15) and in Egypt (6:2–3). Both of these sources, however, disagree with the third source, which declares that the name *YHVH* was known from the beginning of history, from the time of the immediate descendants of Adam and Eve (Gen. 4:26). These facts suggest the existence of different theological perspectives concerning the time of the great turning point in Israelite religion, when it becomes a faith very different from that of the surrounding peoples.

The names that are used for God have served as important clues in the separation and discovery of the sources that make up the Torah. The different names of God have led source-critical scholarship to find independent traditions, each of which uses the divine name in a different way. These traditions are independent of and contradict each other.

How does scholarship explain all of these variations? Different theories have emerged to explain the divergences along theological, geographic, and chronologic lines. Thus there may be a northern and southern version of the same story, which would account for inconsistencies. The stories were written over the course of centuries and reflect an evolutionary process that incorporated interpretations and additions as the text developed.

There is great agreement among scholars that the Torah, the Pentateuch, in its final form, is a work composed and edited from four literary complexes. The oldest of these is the Yahwistic source, designated by the letter J because it consistently uses the name *YHVH* (spelled "Jahweh" in German) and because of its special interest in places located in the southern kingdom of Judah. This tradition seems to have been written in the 10th century B. C. E.

The Elohistic source, designated E, is so named because of its use of the divine name *Elohim* and its interest in the northern tribes, of which Ephraim was the most important. It probably was written between 900 and 800 B. C. E., presenting material parallel and supplementary to that found in J.

The Priestly source, designated P, uses the divine name *El Shaddai* (until Exod. 6) and contains a great many ritual texts. Scholars greatly disagree concerning the date when this source was written. Some place it as early as J and E, but others posit a date as late as the Babylonian exile (6th century B. C. E.).

The Deuteronomic source, designated D, is considered to have been written later (8th to 6th century B. C. E.). It reviews certain stories and presents legislation that sometimes differ from the first four books. It is important to note that contradictions exist not only within narrative material but also within the laws of the Torah. For instance, Exod.

21:2–11 states that a male slave should be released after six years of servitude. This law, however, does not apply to female slaves (v. 7). In Deut. 15:12, the same requirement of release is extended to both male and female slaves.

Most scholars believe that the Torah was compiled and edited by Priestly redactors in Babylonia between 600 and 400 B.C.E.

LITERARY CRITICISM

Though source criticism has contributed a great deal to our understanding of the growth of biblical traditions, by definition it ignores the literary unity of the final form of a text. In reaction, a new form, literary criticism, has arisen, which examines the literary characteristics (including narrative technique, tone, theme, structure, imagery, repetition, reticence, and character) of the texts. In simple terms, source criticism is interested in cutting up the texts to find the different layers of tradition; literary criticism considers the text as it stands now, as a whole, not as it once may have been. Literary criticism is both like and unlike traditional Jewish commentary. It looks at the Bible as a unified whole but has no theological commitment and sees it as the creation of human authors. Source criticism is interested in history; literary criticism treats historical questions as basically unanswerable and understands texts as literary products or objects, not as windows on historical reality. Literary criticism sees texts as coherent wholes that create meaning through the integration of their elements, irrespective of the authors and their intentions. According to source criticism, texts can give us access to the ideas and emotions of great minds of the past.

Earlier I noted that Exod. 6 repeats a great many of the elements present in Exod. 3. The essay "Traditional Methods of Bible Study" points out that the sages of the Midrash and the mystics of the Zohar created stories to explain this repetition. Similarly, literary criticism does not see the two texts as contradictory, but as different parts of an ongoing narrative. Moses receives a renewed call to action in Exod. 6 because he has become so disenchanted by his early failure to convince Pharaoh to let the people go. This new revelation completes the revelation at the Burning Bush. God tells Moses that the mission for which he was called on at the Burning Bush will occur in due time; Moses should not be dismayed by his initial failures in Pharaoh's court and with his fellow Israelites. He reminds Moses that Abraham, Isaac, and Jacob received revelations and promises, and yet it was not in their times that the promise to possess the Land was fulfilled. As the genealogy indicates, the Israelites have gone from being a family to being a people, and so the divine promise will be carried out, the liberation from Egypt will occur, and the Israelites will return to their Land.

Literary criticism finds unity and purposeful repetition where other approaches find disharmony and contradiction.

STRUCTURALISM AND DECONSTRUCTIONISM

In the past, it was thought that texts communicate meaning straightforwardly and simply. Language was supposed to give an exact picture of the world. In modern thinking, however, it is understood that all words have complex relationships with other words and that it is the patterns of language that gives words meaning. All language is figurative. There is a great distance between language about the world and the world itself. Language and literature are cultural phenomena. Structuralism looks at texts and analyzes the basic mental patterns that underlie these social and cultural phenomena.

It was once assumed that the author of a text intended a meaning, and that the reader could understand that intention. In modern thinking, however, it is understood that ambiguities in language and context increase the chances of misunderstanding. Even when a writer and a reader live at the same time and in the same place, a reader could still offer different plausible interpretations of a writer's text. When centuries and geography separate writer and reader, misunderstanding is almost certain.

We assume that any text we read has a clear meaning that it is trying to convey. A method called deconstruction claims that a text itself undermines that meaning by presenting evidence against its own case. A text often makes its case by choosing one alternative over another. In the process, however, the other alternative is brought into the picture, enabling the reader to consider it. The writer's preferred alternative is not necessarily rejected as a result, but it now is seen as only one possible option. The authority of the text breaks down, the text folds in on itself (usually at some weak point), and its center no longer holds.

Let us look at Exod. 6 again, this time to demonstrate how a text deconstructs. As we saw from the perspective of source criticism, Exod. 6 seems to be about the name of God. The patriarchs knew God as El Shaddai, but now Moses and the Israelites will know God by His true name, *YHVH*.

But what does it mean to "know the name of God"? When Moses, at the Burning Bush (Exod. 3–4), asks for the name of the God who has sent him to the Israelites on the mission of liberation, God answers, "I will be what I will be." Moses goes to Pharaoh in *YHVH*'s name: "Thus says the LORD, the God of Israel: Let My people go." Pharaoh replies: "Who is the LORD that I should heed Him and let Israel go? I do not know the LORD, nor will I let Israel go" (5:1–2). Moses thinks that he has met with failure: "O LORD, why did You bring harm upon this people? Why did You send me? Ever since I came to Pharaoh to speak in Your name, he has dealt worse with this people; and still You have not delivered Your people" (5:22–23).

What is the "name" of God? It certainly is neither a description nor a definition of God. God's name seems to be His power. Once both the Egyptians and the Israelites experience the power of God through the plagues, the name of God will be known throughout the world. But God's power is not in His name.

Indeed, the name *YHVH* is a non-name name, a way of undermining the whole idea that God can have a name at all. Moses asks God for His name, and He replies, "I will be what I will be." Thus this text, which seems to be about the revelation of God's name, contains within it the concept that God cannot have a name at all. Admittedly, the Midrash, the Zohar, and the source critics all seek to use the different names of God illustrated in the Book of Exodus as a code by which to crack the meaning of the Torah. But there really is only one name of God—*YHVH*—which is not a name at all but an expression of the namelessness of God.

I must emphasize that this reading of the texts from Exodus is only one interpretation and that these texts, as the other types of criticism indicate, may be about the revelation of God's name and the different names of God may each have its own significance.

When a text is deconstructed, however, we are no longer sure what it is trying to say. "Undecidability" is actually a better description than the term "deconstruction." "Deconstruction" connotes the destruction of a text. "Undecidability" connotes the figurative nature of language and our inability to limit and strictly defend what a literary text means. In the case of the Bible, traditional commentary would agree that no one should claim to have the definitive interpretation of a passage, for every word of the Bible has an infinite range of meanings. Deconstruction tries to be without biases, in contrast to traditional exegesis—which is based on the strongest possible theological basis. Nevertheless it is fascinating that a modern (or postmodern) method joins Jewish commentary in striving to keep the biblical text open for our interpretations and for those who will read the Bible in the centuries to come.

Study Questions

1. The authorship of the Bible is a core question for many students. Is it possible to maintain a belief in the text's sanctity, even if you believe it is a human composition? How is it possible to balance the two beliefs?

2. If the Bible is a "collection of documents" written by many groups, what is the nature of its authority? Should some of the traditions be strictly observed, while we dispense with others? Who gets to decide how we live by the Bible? What is the role of Jewish community in mediating this question?

3. If a book considered holy has contradictions, what might that mean for people looking to religion for "ultimate truths"? Is this a uniquely Jewish way to accept complexity and inconsistency? How does that make you reconsider your understanding of Judaism and what it requires?

4. If you have ever been to Israel and seen the Dead Sea Scrolls, housed in the Shrine of the Book, you can begin to appreciate

what makes them an important archaeological find. They provide modern scholars with important verification of the original text and how it was transmitted. If you have an interest in earlier versions of other biblical narrative, you may enjoy *The Bible as It Was*, by James L. Kugel (Harvard University Press, 1997).

5. Are you particularly attracted to one of the modes of reading that are described in this essay? Why? Why do the others make you uncomfortable?

Study materials by *Jane Sherwin Shapiro*

Revelation: The Divinity of the Torah

BIBLICAL AND RABBINIC PERSPECTIVES

Daniel Gordis

Summary

Revelation—the idea that God has made known to humans the nature of the world and our place in it—is central to Judaism. Yet, as Gordis makes clear, the content of revelation and how it occurred (or occurs) is rife with ambiguity. The central Rabbinic concept of revelation, that *all* of Torah was given to Moses at Sinai, is an idea that is not found in the Torah itself. Neither the Torah nor the Rabbinic tradition agrees on the content of what was given at Sinai. What matters, Gordis claims, is that the people accept that some sort of revelation took place. The content of biblical revelation is primarily law, and it is revealed by written and spoken language. But revelation can also consist of God letting us know that God has a plan for history. The Torah also expresses limits to revelation—there are things about God that humans simply cannot know.

For Gordis, the key aspect of revelation is that it is, by nature, incomplete. No set of revealed laws or commandments could foresee all possible circumstances that may arise. Thus, we see Moses inquiring about how to apply laws of inheritance and *Shabbat*. After Moses is gone, how can we be sure that a new prophet conveys true revelation? It is this inherent difficulty with revelation that gives rise to a different model of revelation from Sinai—namely, the Rabbinic model. In this model, the ability to interpret Torah with the authority of revelation moves from prophets (whose authority is hard to assess) to the sages. The interpretations of the sages were claimed to have the authority of Torah because they, too, were said to have been given to Moses at Sinai as an oral companion to the written Torah. Even those interpretations not yet made by the rabbis, if they are derived from the texts, were themselves given to Moses at Sinai.

The strength of this conception of revelation, argues Gordis, is that it provides Judaism with a form of revelation that is full of content, but allows for many views about what that content is.

Revelation, the claim that God has spoken to mortals and made known to them truths about the world and its nature, is central to Jewish belief. Although modern Jews and Jewish philosophies construe revelation in varying fashions, almost all Jews to whom the religious component of Jewish life is important place some form of revelation at the core of their belief. No document in Jewish tradition is as crucial to our conceptions of revelation as the Torah.

When Jews speak of "the Revelation," they are most commonly referring to the events at Mount Sinai described in the Book of Exodus (19 ff.). In Hebrew, the events at Sinai are known as *Mattan Torah* (The Giving of the Torah). When Moses descends the mountain, he brings a message Jews commonly call "Torah." That message is the core of revelation.

The content of the revelation that Moses brings to the people after his encounter with God atop Mount Sinai is largely legal. The Decalogue or "Ten Statements" (Hebrew: *Aseret ha-D'varim*, Exod. 34:28) primarily define proper behavior, making demands and creating obligations. The same is true for much of the ensuing material in the Torah. The Israelites learn more from God about how they are expected to behave than about enduring philosophical truths.

The Torah does not specify precisely what was revealed to Moses. Much of Rabbinic tradition asserts that the entire Torah (understood as including the Rabbinic oral tradition as well as the Torah's "written tradition") had been revealed by God to Moses at Sinai, although the Torah never states that explicitly. Exodus 20 suggests that the entire content of the Revelation might well have been the Ten Statements, although Rashi and many other commentators understand the Torah as indicating that many more laws were also revealed at Sinai. Shortly after the first revelation from Mount Sinai, Moses is again commanded to ascend the mountain for a revelation (Exod. 24; see also 20:18). Is the content of this revelation to be the same as the first? Furthermore, how does the content of revelation in Exod. 20 or 24 differ from that in Exod. 34, where God orders Moses to return to the top of the mountain yet again? Classic Jewish commentaries all struggle with these questions. Significantly, the Torah does not offer a clear resolution.

This ambiguity continues even at the Torah's conclusion. The Torah tells us that as Moses reached the end of his life, he recorded "the words of this Teaching [*torah*] to the very end" (Deut. 31:24). What constitutes "this Teaching"? Is it the Book of Deuteronomy, as some have suggested, or is it the entire Torah? And how could Moses have recorded Deuteronomy to the very end, when some of it (admittedly, very little) takes place after his death? It is striking that the Torah seems more concerned that the people Israel accept the notion that revelation took place than that they reach any certainty about the content of that revelation.

The major message of the revelation at Sinai is the centrality of law in the relationship between God and the people Israel. That revelation delivers other messages as well. For example, the experience at Sinai serves as a reminder that God communicates to humanity through words. Although this might seem obvious, it is important to note, because there are other revelations that are not verbal. Verbal communication from God to human beings (through direct discourse or through the medium of a prophet) is an essential component of biblical revelation at Sinai, on other occasions during the Israelites' journey through the wilderness, and in the visions of the prophets. Thus the revelation at Sinai is important not only for its content but because of its medium. The timeless Jewish reverence for words, written and spoken, is due in no small part to the verbal nature of many of God's revelations throughout the biblical canon.

Although much of the Torah's revelatory material is legal in nature, not all biblical revelations deal exclusively with law or with specific behavioral commands. There are important moments in which God communicates messages having little to do with law. At times, God communicates a sense of the plan of history. To Abraham, for example, God states, "I will assign this land to your offspring" (Gen. 12:7). To Isaac, God promises, "I am the God of your father Abraham. ... I will bless you and increase your offspring for the sake of My servant Abraham"

(Gen. 26:24). God speaks in similar fashion to Jacob (Gen. 35:9–10) and to Moses (Exod. 6:2–8). Such revelations are not limited to unique individuals. Elsewhere we read that God appears to the entire Israelite community. "The Presence of the LORD appeared to all the people" (Lev. 9:23), although what exactly was communicated is not stated.

The Hebrew word for "appeared" in this last instance is *va-yera,* a term used commonly in passages describing revelation. At times, the Torah uses a less anthropomorphic verb, *noda,* "made known," to connote revelation. The typical biblical notion of revelation portrays revelatory moments as those in which something about God or the universe is made known to humanity as a whole, to the Israelites in particular, or even to an individual.

This is not always the case, however. The Torah records instances in which God's revelation points specifically to realms of understanding that are unavailable to human beings. We read that right after God spoke "to Moses face to face, as one man speaks to another" (Exod. 33:11), Moses asks for more. "If I have truly gained Your favor, pray let me know Your ways, that I may know You and continue in Your favor" (v. 13). Shortly thereafter, Moses asks for even more, beseeching God, "Oh, let me behold Your Presence!" (v. 18). God's response makes it clear that Moses now has gone too far. "I will make all My goodness pass before you, and I will proclaim before you the name LORD, and the grace that I grant and the compassion that I show. But . . . you cannot see My face, for man may not see Me and live" (vv. 19–20). There are aspects of God that no mortal can know; biblical revelation communicates *that* as well.

An aura of power and awe accompanies many of the Torah's central revelatory moments, yet the Torah itself suggests that its revelations are not complete. Even while Moses and the Israelites wander through the wilderness on their way to the Promised Land, new questions arise that Moses, despite having received the Torah, does not feel equipped to answer. On several of these occasions, he turns to God for guidance. The Torah recounts the story of the five daughters of Zelophehad, whose father died without any sons to inherit his property. The daughters insist that basic justice requires that they be allowed to have "a holding among [their] father's kinsmen" (Num. 27:4), although there is no precedent for women to inherit their father's estate. When "Moses brought their case before the LORD" (27:5), God instructed Moses to grant the daughters' request.

Similarly, the Torah recounts the instance of a man found gathering wood on *Shabbat*. Although such activity seemed to violate the spirit of the *Shabbat* laws that Moses had received from God and subsequently communicated to the Israelites, gathering wood had not been prohibited specifically by any revelation up to that point. Indeed, the man "was placed in custody, for it had not been specified what should be done to him" (Num. 15:34). Custody is not the punishment; it is a temporary solution until God gives Moses further instruction on how to deal with this man. In the very next verse, the Torah relates that God orders Moses to put the man to death. Although capital punishment for *Shabbat* violations seems harsh to our modern sensibilities, the point about revelation is clear: Even Moses, who had received the Torah from God atop Mount Sinai, sometimes needs further elucidation about the content of revelation.

The Torah and its revelations contain many examples of ambiguity. Perhaps the classic example is a series of instructions that Deuteronomy offers for distinguishing between a true prophet (who might bring further revelation from God) and a false prophet (whose instructions should always be ignored). God informs Moses that He will select other prophets to follow him. "I will put My words in his mouth and he will speak to them all that I command him; and if anybody fails to heed the words he speaks in My name, I Myself will call him to account" (Deut. 18:18–19). How are the people Israel to discern between a true prophet and one who is false? A few chapters earlier (Deut. 13), the Torah states that any prophet who encourages Israel to abandon the covenant is a false prophet who should be put to death. But what of false prophets who do not encourage the people to abandon the covenant? How could the people know that these prophets are false? The Torah's response is extraordinarily simple (vv. 18:21–22):

> And should you ask yourselves, "How can we know that the oracle was not spoken by the LORD?"—if the prophet speaks in the name of the LORD and the oracle does not come true,

> that oracle was not spoken by the LORD; the prophet has ut-
> tered it presumptuously: do not stand in dread of him.

This method of distinction, however, is problematic at the moment when an Israelite must decide whether or not to follow a given prophet. Many of the Bible's classical prophecies speak of events far in the future. Jeremiah's prophecy of the fall of Jerusalem at the hands of Babylon and his subsequent assurance that God will bring the people Israel back from Babylonia are two cases in point. How were the people to know at the moment of prophecy that Jeremiah was a true prophet whose guidance ought to be heeded? And how would they make sense of the fact that some prophecies by prophets accepted as true prophets did not material-ize? How, in light of Deuteronomy, should we explain Jeremiah's proph-ecy (Jer. 34:5) that King Zedekiah would die in peace, when Zedekiah was tortured, forced to witness the deaths of his own sons, and treated in horrific fashion toward the end of his life (2 Kings 25)?

Ultimately, the Torah's instruction in Deut. 18 does not offer much assistance. Because the Torah itself acknowledges that God's revelations do not address all possible situations and that it would be difficult to determine with certainty in the future whose guidance to follow, it is not surprising that a radically new model of revelation would emerge as tradition developed.

The new model of revelation was the product of the scholars of the Rabbinic period, although it began as early as Ezra. Most modern schol-ars agree that the Torah began to be available as a written document approximately during the lifetime of Ezra, who may well have initi-ated the practice of reading the Torah in public. Although the people's access to the Torah as a written document had immense significance in its own right, this development of interpretation had far-reaching implications because no written document survives for long in the ab-sence of a tradition of commentary and amplification. Over the course of time, the scribes or Pharisees (subsequently, the Sages) developed a rich, complex legal and moral tradition to amplify the Torah. In due course, Rabbinic tradition began to speak in terms of both a written Torah (the Five Books of Moses) and an oral Torah—tradition of ex-plication and interpretation of the written Torah, compiled over many centuries. These rabbis considered the oral Torah to be as authoritative as the written Torah because they held that both had been received by Moses from God at Sinai.

Part of the Sages' intention in advocating their new theological reading of revelation was clearly to remove revelation from the domain of possible future prophets. To be sure, the Sages did not deny the authority of the biblical prophets. Occasionally, they made reference to Moses in prophetic terms and included the prophets in their description of the chain through which revelation was transmitted (as in the quotation from Mishnah *Avot* printed below). Nonetheless, they declared that after the destruction of the First Temple in 586 B.C.E. at the hand of the Babylonians, revelation would no longer be transmitted through prophets. (They seem to have been determined to avoid the anarchy made possible by the Deuteronomic formulation.) They proclaimed, in the name of Abdimi, that "from the day that the Temple was destroyed, prophecy was taken from the prophets and given to the Sages" (BT BB 12a). This tradition does not deny the possibility of future prophecy yet takes it out of the hands of those whose pedigree is difficult to determine and grants it to the Sages, who had created a clearer chain of authority and command.

Then the Sages went further. In an even more acerbic rendition of the same tradition, they seem to deny the legitimacy of all future prophecy by asserting that "from the day that the Temple was destroyed, prophecy was taken away from the prophets, and was given to fools and children" (BT BB 12b). The claim was provocative but disarmingly simple. Anything that God needed to reveal could be revealed through them and their unique tools of textual interpretation. Prophets, long a staple of Jewish religious life, no longer had a place in transmitting God's message.

As revolutionary as this idea seems in retrospect, much of Rabbinic literature describes the process in rather prosaic terms. For example, in the first *mishnah* of *Avot*, the Rabbis describe a long chain of revealed tradition that they inherited but that they certainly did not create: "Moses received Torah at Sinai and handed it on to Joshua, Joshua to the elders, and the elders to the prophets. And the prophets handed it on to the men of the Great Assembly [who in turn passed it on to the Sages]"

(1:1). "Torah" here (not "the" Torah) refers to both the written and the oral Torah. The Sages claim that their own teaching was received at Sinai, an integral part of the authoritative tradition.

Modern Jews are at home with the notion that most cultures evolve over time, that interpretation and development are essential for the vitality of any intellectual tradition. It is important to understand that the Sages were making a very different claim. They presented themselves simply as a new vessel for the transmission of that which had been revealed by God long ago. For them, the entire tradition was a single seamless entity. They insisted even that rabbinic teachings of which they were not yet aware had been given by God to Moses at Sinai. In the Jerusalem Talmud they present a radically ahistorical reading of the entire chain of revelation, arguing that "even what a distinguished student is destined to teach before his master was already revealed to Moses on Sinai" (*Pe·ah* 17a).

So intent were the Sages on asserting their own authority in the chain of revelatory tradition that they began figuratively to minimize God's role in that process. Scholars have long noted with surprise that the Mishnah, the first major document codified by the Sages, quotes Scripture much less than might be expected. What explains the Rabbis' apparent reticence to quote the book at the heart of their world-view? To be sure, they were not denying the centrality of the Torah as the quintessential example of God's revelation. Rather, as several modern scholars have suggested, the Sages styled the Mishnah so as to highlight themselves as the latest, crucial link in a long chain of access to God's revelation. Their intent is evident from a classic talmudic tale in which God's input into a legal debate is not accepted. In this tale, Eliezer disagreed with the other Sages (led by Rabbi Joshua) about whether a certain oven was permissible for use, and neither side could convince the other.

> On that day Rabbi Eliezer brought forward all imaginable arguments, but the Sages did not accept them. Said he to them: "If the *halakhah* agrees with me, let this carob tree prove it!" Thereupon the carob tree moved a hundred cubits from its place. ... "No proof can be brought from a carob tree," they retorted. Again he said to them: "If the *halakhah* agrees with

me, let the stream of water prove it!" Whereupon the stream of water flowed backwards. "No proof can be brought from a stream of water," they rejoined. Again he urged: "If the *halakhah* agrees with me, let the walls of the schoolhouse prove it," whereupon the walls inclined to fall. But Rabbi Joshua rebuked [the walls], saying: "When scholars are engaged in a halakhic dispute, you have no right to interfere." Therefore, they did not fall, in honor of Rabbi Joshua, nor did they become upright again, in honor of Rabbi Eliezer; and they are still standing thus inclined.

Again he said to them: "If the *halakhah* agrees with me, let it be proved from Heaven!" Whereupon a Heavenly Voice cried out: "Why are you disputing with Rabbi Eliezer, seeing that in all matters the *halakhah* agrees with him!" Then Rabbi Joshua arose and exclaimed: "'It is not in heaven'" (Deut. 30:12).

What did he mean by this? Said Rabbi Jeremiah: The Torah had already been given at Mount Sinai; we pay no attention to a Heavenly Voice, because You wrote long ago in the Torah at Mount Sinai, "After the majority must one incline" (a play on Exod. 23:2).

Rabbi Nathan met Elijah and asked him: "What did the Holy One, Blessed be He, do in that hour?" "He laughed [with joy]," he replied, "saying, 'My children have defeated Me, My children have defeated Me'" (BT BM 59b).

Note that the Rabbis portray their decisions in this situation as having met with God's approval. Their sense of their place in the revelatory chain denies neither the importance of revelation nor the obvious claim that God is the ultimate source of revelation. What had changed during the Rabbinic period? A sense of how revelation is transmitted and where the content of revelation is located. The notion that revelation is a contentful, commanding set of instructions and admonitions from God has always been at the core of Jewish belief. At the same time, as we have seen, what that revelation actually commanded was never made entirely clear. If the Torah is ambiguous, the Talmud seems to revel in this uncertainty. That is not a weakness of Jewish tradition but one of its strengths. Ours is a tradition that insists that God has spoken—yet is open to a variety of possibilities of how God spoke and what, in fact, God said.

Study Questions

1. If the idea that all of Torah, written and oral, was given by God to Moses at Sinai, but is not actually specified in the Bible, what reasons are there for the Rabbinic tradition to insist on it?

2. How is Rabbinic interpretation different than prophecy? What are the advantages and disadvantages of each system of "revelation?"

3. Take a look again at the long talmudic story about Rabbi Eliezer. How can the Rabbis claim the authority to ignore a voice from heaven with which most of them disagree? What does this story tell us about the nature of revelation in today's rabbinic Judaism? Is there a problem with people defying the majority of Jews in order to follow the decrees of a "heavenly voice?"

4. How do you feel about the traditional authority of the Rabbis to determine what God has revealed to us?

5. Gordis argues that ambiguity about the content of revelation is a strength of Judaism because it allows for a variety of interpretations. Do you agree with Gordis that this is a strength, or do you see it as a problem?

Study materials by *Jacob Pinnolis*

MEDIEVAL AND MODERN
THEORIES OF REVELATION

Elliot N. Dorff

Summary

In this essay, Elliot Dorff traces how Jews have shaped their justification for the truths expressed in the Torah in light of the cultural contexts in which they lived in the medieval and modern periods. He focuses on early medieval rationalism, the later medieval period of mystical interpretation, and the effect of new rationalist, historical, and literary approaches of the modern period.

Saadia Gaon (10th century) was the first Jewish thinker to justify the use of reason in addition to revelation and tradition as a path to God. Medieval Jewish thinkers balanced reason and revelation in different ways, but their common goal was to demonstrate that Judaism was deserving of respect and loyalty because it was rational and based on the word of God.

Following the dissemination of the Zohar in the 13th century, the influence of the Jewish mystical tradition increased. Philosophical ideas became suspect and dangerous, for they undermined the exclusive true claims of faith. For the followers of what came to be called Kabbalah (tradition), reason was an inferior way of knowing God. The best and most reliable path was through the Torah and its esoteric teachings.

Later, the advent of the Enlightenment in 17th-century Europe challenged this reliance on revelation, and reason was seen as the way to scientific progress and universal citizenship. This cultural shift affected Jews and many Jewish thinkers again felt the need for a rational defense of Judaism. Revelation and religion were now the handmaidens of reason.

By the 20th century, literary, historical, and archaeological forms of study, as well as an increased emphasis on personal and psychological knowledge, altered the cultural context of belief. Traditional claims of the historical authenticity of the Bible were weakened, which led to a "new thinking" about the Bible and revelation.

Along with other existentialist thinkers, Martin Buber and Franz Rosenzweig emphasized the importance of the individual experience. For Buber, Torah was not about precepts or commandments, but about cultivating direct and meaningful relations with other human beings. He believed that these human encounters prepare us for a comparable meeting and relationship with God. Rosenzweig, in contrast, thought that we should strive to experience specific laws as the result of a direct command from God, so that the mitzvot become more than obligations—they become opportunities to establish a link to God.

According to Dorff, the changes that have taken place in methods of Bible study not only reveal much about the origins and composition of the Torah, but can undermine the authority of the Torah as the word of God. Reform thinkers have followed both the historical-critical form of study and the modern emphasis on the "autonomous choice" of each person to determine the content of revelation. This tends to weaken a sense of tradition and community.

Orthodox thinkers have rejected both the historical-critical approach to the study of Bible and the existentialist understanding of Sinai as a contentless encounter. They accept the biblical account of revelation as truthful, but tend to ignore or diminish the significance of the historical and cross-cultural literary scholarship of the past century.

"Conservative thinkers accept the historical method of Bible study, but affirm the legally binding character of Jewish law." The "process and authority of revelation" is understood in three distinct ways: Some conceive of revelation as God's word, but acknowledge that the Torah text was edited over time. Others believe that God inspires certain individuals who "translate that inspiration into human language" so that revelation has both a divine and a human component. A third group of thinkers see revelation as a reaching out *from* God and *to* God.

The Bible and Jewish law are human responses to encounters with God that take on a sacred and binding quality because they are the ways we express our aspiration for holiness. As Dorff explains, all three approaches affirm that revelation is based on a combination of the divine and the human, and that revelation is an ongoing encounter with our Jewish tradition.

REASON VERSUS REVELATION

How do religious people justify what they believe? The answer is often found in the general culture of specific places and eras. What counts as convincing proof of specific statements of belief depends on what a given society at a given time sees as the most reliable path to truth.

Since the founding of each faith, Jewish, Christian, and Muslim teachers have all proclaimed that their beliefs and values are rooted in God's will as revealed in their particular religion's sacred scripture and tradition—in our case, the written Torah and the oral Torah. Basing your beliefs on revelation has the advantage of divine authentication and confirmation of what you believe. You need not depend on your own insights or those of other fallible human beings; none other than an all-knowing God confirms what you take to be true.

You can claim divine authority for your beliefs, however, only if you affirm that a specific record of revelation accurately articulates God's will. Indeed, you would have to believe not only that the founders of that religion experienced a genuine revelation of God but also that their followers possessed an accurate record of that revelation and that they interpreted and applied it correctly. Furthermore, those who argue that their faith alone is the true and accurate statement of God's will, as proponents of the three Western religions do, must also appeal to the willingness of people to discount the theological authenticity of other religions' claims to revelation.

Although the revelational basis for Jewish, Christian, and Muslim beliefs persists in one form or another among believers to this day, in the early 8th century C.E. leaders of these religions looked to other grounds—reason rather than revelation—for justifying their beliefs. The Muslims had conquered the world from Spain to India by 711 C.E., and they then sought to master it culturally as well. To have access to all of the important documents of the people they had vanquished, they translated those materials into Arabic. Through the Arabic translation of Greek sources, Muslims, and then Jews and Christians, learned about Plato and Aristotle. Because Plato and Aristotle had used reason rather than revelation to advance their claims, leaders of these three religions began to augment their claims to authentic revelation with rational justifications for their beliefs.

They did this, in part, because of the advantages of reason as an avenue to truth. A specific revelation is avowed only by those who believe in it, but everyone shares the powers of reason. Assertions based on reason, therefore, are open to everyone's examination and evaluation. Reason provides a level playing field for discussion and debate, unlike every particular revelation, and so reason gained a degree of authority in the Middle Ages beyond that of all specific revelations. As a result, defenders of Judaism, Christianity, and Islam were concerned with showing that their respective faiths were rational in both their origins and their claims. At the same time, they sought to demonstrate that reason alone is not sufficient to capture the whole truth about God and His will, which makes revelation—that of their own tradition, of course—necessary.

Probably the most articulate Jewish spokesman in this regard was Saadia Gaon (882–942). In his *Book of Doctrines and Beliefs* (Prolegomena 4), he maintains that only the ignorant reject rational thinking about religious matters for fear that it will lead to disbelief and the adoption of heretical views. On the contrary, Saadia asserts, God Himself "has commanded us to engage in such inquiry in addition to accepting the reliable Tradition," and he cites Isa. 40:21 and Job 34:4 as proof-texts. We

> inquire and speculate in matters of our religion for two reasons: (1) in order that we may find out for ourselves what we [already] know on the basis of what the prophets of God have imparted to us [through revelation]; (2) in order that we may be able to refute those who attack us through revelation about everything we need to know and do in His service.

Although that revelation is confirmed by signs and miracles, God

> also informed us that by speculation and inquiry we shall attain to certainty on every point in accordance with the Truth

revealed through the words of His Messenger [Moses]. In this way we speculate and search in order that we may make our own what our Lord has taught us by way of instruction.

If rational inquiry is not only permissible but commanded, why do we need revelation at all? Saadia gives several answers. First, because people attain the ability to follow arguments and construct them on their own only after they have lived for a number of years, revelation is necessary so that we know what God wants of us until then. Some people, indeed, never become philosophically adept, either because they lack the ability or patience or because they lack faith in either the reasoning process itself or its results; such people need the divine guidance that revelation provides throughout their lives. Even those who can reason sometimes make mistakes, and revelation is necessary to serve as a check against errors.

Along the same lines, Saadia (in chapter 3) divides the law into two classes: laws known by reason and laws known by revelation. Even for the rational laws, though, revelation is necessary, according to Saadia. First, reason tells us only the general rules about what to do but not the details about how to do it; we need revelation for that. Second, God will reward us not for following what we would do anyway on the basis of our reasoning powers but for obeying Him. God therefore had to include even Judaism's rational laws within the revealed Torah so that we can merit God's blessings for following His revealed will.

In these ways, then, Saadia balances and integrates the traditional reliance on revelation with the new authority of reason. Later Jewish philosophers in the Middle Ages described the relationship between reason and revelation somewhat differently and used both in varying degrees and instances. Maimonides (1135–1204) maintains that in cases of rational ambivalence we should turn to the Torah (*Guide* II:16). For example, reason cannot determine whether the universe has existed eternally or was created at a specific point in time; thus we use the Torah to learn that creation in time is the correct view. Jewish philosophers after Saadia also suggested other grounds for learning about God from both reason and revelation. The goal of all the rationalists, however, was to demonstrate that Judaism is rational and, therefore, deserving of belief and respect on purely rational grounds, even though revelation is nevertheless required.

This changed, at least in degree, with the advent of the *Zohar* in the 13th century and the kabbalistic tradition that followed. For kabbalists, the Torah—the blueprint from which God created the universe—is the only legitimate source of knowledge of God and His will; reason is an inferior way of knowing religious matters and, at that, misleading. Consequently, revelation alone is to be trusted, and it is to be studied not only for its plain and traditional meanings but also—indeed, primarily—for its esoteric ones. So, for example, the biblical verse "Jacob left Beer-sheba and set out for Haran" (Gen. 28:10) appears to be simply a description of Jacob's journey from one physical place to another. For the *Zohar* (1:147a–148b), however, Beer-sheba becomes the symbol of deep knowledge of both the written and the oral Torah. With this understanding, the verse asserts that Jacob had to leave the safe haven of the Torah to encounter Haran, which the *Zohar* takes to be the symbol of evil enticement, "the woman of whoredom, the adulteress," to test whether his knowledge of the Torah was strong enough to protect him from such temptations.

In the 17th century and thereafter, the advent of the Enlightenment radically undermined Jews' confidence in revelation. As the Jewish communities of western Europe and North America gradually came to enjoy political rights on the basis of Enlightenment affirmations of the rationality of each individual and as science developed new theories and new technologies, Jews, like their Christian neighbors, came to rely on reason again as the primary way to know about the world and, inevitably, about God.

It is not surprising, then, that Jewish thinkers in the 18th, 19th, and early 20th centuries expended considerable effort to justify Jewish faith and action on rational grounds. Some followed Immanuel Kant's view that religion (in general) and revelation (in particular) are handmaidens to reason. Reason, for these thinkers, establishes not only what one should believe but the grounds for belief. Because the masses have limited reasoning powers, however, they cannot understand rational argumentation. Therefore, they need the tenets and commandments of religion, with their basis in revelation, to learn what they need to know and do. This sounds like Saadia, who also saw revelation as a method for teaching people who cannot or do not yet understand the deliberations of reason. For 19th-century thinkers, however, unlike Saadia, revelation was clearly an inferior form of gaining knowledge about God. So completely did reason win the day during that era that some philosophers, like Hermann Cohen, thought that revelation derived from, and amounted to, reasoning about God.

SHIFTS IN THE NATURE AND AUDIENCE OF REVELATION: BUBER AND ROSENZWEIG

From the divine appearance on Mount Sinai through the early 20th century, Israelites and their descendants have always understood the audience of revelation to be the people Israel as a whole. The Torah itself is ambiguous as to how much of God's revelation the people heard as a group and how much was relayed through Moses—an ambiguity that later sources develop in differing ways. Some Rabbinic interpretations (e.g., Exod. R. 5:9, 29:1) go so far as to point out that at Sinai each person understood God's revelation in his or her own way, depending on each individual's intelligence and sensitivity. Even with these caveats, though, the audience for the Revelation was always construed as the entire people Israel, and its content was always understood to be both God's will and at least some facets of God's nature and actions. Moreover, with just a few exceptions (Spinoza being the most obvious and radical), Jews always understood the Torah in the form that has come down to us as an accurate record of what God revealed at Sinai.

All these assumptions were challenged in the 20th century. Martin Buber (1878–1965) and Franz Rosenzweig (1886–1929) were most responsible for understanding the nature and audience of revelation in new, nontraditional ways. Both men were part of the existentialist school of thought, an approach popular in the first half of the 20th century. Existentialists believe that one must start with the individual's experience to understand how people come to know anything. Furthermore, one must be wary of generalizing from that experience. Because we experience everything as individuals, we cannot accurately characterize how we all experience a given subject. Thus, despite our pretensions to the contrary, we cannot know general truths.

For Buber, then, revelation at Sinai was not a matter of words; it was a revelation of God Himself. All of the words of the Torah are simply a record of how the people who participated in the revelation at Sinai (and many people thereafter) understood its nature and implications. The Torah's account is important because it attests to an experience of God. The Torah's description of that event, though, and the commandments the Torah bases on it, are only human reactions to being in touch with God. Indeed, in Buber's view, to be constrained to the Torah writers' particular reactions to the experience of encountering God is to confine and squelch the living, ongoing relationships that each individual should have with God. We, therefore, should not see ourselves as obligated to obey Jewish law or to believe anything specific that the Torah or later tradition states about God. Instead, according to Buber, we should cultivate special relationships with other human beings that he called "I—thou" relationships. Here we meet each other face to face and soul to soul without any element of trying to use the other party for one's own purposes—for "in each thou we address the Eternal Thou." In other words, although human beings may think that they can use God as a source to get something, they literally cannot do that, but can only engage in an I–thou relationship with God. I–thou relationships with other human beings thus prepare us for encounters with God and, in fact, are the prime way in which we can meet God.

Rosenzweig agreed with his friend Buber that revelation is not a matter of God speaking words; it is rather what we learn about God from ongoing encounters with Him. "All that God ever reveals in revelation is revelation. ... He reveals nothing but Himself to man." For Rosenzweig, though, the Torah is the record of an encounter of the Jewish people with God and, as such, each Jew is obligated to keep the commandments that he or she can. Rosenzweig stresses that Jews are not free to choose which commandments they want to fulfill; rather, they are obligated to do whatever they can. Sometimes we are not physically able to perform a commandment—for example, when we are ill. Even in traditional Jewish law, under such circumstances we are not held to be at fault for failing to do what the commandment requires. The novelty of

Rosenzweig's thesis is that he sees ability not just as a physical property but as a psychological—or, better, a relational—matter. One's ability to perform God's commands, for Rosenzweig, is primarily a function of one's ability to feel commanded by God. That, in turn, is a function of the depth of one's relationship with God.

The best way to understand this is to think of human relationships. One feels only minimally obligated to help a stranger find the way—although one does feel obliged to some extent. As one moves across the spectrum of one's relationships, from the shallowest to the deepest, one gains more and more obligations. These duties are not a matter of promise or contract; indeed, they are generally not even articulated. They instead grow silently out of the expectations that two people have of each other as they become closer. Ultimately, at the end of the spectrum of relationships farthest removed from those with strangers, one feels many and, in some cases, burdensome duties toward one's family members. Regardless of one's feelings about one's relatives, the very depth of the relationship invokes a sense of duty.

Similarly, says Rosenzweig, the extent of one's obligations to God is a function of the depth of the relationship that one has been able to cultivate with God. Consequently, each of us will have a different level of obligation to fulfill the commandments. One wonderful consequence of this theory is that it minimizes haughtiness. None of us can judge anyone else because none of us knows the depth of anyone else's relationship with the divine and the number or character of laws that are, therefore, incumbent on that person.

At the same time, each of us is obliged to take steps to enhance our ability to obey more of God's commands. God, in other words, is like a family member toward whom there is a duty not only to fulfill one's obligations but to seek to deepen the relationship, thereby becoming even more obligated. Rosenzweig's existentialism is manifest, however, in his concern that as we strengthen our relationship with God, we should not see our increased obligations as simply burdens imposed on us from the outside by God (i. e., as laws). Instead, we must seek to transform the requirements of Judaism into living commandments whose authority comes from within us, as individuals, as well as from God because they derive from the relationship that we have with God. The

Torah's precepts, then, are not only demands but bridges between each individual and God. Until a given rule can function as an outgrowth of one's relationship with God and as a further strengthening of it, the rule is not incumbent on the individual—at least not yet.

Both Buber and Rosenzweig redefine the audience for revelation as the individual Jew rather than the entire Jewish people. And they both redefine the substance of revelation as the encounter with God rather than the specific laws and beliefs that the Torah and later tradition draw from it. However, they disagree about the implications of the Torah's record of revelation for us. For Buber, we are informed by the Torah simply that divine revelation is possible and we each seek it through our I–thou relationships with other human beings and animals. For Rosenzweig, on the other hand, the Sinai event binds us to obey Jewish law to the extent that our own individual relationship with God is deep enough for us to feel a given law as a commandment of God.

LATER VIEWS OF THE AUTHORITY OF REVELATION

In addition to these shifts in understanding the nature and content of revelation, the 20th century brought new understandings of the authority of revelation. Jewish Bible scholars began to use historical methods to understand biblical history and the formation of the biblical text. Archaeologic evidence and cross-cultural legal, linguistic, and literary studies of the text demonstrated that the Torah was not originally written as one book but rather consists of at least four separate documents that were later edited and combined. This approach was not intended to supplant the traditional modes of studying the Torah or the law based on such exegesis; it was intended instead to complement such study with another approach to discover the original meaning of the text in addition to the meanings that Jewish tradition later ascribed to it.

The great advantage of this approach is its honesty; one does not need to protect the Torah, so to speak, from whatever results scholarly study indicates about its origins and formation. On the other hand, though, that mode of study questions the authority of the Torah, because it suggests that the Torah consists of several documents that were edited together rather than of one, authoritative record of the words of God.

Reform thinkers, accepting the historical (or "critical") approach to the biblical text, have asserted, along with Buber, that God meets each person individually and that Jewish law, therefore, is not binding. Each of us must do what his or her conscience dictates in response to our encounters with God. Although the 1999 platform statement of the Reform rabbinate endorses a strong effort to motivate Jews to study the Jewish tradition and to base their decisions on that knowledge, ultimately it is the individual's own autonomous choice that determines the content of revelation for that person. This emphasis on individual autonomy inevitably weakens one's sense of tradition and community; and in practice, it raises serious questions as to whether the Reform community can act as a group, even on such critical questions as intermarriage.

Most Orthodox thinkers, at the other end of the spectrum, deny the legitimacy of using the historical method to understand the Torah, arguing that studying the Torah in that way undermines its authority. They insist that the revelation on Mount Sinai is exactly what is recorded in the Torah. In their view, this preserves the divine authority of the text, even though it is human beings who must interpret and apply it. The Orthodox approach also requires one to discount the evidence of cross-cultural influences on the stories and laws of the Torah, for that too, in their perspective, would compromise the divine authority of the text. Thus even a rabbi in the "modern" or "centrist" wing of Orthodoxy, such as Norman Lamm, president of Yeshiva University, has stated:

> I believe the Torah is … God-given. … By "God-given" I mean that He willed that man abide by His commandments and that that will was communicated in discrete words and letters … in as direct, unequivocal, and unambiguous a manner as possible.
>
> Literary criticism of the Bible is a problem, but not a crucial one. Judaism has successfully met greater challenges in the past. … [It] is chiefly a nuisance but not a threat to the enlightened believer (*The Condition of Jewish Belief,* New York, 1966, pp. 124–125).

Conservative thinkers accept the historical method of Bible study but continue to affirm the legally binding character of Jewish law. This form of Jewish faith preserves consistency in method in that it permits us to use the same methods of analysis that we use in examining the texts of other cultures for our study of the classics of the Jewish tradition, and it leaves us open to what we learn from any form of both traditional and modern scholarship. It nevertheless perpetuates a strong sense of tradition and community. This approach, however, requires a considerable amount of good judgment in deciding how to use the newly emerging historical evidence about the development of the Torah and tradition in applying them to modern times. Moreover, because the text of the Torah is no longer seen as a direct transcription of what God said at Sinai, this method of studying and practicing the Jewish tradition necessitates a thorough treatment of what we mean by claiming that the Torah's laws and theories have the authority of divine revelation.

Conservative thinkers of the past and present have interpreted the process and authority of revelation in three general ways. Some, like Joel Roth, conceive of revelation as God communicating with us in actual words. For such thinkers, revelation has propositional content and is normative as God's word. Unlike Orthodox thinkers, however, these Conservative exponents acknowledge that the Torah text that we have in hand shows evidence of consisting of several documents edited over time. Nevertheless, Jewish law is binding as the word of God interpreted by the rabbis over the generations.

Others within the Conservative movement, like Ben Zion Bokser (1907–1984) and Robert Gordis (1908–1992), believe that God, over time, inspires specific individuals who then translate that inspiration into human language. Revelation thus consists of both a divine and a human component. The human element explains the historical influences on our sacred texts. Nevertheless, Jewish law remains binding because the human beings who formulated it were inspired by God.

Still others within the Conservative movement conceive of revelation as the human response to encounters with God. Some, following the lead of Rosenzweig, think of such meetings in individualistic, personal terms, on the model of human beings meeting each other. Louis Jacobs and Seymour Siegel (1927–1988) do this in their writings, and so does Abraham Joshua Heschel (1907–1972). In Heschel's striking term, the Torah itself is then a *midrash*, an interpretation, of the nature and will of God, formulated in response to ineffable encounters with God. In addition to the existentialists and phenomenologists within this camp are rationalists like David Lieber and Elliot Dorff; the rationalists conceive of revelation as the ongoing human attempts to discover truths about God and the world. Rationalists affirm the importance of our personal encounters with God, but they also call attention to what we can learn about God from nature, history, and human experience as a whole. Revelation, on this theory, comes not only from meeting God but also from our outreach to God. For both approaches, Jewish law is binding on both communal and theological grounds: It is the legal part of our communal midrash, representing our collective aspiration to be holy in response to our interactions with God.

Two factors characterize revelation for all three of these approaches within the Conservative movement. First, the authority of revelation is based on a combination of the divine and the human. That is, whether God spoke words at Sinai, or whether God inspired human beings to write down specific words, or whether human beings wrote down the words of the Torah in response to their encounter with God in an attempt to express the nature and implications of that encounter, the authority of the Torah's revelation is, in part, divine. On the other hand, for all three approaches, it is human as well. Whether the divine input came through words, inspiration, or modeling, human beings had a hand in translating that divine incursion into the words of the written and oral Torah. Moreover, we honor and obey the Torah, at the very least, because our ancestors have done so over the centuries and because we continue to see it as authoritative today.

Second, for all three approaches, revelation is ongoing. The revelation at Sinai is critically important because that is where our ancestors as a people first encountered God and wrote their reactions to that event in the document that became the constitutive covenant between God and the Jewish people. Revelation continues, however, just as the talmudic rabbis said it does, through a continuing encounter with the tradition. Therefore, what the liturgy has us declare when called to witness a public reading of the Torah is not an accident: God not only "chose us from among all nations and gave us His Torah" (in the past); God is also to be blessed now as "giver of the Torah," or, reading the word as a verb, as "the One who gives the Torah." Each time we read the Torah anew, nothing less than God's revelation is taking place again, and we bless God for that continuing relationship with us.

Study Questions

1. Is a true faith and path to God justified by the Torah's own account of its origins?

2. What challenges does the reliance on reason present to the belief in the revelatory authority of Scripture? How did Saadia resolve these? How is this different than the modern rationalism Dorff describes?

3. What were some of the justifications that Saadia offered for continued reliance on revelation?

4. When Martin Buber made aliyah to Israel, he was pointedly not named a professor of Jewish thought; instead, he was appointed professor of social ethics. What in his religious outlook might have led to this administrative decision?

5. When Franz Rosenzweig was queried as to whether he used tefillin in his daily prayers, he reportedly responded, "Not yet." How is this answer related to his outlook on Jewish law and observance?

6. In what ways do historical study, textual criticism, and archaeological research challenge the presumptions of traditional Judaism? How might a sophisticated Orthodox thinker respond to the claims of these disciplines?

7. How does the Reform emphasis on individual autonomy build on earlier talmudic claims of the personal nature of revelation?

8. What is common to all Conservative Jewish thinkers as they reflect on the nature of revelation?

9. How do the three groups of Conservative rabbis differentiate between divine and human elements of revelation? How might this affect their understanding of the process, precedence, and prescriptiveness of *halakhah* (Jewish law)?

10. Does your own sense of the Torah's authenticity derive from a belief in revelation? Of the modern approaches (Reform, Orthodox, Conservative), which makes the most sense to you?

11. How does the mix of revelation vs. reason affect your sense of the need to carry out Judaism's rituals and laws?

Study materials by *Baruch Frydman-Kohl*

THE NATURE OF REVELATION AND MOSAIC ORIGINS

Jacob Milgrom

Summary

Jacob Milgrom tackles the difficult issue of how one can rationally believe in the Mosaic origin of all of Torah and *halakhah* given that the laws of the Torah have undergone enormous change over time. Milgrom suggests that one can believe that Moses laid down the fundamental principles in the Torah, and that each generation must interpret those principles to deal with its own circumstances. Milgrom argues that this process is already described within the Bible in cases such as Nehemiah's *amanah* and the stations for Priests and Levites in Chronicles. Neither of these laws can be found in the Torah, but Milgrom shows how they can be seen as limitations or extensions of laws that can be found there. This "minimalist" idea that laws derived from Mosaic principles are also Mosaic, is contrasted with the "maximalist" position that every future rabbinic interpretation of the Torah was already given orally to Moses at Sinai.

When the Torah Scroll is raised after it has been read during the synagogue service, the congregation chants *"v'zot ha-Torah asher sam Mosheh lifnei b'nai Yisra·el al pi Adonai, b'yad Mosheh"* (This is the Torah that Moses set before the Israelites by the command of *YHVH* through Moses!; Deut. 4:44, Num. 4:37). Is that statement truly believed?

This is not a new question. Both Judah ben Ilai in the Talmud (BT BB 15a, BT Men. 30a, Sifrei Deut. 357) and Ibn Ezra in his commentary (to Gen. 12:6, 22:14; Deut. 1:2, 3:11, 34:1,6) realized that several verses in the Torah are post-Mosaic. Joseph Bonfils, in his supercommentary to Ibn Ezra's commentary on Gen. 12:6, commented that this fact does not affect the belief in the revealed character of the Torah. But how is it possible to affirm the Mosaic origin of the entire Torah, not as blind faith but with conviction—rationally? I resort to a Rabbinic story.

During a discussion about how the Torah would be interpreted in the future, Moses requested of God that he be allowed to visit Akiva's academy. The request was granted. Moses sat down in the back of the classroom and listened to Akiva exposit a law purportedly based upon the Torah. Moses didn't understand a word. As a result, he felt faint, "his energy was drained." At the end of Akiva's discourse, the students challenged their teacher: "What is your source?" Akiva replied, *"Halakhah l'Mosheh mi-Sinai"* ([It is] an oral law from Moses at Sinai). The story concludes that Moses was reinvigorated—"his mind was put to rest" (BT Men. 29b).

This story leads to an obvious deduction. Between the times of Moses and of Akiva, the laws of the Torah underwent vast changes, to the extent that Moses was incapable even of following their exposition. But the story conveys a deeper meaning. After all, why was Moses pacified when Akiva announced that his law is traceable to Moses? It couldn't be true. Moses never said it! The answer, however, lies on a different plane. After Akiva announced that the specific law was given by Moses at Sinai, Moses recognized that it was based on Mosaic foundations. Akiva was not creating a new Torah, but was applying the Torah's law to new problems. Moses had been given general principles; successive generations derived their own implications. Presumably, although Moses was not the author of Akiva's legal decision, he might have intended it. That is, had Moses lived in Akiva's time he might have concurred with Akiva's conclusion.

This interpretation is explicitly confirmed in Scripture. Let me cite two examples: The priests and Levites took their accustomed stations *"k'torat Mosheh ish ha-Elohim"* (according to the Teaching of Moses, man of God; 2 Chron. 30:16). No such stations are attributed to priests and Levites in the Torah. According to the Torah, the priests and Levites indeed did have stations in the Tabernacle, though they were different ones (Num. 3:5–10, 18:67). This suffices for the chronicler to declare that the clerical stations in his or her own time are of Mosaic authorship.

A more impressive example is Nehemiah's *amanah* (covenant, agreement) subscribed to by Israel's leaders and accepted on oath by the people (Neh. 10:1 ff.). The *amanah* comprises 18 laws, *"b'yad Mosheh eved ha-Elohim"* (given through Moses the servant of God; Neh. 10:30, cf. vv. 35–37), yet none of them can be found in the Torah precisely as prescribed in Nehemiah's *amanah*. Nonetheless, Nehemiah feels authorized to attribute the 18 laws to Moses since they are built on Mosaic foundations. Each law can be derived from a precedent in the Torah.

Even though it must be conceded that Nehemiah and the chronicler had the complete written Torah before them, the question still remains: What were the Mosaic principles that lay behind the traditions within the Torah? It could well be that each such tradition derives from the Decalogue. The kernel of the Decalogue is terse. Without the inclusion of penalties, it reads more like directions or principles rather than laws. The second commandment orders: "You shall not make for yourself a sculptured image" (Exod. 20:7). Does this mean that images are forbidden in our homes and synagogues? The earliest opinion is found in the appendix to the Decalogue, which prohibits gold or silver images of the Lord, who should be worshiped on imageless altars of wood or unhewn stone (Exod. 20:19–23). Other interpretations are found in the Torah: This prohibition includes imageless pillars (Lev. 26:1, Deut. 16:22). Yet the absence of pillars from the second commandment indicates that they were tolerated in Israel's early worship—thus Jacob (Gen. 28:18,22; 31:52–53; 35:14), Moses (Exod. 24:4), and the Israelite sanctuary unearthed at Arad. Indeed, they were situated in the Temple itself until destroyed in the 8th century by Hezekiah (2 Kings 18:4) and in the following century by Josiah (2 Kings 23:14).

Thus, the second commandment was limited in one interpretation (Exod. 20) and expanded in another (Lev. 26)—showing that various traditions were at work, applying the Decalogue to questions that arose in their age (see also Deut. 4:19–20). Each tradition could rightfully claim that it is "an oral law from Moses at Sinai." This specifically is the case for some of the priestly and Deuteronomic traditions. No wonder, then, that these traditions stemming from different authors might differ in form and content.

In effect, the Torah's *"va-y'daber YHVH elMosheh leimor"* (*YHVH* spoke to Moses, saying …) is equivalent to the rabbinical *"halakhah l'Mosheh mi-Sinai"* ([it is] an oral law from Moses at Sinai). The anonymous authors of the Torah's legislation were certain that the laws they proposed were not of their invention but were derivable from Mosaic principles, i. e., traceable to Moses himself. They might have agreed, for example, that the dire economic conditions of their time, probably 8th-century-B. C. E. Judah, would have been remedied by the laws of jubilee and redemption. On that basis, they attributed these laws to Moses, even though he himself had not been their author.

Talmudist David Weiss Halivni presents a systematized perspective on divine revelation in Rabbinic literature. He refers to the story of Moses and Akiva as the "minimalist" position, arguing that only general principles were revealed at Sinai. This is in contrast to the "maximalist" position that dogmatically asserts that the entire oral and written Torah, including "whatever text an earnest scholar [*talmid ḥakham*] will someday teach, has already been declared to Moses at Sinai" (JT *Pe·ah* 17a). Halivni cites another minimalist position, illustrated by the following *midrash*: "R. Yannai said: The words of the Torah were not given as clear-cut decisions. … When Moses asked, 'Master of the Universe, in what way shall we know the true sense of the law?', God replied, 'The majority is to be followed' [a play on Exod. 23:2]—when a majority declares it is impure, it is impure; when a majority says it is pure, it is pure" (Mid. Psalms 12:4; cf. BT Ḥag. 3b). As Halivni perceptively concludes:

> Contradictions are thus built into revelation. Revelation was formulated within the framework of contradiction in the form of argumentation pro and con. No legitimate argument or solution can be in conflict with the divine opinion, for all such arguments and solutions constitute a part of God's opinion.

These two minimalist stories about Moses portray the human role throughout the generations in the revelatory process. Revelation was not a one-time Sinaitic event. It behooves and indeed compels each generation to be active partners of God in determining and implementing the divine will.

I submit that what Halivni discovered in Rabbinic tradition applies as well to the written Torah. If it can be maintained that insights of, or disagreements among, the Sages are traceable to Sinai, this is also true for innovations or discrepancies ensconced within the biblical text. Legal formulations may be presuming earlier, reputedly Sinaitic precedents

(Moses in Akiva's academy); and conflicting laws may be justifiable claimants to Sinaitic origin (Moses in Yannai's *midrash*).

We should, therefore, acknowledge that each of the schools that contributed to the composition of the Torah had a valid claim to its conviction that its laws were traceable to Mosaic origins; and as for their differences, we might adapt the coinage of a later generation of rabbis concerning the differing schools of Hillel and Shammai: *"Eilu v'eilu divrei Elohim ḥayyim"* (Both [statements] are the words of the living God; PT Ber. 1:7, BT Er. 13b).

Study Questions

1. Besides the passages about Moses' death, what other evidence can you think of that suggests Moses was not the author of all of Torah?

2. Do you agree with the commentator Joseph Bonfils, a 15th-century rabbi, who claimed in an explanation of Ibn Ezra's Torah commentary that whether or not Moses wrote a section of Torah does not affect its authority as divinely revealed?

3. Does it make sense to think that laws derived from Torah principles can be said to have been revealed at Sinai? Would such laws have the same authority as those directly revealed to Moses?

4. In the story from the Talmud about Moses visiting Akiva's academy, can Moses' confusion be consistent with either the minimalist or maximalist positions? How so? In your own theology, do you consider yourself a "minimalist" or a "maximalist"?

Study materials by *Jacob Pinnolis*

Biblical Foundations: Beliefs

THE GOD OF ISRAEL

Howard Avruhm Addison

Summary

The essential point of Howard Addison's essay is that the concept of God in the Bible evolved over time. The overall trend of this evolution was from a family deity (much like the pagan gods of the surrounding culture) to an increasingly abstract, universal, and monotheistic concept of God. Writers of early sections of the Bible, influenced by contact with Mesopotamia, see God as the protector of a family who is owed loyalty. Canaanite influence can be detected in the later development of God as a ruler or father. The key evidence for understanding the different concepts of God can be seen in the use of different names for God; the characteristics attributed to God; and the ways in which God is manifested to humans. Each piece of evidence, when connected to what is known about its historical context in the ancient Near East, helps fill in the picture of a gradual development toward a thorough monotheism. For example, the name "*El,*" for God, connects the Torah to Canaanite tradition and the concept of god of a clan. In another example, early biblical texts tend to describe God in thoroughly anthropomorphic ways, reflecting the idea of a personal and intimate relationship with God. Later texts, particularly those of the Prophets and Deuteronomy, portray God as essentially unknowable and not limited to a particular place, thus reflecting a more abstract concept of God. Addison ends by noting that the development of the concept of God did not end in the biblical period, but continued throughout Rabbinic literature to the present.

How did the God of Israel differ from pagan deities in biblical times? Yehezkel Kaufmann, in his seminal work *The Religion of Israel*, demonstrates that the God of Israel, unlike the pagan deities of the surrounding nations, had no pedigree or genealogy. This does not mean, however, that Israel's conception of God did not evolve over a period of time. One way of tracing this evolution is by examining various names by which God was known in the Torah, examining in this way the development of Israel's understanding of God.

THE EVOLUTION OF ISRAEL'S GOD IDEA

An understanding of the patriarchs' relationship to God can best be approached by examining their patterns of marriage, rather than their patterns of worship. Abraham insisted that his servant find a wife for Isaac in Mesopotamia and not from among the women of Canaan (Gen. 24:1–10). Later, Rebekah persuaded Isaac to send Jacob to Mesopotamia, not ostensibly to flee Esau's wrath but for the stated purpose that Jacob there find a wife (27:46–28:9). Given the popular assumption that only Abraham and Sarah's family recognized the one God at that time, these demands seem strange if they were motivated by religious rather than ethnic concerns. Stranger still is the oath that Laban uttered before leaving his nephew Jacob at Gilead (31:53), identifying "the God of Abraham and the god of Nahor" as the same ancestral deity.

These tales indicate the deep familial context that conditioned the ancestors' view of the divine as they traveled from Mesopotamia to Canaan. For them God was the unseen head of the household whose members were members of God's family. This God of the ancestors entered history by concluding a covenant with the elect (Gen. 15, 17) and was invoked in matters of war and its spoils (14:19–24). Not restricted by locale, God guided the clan in its travels (12, 26, 31:3) and cared for them (18, 26:12). In turn, the clan recognized this God and showed its loyalty through worship and tithes (28:20–21). Far from unapproachable, the God of the patriarchs was not only questioned by the patriarchs and matriarchs (16:2,3; 18:12) but could be the subject of moral indictment and negotiation as well (18:23–33).

The strong bond between God and the clan is evidenced by the inclusion of the name of the family head as part of God's title. God identifies Himself as Abraham's "shield" (Gen. 15:1) and is later termed the "Fearsome One" or "the kinsman" of Isaac (31:53) and the "Mighty One of Jacob" (49:24). It is unclear to modern scholars if God was known only by these names and what the relationship of this deity was to *Shaddai* (possibly, the "Exalted One of the Mountain"; Gen. 48:3; Exod. 6:3).

Upon their arrival in the Promised Land, the ancestors' clan came in contact with the Canaanites who worshiped the divine figure *El*. Although suggested derivations of *El*'s name include "going in front," "going toward," and "whose ties cannot be shed," its root meaning is most likely "power" (Gen. 31:29). Far greater than a local deity, *El* was the head of the Canaanite pantheon, a high god, whose manifestations were associated with specific Canaanite altars and locales (*El-Elyon* at Salem, 14:18; *El Olam* at Beer-sheba, 21:33; *El Beth El* at Bethel, 35:7).

Like the God of the ancestors, *El* was also seen as a divine father, guide, and ruler. His attributes influenced the ancestors' view of God, and literary allusions to God standing preeminent among the *Elim* and judging in the council of *El* persist both in the Torah (Exod. 15:11) and in Psalms (82:1). The Hebrew Bible, however, stripped these images of their polytheistic associations with *El*'s family and with *El*'s cabinet of gods.

Looking at the language of the Torah, we can see a growing association between the God of the ancestors and *El*. The poetic passages uttered by the heathen seer Balaam praising, rather than cursing, Israel set a parallelism between *El* and *Shaddai* (Num. 24:16). The tandem use of *"El Shaddai"* can be found throughout the Hebrew Bible but appears mostly in Genesis and in the poetry of other scriptural books. This association between *El* and the God of the ancestors becomes an identification when Jacob consecrates an altar in Shechem and names it *El-elohei-yisra·el* (Gen. 33:20).

When was God first addressed by the now ineffable four-letter name, *YHVH* (יהוה) the name we pronounce as *Adonai*? This is a matter of serious debate. Although in Exod. 6:2, God seems to have revealed Himself to the patriarchs only as *El Shaddai*, the divine name *YHVH* was not a totally new revelation to Moses. Archaeologists have discovered lists of Edomite place-names from 13th- and 14th-century-B.C.E. southern Palestine that use forms of the root הוה to designate the existence of God. Similar verb forms employed in western Semitic personal names date from the time of Hammurabi (d. 1750 B. C. E.). The Torah claims that Enosh, Adam's grandson, was the first to call on *YHVH* by name (Gen. 4:26), whereas Gen. 9:26 identifies *YHVH* as the God of Shem. Among the descendants of Leah, the names Jochebed (*Yo-kheved; YHVH* is powerful) and possibly Judah (*Y'hudah;* the etymology is uncertain) indicate a recognition of *YHVH* among the Israelites before Moses. The lack of resolution as to when the Hebrews first referred to God as *YHVH* led to the documentary hypothesis. This theory argues that the patriarchal narratives that refer to God as *YHVH* and those that call God solely *Elohim* (an expanded plural form of *El,* "divinity" or "godhood") represent separate literary sources.

Although some scholars have suggested that *YHVH* might derive from a cultic interjection (*Yahu,* "It is He!"), most consider it more probable that the name is related to the Hebrew verb "to be," הוה. When God refers to Himself as *Ehyeh-Asher-Ehyeh* (Exod. 3:14), this distinguishes Him from the lifeless idols as well as from the ephemeral and fleeting in the world. It is God who is ever present or who causes to be that which is—and therefore will fulfill God's redemptive vows to the Israelites.

Some scholars suggest that *YHVH* might first have been a cultic name for *El* in the Midianite and Semitic communities of Sinai and Seir (Deut. 33:2–5). The name *YHVH* replaced the imagery and functions of *El,* as is found in the Torah's numerous descriptions of *YHVH*'s kingship (Exod. 15:18) and role as a wise, compassionate father and creator (Gen. 49:25; Deut. 32:6). Among the Israelites under Moses, the roles, epithets, and attributes of the God of the ancestors and of *El* were subsumed by the divine figure of *YHVH.*

THE ATTRIBUTES OF GOD

Although the Decalogue prohibits physical images of the divine, a rich verbal imagery of God pervades all of Hebrew Scripture. Medieval Jewish thinkers, influenced by Greek philosophy's spiritual/physical dualism, tended to view the Bible's descriptions of God—as having human form and emotions—as a concession to a prebiblical mind-set. Maimonides' *Guide of the Perplexed* was not alone in its quest to preserve

God's exclusively sublime nature by reinterpreting these human images of God.

Because the Israelites in the Bible maintain a concrete, personal relationship with *YHVH,* it is hardly surprising that the source of life was conceived among them as a living personality—possessing self-consciousness, will, and imagination. All descriptions of God are by analogy. The Hebrew Bible drew its analogies not from the conceptual or from the spheres of impersonal substance or force but rather from the personal and intimate.

This is reflected in the titles, attributes, and emotions ascribed to God in the Bible. God is infrequently referred to as *Adon,* "Lord." (Its derivative, *Adonai,* became a substitute epithet for the ineffable *YHVH.*) More often used are *Melekh* (king), denoting God's sovereignty, and *Av* (father), an expression of God's relationship to God's human sons and daughters.

God acts as chieftain or judge (*Shofet*) by meting out reward to the good and punishment to the wicked in conformity to the norms of righteousness (*tzedek*). God's wisdom distinguishes good and evil and can endow the knowledge necessary for success. Showing love to the elect, God guarantees the covenant with them in loyalty and security. However, God uses rejection and outbreaks of heat and fury, sometimes mysteriously, to establish His purpose and rule when that rule is violated.

A tension, however, does exist in Scripture between the impulse to describe God as humanlike and God's sanctity as the unknowable. God's ability to assume a human form is seen in Gen. 18 and 32, Amos 9, and Isa. 6. Yet Ezekiel's description of the divine Presence (*Kavod*) on the chariot throne (*merkavah;* Ezek. 1) is hedged in by so many qualifying terms (e. g., image and likeness), that it suggests that what was observed was only a semblance, not the reality of God. Descriptions that seem to limit God in place or knowledge (Gen. 3:8–10, 22:12) are more than balanced by those claiming divine omniscience and omnipresence (Deut. 29:28, 30:4). Scripture's depictions of God's emotions are at times so pronounced that they portray God as the Bible's tragic hero—admitting mistakes, rethinking decisions, and more often than not being disappointed by His own creatures (Gen. 6:5–7; 1 Sam.

15:11). In contrast to these metaphors stands the assertion by Hosea proclaiming God's insistence that "I am God, not man" (Hos. 11:9). Not bound by procreation, mortality, or physical constraint, God has neither ancestors nor spouse. For Hosea, God's only consort is Israel, betrothed through an act of divine grace.

THE DIVINE BEING, UNITY, AND MANIFESTATIONS OF GOD

The Hebrew Bible portrays a world dominated by the figure of *YHVH*. Exclamations stating, "God does not care"—literally, "there is no God" (Ps. 10:4, 14:1, 53:2)—question God's providence, not God's existence. Comparisons identifying *YHVH* as the God of history and pagan deities as gods of nature prove facile on further examination. The God of Israel is revealed in fire, lightning, wind, and storm (Pss. 29, 89, 97). When God causes the Sea of Reeds to flee and establishes both divine sanctuary and eternal rule (Exod. 15:1–18), this sea (*yam*) is not a vanquished rival god, but His instrument for defeating the Egyptians through His rule over nature. Though pagan deities shift in relationship both to the seasons and to the fleeting political fortunes of their adherents' city-states, the God of Israel controls history as the dynamic arena for enacting His own purposes. Idols are feeble and inert, but the "living God" (*Elohim ḥayyim;* Deut. 5:23) is vital and bestows life.

The unity of God in Israel was not a mere intellectual construct, but a response to His demand of total loyalty, "with all your heart and with all your soul and with all your might" (Deut. 6:5). The verb for "creating" used in Genesis, *bara* (literally "cut out"), is reserved only for God, indicating that He alone is the power responsible for the new and the unprecedented.

The Hebrew Bible occasionally describes God as being represented by a manifestation or an emissary, similar to the way that a human emperor is represented by a legate. These representations reveal God's power and purpose to different people in different places while preserving the essential unity and invisibility of God. Chief among these manifestations is *shem*, God's "name." Ancient belief held that people's names are the emblem of their essential nature and could be separated from them even to be used against them. God's "name" is sometimes used synonymously with *YHVH*. When caused to dwell in the Temple, the *shem* indicates that the sanctuary is *YHVH*'s property (Deut. 12:4–12).

Other manifestations of God include *mal·akh* (angel), *panim* (face), and *Kavod* (Glory or Presence). As divine messengers, *mal·akhim* are ambassadors who identify with their divine sovereign while remaining distinct from God. Although angels appear in many places to speak God's message, God remains ultimately one; and it is God who answers prayers. Because the face is an individual's most recognizable and expressive feature, *panim* is used to indicate the manifestation of God's presence. The lifting up of God's face (*yissa panav;* Num. 6:26) indicates favor and blessing, whereas its concealment (*astir panai;* Deut. 31:17) denotes abandonment and curse. Although the Torah is equivocal about whether humans can see God's *panim* (Exod. 33:11,20; Num. 12:8), the *Kavod* confirms God's message and will indicate God's redemptive acts (Isa. 60:1–2).

THE TRIUMPH OF MONOTHEISM

Overtly mythologic statements are foreign to the Torah. Despite one strange, brief passage concerning "sons of God" or divine beings (Gen. 6:1–4), God alone dominates life. God's manifestations are that and nothing more; God's "Hosts" (*YHVH Tz'va·ot*) are not armies of gods, but troops of stars, constellations, or spirits that do battle with the political enemies of Israel and the morally perverse. God is the ultimate source of *k'dushah* (holiness), a mysterious supernatural force, both beneficial and dangerous, on which life depends and is renewed. God's unconditional holiness radically distinguishes Him from the creatures. It is God who imbues chosen times, objects, and persons with this special quality (e. g., *Shabbat,* the Ark, the priests) and conditionally sanctifies Israel with this fullness of power and life through the Covenant (Lev. 19:2, 20:7–8).

Despite *YHVH*'s covenant with Israel and demand for exclusive fealty in the Decalogue, Israel's loyalty was severely tested during the 9th century B. C. E. by the faith and devotees of *Baal* (Master). Identified with the Aramean storm god *Baal Hadad*, he was the god of rain, life, and fertilization, a cultic manifestation that ultimately rivaled and then supplanted *El* (Judg. 9:4,46). *YHVH* subsumed some of *Baal*'s functions, as evident in the storm poetry of Ps. 29 and the divine honorific "Rider of the Heavens" (*Roḥev Shamayim;* Deut. 33:26). The co-use of *Yahu* and *Ba·al* in Israelite personal names, including Jonathan and Eshbaal, sons of King Saul (1 Chron. 9:39), suggests that *Ba·al,* as owner or master, was at one time an accepted epithet for *YHVH.*

An attempt to establish the cult of Baal, an agricultural rain god, and to eclipse *YHVH,* God of Israel's nomadic desert past, was undertaken by Samaria's murderous Queen Jezebel, a former Phoenician princess. A furious counterattack was mounted by the prophet Elijah, who is portrayed in Kings as a second Moses. Like his predecessor, Elijah built an altar of 12 stones, split a body of water, killed the ringleaders of idolatry, and experienced a revelation of God at Sinai. The final resting place of neither is known. They differed, however, in that Moses received the Tablets of the Covenant amid thunder and lightning, storm manifestations that in Elijah's time had become overly associated with Baal. Elijah's divine revelation clearly indicated that although *YHVH* controlled the lightning and whirlwinds, *YHVH*'s message was to be heard only in the still, small voice that followed the storm. The final expunging of Baal from family names (replaced by the derogatory *boshet,* "shame") and the Israelite lexicon was proclaimed in Hosea's prophecy to Israel (Hos. 2:18), "You will call [Me] Ishi [My Husband], / And no more will you call Me Baali."

The seeds of monotheism, present from the earliest stages of Israelite history, came to full bloom toward the end of the first commonwealth, beginning with the reform of Josiah at the end of the 7th century B. C. E., during the Babylonian exile and throughout the Second Temple period. The attacking Assyrian and then Babylonian armies are described as *YHVH*'s instruments to punish Israel for its sins (Isa. 7:17–22, 10:5–11; Lam. 2:17). Jeremiah maintained that *YHVH*'s covenantal providence and worship extended outside the Land of Israel (Jer. 29:4–7), an issue that in former times was questioned (1 Sam. 26:19). Deutero-Isaiah, the anonymous prophet of the exilic age whose writings are found in chapters 40 to 55 of the Book of Isaiah, categorically dismissed the possibility of two or more divine powers, lampooning pagan idols as worthless man-made fetishes (Isa. 44, 45:7). Visions of an eschatologic future portrayed *YHVH* as the recognized universal king whose reign would even vanquish the power of death (Isa. 2:1–4, 25:8; Dan. 12:2).

CONCLUSIONS

Later Judaism's monotheism would not remain seamless, as evidenced by ongoing debate over the nature of God and God's attributes. Contemporary thinkers disagree over whether God is ultimately a personal being, the boundless source of life transcending description and personality, or a force making for salvation within nature and humanity. Is God all-powerful, all-powerful but self-limiting, or essentially limited in nature? Are God's attributes (e. g., wisdom, mercy) essential aspects of God, merely manifestations of God's activity, divine names, potencies, or actual hypostases? All of these have been explored and expounded on in centuries of rabbinical, philosophic, and kabbalistic literature. The question of whether God can be both omnipotent and just took on new poignancy after the *Sho·ah*. However, when the Midrash identified *YHVH* and *Elohim* as God's attributes of mercy and judgment—with no acknowledgment of their historic connotations—one thing became clear: The Judaism that emerged from the biblical period—and that continues to engage our hearts and our minds—is a monotheism of the unique, universal God.

Study Questions

1. Addison notes that there is "a tension … in Scripture between the impulse to describe God as humanlike and God's sanctity as the unknowable." What are the reasons people, even today, might be pulled in both directions—seeing God sometimes as having personality and emotions, and other times as more distant and omnipotent?

2. Ancient Israelites appear to have appropriated both the imagery and language of surrounding pagan cultures. What do Jews today look to for imagery and language in understanding God—to

psychology, to environmentalism, to philosophy, to film and literature?

3. Is it a religious problem for us if much of the Bible seems less than completely monotheistic? Is it disturbing to think that the Bible subsumes in God many of the characteristics of pagan gods (such as Ba'al's control of the weather)?

4. Which of the various theories Addison cites about the origin of the name *YHVH* do you find most convincing and why?

5. Take one prayer service, such as *Kabbalat Shabbat*, and look closely at its prayers for the characteristics of God they portray. Which of the different concepts Addison describes can you find? What sorts of attributes are emphasized? Are these features of God particularly connected to *Shabbat*?

Study materials by *Jacob Pinnolis*

THE COVENANT AND THE ELECTION OF ISRAEL

David L. Lieber

Summary

Belief in a covenant (*b'rit*) of the people of Israel with God, and in the divine election of that people, are core beliefs of the Bible that have sustained the Jewish people throughout history. That special relationship is anticipated in Genesis, serves as the basis for the Exodus, is articulated in the Sinai Revelation, detailed in the laws of Leviticus, and refined in the discourses of Deuteronomy.

The narratives of Joshua are particularly important, since they show the people of Israel entering the land in fulfillment of the divine promise, and replicate three elements of the Sinai commitment: the divine "election of Israel, the covenant between God and Israel, and Israel's covenanted obligations."

Although other forms of covenant existed in the ancient Near East, only Israel viewed itself as a group of clans united into a people through this special relationship with God. While there were examples of Hittite and Assyrian treaties, the covenant of Israel was unique. It indicated that God and a single people had freely entered into a bond that called upon Israel to become "a kingdom of priests and a holy nation," with precise prescriptions to achieve this ideal.

Notably, this agreement limited human authority. Kings could be called to account by prophetic messengers, and individuals had responsibilities to the community and to God. Even the sacrificial cult required righteous living as part of the covenant. Israel was assigned a central role in God's plan for humanity, to be a "light to the nations." This privilege entailed significant obligations, and failure to fulfill God's demands could elicit terrible punishment. Nonetheless, the covenant was essentially hopeful because it was understood to be an eternal challenge.

Rabbinic Judaism prescribes specific observances that affirm, renew, and reinvigorate this covenantal relationship, such as pilgrimage festivals, *Shabbat*, *t'fillin*, daily prayer, recitation of the *Sh'ma*, and circumcision.

In modern times, the belief in election has been challenged as being out of step with efforts to create democratic societies with universal ideals. In addition, both the Reform and Reconstructionist movements have sought to reinterpret or modify the concept of covenant. Still, according to Lieber, "the uniqueness of Israel's calling to be a holy people, by virtue of Torah, remains fundamental to the faith of the Jew."

One who is called to the Torah during synagogue services recites a blessing (*b'rakhah*) thanking God "who has chosen us from among all peoples by giving us His Torah" (BT Ber. 11b). This *b'rakhah* affirms two of Judaism's fundamental doctrines, both of which have had far-reaching implications for ancient Israel's political institutions and its religious worldview. These doctrines are the election of the people Israel, and its covenant with God. Both of these stem from Israel's origins, providing the rationale for its existence and the foundation on which its system of government was established. In fact, the belief in Israel's special relationship to God, as defined in the covenant at Sinai, is the central theme of the Torah (see Exod. 19:5, 24:7–8; Deut. 26:17 ff., 29:9–14).

This is underlined by the covenant Joshua made with the Israelite tribes after he reviewed the early history of Israel at a public gathering of the tribes in Shechem (Josh. 24). As at the covenant of Sinai, the people affirmed three times that they would worship the Lord alone and obey Him. Unlike the first covenant between God and Israel, however, the gathering at Shechem was an occasion for reaffirming an existing covenant—not entering into a new one. This account differs from the one at Sinai, suggesting, as it does, that the people were free to reject the God of Israel (Josh. 24:15). This led some to conjecture that it presents an alternate tradition to the Sinai account, describing, perhaps, the admission of additional tribes to the covenanted union. In any event, the Shechem story does contain the three basic elements found in Sinai narrative:

- It is God who takes the initiative in choosing and delivering Israel (Josh. 24:3,6; cf. Exod. 19:4).
- Israel's relationship with God is defined by a covenant (Josh. 24:25; cf. Exod. 19:5, 24:3 ff.).
- The covenant brings with it obligations (Josh. 24:25; cf. Exod. 19:5,8, 20:1 ff., 21:1 ff.).

These elements may be summarized as: the election of Israel, the covenant between God and Israel, and Israel's covenanted obligations.

From the earliest period of its recorded history, Israel was conscious of its uniqueness as "the people of God." This claim was immortalized in the name "Israel," which, according to the biblical narrative, originated when Jacob wrested a special blessing from God, having "striven with beings divine and human, and ... prevailed" (Gen. 32:29). Whatever the name meant originally, it could also be interpreted as "[the domain in which] God rules," as the ancient blessing of Moses suggests (Deut. 33:5). Genesis anticipates this special bond between God and Israel with the divine promises made to the patriarchs. These promises move to their dramatic fulfillment with the exodus from Egypt and the encampment at Sinai, where God enters into a solemn covenant (*b'rit*) with the people and provides them with instructions, statutes, and judgments. Deuteronomy spells out the implications of the covenant for future generations; and finally, Joshua marks the fulfillment of the promise to Israel's ancestors and the renewal of the covenant in the Promised Land.

Of all the peoples in the ancient Near East, only Israel seems to have viewed its relationship with a deity as covenanted. Since covenants generally played an important role in the political and social life of the ancient world, this may appear surprising. A covenant might serve as a treaty between nations, such as that between Israel and the Gibeonites (Josh. 9:15). It could solemnize a compact between individuals, as in the case of Jacob and Laban (Gen. 31:44). It could assume the form of a land grant, as in the patriarchal stories (e.g., Gen. 15:18 ff.). A covenant could also define relationships that were not primarily legal, such as the friendship of David and Jonathan (1 Sam. 18:3), or not exclusively so, such as marriage (Mal. 2:14). In such cases, it formalized the relationship, lending it an enduring quality and adding a sense of commitment and obligation that had not been there before. Generally, a covenant clarified a relationship, spelled out the nature of the obligations that flowed from it, and sealed it with a religious rite or symbolic affirmation at a shrine (e. g., Exod. 24:4 ff.; Josh. 24:19 ff.; 2 Kings 23:1 ff.).

Law codes sanctified by a covenant between a god and a "chosen" king existed in the earlier Sumerian and Old Babylonian traditions. What was new at Sinai was not the linkage of covenant with law giving, but the entry of disparate clans into a covenant with God, which welded them into a people united by a system of laws. Israel's God transcended the forces of nature and thus had no need for worshipers to wait in attendance or assist in preserving the order of a world constantly threatened by the forces of chaos. The function of the covenant, then, was to define the people's exclusive relationship to God and to institutionalize the paramount nature of God's rule. This is given expression in the first two statements of the Decalogue, which also define the relationship as personal, one in which God has a special interest. The Decalogue's use of the term *"kana,"* which literally means "jealous," is an instructive characterization of God. The term clearly intends to convey that God considers it a personal betrayal for Israel to turn to other gods.

The Sinai covenant did not follow either the model of the Hittite treaties of the 14th century B. C. E. or the Assyrian treaties of the 8th or 7th centuries B. C. E., because it was not a treaty. It did not contain the language of the land grants associated with the Abrahamic or Davidic covenants, because it was not a land grant. The covenant was unique: an agreement entered into freely by a deity with a people to create a new relationship or, rather, to redefine an earlier one initiated by God through the gracious act of deliverance from bondage. It called for a response from the people, who were to be "a kingdom of priests," "a holy nation" (Exod. 19:6), and who were provided with specific directions to attain this goal. They accepted God's charge, participating in an elaborate rite to seal their agreement (Exod. 24:4 ff.). God undertook to dwell among them and to give them the land promised to their ancestors, providing that they carried out their part of the agreement. This differed from the covenant entered into with Abraham (Gen. 15), which was modeled after the ancient land grant to a loyal servant for services rendered and in which no future acts were required.

The most detailed presentation of the covenant between God and Israel is found in the Book of Deuteronomy, which almost precisely follows the form of neo-Assyrian vassal treaties, such as the one of Esarhaddon (672 B.C.E.). Presumably, the authors of Deuteronomy spelled out God's original covenant with Israel in the explicit, carefully structured form devised by the Assyrians to emphasize that God—not the Assyrian king—is sovereign over Israel.

The early belief that God had entered into a covenant with the Israelites' ancestors did not allow the establishment of the monarchy in the 11th century B.C.E. to displace the "king-ship of God." This limited the king's authority and led to uprisings, on occasion, when he abused it. The people ultimately did accept the notion of a covenant between God and the house of David, but this covenant was limited by the requirements of the divine law (cf. Deut. 17:14–20).

Nowhere is this better illustrated than in the actions of the prophets. Samuel is depicted as remonstrating with Saul, the first king of Israel: "Does the LORD delight in burnt offerings and sacrifices / As much as in obedience to the LORD's command?" (1 Sam. 15:22). Prophets, viewed as the messengers of God, did not hesitate to speak the truth to reigning monarchs, who accepted their harsh pronouncements. This is indicated by the messages of doom pronounced against David by Nathan in the wake of the Bathsheba outrage (2 Sam. 11–12) and against Ahab's house by Elijah after Ahab had Naboth slain to expropriate his vineyard (1 Kings 21).

The prophets, however, did more than take kings and princes to task for violating the law of God. They insisted that the covenant was binding both on the people as a whole and on each individual Israelite as a responsible member of the community. Each of them shared equally in both the obligations and the privileges of the *b'rit*. This is stated dramatically in Deuteronomy (5:2–3) when Moses declares: "The LORD our God made a covenant with us at Horeb. It was not with our fathers that the LORD made this covenant, but with us, the living, every one of us who is here today." To be sure, some bore greater responsibility than others because of their power and wealth, but none could ultimately escape the divine judgment. People had to be at peace with others as well as with themselves and with God. The cult, the organized system of Israelite worship, enabled them to come into the presence of God and express their heartfelt emotions to the divine. Its efficacy, however, depended on their obedience to God, as the prophets insisted, on the proper response to the divine call for righteous living. If this was not forthcoming, God threatened to destroy the holy places and abandon the people.

This message was brought home by virtually every prophet who lived before the destruction of the Temple in 586 B. C. E. They stressed, however, that God's relationship with Israel remained constant and that the covenant was eternal. That is why all of the prophets, without exception, saw beyond the destruction they prophesied to a glorious future. Even as severe a critic as Jeremiah, who announced the forthcoming demise of the Judean state, proclaimed in the name of God: "They shall be My people, and I will be their God. ... And I will make an everlasting covenant with them that I will not turn away from them and that I will treat them graciously" (Jer. 32:38–40). To effect this, God intended to give them a "new covenant" and inscribe divine Teaching in their hearts (31:31,33). Almost as if anticipating the later claim of the Christian church that this implied the rejection of Israel, the prophet added (31:35–36):

> Thus said the LORD,
> Who established the sun for light by day,
> The laws of moon and stars for light by night,
> Who stirs up the sea into roaring waves,
> Whose name is LORD of Hosts:
> If these laws should ever be annulled before Me
> ...
> Only then would the offspring of Israel cease
> To be a nation before Me for all time.

God's justice was tempered by compassion. While making demands on people, God was "slow to anger," providing many opportunities for both individuals and societies to make amends. Beyond that, God provided the Israelites, and indeed all of humankind, instructions and guidance to enable them to live in peace with one another and to enjoy the bounties of the earth. Having created humankind in the divine image, God hoped people would walk in fellowship with Him and in obedience to His will.

The everlasting nature of the covenant was grounded in the divine promise to the Israelites' ancestors. Although it certainly was not considered arbitrary, the covenant was recognized as an unmerited expression of divine love (Deut. 4:37, 7:6–7). The "election" of Israel went hand in hand with the covenant and provided a theological explanation for it. This is most clearly crystallized in Exod. 19:3–6, where Israel is called on to be "a kingdom of priests and a holy nation." As such, Israel was assigned a central role in God's purpose for all of humankind—a role that the great prophet of the exilic period defined as "a light unto the nations" (Isa. 49:6).

The conviction that God had entered into a covenant with its ancestors shaped Israel's entire worldview. It taught the Israelites that God cares about human beings, particularly for those who, like the people of ancient Israel, were helpless and oppressed. The covenant also made it plain that Israel's election was not for Israel's sake but to serve God's purpose for the rest of the world. It entailed obligation, not special privilege. As Amos, the first of the literary prophets (8th century B. C. E.), stated explicitly: "You alone have I singled out / Of all the families of the earth— / That is why I will call you to account / For all your iniquities" (Amos 3:2). The world required the example of a covenant community because it was unredeemed. This message was stated clearly by the anonymous prophet whose words appear in the second part of the Book of Isaiah: "My witnesses are *you* / . . . / My servant, whom I have chosen" (Isa. 43:10). These words were addressed to Babylonian exiles, calling on them to cast off their gloom and engage in a new exodus that they might be, as cited earlier, "a light unto the nations" and that God's salvation might reach the ends of the earth (49:6).

It was an extraordinary challenge. Not surprisingly, it was never fully met. The Bible recounts at least three instances when the covenant was renewed: at Shechem, before Joshua's death (Josh. 24); in Jerusalem, at the time of King Josiah's reformation (2 Kings 23); and in Jerusalem again, during the time of Ezra (Neh. 10). These renewals succeeded in consolidating the community and setting it on a new course, demonstrating the power of the covenant concept, both as an ideal to be aimed at and an obligation to be met, rather than as a final achievement.

This concept had an effect on the development of the apocalyptic communities, which held the belief that the final judgment was at hand, such as the Qumran community near the Dead Sea (from the 2nd century B.C.E. through the 1st century C.E.) and, of course, on Christianity, which called on its faithful to adopt a "New Covenant." It is perhaps for this reason that Rabbinic Judaism played down the use of *"b'rit,"* restricting it almost exclusively to the rite of circumcision, one sign of the covenant. The concept itself, however, has remained central to the Rabbinic view of the Jewish relationship to God. The covenant is celebrated annually in the three pilgrimage festivals that recall God's great acts on Israel's behalf, as well as weekly on *Shabbat,* which is seen as a sign of the covenant. It is re-enacted every weekday morning in the putting on of *t'fillin.* The morning service itself reminds worshipers of the election of Israel and God's love for it, as expressed in the liberation from Egyptian bondage and the gift of Torah. The recitation of the *Sh'ma* is a daily reaffirmation of the sovereignty of God and the authority of the divine commandments.

The Sages also grasped the dynamic significance of the covenant concept for rebuilding Jewish life, through its institutions and laws, to meet the altered circumstances presented by the destruction of the Second Temple and the growth of the Diaspora. The development of the oral Torah would not have been possible without the view that the Sages had the right to interpret the written Torah to maintain God's presence among the Jewish people. They derived this from the scriptural injunction: "You shall act in accordance with the instructions given you [by the Levitical priests] and the ruling handed down to you" (Deut. 17:11), which they interpreted as granting them the rightful authority to carry on the work of Moses and his successors so that the everlasting covenant might be applicable to their time as well (cf. 5:3, 29:13–14).

With the spread of the Enlightenment and of the Emancipation in the 19th century, some western Jewish thinkers considered the doctrine of the election to be too exclusive. In an effort to universalize it, Reform leaders preferred to speak of "the mission of Israel," designed to spread ethical monotheism throughout the world. In the second quarter of the

20th century, Mordecai Kaplan, the founder of Reconstructionism, also suggested the abandonment of "the Chosen People doctrine," because it not only drew invidious distinctions between Jews and others but also lent itself to misinterpretation both by anti-Semites and Jewish chauvinists. In its place, he substituted the "doctrine of vocation," whereby Jews might acknowledge that God manifested His love to Israel. However, Kaplan considered the concept of the covenant valuable, calling on Jews worldwide to enter into a pact, as in the days of Ezra, to reconstitute themselves as a people dedicated to ethical nationhood and to the furtherance of their religious civilization.

Historically the belief in both the election of the people Israel and God's covenant with them has played a major role in the growth and survival of the Jewish people and of Judaism. Today, as well, whether one speaks in terms of election or of vocation, the uniqueness of Israel's calling to be a holy people, by virtue of Torah, remains fundamental to the faith of the Jew.

Study Questions

1. Conduct your own comparison of Josh. 24 with Exod. 19–20. Can you discern the three basic elements Lieber identifies? Why is each one so significant?

2. Review the section where Lieber contrasts the biblical concept of covenant with contemporaneous relationships between other peoples and their deities. In what ways is the covenant between God and Israel unique?

3. How essential to the covenant is possession and settlement of the Land of Israel? Do you think that being a landed people is part of a life of holiness? What might this mean to Diaspora Jews? What are some contemporary implications of the linkage between land, loyalty to the covenant, and leading a life of holiness?

4. How does the idea of covenant affect or define the role of the king in ancient Israel? The prophet? The priest? Is the idea of covenant compatible with a sense of "democracy?"

5. Does the idea of covenant give you a sense of privilege and/or security? In what way does it present you with obligations and challenges?

6. Three classical "signs" of the covenant are *Shabbat*, circumcision, and tefillin. Do you see "election" or "covenant" as important in your observance of mitzvot? What are other ways you affirm the covenant?

7. Why is it easier to speak about peoplehood and community rather than election and covenant?

Study materials by *Baruch Frydman-Kohl*

REWARD AND PUNISHMENT

Harvey Meirovich

Summary

Harvey Meirovich surveys some of the traditional responses to the problem scholars refer to as "theodicy," a term derived from a Greek word that literally means "the justice meted out by God," but which is more often used to describe the vindication of the holiness and justice of the Divine despite the existence of physical and moral evil in the world. In the spirit of that definition of theodicy, Meirovich categorizes the many approaches in biblical and Rabbinic literature that seek to justify the injustices and sufferings that are a part of our experience. As we read, we sense the Bible's mighty struggle to interpret order and a sense of God's control in a world that often seems perched on the brink of chaos.

The concept of divine reward and punishment in the Bible is linked to the perception that God cares enough about His creatures to be deeply moved by their behavior. God's essence is beyond human comprehension, yet the prophets make the concept of God's relationship to humanity accessible by presenting it in association with two primary traits: sympathy and rejection. Human beings perceive sympathy through blessings, rewards, and redemption. They perceive rejection through punishments, curses, and affliction.

God's sovereignty over individuals and nations is identified with the pursuit of justice. In the Bible, there is a direct correlation between behavior on the one hand and reward and punishment on the other. Israel's obedience ensures crop abundance, human and animal fertility, wealth, and military success. Deeds, in the exercise of free will, determine destiny (Exod. 23:25–27; Lev. 26; Deut. 4:25–28, 7:12–16, 11:13–21; Jer. 5:15–17, 19:9).

This strict demand for justice was tempered by a perception of God's quality of mercy. The Bible basks in God's intimate relationship with Israel. It apprehends the Creator as both transcendent judge and forgiving, compassionate father. Divine love is the counterpart to divine wrath.

The radical notion of intercession is prominent in the Bible's teaching that prophets prevailed on God to delay, or even cancel, divine punishment. The prophets availed themselves of their power of persuasion (Exod. 32:11–14; Num. 14:13–16), as well as prayer (Num. 11:2, 12:13, 21:7), direct pleading (Num. 16:22; Amos 7:2–3), and reliance on God's grace (Ps. 103:10–14). Prophetic intercession is necessary because of the moral imperfection of human beings (Gen. 8:21). Prophets view people as pitiable creatures, incapable of moral reformation (Jer. 31:31–34; Ezek. 36:25–27). This will compel God in the future to replace human choice and free will with robot-like behavior; the human heart will be replaced with a model guaranteed to seek only goodness and righteousness. At one point in history, the notions of reward and punishment will cease to hold any relevance for mortals!

TRANSGENERATIONAL RETRIBUTION

The doctrine of transgenerational retribution (in which one generation suffers punishment for the sins of a previous generation) is based on two principles: (a) Strict justice in the distribution of reward and punishment. (b) A conviction that the family unit, not the individual, forms the basis of society. Thus the individual is an extension of his or her family's good or bad fortune. Communal and national solidarity outweigh personal destiny. The deeds and the misdeeds of the individual inevitably have repercussions for the whole House of Israel in the future.

Strict Justice

In the strict application of retribution, vicarious punishment and reward are administered on future generations without qualification.

> The LORD passed before him (Moses) and proclaimed: "The LORD! The LORD! A God compassionate and gracious, slow to anger, abounding in kindness and faithfulness, extending kindness to the thousandth generation, forgiving iniquity, transgression and sin; yet He does not remit all punishment, but visits the iniquity of parents upon children and children's children, upon the third and fourth generations (Exod. 34:6–7).

A More Temperate Perception

A more temperate view holds that the strict measure of the law is quali-
fied in the two versions of the Decalogue (Exod. 20:5–6; Deut. 5:9–10).
In this scenario, the threat of suffering or the assurance of blessing for
future generations depends on the ancestors' behavior. This knowledge
could deter the ancestors from wayward acts and inspire them to the
performance of righteous deeds. "For I the LORD your God am an im-
passioned God, visiting the guilt of the parents upon the children, upon
the third and fourth generation of those who reject Me, but showing
kindness to the thousandth generation of those who love Me and keep
My commandments."

An Interpretation of Greater Leniency

In the view of greater leniency, there is no notion of transferring punishment to the sinner's offspring. God rewards the faithful to the thousandth generation but metes out punishment to the offender personally
and immediately. The divine blessing connotes boundless beneficence.
"Know, therefore, that only the LORD your God is God, the steadfast
God who keeps His covenant faithfully to the thousandth generation of
those who love him and keep His commandments, but who instantly
requites with destruction those who reject Him" (Deut. 7:9–10).

All of these passages, addressed to the entire people of Israel, highlight God's primary attributes of justice and mercy. In this portrayal,
God's abiding compassion, based on an implicit desire for reconciliation, exceeds by far His short-term, legitimate outbursts of exasperation.

The Bible's insistence on communal solidarity and mutual responsibility is crystallized in the plural form of most Jewish prayers. For
example, the formal confession of sins on the Day of Atonement assumes community consciousness, because it is couched in the plural.
The individual is held personally responsible for the moral state of the
community.

Rejection of Transgenerational Retribution

Jeremiah and Ezekiel championed a counter-belief in individual retribution, categorically denying that any person is morally an extension

of another. "The person who sins, only he shall die. A child shall not share the burden of a parent's guilt, nor shall a parent share the burden of a child's guilt" (Ezek. 18:20). This prophetic rejection may have been inspired by a pressing need to counter a pervasive hopelessness in the period after the national catastrophe, which included the destruction of the Temple. If ancestral guilt indeed was the cause of current suffering, to what avail is the moral struggle?

Two More Radical Beliefs

The more traditional belief affirms that sin invariably generates punishment (Exod. 32:33–34). Later, postexilic traditions, however, affirm that repentance renders punishment null and void. Repentance, in this view, even obliterates sin. For example, God renounced punishment against the people in Nineveh when they turned from their evil ways in repentance (Jon. 3:10). Isaiah went a step further. God would wipe away Israel's transgressions and remember them no more (Isa. 43:25, 44:22). At the root of this lay a heartfelt conviction that human repentance could so overwhelm God's justice that only His compassion remained operative.

"Why does the way of the wicked prosper?" (Jer. 12:1). This echoes the searing challenge of the psalmist: "Why, O LORD, do You stand aloof, heedless in times of trouble?" (Ps. 10:1). The complaint resonates in Rabbinic conversation as well. Yannai said: "It is not within our grasp to explain the tranquility of the wicked or even the suffering of the righteous" (M Avot 4:15). Yet the human need to justify God's ways led biblical and Rabbinic sources to seek solutions to the problems raised by suffering.

Retribution

The most conventional explanation of human suffering is provided by the doctrine that sinful behavior leads to punishment. Adam and Eve were punished for failing to heed God's command (Gen. 3). God's judgment of moral corruption led to the destructive flood of Noah's day and the annihilation of Sodom and Gomorrah (Gen. 6, 18). The severe price to be paid for disobedience reaches a crescendo in the stern warnings recorded in Lev. 26 and Deut. 28. The historical books of the Bible are replete with the conviction that the outbreak of communal idolatry was a direct cause of punishment and suffering (Judg. 2:10–19, 3:7, 4:1, 8:33). The theme was highlighted in Deuteronomy (11:16–17, 28). The prophet Amos reduced the doctrine to "Seek good and not evil, that you may live" (Amos 5:14).

The exile of the northern and southern kingdoms was explained by the same rationale (2 Kings 17:7–23). Israel's wisdom teachers also understood the principle of retribution determining the individual's fate. "There is no wholeness in my bones because of my sin" (Ps. 38:4). "Misfortune pursues sinners, but the righteous are well rewarded" (Prov. 13:21).

This theological construct surfaced in Rabbinic tradition as well. A classic expression of retribution is the claim of Ami: "There is no death without sin, and no suffering without transgression" (BT Shab. 55a). A pious rabbi who survived the bite of a poisonous lizard observed: "It is not the lizard that kills, it is sin that kills" (BT Ber. 33a).

Measure for Measure

Jacob tricked his father Isaac into giving him the blessing that belonged to his firstborn brother, Esau (Gen. 27). Jacob was therefore outwitted by his father-in-law, Laban, who tricked him into marrying his eldest daughter, Leah, in place of her younger sister, Rachel (Gen. 29:21–30). This twist wove its way as well into Rabbinic tradition, which taught that because the Egyptians tried to destroy Israel by water they were annihilated by the waters of the Sea of Reeds (Exod. 1:22, 14:26–28; Mekh. B'shallah).

Deterrent

The suffering of the guilty was to be considered a deterrent, warning the Israelites against disobeying the divine commandments. They were to internalize the concept "fear of the LORD" by witnessing God's destruction of the Egyptian enemies (Exod. 14:30–31; Deut. 11:2–9). Israel's sufferings were to serve as a warning to the nations around it (Ezek. 5:15).

Discipline

Suffering is not strictly a punishment but rather a catalytic agent brought into service by a caring God to purge and purify individual waywardness, at the root of which often lay arrogance and pride (Job 33:14–17). Biblical wisdom teachers found this explanation especially attractive. "Do not reject the discipline of the LORD, my son: do not abhor His rebuke. For whom the LORD loves He rebukes, as a father the son whom he favors" (Prov. 3:11–12). The psalmist perceived Joseph's stay in an Egyptian dungeon as a necessary chastening that transformed his character (Ps. 105:17–19). Distress is the gateway to understanding (Job 33, 36:8–10,15).

The same principle operates on the collective level. "Shall He who disciplines nations not punish, He who instructs men in knowledge?" (Ps. 94:10). Critical, however, is the corollary that although God chastened His people for their own good, He would not destroy them completely (Lev. 26:44; Deut. 4:31; Jer. 30:10–11).

Israel will come to a knowledge of God's existence by passing through the crucible of calamity (Ezek. 22:22, 33:29). Ezekiel also submitted that the hardships suffered by foreign nations awakened them to a recognition of divine might and the ethical dimensions of monotheism (Ezek. 25–26, 28–30, 39). In this context, Isaiah, with theological daring, envisioned Egypt—to the exclusion of all other nations—returning to the LORD after suffering divine punishment (Isa. 19).

"Sufferings of love" was the concept in Rabbinic parlance, articulating the belief that suffering is an expression of divine love (Ber. 5a). The inspiration for this idea is found in Deut. 8:5: "Bear in mind that the LORD your God disciplines you just as a man disciplines his son." The remedial effects of discipline led later Rabbinic masters to posit that God inflicts pain as a test, but only for the righteous who are able to endure the suffering (Gen. R. 34:2, 55:2). From another quarter came speculation that the rich are reproved by God to see if they will open their hands to the poor, whereas the poor suffer to ascertain if they accept discipline (Exod. R. 31:3).

Both biblical and Rabbinic sources concur that disciplinary punishment is meant to trigger genuine remorse and regeneration, coupled with a desire to return to God in sincere repentance (Jer. 31:18–19; Ps. 78:34). "One should rejoice more in chastisement than in prosperity, for if one is prosperous all his life, no sin of his will be forgiven. What brings forgiveness of sin? Suffering" (Sifrei Deut. 32).

VOICES OF RESISTANCE AND OPPOSITION

"It was for nothing that I kept my heart pure and washed my hands in innocence, seeing that I have been constantly afflicted" (Ps. 73:13–14). There was always the possibility that people would refuse to accept divine chastisement by closing themselves off to the best intentions of the Almighty. "To no purpose did I smite your children; they would not accept correction" (Jer. 2:30).

The Bible and the Sages legitimized the right to protest against God for the infliction of what humans perceived to be unjust suffering. The outbursts of Job in the Bible have their counterpart in the Midrash, which states that Abraham was so traumatized by binding his son Isaac that he warned God he could bear no further trials by ordeal (Gen. R. 57:4).

Voices of opposition arose within Rabbinic tradition to invalidate the educational rationale that justifies pain. When the sage Johanan fell ill, his colleague Ḥanina urged him to place his trust in God. When Ḥanina was racked with pain, however, he uttered: "I want neither the sufferings nor any reward associated with them" (Song R. II, 16:2).

Atonement

The prophet of consolation, Second Isaiah, articulated a revolutionary doctrine when he depicted the vicarious sufferings of the anonymous servant of the LORD (Isa. 52:13–53:12). In this powerful expression of human solidarity, the servant's self-sacrificing readiness to bear misery relieved and delivered the wicked from retribution. It was hoped that the suffering of the servant who allowed his own life to be consumed as a guilt offering would lead the guilty to forsake sin. The appeal of this argument lies in the belief that the misery or the death of an innocent victim can generate moral repair in the souls of sinners who are horrified at the consequences of their own errors or those of others.

This notion is found in Rabbinic circles as well. "The death of the righteous atones [for the living left behind]" (MK 28a). Echoes of the atonement principle resonate in the ruling that the death of the high priest procured atonement for the person banished to a city of refuge after having committed unintentional homicide (Num. 35:11–15; Mak. 11b). In a dramatic personal identification with this motif, the distinguished Ishmael prayed that he might serve, if necessary, as an atonement victim for any punishment that might befall his people (M Neg. 2:1).

Some talmudic authorities tried to neutralize the virtue of vicarious suffering, arguing that afflictions atone only for one's own transgressions. An individual's own sufferings were considered more appealing to God than sacrifices, for sacrifices involve only the outlay of money, not physical pain (Sifrei Deut. 32; Mekh. B'hodesh 10). Similarly, if a person transgressed commandments punishable by execution at the hands of either Heaven (*karet*) or the court, repentance on the Day of Atonement served to suspend the sentence, and that person's sufferings during that year atoned for the sin (ARN 29).

Strangely, not until the Middle Ages did midrashic license adroitly adapt the notion of the single suffering servant, identifying him collectively with the Jewish people.

Meaningless Suffering

After all explanations have been exhausted, the brutal candor so prominent in Ecclesiastes remains: "In my own brief span of life I have seen both of these things: sometimes a good man perishes in spite of his goodness, and sometimes a wicked one endures in spite of his wickedness" (7:15). Reward and punishment are not meted out according to a person's deeds. This is a bitter pill to swallow.

The evidence of everyday reality pressed Rabbinic tradition to admit that indeed "there is death without sin and there is suffering without transgression" (BT Shab. 55b). The proof-text was drawn from none other than Ecclesiastes: "The same fate is in store for all: for the righteous and for the wicked; for the good and pure and for the impure. . . . That is the sad thing about all that goes on under the sun" (9:2–3).

Study Questions

1. Consider the spectrum of attitudes Meirovich finds within the Torah itself by reading the story of the Golden Calf in Exodus chapters 32 through 34. The text's stance seems clear: all sin must be requited, even if it takes several generations for that to happen. Does this seem like a reasonable way to explain the suffering of the righteous in our world and the prosperity and good health of criminals, or does it feel more like an after-the-fact effort to convince people already invested in the system? What advantages are there for a generation to believe they are being punished for the deeds of their ancestors?

2. Now move on to the Decalogue text discussed under the rubric, "A More Temperate Perception." Locate the original text as it appears in Exod. 20:5–6 and Deut. 5:9–10. Determine if the text is identical in both places; then consider it in terms of the text from Exodus 34 cited above. Meirovich seems to suggest that the Decalogue text constitutes an elaboration or refinement of the earlier idea. Do you feel this is really different than the earlier text? Or do you prefer the view of Deut. 7:10, that God instantly requites sin?

4. Read Ezekiel 18 and then compare it to Jeremiah 31 (especially verses 27–34.) It is in the work of these two prophets, especially Ezekiel, that the doctrine of absolute responsibility for one's own deeds is propounded to the greatest effect. How do you respond to the prophet's words? Do these chapters mean that no one is ever punished for sins other than his or her own, but that there is still suffering in the world unrelated to the punishment of sin? That would be easy to defend, but does it adequately explain the suffering of the righteous?

5. In the section of his essay labeled "Voices of Resistance and Opposition," Meirovich presents the concept that "Israel will come to a knowledge of God's existence by passing through the crucible of calamity." Review his prooftexts, Ezek. 22:22 and 33:29. Do you find them convincing in making this point? Consider the idea that divinely inspired (or not prevented) suffering can be remedial, not

merely punitive. How do you react to the idea that one reason for the existence of suffering in the world is to bring to God those who were previously indifferent? Does this seem cruel and impossible to reconcile with what you know of God, or is it an effective strategy for dealing with the issue of theodicy?

6. Consider a time in your own life when you experienced suffering or loss. Which of the ideas in the essay resonated with you at the time? Did you consider the experience to be a kind of punishment for some (obvious or presumed) misdeed? Or did it feel more like a wake-up call or a divinely inspired effort to teach you something? Looking back, are your answers different now than they were when the pain was at its worst?

Study materials by *Martin S. Cohen*

ESCHATOLOGY

Neil Gillman

Summary

In his essay, Professor Gillman presents an outline of the traditional way in which the greatest of human prayers—that life have meaning, that it be "going somewhere"—has been translated into the realm of hopeful philosophy. In fact, all of the authors cited by Gillman, both biblical and postbiblical, express the great hope that history is a line, not a circle, and that we are therefore moving toward some sort of great and climactic denouement.

By finding traces of this kind of linear historical thinking in the Torah, in the work of the pre- and postexilic prophets, in the Persian-Hellenistic era, and in the postbiblical period, the author shows how a single idea can wear the garb of its historical period, yet be unmistakably linked to its own forebears and descendants. Gillman illustrates how ideas as diverse as the so-called Day of the LORD, the doctrine of the resurrection of the dead, the messianic idea, and political Zionism are all features of the same kind of eschatological belief. He effectively demonstrates how an idea can weave its way through millennia of thinking about the nature of history without compromising its essential nature or losing its ability to stir the souls of those individuals who, unable to escape history, are still able to see it from a sufficient distance to reflect thoughtfully about its nature.

THE ESCHATOLOGIC IMPULSE

What does the future hold for us? Can we hope for a time when the world will be a better place and human life somewhat easier? From the time human beings began to reflect about themselves and their world, these questions have been posed, somewhat intuitively, in every human society. The discussion of these questions and the range of answers that have been offered are covered by the term "eschatology."

"Eschatology" (from the Greek *eschatos,* "last," and *logos,* "discourse") designates a doctrine that describes both an ideal state of affairs that will be realized some time in the future and the sequence of events leading to the emergence of that state. It usually is understood to be a dimension of religion, although we also speak of "secular" eschatologies. Marxism, for example, is often cited as incorporating a secular eschatology, although some would say that precisely because it deals with issues of this kind, Marxism is really a religion.

Eschatologies are imaginative visions of an ideal or perfected world or age that contrasts sharply with the current state of affairs, which is perceived as flawed. Whenever a human being or a community becomes fully aware that human life as currently experienced is in some way imperfect, the natural response is to dream of a future age in which the imperfections of this age will vanish. What the perfected age will look like and how it will come to be is the common agenda of all eschatologies; the differences in these visions reflect the differences in the value systems of the cultures that produce them.

We have called these eschatologies "visions," and so they are. They are all imaginative projections—none of them based on any solid experiential data—because the "age to come" has not as yet come. Some religions do suggest that we now have anticipations of that perfected age. Judaism, for example, understands *Shabbat* as "a foretaste of the age to come"; and Christianity claims that since the advent of Jesus, the ultimate state of affairs is already "here" mysteriously. These anticipations, however, are only pale reflections of the full glory of what will be in the hereafter.

JEWISH ESCHATOLOGY

Jewish eschatology is one of the richest in the history of humanity. It decisively shaped the thinking of Christianity and Islam and, through them, the culture of Western civilization to this day. As with every other theme in Jewish thought, Jewish eschatology has a history of its own. Its full flowering is the product of talmudic (Rabbinic) Judaism. But almost every eschatologic theme elaborated in talmudic literature has its roots in the Bible. In what follows, I will concentrate on the biblical material, only suggesting how it was transformed by the later tradition.

Jewish eschatology is structured in three dimensions: the individual, the national, and the universal. It answers three broad questions: What will be the ultimate destiny of the individual human being (usually, but not only, the individual Jew), of the Jewish people, and of human civilization or even the cosmic order as a whole? It is not always easy to separate out these three dimensions, particularly the universal and national dimensions, but they will be kept in mind. As I proceed, I will also trace the evolution of these dimensions through four broad periods of history: the Pentateuchal era; the time of the pre-exilic prophets; the time of the postexilic prophets; and the Persian and Hellenistic period, which brings the Bible to a close.

THEOLOGICAL ASSUMPTIONS

The ground for all of Jewish eschatology lies in the three basic assumptions of biblical religion: First, the God of Israel is the ultimate reality whose will governs everything that transpires on earth. Second, God has entered into a unique relationship with the people Israel. Third, God cares deeply about the world, about human society, and about human history—and will intervene to shape events to reflect an ultimate purpose.

Immediately obvious from this listing is the direct interrelationship between the national and the universal dimensions of biblical religion as a whole and hence of biblical eschatology as well. God's intentions for Israel are part of a broader plan for humanity, and God cares enough and has the power to bring this vision into place.

THE TORAH BACKGROUND

But the eschatologic implications of this relationship become explicit only in prophetic literature, dating roughly from the 8th to the 5th centuries B. C. E. The fate of human civilization apart from the people Israel is of little concern in the Torah itself. In fact, whereas the prophets envision an age when all nations will worship the one true God, the God of Israel, Deut. 4:19 seems unperturbed by the fact that "other peoples" worship the sun, moon, and stars; this seems to be their legitimate lot.

But what is of central concern in the Torah is the ultimate destiny of the people Israel. At this stage of development, however, that destiny does not go beyond Israel's entry into the Promised Land. Israelite history—in the Torah itself—is the story of a community that journeys from Egyptian slavery to its promised homeland.

Again and again, the Torah describes what will take place when "you enter and possess the land that the LORD your God is assigning to you" (Deut. 11:31). The following chapter details some of the laws that are to be observed in the Land, concluding that if these commands are heeded, then "it will go well with you and with your descendants after you forever" (12:28). Note the term "forever"; it is the hallmark of a genuine eschatologic vision. The Land itself is portrayed in ideal terms, in stark contrast to the desert wilderness through which they are now journeying and to the Egypt that they have left behind. Their destiny in this Land is also portrayed in ideal terms: "You will dominate many nations, but they will not dominate you" (15:6). It is the place that God has chosen (16:16), or has chosen "to establish His name" (14:24).

Much later, biblical religion postulated that the ultimate destiny of the individual does not end with death. There is not a hint of this suggestion in the Torah, however, or in most of the Bible. There, human death is final. Whatever ideal state an individual Israelite can hope to achieve is restricted to one's lifetime and is conditional on heeding God's commands: material prosperity, good health, length of days, self-determination, posterity, and peace (28:1–14). With the possible exceptions of Elijah and Enoch, all biblical personalities die and their death is final.

PRE-EXILIC PROPHECY

This rather restricted eschatologic canvass expands considerably with the emergence of prophetic religion in the years preceding the destruction of Jerusalem and the Temple at the hand of the Babylonians (586 B. C. E.).

Four eschatologic themes pervade the writings of this period: (a) the anticipation of a "day of the LORD," a transforming event portrayed in cosmic terms that will mark God's ultimate triumph over Israel's idolatrous enemies and will inaugurate an everlasting age of peace and prosperity. (b) Out of the ruins of this cosmic upheaval, a "remnant of Isra-el"—those who kept faith with God throughout the tribulations of the age—will emerge to become the foundation for a new world order. (c) In this ideal society, Zion will become the religious center of the world, and all the nations will stream there to learn the ways of the LORD from Israel. (d) This entire scenario will be presided over by a charismatic fig-ure, an ideal king—the "messiah" (from the Hebrew: *mashi·aḥ,* "anoint-ed one"; Israelite kings were crowned by being anointed with oil). All of these themes figure in the writings of this pre-exilic period.

Amos, the earliest of this group of prophets (mid-8th century B. C. E.), describes the approaching day of the LORD as a day of ultimate judg-ment when God will destroy all evildoers, both among the nations and in Israel. This upheaval will affect the structures of nature as well. It will be "a day of darkness, not light" (Amos 5:18), a day when "the sun will set at noon" (8:9).

This theme is echoed even more forcefully by Amos's later con-temporary Isaiah (commonly understood to be the author of most of chapters 1 to 39 of the Book of Isaiah). On that day, "all will be over-come by terror," the earth will be desolate, sinners will be wiped out, stars will not give out light, the sun will be dark when it rises, heaven will be shaken, and the earth will "leap out of its place, at the fury of the LORD of Hosts." God will "requite the world its evil ... and put an end to the pride of the arrogant and humble the haughtiness of tyrants" (Isa. 13:6–16).

This vision of a universal, cosmic day of judgment marks the dra-matic transformation from the familiar age to its eschatologic ideal. It is a purgative event, cleansing the world of its evil. But out of the destruc-tion, there will emerge those who "seek Me" (Amos 5:4), or those who "seek good and not evil" (5:14), "the remnant of Joseph" (5:15) with whom God will deal graciously. This theme of "the remnant of Israel" is echoed again by Isaiah (Amos 10:20, 11:11), who gives his son the symbolic name *Sh'ar Yashuv,* "a remnant shall return" (7:3).

In the work of Amos's contemporary Hosea (and later, more explic-itly, in Jeremiah), this theme is enlarged by the promise that God's love for this saving remnant will lead to a renewal of God's covenant with Israel as in the days following the Exodus (Hos. 2:17). This renewed covenant will be such that, in contrast with the "old" covenant, it will be incapable of dissolution (2:21–22).

The tight connection between the national and the universal dimensions of this ideal age to come is most explicit in the prophecies of Isaiah. No eschatologic vision in the entire body of classical Jewish literature is more eloquent than Isaiah's prophecy of the events that will take place "in the days to come" (Isa. 2:2– 4; Mic. 4:2). The nations will come to Israel to learn God's ways, "for instruction (*torah*) shall come forth from Zion, the word of the LORD from Jerusalem." Then follows Isaiah's promise of the end of warfare: "Nation shall not take up sword against nation; they shall never again know war."

Isaiah 11:1–9 expands the vision of this ideal age. It will be an age of justice and equity, an age when even the tensions of nature will be abolished, when wolves will dwell with lambs, when little boys will herd calves and beasts of prey, when oxen and lions will eat straw. Finally, Isaiah prophecies the end of idolatry: "For the land shall be filled with devotion to the LORD as waters cover the sea."

All of this will be brought to pass under the aegis of an ideal king of the Davidic dynasty; he will be guided by "the spirit of the LORD," a spirit of wisdom and insight, of counsel and valor, of devotion and reverence for God (Isa. 9:5–6, 11:1–2). These are the original proof-texts for the doctrine of a messianic figure who will initiate and reign over the ideal age to come. In the later literature, this doctrine will undergo major transformations toward a supernatural or angelic being; but at this stage, the king is very human—albeit endowed with charisma, political savvy, and religious gifts.

Note also that at this stage, the eschatologic age will be thoroughly within history, not in some new age that follows the "end" of history (or of time as we know it). Isaiah 2:2 refers to the events that will take place "in the days to come," not, as in the later tradition, "at the end of days." That understanding of the phrase will emerge only much later.

The prophet who bridges the pre-exilic and postexilic traditions is Jeremiah. Jeremiah prophesied in the years immediately before and after the destruction of Jerusalem and the First Temple in 586 B.C.E. He witnessed the destruction and went into exile with his people.

In Jeremiah's day, his predecessors' vision of God's day of judgment assumed a vivid and imminent reality; the Babylonian army was literally at the gates of Jerusalem. Jeremiah also understood the trial to come as God's inescapable purging of the nation from its sins. But again, despite the gloom that pervades much of his book, Jeremiah's vision of consolation and return are among the most poignant in all of prophetic literature. The streets of Jerusalem will once again resound with the sounds of marriage celebrations (Jer. 33:10–11). Jeremiah 31 is the single most eloquent prophecy of return and redemption in all of prophetic literature. Jeremiah envisions the re-establishment of the Covenant. This time, however, it will be placed in "their innermost being" and inscribed "in their hearts" so that it will never again be dissolved. Most important, God promises to reach into the heart of Babylonia and bring the exiles back to their homeland (29:10–14), for God is the LORD of history, and God's power is not limited by geography.

POSTEXILIC PROPHECY

The destruction of Jerusalem and the subsequent exile totally transformed the national dimension of Jewish eschatology. The themes of return to Zion, the rebuilding of Jerusalem, and the reinstitution of the Temple sacrificial cult become central in all postexilic prophecy. After the destruction of the Second Temple at the hands of Rome in 70 c. e., they remain central in all of talmudic and post-talmudic eschatology until the dawn of modernity.

Ezekiel's prophecies, like those of his slightly older contemporary Jeremiah, bridge the pre-exilic and postexilic periods, although he prophesied only in Babylonia. For Ezekiel, Israel's national rebirth is a form of bodily resurrection as in his vision of the dry bones that come to life again (Ezek. 37). He describes in great detail his vision of Jerusalem and the rebuilt Temple as the center of a new Israelite polity. Following Jeremiah, he insists that the new Israel will enjoy "a new heart and a new spirit" to follow God's rules faithfully, and then, the old intimacy will be re-established: "You shall be My people and I will be your God" (36:26–28). Ezekiel's vision of God's final war against the evil kings of Gog and Magog echoes the earlier visions of a "day of the LORD" and was elaborated in the apocalyptic visions of the later Jewish and Christian eschatologies. In these visions, the setting for the eschatologic scenario transcends history. We are no longer in Isaiah's "days to come," but rather at the end of history as human beings know it.

This cosmic eschatologic vision is echoed by the anonymous author of Isa. 40 to 55, commonly called "Deutero-Isaiah" or "Second Isaiah," who prophesied in the middle of the 6th century B.C.E. This prophet portrays the age to come as a total transformation of nature: "I will turn the desert into ponds, the arid land into springs of water" (Isa. 41:18). But Deutero-Isaiah's most notable contribution to the development of biblical eschatology is his portrayal of the "Servant of the LORD" (49:3) who suffers, is ultimately vindicated, who bears the sins of his generation, and who will carry out God's ultimate plan for civilization. The precise identity of the servant is hotly debated in scholarly circles. Is the reference to Israel, to an elite body of Israelites, to a single person? The very notion of a suffering servant is a significant step in the development of the messianic idea in Judaism and, later, in Christianity.

THE PERSIAN-HELLENISTIC PERIOD

The edict of Cyrus, king of Persia, permitting Israelites to return to their homeland and to rebuild their Temple (539 B.C.E.) transformed the terms of biblical eschatology in yet another way. Jeremiah's vision of a return to Zion and Ezekiel's vision of the rebuilt Temple now assume a much greater immediacy. However limited and compromised the work of rebuilding might have been, the prophecies of Haggai and Zechariah (late 6th century B.C.E.) and of Malachi (early 5th century B.C.E.) exude a messianic fervor. They spur the people to rebuild the Temple and see its completion as the mark of God's forthcoming kingdom. They view the appointment of Zerubbabel, a scion of the Davidic monarchy, as governor of the Judean province, to be a fulfillment of Isaiah's messianic promises (Zech. 4:6–7, 6:9–14). Malachi is the source for the notion that Elijah will return as the herald of "the awesome, fearful day of the LORD" (Mal. 3:23), i.e., of the messianic age.

The author of Isa. 56 to 66—whose writings are commonly understood to be yet a third distinct text collected within the Book of Isaiah, dating roughly from the same period—brings together many of the eschatologic themes echoed throughout prophetic literature. God will gather all the nations of the earth to a new Jerusalem for the final judgment, the righteous will rejoice but the evildoers will be rebuked "in flaming fire." And just as "the new heaven and the new earth" that God will then create will endure, so will the new Israel, and "new moon after new moon, and Sabbath after Sabbath, all flesh shall come to worship Me" (Isa. 66).

THE DESTINY OF THE INDIVIDUAL

It is only at the very end of the biblical period that the ultimate destiny of the individual is viewed as transcending death. In almost all of the Bible itself, death is viewed as final. The most that one can hope for is to achieve a measure of blessing here on earth. Then we die, and after death God has no power over our destiny, nor can the dead enjoy any relation with God (Ps. 30:10, 115:17, 146:3–4). The probable reason for this silence reflects the wish to keep the realms of the human and the divine quite separate. Only God is eternal.

There are only three biblical texts that announce some form of life after death: Dan. 12 and Isa. 25:8 and 26:19. The first of these can be dated with some precision to 166–165 B. C. E. The latter two, from still another unit of the Book of Isaiah called the Isaiah Apocalypse (Isa. 24–27), are probably slightly earlier.

The Daniel text was written within the context of the persecutions of Antiochus IV, the villain of the Ḥanukkah story. It reflects the dilemma of the Jewish pietists who were being martyred precisely because of their loyalty to God. If there is no reward for piety, why die the death of a martyr? The author answers that there is reward for the righteous and punishment for the evildoer, but only after their death. Therefore, "Many of those that sleep in the dust of the earth will awake, some to eternal life, others to reproaches, to everlasting abhorrence" (Dan. 12:2). The reference here is clearly to bodily resurrection.

Of the two Isaiah texts, the more interesting is Isa. 25:8: "(God) will destroy death forever." This presages the later tradition's claim that at the end, not only will the dead be resurrected but also death itself will die.

Not reflected in the Bible itself but of central importance in the later tradition is the Greek notion that human beings are a composite of two substances—a material body and a spiritual soul—and that what never dies is the human soul. It leaves the body at death and enjoys eternal life with God. In time, the two doctrines of bodily resurrection and spiritual immortality were conflated: The body disintegrates at death, the soul remains with God. Then, at the end of days, God reunites the body and the soul; and the individual, now reconstituted as in life on earth, comes before God for judgment. That doctrine was central to all of Jewish eschatology until the dawn of modernity in the late 18th century.

POSTBIBLICAL JUDAISM

In the later tradition, the three dimensions of Jewish eschatology—the universal, the national and the individual—undergo significant transformations. Of the three, it is only the most ancient, the universal dimension, that retains its hold on the Jewish consciousness almost without change, to our day. All denominations continue to recite *Aleinu,* the prayer that articulates Isaiah's vision of an age of universal peace and justice under the dominion of the God of the people Israel. Meanwhile, with the dawn of the Jewish enlightenment at the end of the 18th century, the Reform movement in Judaism denied the national dimension of the Jewish identity, and with it the dream of a return to Zion and a reconstitution of the Temple service. A part of that dream, at first in a starkly secular form, came to be embodied in political Zionism.

Of the twin doctrines of bodily resurrection and spiritual immortality, medieval Jewish philosophy (particularly in the thought of Maimonides) and Jewish mysticism clearly preferred the latter. Most modern Jewish thinkers have agreed with this predilection. Modern prayer books from the liberal (Reform and Reconstructionist) movements modified the traditional liturgy to reflect this preference. That process has begun to be reversed in recent decades, but that reversal is still in its beginning stages.

Jewish eschatologic thinking may be elusive and imaginative. Nevertheless, its centrality to any authentic reading of Jewish thought is beyond dispute. What divides modern Jewish thinkers is precisely how to understand these teachings. Are they literally true prophecies or events that will occur in some indefinite future (as traditionalists would have it)? Or are they subjective, poetic, or, to use a more technical term, mythic constructs, designed to help us structure and give meaning to our lives here on earth (as liberal thinkers suggest)? That difference, of course, reflects a far more profound division on how modern Jews understand Jewish religion as a whole.

Study Questions

1. In his section called "The Torah Background," Gillman suggests that the narrative of the Torah and its recounting of the journey of the Israelites to the Promised Land suggest the great journey of humankind through time toward the end of history. What details of the Israelites' journey through the wilderness seem evocative of the journey of humanity through history? How does the fact that the biblical journey begins with the Israelites enslaved to a tyrant and ends with them on the verge of entering the Promised Land agree with this view of human history? How does the account of the revelation at Sinai work in terms of reinterpreting the story of the Torah in eschatological terms?

2. Locate biblical sources that speak about the great Day of the LORD—primarily the ones mentioned in the essay, such as Isaiah 2 and 13, Ezekiel 1, and Joel 1–4. What do all these descriptions of the Day of the LORD have in common?

3. Note that the imagery in these passages is meant to be terrifying, but also comforting, by suggesting that humanity can enter the next age by passing through the portal of divine judgment. Imagine that you wanted to "sell" this idea of a great day of divine wrath as the threshold experience for humanity on its way to an age of messianic bliss. If you needed to write your own material, not simply cite the works of your biblical predecessors, what imagery would you use to make the idea sound most plausible?

4. Gillman labels Isaiah 9 and 11 as "the original proof-texts for the doctrine of a messianic figure who will initiate and reign over the ideal age to come." Compare these passages to the following prayer, recited three times daily in the *Amidah*: "May You quickly bring forth a scion of David, Your servant, into our midst and may his horn be raised up as a sign of his salvation in You, for it is precisely that sign of Your imminent salvation that we await daily. Blessed are You, LORD, Who will surely bring forth a scion of David to lead us to salvation." How do the texts from Isaiah affect the way you understand the words of the liturgy? What does the idea of a Davidic messiah mean to you?

5. Gillman mentions Jeremiah 31 as "the single most eloquent prophecy of return and redemption in all of prophetic literature." Read that chapter and consider the progression from subtopic to subtopic. Can you discern a motivating factor in the prophet's progression of ideas? Do you find the prophet's words ultimately comforting, or would they only have been reassuring to people in the prophet's own time and place? The concept of a "new covenant" that God promises to make with the House of Israel and the House of Judah is among the most challenging ideas put forth in the chapter. Can you relate to that idea? How would you summarize its terms? And how does that notion relate to the strong Zionist flourish at the end of the chapter?

6. Consider the question Gillman poses at the end of his essay. The texts that develop the eschatological idea can be understood in two distinct ways: as literal truths (that is, as authentic prophetic oracles) or, in Professor Gillman's own words, as "subjective, poetic, or … mythic constructs designed to help us structure and give meaning to our lives here on earth." Which line of thinking seems most convincing? Which do you find most appealing? Have you developed a private eschatological theory that explains where humankind is going as it evolves, for the better or the worse, through the course of history?

Study materials by *Martin S. Cohen*

Biblical Foundations: Law

CIVIL AND CRIMINAL LAW

Ben Zion Bergman

Summary

In this essay, Ben Zion Bergman presents five assertions concerning his understanding of biblical law:

1. The Bible affirms that the laws it contains are divinely commanded. Therefore it does not reflect a separation of "church and state" and it is premised on a set of "obligations" rather than "rights."
2. Biblical laws reflect a simple, agricultural society.
3. The procedural aspects of biblical law also reflect a "primitive," agrarian society.
4. In its time, biblical law functioned as an instrument of public policy whose goal was to establish a "just society."
5. Biblical law is "neither systematic nor monolithic." In addition, Berman shows that a set of earlier oral traditions must have existed alongside the biblical material. While biblical law reflects its origins in a simpler society, it became the basis for a dynamic and evolving legal system developed by the Rabbis.

The Bible sometimes uses different terms to designate various categories of laws; for example, *hukkim* (primarily ritual or cultic ordinances) and *mishpatim* (civil and criminal statutes). Underlying the entire system of law in the Bible and unifying its various components, however, is the assertion that it is all divinely commanded. This basic premise accounts for many of the salient characteristics of biblical legislation.

Because the law in all its aspects represents the will of God, rules governing relations between persons and rules delineating one's obligations to God and how they are to be fulfilled are equally sacred. Therefore, the laws of the Bible are not always conveniently categorized in the definitional framework of Western and modern legal systems. Although

117

we would clearly label the willful violation of *Shabbat* as the infraction of a religious norm, not to be subsumed within a civil or criminal legal system, the Bible mandates the death penalty in that instance (Num. 15:32–36). The intentional violation of *Shabbat* is thus a capital crime subsumed under the biblical criminal code. The same is true for witchcraft (Exod. 22:17), idolatry (Exod. 22:19), and other cultic offenses that lead to the death penalty.

On the other hand, the rape of an unmarried or betrothed maiden (which, in a modern legal system would be classified as a crime) is treated in the Bible as a tort. It is seen as a wrongful act penalized only by a monetary payment to the woman's father (as compensation for her reduced value on the marriage market) and by the rapist's consequent obligation to marry the maiden (Deut. 22:28–29).

It is characteristic of biblical law that it rarely delineates rights; rather it encodes obligations. Indeed, a case can be made that Jewish law in general is primarily duty oriented rather than rights oriented. This too is symptomatic of the overlapping of the civil and the ecclesiastical, unified by the authority of a divine lawgiver. The law is thus given a religious underpinning—and it is in the nature of religion to impose duties, not to confer rights. It is also characteristic that a divinely ordained law should be couched primarily in terse statements with little elaboration, in categorical style. The most typical examples of this are from the Decalogue: "You shall not murder. You shall not commit adultery. You shall not steal. You shall not bear false witness against your neighbor" (Exod. 20:13; Deut. 5:17).

The biblical codes, in contrast to postbiblical talmudic legislation, reflect a comparatively simple society, engaged mainly in agriculture. As land was the primary source of economic productivity, its sale was severely limited. In the sabbatical year, debts were cancelled (Deut. 15:1–4); and in the jubilee (every 50 years), agricultural property that had been sold reverted to the seller or his or her heirs (Lev. 25; Deut. 15). These practices were designed to prevent the accumulation of the source of wealth in the hands of the few to the detriment of the many. They also ensured the integrity of the original tribal division of the Land, which was further protected by the decree that a daughter who inherits (in the absence of sons) must marry within the tribe (Num. 36:6).

Thus the Torah prevented the sale of land in perpetuity, providing the religious rationale "for the land is Mine; you are but strangers resident with Me" (Lev. 25:23).

A similar motivation and rural setting are reflected in the law of levirate marriage (*yibbum*): "When brothers dwell together" and one dies childless, the widow cannot marry a stranger; the brother of her deceased husband must marry her. The firstborn son of that marriage is considered the son of the deceased, and the deceased's property thus remains within the family. So strong was the brother's obligation that if he refused to marry his sister-in-law, he invited censure. If he remained adamant in his refusal, he was subject to public humiliation (Deut. 25:5–10).

Outside of the general admonition to have just weights and measures (Lev. 19:36; Deut. 25:13–15) and not to take unfair advantage in buying and selling (Lev. 25:14), there is a paucity of commercial legislation. This further reflects the rural setting, as are the torts enumerated in the Bible: the goring ox (Exod. 21:28–32,35–36), the conversion of a bailment (22:6–7), arson (22:5), and depredation by one's animals (22:4), to give just a few examples. In the case of the goring ox, the Torah distinguishes between a first-time offender and an ox that had previously exhibited vicious behavior. In the latter case, the owner of the ox, being under a greater duty of care, was subject to greater liability. Although the repeat offender was liable for full damages, the ambiguous statement in Exod. 21:35 was interpreted to make the owner of the first-time offender liable for only half the damages. Thus the loss was borne equally by the owners of both oxen. Evidently, the realities of rural and village life were such that both offender and victim shared an assumption of risk.

The rural societal setting is also reflected in the fact that criminal penalties were limited. An offender could be flogged, although the nature of the offenses for which flogging was to be administered is not specified (Deut. 25:1–3). The only other criminal punishment was execution, which was the punishment for murder (Exod. 21:12), adultery (Lev. 20:10), bestiality (Exod. 22:18), and a number of other capital offenses. Incarceration, however, was not mandated as a punishment for any crime. Indeed, to maintain a prison system requires a highly developed society with elaborate governmental organization and bureaucracy, impossible in the primitive setting of the Pentateuchal laws. Any incarceration was only for the limited period required for trial and judgment (Num. 15:34).

Therefore, the Torah does not mandate incarceration for theft. Instead, the thief reimbursed the victim twofold. Significantly, if the stolen object was a sheep or an ox—both vital to the rural economy—and it had been either sold or slaughtered and could, therefore, not be returned to the owner, the reimbursement was fourfold for the sheep and fivefold for the ox (Exod. 21:37, 22:3).

The procedural aspects as well as the substantive aspects of the law similarly reflect both the comparatively simple societal structure and the divine rationale. Although the Torah ordains the establishment of a judicial system operating in all cities within each tribal territory (Deut. 16:18), there is no explicit description of its composition. Though not specifying an appeal system, the Torah assumes that there is a higher judicial authority to whom local judges could turn in cases beyond their competence (Deut. 17:8–12). The alternate use of "judge" and "priest" in this passage is indicative of the ecclesiastical underpinning of the law. Even more striking is the use of *elohim* (a generic term for God) to designate the judges (Exod. 22:7–8, 22:27).

The city gate was evidently the place where judicial transactions took place. Abraham bought the field of Machpelah from Ephron the Hittite in the presence of those at the city gate (Gen. 23:10). It was at the city gate that Boaz transacted the waiver of Naomi's nearest kinsman and thus acquired the right to redeem the lands of Elimelech and to marry Ruth (Ruth 4:1–10). Because written contracts were unknown at an early period, for transactions to become a matter of public record they had to be contracted in the presence of witnesses and in the most public place, which was the city gate. The contract was formalized by an overt act that signified the consent of the parties, such as the removal of a shoe (Ruth 4:7). Written documents evidently came into use at a later period. Jeremiah acquired the field of his cousin Hanamel via a deed of purchase (Jer. 32:10–12). That incident, however, does not necessarily indicate that written documents were becoming common at that time. Jeremiah had a special purpose in committing his purchase to writing and preserving it for safekeeping. It was symbolic of his belief that God would bring His people back from their impending exile. The only legal document mentioned in the Torah is the bill of divorce (Deut. 24:1), although the formalities of its language and form are uncertain. It was certainly not the Aramaic document later formulated by the Sages.

The judges are commissioned to effectuate justice (Deut. 16:18). A number of biblical ordinances are, therefore, directed particularly to judges. They are not to favor persons or take a gift from a litigant (Deut. 16:19). They must treat rich and poor alike (Lev. 19:15); likewise, the stranger and the native born (Lev. 24:22).

Evidentiary rules were simple. Eyewitness testimony was the best (possibly the only) evidence, but judgment could be passed only upon the testimony of two witnesses. One witness was insufficient (Deut. 19:15). The penalty for perjury varied with the nature of the case. As punishment, the perjurer was to suffer whatever effect the perjurious testimony would have had. Thus a false accusation of a capital offense would mean the death penalty for the lying witness. False testimony that would have resulted in a monetary loss to one of the disputants would result in an equal loss to the perjurer (Deut. 19:19). The Torah explicitly delineates that the purpose of this was not only to punish the miscreant but also to act as a deterrent to false testimony. Therefore, the punishment was to be carried out in all its severity—"Nor must you show pity" (Deut. 19:20–21).

The law was thus seen as an instrument of public policy. As the establishment of a just society is God's will, the law mandated by God was designed to accomplish that end. That explains the abundance of "poor laws" that placed a duty on every Israelite to care for the fatherless, the widow, the stranger, and other disadvantaged members of society (e. g., Exod. 22:19–23; Deut. 24:17–22). Farmers were forbidden to glean their field but were to leave the gleanings for the poor and the stranger. They also had to leave a corner of each field unharvested, relinquishing its produce to the disadvantaged (Lev. 23:22). For an example of this law in practice, see Ruth 2. A sheaf left by chance in the field as well as olives and grapes ungleaned were also to be left for "the stranger, the fatherless, and the widow" (Deut. 24:19–22).

The wages of a day laborer had to be paid promptly, for "he is poor" and depends on it (Deut. 24:14–15). One was commanded to lend to the poor unhesitatingly (Deut. 15:7–11) and no interest was to be exacted from them (Exod. 22:24; Deut. 23:20–21). And although slavery existed, the law distinguished between Hebrew slaves and non-Hebrew slaves. Whereas the latter were property and could be bequeathed, the former were only indentured servants. Their term was limited to six years, although they could elect to remain in perpetual servitude (Exod. 21:2–6; Deut. 15:12–18). Their gentler treatment was motivated by the historical memory of Israelite slavery in Egypt: "and the LORD your God redeemed you; therefore I enjoin this commandment upon you today" (Deut. 15:15).

For those who are so poor as to be reduced to pawning a garment, the pledge must be returned each night so that they have a covering during sleep (Exod. 22:25–26). Characterization of God as "compassionate"—as in this last passage—is the basic premise that informs the unique moral and ethical stance of biblical law. A touching example of this compassion translated into law is found in the prohibition against taking both the mother bird and the eggs from the nest. The mother bird must be sent away before the eggs or fledgling are taken (Deut. 22:6–7).

That the community as a whole bore some measure of guilt for the unrequited crime committed in its midst was a unique moral and ethical concept for that era. It is exemplified in the exotic ritual of the beheaded heifer. When a corpse was found in the field—the victim of foul play with the perpetrator unknown—the elders of the nearest city (representing the body politic) took a heifer into the valley, where its neck was broken. They then uttered an expiatory prayer: "'Our hands did not shed this blood, nor did our eyes see it done. Absolve, O LORD, Your people Israel, whom You redeemed, and do not let guilt for the blood of the innocent remain among Your people Israel.' And they will be absolved of bloodguilt" (Deut. 21:1–9). The necessity to seek expiation for the murder arose from the conception that this heinous crime, the perpetrator of which could not be brought to justice, contaminated the community in whose vicinity it took place. Were the perpetrator known, justice could be done and the punishment meted out to the murderer would expiate the crime. Failing this, the community had to remove the defilement of the "innocent blood" by this expiatory ritual.

Although in all of the above examples we have treated the biblical law as if it were embodied in a uniform code, in reality, the biblical law is neither systematic nor monolithic. One can find change and development within the Torah itself. Even in the two versions of the Decalogue (Exod. 20:2–14; Deut. 5:6–18) one finds significant differences (e. g., in the commandment forbidding coveting and in the motivation and rationale for *Shabbat*). So too, whereas in the earlier Exodus code (21:7–11) the daughter sold into slavery by her father did not automatically go free after six years as did the male slave, and could be forced to become her master's wife, in the later Deuteronomic code (15:12) her status is equalized with the male Hebrew slave. Similarly, the Torah records a revolutionary amendment of the law of inheritance. Through the plea of the daughters of Zelophehad, the right to inherit, previously the exclusive prerogative of males, was awarded to daughters when the deceased leaves no sons (Num. 27:1–11). Thus it is clear that biblical law reflects development occasioned by change of time, place, and ethical conception.

It is equally clear that the laws encoded in the Torah do not comprise the totality of the law operative in biblical times. Two outstanding examples show that there was a body of customary law that preceded the writing of the biblical codes and that continued to be operative.

> If a man has two wives, the one loved and the other unloved, and both the loved and the unloved have borne him sons, but the first-born is the son of the unloved one—when he wills his property to his sons, he may not treat as first-born the son of the loved one in disregard of the son of the unloved one who is older. Instead he must accept the first-born, the son of the unloved one, and allot to him a double portion of all his possessions; since he is the first fruit of his vigor, the birthright is his due" (Deut. 21:15–17).

The Torah's assumption here that the firstborn son was entitled to a double portion of the inheritance is nowhere else to be found in the biblical codes. There is no specific statute to that effect. Yet it is clear that such a customary law was operative.

The existence of customary law precedent to the biblical enactments is also adumbrated in the unique treatment of manslaughter, as opposed to premeditated murder. Six towns, strategically placed for easy access, were to be set aside as "cities of refuge" to provide asylum to the manslayer from the "avenger of blood," a near kinsman on whom evidently devolved a duty to avenge the death of an innocent victim. Manslayers had to remain in a city of refuge until the death of the current high priest. If they left the city before then, the blood avenger could kill them with impunity (Num. 35:9–34). Again, the Torah nowhere specifically gives kin the right to kill manslayers. The position of the blood avenger was evidently a prebiblical institution that continued into biblical times and whose consequences the Torah sought to ameliorate.

Nor did the development of law cease with the Bible's canonization. In the Torah, cities of refuge are characterized as providing asylum and protection for the manslayer; however, later talmudic law viewed the institution (which it called *galut,* banishment) as punishing the manslayer for fatal negligence. Similarly, whatever "an eye for an eye" (Exod. 21:24) may have meant in its day, by the time of the Mishnah it had been transmuted into five elements of damage for which the wrong-doer was liable: loss of economic value, pain and suffering, medical costs, loss of earnings during convalescence, and emotional distress prompted by bearing a permanent injury. One should not make the mistake of equating the biblical codes with the totality of Jewish law. On the contrary, the initial work of biblical codifiers has been expanded into a vast legal literature—as generations of talmudic sages, medieval commentators and codifiers, and modern legalists have continuously brought God's law to bear on all facets of human endeavor.

Study Questions

1. The modern, democratic tradition maintains a tension between a "separation of church and state" and the desire to inform society with sacred or moral values. How might Bergman's interpretation

of biblical law allow an open, democratic society to protect religious freedoms while applying sacred values at the same time?

2. Bergman notes that the Bible's vision of legal authority tends to frame norms in terms of obligations rather than rights. How might this difference influence our outlook on some contemporary controversies such as homosexuality, abortion, and end of life issues?

3. Bergman gives examples of laws that clearly reflect the agrarian nature of biblical society, such as the sabbatical and jubilee years, levirate marriage, and "goring oxen." In what sense are these laws meaningful or applicable to us today?

4. What do you think of the biblical legal process (judges, witnesses, and standards of evidence) described by Berman? Would it have been effective in its own time? What about in our own?

5. Note the list of laws cited in the article that deal with social justice. How does this compare to our modern legal system? (If this topic is of interest, you might also read the essay "Justice" by Elliot Dorff in this volume).

6. What does Bergman mean by a "monolithic" system of law? What are the implications of his suggestion that the Bible does not present us with a complete code of law?

Study materials by *Dov Lerea*

MIDRASH AND LEGAL PROCESS

Joel Roth

Summary

Joel Roth's essay provides a conceptual framework for understanding the relationship between law and *midrash*. Law, according to Roth, serves as the medium through which God's will becomes known on earth and *midrash* becomes the indispensable key to interpreting and understanding divine revelation.

Roth clarifies two important technical aspects of *midrash*. First, he presents some biblical usages of the word and suggests that the meaning, "to set his heart to examine God's Torah in order to fulfill it, and to teach laws and rules to Israel," based upon *Ezra* 7:10, is the biblical usage most aligned with subsequent rabbinic application. He also distinguishes between two different genres of *midrash*: *midrash halakhah* (legal midrash) and *midrash aggadah*. *Midrash aggadah*, or nonlegal *midrash*, was not concerned with legal exegesis, but provided the ancient rabbis with a vehicle for interpreting the Torah in ways that could speak to issues of "moral values and social commentary," issues which, Roth notes, are as important as legal norms to a "viable, vibrant society."

Roth constructs a paradigm based on the distinction and tensions between two different forms for transmitting revelation: *mishnah* and *midrash*. In this paradigm, the *mishnah* form of transmission characteristically presents legal norms without identifying either the biblical sources of the law or the argumentation that led to the conclusions. The midrashic style of transmitting God's will and translating it into law, in contrast, usually links norms to their biblical source and also presents some form of argumentation or interpretation. Roth notes that these two modes of thinking represent different "manners of transcription and transmission" rather than traditions that reach conflicting conclusions.

Roth's paradigm also serves as a lens through which we can understand the history of the codification of Jewish law. He uses the *Mishneh Torah* of Maimonides which omits sources or explanations of laws, as a medieval reflection of *mishnah* style. This style resulted in generations of commentary that served to redress the imbalance created by Maimonides, who spoke as a lone voice of unchallenged authority. Roth sees the relationship of the *Mishnei Torah* to the *Beit Yosef,* the *Shulḥan Arukh,* and even to the *Tur* in terms of the tension between *mishnah* and *midrash.*

Roth goes on to describe the conceptual differences and practical applications of two differing ancient schools of legal interpretation: the schools of Akiva and Ishmael. He characterizes Ishmael as a strict constructionist, who believed that the Torah was written in human language and that we must not read extraneous meanings into divine text. Akiva, in contrast, was a loose constructionist and believed that every aspect of the Torah text—every individual letter as well as the crowns on the letters—contains implicit spiritual meaning from God, and challenges us to interpret them as sources of Jewish law. Just as in the American legal system where traditions of legal interpretation no longer tend to directly interpret the Constitution itself, but rather respond to later authoritative texts, contemporary decisors of Jewish law today interpret talmudic and post-talmudic works rather than continue the traditions of midrashic interpretation of the written Torah.

Normative Jewish tradition is a legal tradition, the foundation of which is the Torah. The goal of the tradition is to make clear in detail the commands of God's revealed will. In the earliest eras, God's will was revealed either directly through the biblical prophets, starting with Moses, or indirectly through other media of revelation in the Temple in Jerusalem, like the Urim and Thummim (Exod. 28:30; Num. 27:21; 1 Sam. 14:37–41, 28:6). However, "Ever since the Temple was destroyed, God's place in the world has been restricted to the four cubits of the law" (BT Ber. 8a). The entire legal system (*halakhah*) is based on the conviction that through it God's will becomes known. If that legal system is to remain viable, the Torah must be able to serve as the ultimate source for the resolution of legal questions, even in times far removed from the period of the Torah's composition. In other words, the Torah must be eternally relevant if the halakhic system is to remain vibrant.

The key to understanding the evolution of the legal system, as G. D. Cohen once noted, is *midrash*. *Midrash* is the method and process by which the words of the Torah are interpreted, explained, analyzed, and understood. Through the process of *midrash*, the Torah has remained a living document, eternally relevant and able to serve as the basis of an ever-evolving Jewish law.

The term *midrash* in the Bible means "to examine," to "investigate," "to seek or search out" (Lev. 10:16; Deut. 13:15). It is derived from the root דר"ש. Probably the most illustrative use of this root in the Bible, for our purposes, appears in the verse that informs us that Ezra "set his heart to examine [*lidrosh*] God's Torah in order to fulfill it, and to teach laws and rules to Israel" (Ezra 7:10). The term *midrash* in the Dead Sea Scrolls, too, refers to a method of inquiry into the meaning of biblical verses.

Even though *midrash* is a key to understanding the legal tradition, it is important to note that there is a vast literature of *midrash* that is not legal. That body of literature is called *midrash aggadah,* the nonlegal interpretation of the Bible. Indeed, the term *midrash* without any modifier usually refers to *midrash aggadah* and not to legal (halakhic) *midrash*. There are collections of *midrash aggadah* compiled from the 5th through the 12th centuries. Some of the older collections, such as Genesis Rabbah, contain elaborate literary structures, which probably reflect a long period of development. There are two basic types of *midrash aggadah*. Those that interpret the verses of the Torah in consecutive order, with comments on almost every verse, are called "exegetic." Those that explain and expound only the first verses of a section of the Torah that is read publicly on a *Shabbat* or on a festival are called "homiletic."

Nonlegal *midrash aggadah,* like the legal *midrash* discussed below, enables the Torah to speak to every generation everywhere. The contents of *midrash aggadah* reflect how the preachers of each generation used the Torah as the starting point of moral instruction and social commentary—which are no less important to a viable, vibrant tradition than are its legal norms. Indeed, the values of *midrash aggadah* are often translated into normative legal behavior.

Behavior norms at the beginning of the Rabbinic era (through the early 3rd century C. E.) were transmitted in either *mishnah* form or in the form of legal *midrash* (*midrash halakhah*). In *mishnah* style, norms are presented almost always without their source or basis in the Bible and without the argumentation that led to the conclusion. In *midrash* style, the norms are linked directly to the biblical verses that serve as their basis, and usually the argumentation is also presented. Many legal conclusions are identical in the works of both styles. They are not the result of conflicting processes that must lead to different conclusions; more accurately, they are different manners of transcription and transmission. Obviously, *midrash* style highlights the fact that the Torah is at the core of legal decisions. On the other hand, *mishnah* style (severing the laws from their scriptural basis) allows for organizing the material more systematically, making it easier to follow.

The *mishnah* style did not eliminate the need for *midrash halakhah* to link the law to the Torah. Even after *mishnah* style became the predominant method of transmission, passages of the Talmud that discuss a clearly established *mishnah* often begin by citing the biblical source on which the *mishnah* was based, as well as the argument that led to the conclusion. Both methods were used by the Sages of the early Rabbinic period. Virtually the same Sages appear in both the Mishnah (and Tosefta) and the literature of *midrash halakhah*.

This tension between *mishnah* style and *midrash* style is also reflected in the history of the codification of Jewish law. For example, Maimonides wrote his classic legal compilation (*Mishnei Torah*) in *mishnah* style. His code rarely quotes a source, offers a justification of his view, or records differences of opinion. Shortly after its publication in 1177, it began to spawn commentaries that essentially restored the sources of his decisions as well as the argumentation that led to them. This is the same process of reinserting *midrash* style into *mishnah* style that we find often in the Talmud.

Maimonides was widely criticized for his audacity in composing a legal code without citing any sources or justifications of his decisions. Joseph Karo, the 16th-century author of the classic Jewish code of law *Shulḥan Arukh,* attempted to meet that objection by composing a lengthy work (*Beit Yosef*) that quotes the relevant sources and argumentation. His work is actually a commentary to a 14th-century legal code, called the *Tur,* by Jacob ben Asher. Karo's *Shulḥan Arukh* itself was more a digest of the *Tur* and his own *Beit Yosef* than a new code. Nonetheless, the sources and argumentation were reinstated into the *Shulḥan Arukh* by its commentators as well—even though they already had been spelled out in the *Beit Yosef.*

The *mishnah* style—clear, definitive, and unencumbered by sources and justifications—has a special appeal because it is so easy to use. That style was necessary at certain times in Jewish history, and most codifiers who resorted to it did so due to the compelling circumstances of their time and place. So, for example, Maimonides justified writing his code in *mishnah* style because the proliferation of legal materials had made it difficult to determine the law or to understand how it was to be derived. The *mishnah* style allowed him to record and organize the law "so that all the laws shall stand revealed to great and small." Similarly, Karo indicated that the movement of Jews from country to country produced conflicts between new arrivals and long-time residents, with the result that "the law has come to be many *torot* [laws]," which needed to be summarized and codified in a systematic and useful way.

However, in the long run Jewish law does not rely on the pronouncement of one sole authority, one codifier, but flows from reasoning and cogent proofs. The *mishnah* style omits reasoning, and it offers no proofs. The *midrash* style retains them. Although *mishnah* style is useful, it cannot replace the need for *midrash*. What is recorded and transmitted in the *mishnah* style is the result of *midrash*, not its replacement. Often, short and clear statements are used to transmit God's will. Determining the specifics of that will, however, is rarely achieved without extensive discussion, deliberation, and analysis—of sources, precedents, and arguments.

In a legal system that ultimately depends on the reasoned analysis and interpretation of texts, it is most plausible to expect that the interpreters of those texts may have differing approaches to interpreting those texts. Those differences may reflect more than varied opinions of interpretation that legitimately can be deduced from texts. In the United States, such differences are often reflected by what we call strict constructionists and loose constructionists. Strict constructionists, for example, tend to be more concerned with the original intent of the framers of the Constitution, whereas loose constructionists believe that the court should be creative in its interpretation of the Constitution, so that it can meet the challenges of new times more expediently. The devotees of these two schools are in fundamental disagreement about the limits of legitimate interpretation. In terms that we have been using, these differences reflect conflicting views about what is a legitimate *midrash*. Both schools agree that *midrash* is the most significant tool for understanding the meaning of the text. Their dispute is about the legitimacy of specific approaches to *midrash*.

It should come as no surprise that there were different schools of midrashic interpretation of the Torah. In the 2nd century c. e., the period of the greatest flowering of Rabbinic *midrash*, there were two such schools—the school of Akiva and the school of Ishmael. There has been a great deal of scholarly debate about the distinctions between these two schools. I offer here two examples (of about 15 differences between them) to show how the schools reflect different approaches to the interpretation of Torah.

For the school of Akiva, no word or letter in the Torah can be the result merely of linguistic style or usage. Every word, even every letter, has significance and, therefore, can become the basis of *midrash halakhah*. The Talmud discusses the punishment decreed for the daughter of a *kohen* who has violated the Torah as noted in Lev. 21:9: "And the daughter of any priest, if she profane herself by playing the harlot, she profanes her father; she shall be burned with fire." The Talmud affirms that this applies only to one who is engaged. Akiva determines that this punishment applies also to a married woman. He determines it on the basis of one extraneous letter (*vav*) in the verse from Leviticus. His disputant, Ishmael, replies: "Because you make a *midrash* on a superfluous letter *vav*, we should take this woman out to be burned?" (BT Sanh. 51b). For Ishmael, the divine Torah is written in human language. A matter of style, grammar, or usage is not to be interpreted as indicating a divine message. For Akiva, all statements, all letters, in the Torah are divine and are sources for midrashic interpretation and legal application. Ishmael was a strict constructionist; Akiva a loose constructionist.

Akiva declared that even words like "all" (*kol*), "also" (*gam*), and "the" (*et*, when used to indicate a direct object) imply teachings that are unstated in the words of the text. The fifth commandment illustrates his method. "Honor your father and your mother." The Hebrew reads: *kabbed et avikha v'et immekha*. The school of Akiva interprets the first *et* to teach that one's stepmother is included in this commandment and interprets the second *et* to teach that one's stepfather is included. The connective prefix *v'* is interpreted to teach the obligation to honor one's older brother, also. For Ishmael and his school, these words do not serve as the source for the derivation of any law.

Both schools agree that God's will is to be learned from the Torah through the process of *midrash*. Often both schools will agree on the actual law, although each school will use a different method of interpretation to deduce it. Sometimes, though, the different views of what constitutes legitimate *midrash* produce different understandings of what God demands of us. Such conflicting understandings result in different behaviors, each consistent with what that school believes to be the will of God.

Abraham Joshua Heschel's monumental work in Hebrew, *Torah Min Ha-Shamayim Ba-Aspaklaria Shel Ha-Dorot* (*Theology of Ancient Judaism*), demonstrates that the differences between the school of Akiva and the school of Ishmael extend beyond legal matters to issues of *aggadah* and theology. Furthermore, Heschel demonstrates, the principles and methods of the schools survive long after the schools themselves cease to exist.

Some things have changed since the end of the Rabbinic period, which has been the focus of most of the discussion here. Mainly, new *midrash halakhah* on the Torah itself is rare. In fact, it has been rare since about the 10th or 11th centuries C. E. (There continues to be *midrash aggadah* directly on the Torah even in our own day.) Instead, the focus of *midrash halakhah* has shifted from the Torah itself to the subsequent layers of authoritative texts: Mishnah, Talmud, medieval codes of law and their commentators, and the volumes upon volumes of legal responsa written throughout the centuries. There is some similarity between this process and what is recognizable in the United States too. Although, admittedly, the Supreme Court sometimes still engages in the direct interpretation of the Constitution itself, its decisions often are focused not directly on the Constitution, but on how the Constitution has been interpreted by earlier courts. And this is surely true of lower courts, which rarely interpret the Constitution itself. Most Jewish legal authorities since the close of the Talmud would surely have considered themselves "lower courts" compared to the Sages of the talmudic period itself. Thus it is logical that the focus of their *midrash* would shift from the actual Torah to the authoritative interpretations of the Torah in earlier generations. And each generation's contribution to this process becomes a focus of halakhic midrashic attention for those that follow. Furthermore, because subsequent authoritative texts are themselves a *midrash* on earlier authoritative texts, the latest links in this continuous chain are linked directly to Torah through the chain itself.

Some things, however, have remained quite unchanged. Just as there were different schools of interpretation in the early Rabbinic period, so, too, every era has had differing schools. The schools may not have been as easily distinguished from each other as the earliest schools were, but every generation has had its strict constructionists and its loose constructionists. In later generations, though, the Akiva-like or Ishmael-like interpretations were no longer directly focused on the Torah but on later authoritative texts. Thus, for example, decisors of this generation engage in midrashic interpretations of several talmudic passages and several responsa and come to differing conclusions about how to define the moment of death according to Jewish law. Many feel constrained by the texts of the tradition that seem to define death as the cessation of respiration and heartbeat, whereas others offer a liberal interpretation of a *mishnah* (one never used for this purpose before) to accept brain death as a halakhic definition of death. It may be that in the future even those who now retain the more traditional view will find a *midrash* that fits their framework of legitimate *midrash halakhah* and thus adopt the other view. If and when that happens, we will see an instance of two schools coming to the same conclusion via differing *midrash,* a phenomenon emphasized in the discussion of the schools of Akiva and Ishmael. If that never happens, we shall see an instance of the differing midrashic views of differing schools leading to differences of opinion that translate into different legal decisions.

In the final analysis, each generation and era is distinguished from all others, and the distinctions between them are often the subject of historical research. But, in terms of Jewish law, all eras share several constants: the centrality of *midrash* to the evolution of law, the existence of differing views as to what constitutes legitimate *midrash*, and the possibility of divergent behaviors within the framework of Jewish law.

Study Questions

1. How is the process of *midrash* central to Jewish law?

2. How does the difference between *midrash* and *mishnah* help us understand the history of the development of Jewish legal codification?

3. What are the advantages of a *mishnah* form of transmission, if that form does not identify biblical sources and present interpretive arguments? Alternatively, what are the disadvantages of a midrashic style of transmission?

4. Think about the differences between law and prophecy. In terms of transmitting God's will on earth in a way that speaks to ordinary people, which form seems most compelling today?

5. What are the implications of midrashic thinking for the power or limitations of human language?

6. A classic problem in the history of religious thinking is the dichotomy between inner experience and outer performance. For example, a person may be saying the words of a prayer without actually feeling them in his or her heart. Compare Akiva's and Ishmael's interpretations of Lev. 21:9. Which school of midrashic thinking emphasizes the spirit of the law, and which the letter of the law, and why?

Study materials by *Dov Lerea*

MEDIEVAL AND MODERN HALAKHAH

Elliot N. Dorff

Summary

Elliot Dorff's essay is concerned with three aspects of *halakhah*. First, he describes the ways in which Jewish law was preserved and transmitted in the medieval period. Dorff then discusses the impact that changes in society from the medieval to early modern period had on the authority of Jewish law. He concludes his essay with a detailed explanation of how the various movements in Judaism, and Conservative Judaism in particular, have responded to ongoing challenges to the authority of Jewish law.

Dorff notes that Jews in the medieval period produced three forms of literature to preserve and develop Jewish law: codes, responsa, and amendments to law, which include enactments and decrees. Codes provided a way for the majority of Jews to learn the laws that would enable them to lead Jewish lives without having to acquire the skills or allocate the time necessary for studying the Talmud. Responsa (*t'shuvot*) were written by individual rabbis, drawing on earlier legal precedents to address new situations to respond to "questions" posed by individuals or communities. Local authorities also sometimes established statutes (*takkanot*) and or decrees (*g'zerot*) to address a situation. Finally, since Jews were scattered throughout the diaspora, local custom (*minhag*) assumed the importance of law in these communities.

Dorff maintains that the authority of Jewish law rested upon a medieval societal structure in which religious communities governed themselves in most instances, and where there existed a strong pressure within each community to conform to religious norms. The Enlightenment challenged this structure and stressed instead the importance of the individual over the group. Dorff maintains that the denominations of modern Jewish life emerged as a response to the crisis caused by the shift in society from a corporate structure to an enlightened, individualistic one. Reform Judaism reconceptualized

Jewish law as guidelines for living. Reconstructionists naturalized Judaism and viewed *halakhah* as a pathway, rather than as an expression of God's will. Orthodox thinkers asserted that Jewish law derives its authority from God and remains immutable; only changes in context warrant the possibility for a new ruling, while changes in human perceptions or values cannot force God's hand in establishing norms for behavior. Conservative Judaism asserts the divine quality of Jewish law, but also presents a range of interpretations for explaining the relationship between God's will and the historical development of the Torah and its teachings, including the possibility that the Torah was inspired by God but composed by people over a long period of time.

Dorff's long final section presents two sets of rationales for the continued authority of Jewish law: theological responses and functional ones. Theological reasons include the historical dedication to the sanctification of God's name in the world (*kiddush ha-Shem)*, the human need to express gratitude to God about life, and the fact that we are partners in covenant with God. Functionally, Jewish law provides a structure for communal life, it sensitizes us to moral values, and it preserves the wisdom of the ages for our own lives.

During the Middle Ages, Jews were scattered all over the globe, and after the close of the Babylonian academies in the 11th century c. e., a centralized authority to teach and make Jewish law no longer existed. Under these conditions, biblical and talmudic commentaries were written to help people understand Judaism's sacred books even in the absence of teachers. Thus three types of legal literature were produced—legal codes, responsa, and amendments to the law (*takkanot*)—in an effort to make it possible for Jews to know what Judaism required of them and to make Jewish law viable in totally new circumstances.

The most famous of the medieval codes were those of Moses Maimonides and Joseph Karo, completed in 1177 and 1565, respectively. Maimonides titled his code *Mishnei Torah*, cleverly using a biblical phrase meaning "copy of the Torah" (Deut. 17:18) to signify also, through a play on words, "second to the Torah" and "the learning [lessons, import] of the Torah." As he states in the introduction, he wanted people to be able to read the Torah and then read his code and thereby know how to live their lives as Jews. After that, any time they had to spend learning the intricate legal discussions in the Talmud would be all to the good. The vast majority of Jews, however, had neither the time nor the expertise to follow those arguments; therefore, Maimonides presented to them the practical conclusions of those discussions so they could live their lives in conformity with Jewish law. Similarly, Karo titled his code *Shulḥan Arukh,* "the set table," because he was effectively spoon-feeding the requirements of Jewish law to those who could not delve into its rationales and nuances.

The very process of summarizing Jewish law in the form of codes caused great controversy. First of all, because the whole point of writing a code was to create a short, clear, unequivocal statement of what is required, the codifiers generally did not cite their sources or the reasoning that led them to their conclusions. That detached Jewish law from its sources and from its process of ongoing development, freezing it in the form that the codifier created. The reader thus totally depended on the codifier's interpretation of the sources. Furthermore, because none of the reasoning behind the law was provided, readers might well make mistakes if they tried to apply a section of the code to a question that it did not cover. Finally, rabbis like Abraham ben David of Posquieres ("Ravad," 12th century C. E.), a harsh critic of Maimonides, objected to the arbitrariness of the form, for it presented Jewish law the way one particular codifier understood it, with no mention of why or of alternate opinions and practices. Karo acknowledged some of these difficulties, but the need to make Jewish law available to the masses prompted him to write his code nonetheless.

The *Mishnei Torah* still governs the practice of many *S'fardim* (Mediterranean and Middle Eastern Jewish communities). Other *S'fardim* follow the *Shulḥan Arukh* because Karo himself was a rabbi from that tradition, living first in Spain and then in the Levant. Meanwhile, *Ashk'nazim* (originally from France and Germany and then from eastern Europe) generally follow the *Shulḥan Arukh,* because Moses Isserles (a 16th-century Polish rabbi) wrote glosses to it—and cleverly called it *Mappah,* "tablecloth"—indicating wherever the practices of *Ashk'nazim* differed from *S'fardim*. Other codes (or partial codes) have been written more recently. But Karo's code still is the primary one because it is the last that, with the notes of Isserles, can legitimately claim to reflect the practices of worldwide rabbinic Jewry of its time (with the exception of the Jews of the Far East and Yemen).

Far more extensive is the literature of responsa (Hebrew: *t'shuvot; singular:* responsum, *t'shuvah*), rabbis' rulings dating from the 8th century C. E. to our own in answer to specific legal questions asked of them. Indeed, it is estimated that some 300,000 responsa are extant, and new ones are being written all the time. This genre of legal literature has the distinct advantage of being focused on specific questions and contexts. Thus responsa can be produced far more quickly than can comprehensive codes, and responsa can attend to the particular details of a case at hand. Moreover, responsa by nature require the authors to cite sources and explain their reasoning, and they deal only with given cases. These features give rabbis in other times and places a choice: They can depend on a given responsum for their ruling, or they can dismiss it—claiming that its embodied precedent is too different from the present case. The resulting process preserves both the continuity and the flexibility of the law. No wonder, then, that the vast majority of the business of Jewish law over the last 1,300 years has been accomplished through the genre of responsa. The one drawback of responsa is that—written in many times and places—they are poorly collected and organized, making it difficult to know whether relevant responsa exist on a given topic. But that problem has diminished in our time by the creation of computer databases that catalog many medieval and early modern responsa.

Because medieval Jews found themselves living in new places under new economic, political, and religious conditions, some aspects of Jewish law had to be adjusted to the new circumstances. Most of the time, that was accomplished by new legal interpretations and applications of the sources or by changing customs. Sometimes, however, the law had to be formally amended, accomplished through *takkanot* (literally, "fixings") or *g'zerot* (decrees) that were enacted by, or in the name of, the rabbis of the community or communities that were to follow the laws and on the combined authority of those rabbis and communities. Some of these enactments were highly localized and temporary, establishing, for example, the ways in which Jews were to interact with the non-Jewish authorities of the region or the specific method by which honest weights and measures were to be ensured. Others were intended to be, or were taken by later authorities to be, more permanent, e. g., the enactments attributed to Gershom (ca. 1000 C. E.), limiting a man to one wife and requiring the wife's consent to a divorce.

Finally, with Jews scattered throughout the world and with many living in small communities, it is not surprising that local custom became an important source for the law. In some cases, it even superseded laws of the Talmud. So, for example, although the Mishnah requires a year's waiting period between betrothal and marriage, the medieval conditions in which Jews lived were too precarious to trust that a wedding postponed for a year would take place. In addition, Jews were too poor to host both an engagement party and a wedding feast, and so medieval custom combined the two into one ceremony, as we do to this day. Similarly, although the Mishnah and the Talmud establish beyond any shadow of a doubt that the sale of movable property is legally valid only when it has been transferred to the domain of the purchaser, medieval custom determined that a handshake would seal the deal.

In some cases, commercial custom all but abrogated even the laws of the Torah, as, for example, the commercial customs that ultimately led to the rabbinical *heter iska*, literally, "the permission to engage in business," which by medieval times required the charging of interest, against the Torah's express words. The rabbis of the time created a legal fiction whereby such transactions were not to be considered interest on loans but rather profits from a partnership. (Thus, to this day, when one deposits money in an Israeli bank owned by religious Jews, one is actually investing as a partner in the bank, as a notice in the bank attests.) This is also a good example of the interaction of these various sources of law—codes, responsa, legislation, and custom—because pervasive commercial custom ultimately prodded the rabbis to issue a ruling legitimating the practice.

Jewish law governed the daily lives of most of the world's Jews throughout the Middle Ages and until World War I. That was because societies were organized corporately, such that the government let specific communities within their realm govern themselves as long as they produced the required taxes and (sometimes) men for the army. As a result, Jews who had a dispute with one another would bring it to Jewish courts for resolution. (Filing suit instead in a gentile court would undermine the authority of Jewish courts; and it might subject the other party—and perhaps even the Jewish community—to penalties exacted by the usually anti-Semitic government. Therefore, "outside" suits were subject to fines and more severe punishment imposed by the Jewish courts.)

This ceased being true with the advent of the Enlightenment, according to which each person was to be seen as an individual and not as a member of a group. Until the end of World War II, however, the Enlightenment affected the political and legal structure only of countries in western Europe and the United States while most Jews lived in eastern Europe and in the Muslim world, where the old, corporate system still held sway. Consequently, it is only since then that the majority of the world's Jews have no longer been governed by the decrees of Jewish courts, enforced, if necessary, by government authorities.

It is thus not surprising that the problem of delineating the authority of Jewish law was not an issue for most Jews before World War II; it was authoritative at the very least because it was enforced by courts and police. In Germany, however, and in other countries of western Europe and the United States, the Enlightenment affected the structure of government beginning with the end of the 18th century; and so Jewish courts from then on no longer had such authority over Jews. Therefore, German thinkers of the 19th century argued for delimiting and justifying the ongoing authority of Jewish law, despite the inability of the Jewish community to enforce it, and that thinking continued primarily in Germany and in the United States in the 20th century. The modern Jewish movements—Conservative, Orthodox, Reform, and Reconstructionist—are all responses to this historical and philosophical dynamic, which in many ways continues to our own day.

How, then, can the authority of Jewish law be justified when Jews living in free societies cannot be forced to abide by it? Indeed, in what sense is Jewish law still "law"?

Reform thinkers in the 19th and early 20th centuries maintained that Jewish law no longer existed, that what went by that name was, at best, a series of customs and guidelines and, at worst, antiquated norms that were best abandoned. In recent decades, Reform thinkers, professionals, and laypeople are more open to having Jewish norms shape parts of their lives; but the extent to which they do so is totally a function of each Jew's autonomous choice. The Reform Movement's 1976 *Centenary Perspective* does call on Reform Jews to study Judaism so that they can make informed choices, and the Reform rabbinate's 1999 *Pittsburgh Platform* goes even further in encouraging Jewish observance. In the end, though, it is not Jewish law that governs; people individually have the freedom to choose when and how their Jewish commitments will influence their thinking and behavior.

The Reconstructionist movement, founded by Mordecai Kaplan, rejected supernaturalism and with it the divine authority for Jewish law. In Kaplan's view, although moral norms are binding not only on Jews but also on all people, religious rituals derive from folkways. Jewish ritual behavior, then, is important because it provides a unifying force for the community and dramatizes its values. It is not, however, "law" and hence can be modified to meet changing needs and circumstances. More recent exponents of Reconstructionism have moved away from Kaplan's emphasis on the central role that the community plays in Jewish religious practice and belief and have adopted positions more similar to those of the Reform Movement.

Orthodox thinkers maintain not only that Jewish law derives its authority from God but also that it has and should remain the same as Moses received it on Mount Sinai. Moreover, the written Torah that we have in hand is, in the Orthodox view, the exact copy of the text that Moses wrote down at God's command, and the oral Torah is what he learned there and passed down in unwritten form. If this is so, then we must assume that historical development did not, and should not, occur in Jewish law; God's word stands forever. What does need to be addressed, however, is how to apply precedents from the past to modern times, which is often difficult, because the Enlightenment has substantially changed social structure, and science and technology have radically altered the physical environment in which we live. In response to these new circumstances, the Orthodox have produced many responsa—more, in fact, than any other group. The assumption underlying all of them, however, is that only changes in context can warrant a new application of law; changes in human perceptions or values cannot, for God's word as it has come down to us always takes precedence over human ideas and values.

The Conservative Movement, like the Orthodox, affirms the divine root of Jewish law and its binding character. It studies the Jewish past, though, with the same intellectual tools by which we examine the past of any other people. When those techniques are applied to the Torah, one discovers that the text we have in hand shows signs of being composed of several documents that were later edited together. The laws that governed the Israelites, like their stories and traditions, were undoubtedly passed down from generation to generation primarily in oral form. People learned how to behave as Jews by observing how Jewish law was practiced in their own homes and communities and by hearing answers to their questions from parents, rabbis, and friends. In this process, elements were borrowed from nearby cultures and then sometimes changed by the Israelites to fit their own emerging view of life and their own circumstances. Only much later were some of these stories and laws written down, and still later these documents were edited together.

Conservative thinkers generally accept the documentary theory about the origins of the Torah and agree that it nevertheless bespeaks God's will, but they differ as to why and how. Some think that the divine authority of the Torah, and of later Jewish law based on it, ultimately depends on the words that God spoke at Sinai and the rabbis' interpretations of those words in all succeeding generations. Others believe that the process of God's revelation at Sinai was more akin to inspiration: God inspired (literally, "breathed into") the writer(s) of the biblical texts the divine spirit, but it was human beings who wrote down what they understood God to mean and want. Still others are uncertain about such divine origins of the law but maintain that the Torah is "divine" at least in the sense that it represents what our ancestors understood God to demand. Similarly, Jewish law in our day is "divine" minimally in its aspiration to articulate what God wants of us now, what God, indeed, commands.

Because Jews historically have seen the Torah as the source of our knowledge of God's will, they have considered it the authoritative guide for how we should live our lives—so much so that for them life ceased to be worthwhile if they could not live according to its laws. Jews have, indeed, given up their lives for the sanctification of God's name, *al kiddush ha-shem,* rather than publicly violate Jewish law. Jews have also put themselves at great risk to carry out its observance. Numerous examples of both of these affirmations of the importance of Jewish law in extremely adverse circumstances can be found during the Middle Ages, especially in response to the Crusades and the Inquisition. Examples also abound in recent events, in particular during the *Sho·ah* and during the communist reign in Russia and in eastern Europe. Jewish law, then, may also be considered "divine," or at the very least "sacred," because our people have been willing even to sacrifice their lives to uphold it. As the Mishnah (Ber. 9:5) maintained, when the Torah says, "You shall love the LORD your God with all your heart, with all your soul, and with all your might" (Deut. 6:5), it means, by the second phrase, "even if God takes your soul" (life). Unfortunately, Jews in times past have had to make that sacrifice, and that should give us today yet another reason to honor Jewish law and seek to uphold its provisions.

Jews from biblical times to our own have obeyed Jewish law for other theological reasons, too. We obey the commandments in gratitude for our very lives and for the special favors God has done for us individually and as a people (Deut. 4:32–40). Moreover, we are, according to the Torah, partners in a covenant with God. Through that covenant, we are bound to the promises that our ancestors made at Sinai (Deut. 5:2–3, 29:13–14,28). That covenant also establishes the ongoing relationship between God and the people Israel, and so we obey the commandments to maintain that relationship. We obey Jewish law, in other words, out of love for God (Deut. 11:1). Furthermore, we obey Jewish law because we aspire to be "a kingdom of priests and a holy nation" (Exod. 19:5–6), indeed, "a light unto the nations" (Isa. 49:6); that is our divinely ordained mission in life. Finally, aspiring to holiness enables us to be like God: "You shall be holy, for I, the LORD your God, am holy" (Lev. 19:2).

In addition to these theological reasons to obey Jewish law, contemporary Jews, like our ancestors over the generations, also have been motivated by the functions Jewish law serves on the human level. The law maintains the identity and structure of the Jewish community; if everyone were to make completely independent choices, there would be little chance for communal cohesiveness and the sharing it brings. Furthermore, the law sensitizes us to the moral dimensions of life; we may not do whatever we wish or even whatever we think is right but must rather conform to communal norms. It also enables us to call on the wisdom of the ages in making our own moral decisions, for the law is a repository of centuries of experience and the wisdom gained in the process (Deut. 4:6–8).

However one understands the grounds for the authority of Jewish law, it is clear from the historical record that the content of Jewish law in the Torah itself and in later periods has changed over time: many things have been added, others dropped, and some changed in form. This was historically done, in part, through the official acts of rabbis and, in part, through the customs of the people. In technical terms, Jewish law has evolved out of the interaction between *din* (law) and *minhag* (custom), between the way in which rabbis over the generations have interpreted and applied it and the way in which Jews have observed it. To be authentic to the Jewish past, then, and to be a living, vibrant tradition now, Conservative Judaism would have us determine the content of Jewish law as it has always been determined—namely, through an ongoing interaction between the rabbis and the masses of Jews who take Jewish law seriously and who practice it in their lives.

As it has been within Jewish communities for at least the last 1,000 years, the burden of that determination within the Conservative Movement rests primarily on the congregational rabbi, the *mara d'atra*, the teacher of the local community. When a rabbi thinks that a question has not been addressed in Jewish law, at least not in the contemporary context, or that modern circumstances or sensitivities warrant a reexamination of traditional Jewish law on a given issue, he or she may address a question along those lines to the movement's Committee on Jewish Law and Standards (CJLS). Ultimately it will issue one or more responsa articulating the committee's advice to the rabbis of the movement on the issue. The local rabbi, however, remains the one to decide the issue for the specific congregation.

In rare circumstances, the committee issues a standard that binds all of the rabbis and synagogues of the movement. So, for example, no Conservative rabbi may even attend, let alone officiate at, the wedding of a Jew to a non-Jew, because that has been made a standard of the movement. Similarly, Jewish identity, according to another standard of the movement, is defined by being born to a Jewish woman or by being converted to Judaism according to the requirements and procedures of Jewish law.

Although the Conservative Movement has not officially adopted many standards, many commonalities exist in how Conservative congregations observe Jewish law, most of which have grown out of the shared customs and perceptions of the movement. One would expect such a development from a group of people who take Jewish law seriously, who demand intellectual honesty in studying its history and in making contemporary decisions, and who deeply want it to shape Jewish life in the modern world as a prime, indispensable way in which to carry out the will of God as we understand it in our time.

Study Questions

1. What are the strengths and weaknesses of codes, *t'shuvot, takkanot,* and *minhagim* as ways of applying and preserving Jewish law?

2. Dorff suggests strongly that Conservative Judaism determines "the content of Jewish law as it has always been determined—namely, through an ongoing interaction between the rabbis and the masses of Jews who take Jewish law seriously and who practice it in their lives." Find examples of ways in which Jews from within the Reform, Reconstructionist, and Orthodox movements have grappled with challenges posed by modern life or values (e.g., driving on *Shabbat*, attitudes toward homosexuality, the role of women in worship) and compare them to Dorff's statement about the Conservative movement. How do you evaluate his statement after your analysis? Dorff provides theological as well as pragmatic reasons for asserting the authority of Jewish law. Are

his reasons compelling to you? Why or why not? Can you think of other compelling reasons to regard Jewish law as authoritative?

3. We live in what many call a post-denominational period. How might transcending denominations provide an alternate response to the threats to the authority of Jewish law, as Dorff presents them?

4. Compare the notion of God as divine law-giver to the fact that on American currency the phrase: "In God We Trust" appears. What do those words mean to us as members of a secular, democratic society? In what sense might the American founding fathers have regarded the Constitution as a "sacred" document? How does this compare with your understanding of the divine nature of Jewish law?

Study materials by *Dov Lerea*

Biblical Foundations: Social and Ethical Responsibilities

BIBLICAL CONCEPTS OF HOLINESS

Baruch A. Levine

Summary

From the outset, Baruch Levine notes that "Holiness is difficult to define or to describe; it is a mysterious quality." Nevertheless, Levine focuses on several aspects of holiness: it relates to a sense of distinctiveness, it is achieved not only by individuals but by the community, and it is associated with certain divine attributes and with human efforts to imitate those attributes. The Torah thus creates a program of ritual and interpersonal mitzvot that create a blueprint for creating a holy people. Finally, Levine explains that "the gulf between the sacred and the profane was not meant to be permanent," and suggests that it is the work of religion to assist regular people in bridging that gulf.

Consider these words of Abraham Joshua Heschel, taken from his great work, *God in Search of Man:*

> In other religions, gods, heroes, priests are holy; to the Bible, not only God but "the whole community is holy" (Numbers 16:3). "Ye shall be unto me a kingdom of priests, a holy people" (Exodus 19:6), was the reason for Israel's election, the meaning of its distinction. What obtains between man and God is not mere submission to His power or dependence upon His mercy. The plea is not to obey what He wills, but to *do* what He *is*. It is not said: Ye shall be full of awe for I am holy, but: Ye shall be holy, for I the Lord your God am holy (Leviticus 19:2). How does a human being, "dust and ashes," turn holy? Through doing His *mitzvot*, His commandments.

Reading Heschel's observations about the relationship of spirituality and the Jewish quest for holiness in light of Professor Levine's remarks about the universal nature of holiness creates a challenging context in which to consider the most basic of all spiritual questions: What is the source of holiness and how can it be attained?

"Holiness" is difficult to define or to describe; it is a mysterious quality. Of what does holiness consist? In the simplest terms, the holy is different from the profane or the ordinary. It is "other," as the phenomenologists define it. The holy is also powerful or numinous. The presence of holiness may inspire awe, strike fear, or evoke amazement. The holy may be perceived as dangerous, yet it is urgently desired because it affords blessings, power, and protection.

The *Sifra* conveys the concept of "otherness" in its comment to Lev. 19:2, which teaches that "you shall be holy" means "you shall be distinct [*p'rushim tihyu*]." This means that the people Israel, in becoming a holy nation, must preserve its distinctiveness from other peoples. It must pursue a way of life different from that practiced by other peoples. This objective is epitomized in Exod. 19:6: "You shall be to Me a kingdom of priests and a holy nation [*goy kadosh*]." This statement also conveys the idea, basic to biblical religion, that holiness cannot be achieved by individuals alone, no matter how elevated, pure, or righteous. It can be realized only through the life of the community, acting together.

The words of Lev. 19:2 pose a serious theological problem, especially the second part of the statement: "For I, the LORD your God, am holy." Does this mean that holiness is part of the nature of God? Does it mean that holiness originates from God? The predominant view in Jewish tradition has been that this statement was not intended to describe God's essential nature but, rather, His manifest, or "active," attributes. To say that God is "holy" is similar to saying that He is great, powerful, merciful, just, wise, and so forth. These attributes are associated with God on the basis of His observable actions: the ways in which He relates to mortals and to the universe. The statement that God is holy means, in effect, that He acts in holy ways: He is just and righteous. Although this interpretation derives from postbiblical Jewish tradition, it seems to approximate both the priestly and the prophetic biblical conceptions of holiness.

In biblical literature, there is a curious interaction between the human and the divine with respect to holiness. Thus in Exod. 20:8, the Israelites are commanded to sanctify *Shabbat* and to make it holy; and yet verse 11 of the same commandment states that it was God who declared *Shabbat* holy. Similarly, God declared that Israel had been selected to become His holy people; but this declaration was hardly sufficient to make Israel holy. To achieve a holiness of the kind associated with God and His acts, Israel would have to observe His laws and commandments. The way to holiness, in other words, was for Israelites, individually and collectively, to emulate God's attributes. In theological terms, this principle is known as *imitatio dei* (Latin: "the imitation of God"). The same interaction is evident, therefore, in the commandment to sanctify *Shabbat,* with God and the Israelite people acting in tandem to realize the holiness of this occasion. God shows the way, and Israel follows.

The biblical term for holiness is *"kodesh."* Although the noun is abstract, it is likely that the perception of holiness was not thoroughly abstract. In fact, *"kodesh"* had several meanings, including "sacred place," "sanctuary," and "sacred offering." In addition, in certain syntactic positions, Hebrew nouns function as adjectives. The Hebrew phrase *shem kodsho,* for example, does not mean "the name of His holiness" but, rather, "His holy name." This leads to the conclusion that in the biblical conception holiness is not so much an idea as it is a quality, identified both with what is real and perceptible on earth and with God. Indeed, the only context in which a somewhat abstract notion of holiness is expressed relates to God's holiness. God is said to swear by His holiness, just as He swears by His life, His faithfulness, and His power. Mortals speaking of God recognize that holiness is inextricable from Him; it is a constant, divine attribute.

The overall content of Lev. 19, with its diverse categories of laws and commandments, outlines what the Israelites must do to become a holy people. It includes many matters of religious concern, as we understand the term: proper worship; observance of *Shabbat;* and the avoidance of actions that are taboo, such as mixed planting and consumption of fruit from trees during the first three years after planting. What is less expected in ritual legislation is the emphasis on human relations: respect for parents, concern for the poor and the stranger, prompt payment of wages, justice in all dealings, and honest conduct of business. Even proper attitudes toward others are commanded.

In this latter respect, Lev. 19 accords with prophetic attitudes, indicating that the priesthood was highly receptive to the social message of the Israelite prophets. Holiness, an essentially cultic concept, could not be achieved through purity and proper worship alone; it had an important place in the realm of societal experience. Like the Decalogue and other major statements on the duties of humans toward God, this chapter exemplifies the heightened ethical concern characteristic of ancient Israel.

Holiness, as a quality, knows no boundaries of religion or culture. Very often, the reactions it generates are perceived by all, regardless of what they believe. Similarly, places and objects as well as persons considered to be holy by one group may be perceived in the same way by those of other groups. There is something generic about holiness, because all humans share many of the same hopes and fears and the need for health and well-being. A site regarded as holy by pagans might continue to be regarded as such by monotheists; indeed, some of the most important sacred sites in ancient Israel are known to have had a prior history of sanctity in Canaanite times. (The Bible ignores the pagan antecedents and explains their holiness solely in terms of Israelite history and belief.)

Despite many differences between Israelite monotheism and the other religions of the ancient Near East, the processes through which holiness was attributed to persons, places, objects, and special times did not differ fundamentally. Through ritual, prayer, and formal declaration, sanctification took effect. In biblical Hebrew, these processes are usually expressed by forms of the verb קדשׁ especially the *pi·el* stem *kiddesh,* "to devote, sanctify, declare holy."

The gulf between the sacred and the profane was not meant to be permanent. The command to achieve holiness, to become holy, envisions a time when life would be consecrated in its fullness and when all nations would worship God in holiness. What began as a process of separating the sacred from the profane was to end as the unification of human experience, the harmonizing of people with their universe and of people with God.

Study Questions

1. When we perform a mitzvah—an act defined as one of worship in the context of Jewish tradition—we often recite a blessing that praises God for having sanctified (i.e., made holy) Israel through the commandments. What do you think it means to say that ritual observance can make an individual holy? In his essay, Levine refers to the various powerful and supernatural aspects of holiness. Can those aspects be accessed through ritual observance?

2. Professor Levine refers frequently to Leviticus 19. Review the chapter and organize the commandments it contains into different categories, for example: commandments relating to worship vs. those relating to daily life, commandments that appear to mirror one of the Ten Commandments (as presented in Exodus 20 and Deuteronomy 5) vs. those that appear to have no obvious link to the Ten Commandments, commandments that are still considered binding on the faithful today vs. those that do not seem applicable, commandments that are presented in Scripture with the tagline "I am the Lord" or "I the Lord am your God," and those that are presented without any tag line at all. Which of your efforts at categorizing these commandments, presented in Scripture as the elaboration of the opening injunction to be holy even as God is holy, seems most cogent to you? Which has the most resonance with your own spiritual life?

3. What do you think it means to say that God is "holy?" What aspects would you describe this way? How do we go about emulating those traits?

4. What does it mean to be a "kingdom of priests; a holy nation"? In what ways are the Jewish people fulfilling this mission today? Where do we fall short?

5. In your own life, how does ritual assist you in your search for holiness? How does this compare with the way you feel about your ethical responsibilities?

6. Levine's closing statement is powerful, but potentially overwhelming: "The command to achieve holiness, to become holy, envisions

a time when life would be consecrated in its fullness and when all nations would worship God in holiness. What began as a process of separating the sacred from the profane was to end as the unification of human experience, the harmonizing of people with their universe and of people with God." What does this statement mean to you? What can you do to contribute to this goal?

Study materials by *Martin S. Cohen*

JUSTICE

Elliot N. Dorff

Summary

In his discussion of justice as "a divine imperative," Elliot Dorff begins by citing the famous verse from Deuteronomy: "Justice, justice
shall you pursue." (Deut. 16:20). The verse illustrates the centrality
of justice in the biblical worldview, as well as the elusive nature of
the goal. Human beings may "pursue" justice, but neither human beings nor their legal systems are perfect arbiters of what is just. That
is possible only for God. Nevertheless, "the Torah obligates us to
establish courts to dispense justice as well as we can." The Torah's
many laws about legal procedures and social justice present us with
a goal that is impossible fully to achieve.

Recognizing the limitations of its own system of justice, the Torah
calls on us to go beyond the letter of the law. We are to do "what is
right and good in the sight of the Lord." At times, Dorff insists, this
moral duty requires "reshaping the law, so that in each new age, it
can continue to be the best approximation of justice."

The Bible assumes justice as an essential characteristic of God's
divine plan, though God's justice may, at times, be beyond human
understanding. By striving to effect justice in human society, we respond to God's will and imitate God's example. Like a parent with
demanding expectations, the divine imperative for justice is an expression of God's love. Our "pursuit" of justice is thus an expression
of our mutually loving, covenantal bond with God.

"Justice, justice shall you pursue" (Deut. 16:20) rings through the ages
as one of the Torah's major principles. The biblical prophets rail against
the people for their failure to achieve justice and issue clarion calls to
reform that have shaped the conscience of Western civilization for thousands of years.

The demand for justice appears at the end of verses that call for the
location of courts in all regions where the people dwell, that prohibit

bribes, and that warn against prejudice in court judgments. By mixing procedural concerns (like the placement of courts in convenient places) with substantive issues (like the prohibitions against bribes and prejudice), the Torah indicates its awareness that the two are inextricably intertwined, that procedure affects substance and substance demands certain procedural rules.

No human being can always know whose cause is right; only God is privy to all the actions and intentions of every individual. Nevertheless, the Torah obligates us to establish courts to dispense justice as well as we can, and it specifies procedural rules to help us do that well.

For example, at least two witnesses are required to establish a fact in court to forestall collusion (Deut. 17:6, 19:15). To accentuate its prohibition of false testimony, the Torah includes it in the Decalogue (Exod. 20:13), announced amid thunder and lightning at Mount Sinai (see also Exod. 23:1–2; Deut. 5:17). Moreover, a 20 percent fine is levied against witnesses who knowingly lie in a civil case (Lev. 5:20–26), and full retribution is required of those who testify falsely in a criminal case (Deut. 19:15–21). A judge's acceptance of bribes is roundly condemned, "for bribes blind the clear-sighted and upset the pleas of those who are in the right" (Exod. 23:8; Deut. 16:19). Each person is to be judged for his or her own actions exclusively (Deut. 24:16). (This principle is assumed without question in modern Western societies; but in many societies in ancient, medieval, and even modern times, people have been punished for the crimes of their family members.) The Torah insists that neither rich nor poor may be favored: "You shall not be partial in judgment: Hear out low and high alike. Fear no man, for judgment is God's" (Deut. 1:17; see Exod. 23:2,6). The alien, too, is to be treated fairly: "Decide justly between any man and a fellow Israelite or stranger" (Deut. 1:16).

The sages of the Talmud and Middle Ages added many more procedural rules to ensure impartial treatment. For example, one litigant may not be required to stand while the other is sitting, both parties to the case must wear clothing of similar quality, judges must understand the languages spoken by the people before them, and witnesses may not be related to each other or to the litigants. Through rules such as these, procedural justice is strengthened and made a reality.

Substantive justice speaks not to the method by which a judicial decision is made but to the character of the results of court procedures and, more broadly, of society's policies. In Plato's *Republic,* substantive justice amounted to social harmony, which could be achieved only when everyone did what his or her station in society demanded. The biblical view of substantive justice is radically different, stressing the equality of all human beings and their right to equal protection of the law. Thus the Torah demands that aliens, widows, and orphans not be oppressed either in court (Deut. 24:17) or in society generally (Exod. 22:21), that they be cared for because they have no protectors (Deut. 14:29, 16:11,14). Indeed, the mistreatment of the defenseless and the failure to protect them in court was denounced by the prophets as a sign of the decadence of the Israelite society of their time (e. g., Isa. 1:17,23, 10:1–2; Jer. 5:28; Ezek. 22:7). The poor were also to be treated honorably and justly (e. g., Deut. 24:10–15; Jer. 22:16) and to be cared for (e. g., Deut. 15:7–11), and the failure to do that was also part of the prophets' complaints against their society (e. g., Ezek. 16:49, 22:29; Amos 2:6–7, 8:4–7).

It is not only the downtrodden, however, whose cause the Torah champions as part of its insistence on substantive justice. All members of society must be treated justly. The Torah, therefore, includes lengthy lists of civil and criminal legislation for society as a whole (e. g., Exod. 21–24; Deut. 20–25), and the sages developed this extensively, beginning with the Mishnah's order *N'zikin.* By formulating rules of procedural and substantive justice, then, the Torah and its Rabbinic heirs transform justice from a pious hope to a concrete reality.

Although the Torah and the later Jewish tradition went about as far as any society could go in translating its moral and spiritual commitments into legal terms, Rabbinic authorities recognized that justice never can be captured totally in law. As a medieval Jewish phrase puts it, one can be a "scoundrel within the limits of the law" or, interpreted somewhat differently, "a scoundrel with the sanction of the Torah" (*naval birshut ha-Torah*). Consequently, the Bible is not content to depict the substance of the law as both life-giving and the source of goodness (Deut. 30:15; Ps. 19:8–10, 119:33–40), in sharp contrast to the abominable acts of the other nations (e. g., Lev. 18, 20). In addition, it requires doing "what is right and good in the sight of the Lord" (Deut. 6:18). The sages of the Talmud take that and other Torah verses as the basis for declaring that people are obliged to act "beyond the letter of the law" (*lifnim mi-shurat ha-din*). Indeed, they state that the Second Temple was destroyed because people did not acknowledge or fulfill such moral duties (BT BM 30b). Thus, while the Torah and the Rabbinic tradition help make justice a reality by giving it concrete expression in law, Jewish law itself recognizes that justice sometimes demands more than the law does, that moral duties go beyond the letter of the law. Moreover, those moral duties sometimes require reshaping the law, so that in each new age it can continue to be the best approximation of justice.

The Torah thus goes beyond defining justice in its procedural and substantive aspects. It insists that justice is a divine imperative. In Western legal systems, justice is an instrumental good, a commodity important for social peace and welfare. That motivation to achieve justice appears in Jewish texts as well, but Jewish sources add another important motive. God demands justice and makes the existence of the world depend on it, because God Himself is just. In fact, He is the ultimate judge who "shows no favor and takes no bribe, but upholds the cause of the fatherless and the widow, and befriends the stranger, providing him with food and clothing" (Deut. 10:17–18). As Moses proclaims in his parting poem:

> For the name of the LORD I proclaim;
> Give glory to our God!
>
> The Rock!—His deeds are perfect,
> Yea, all His ways are just;
> A faithful God, never false,
> True and upright is He (Deut. 32:3–4).

It is precisely because God is just that Abraham can call Him to account for His plan to destroy Sodom, regardless of the innocent people in it. His words ring through the ages: "Far be it from You to do such a thing, to bring death upon the innocent as well as the guilty, so that innocent and guilty fare alike. Far be it from You! Shall not the Judge of all the earth deal justly?" (Gen. 18:25). God's justice is also at the heart of Job's complaint (Job 9:22), and God thunders in reply, "Would you impugn My justice? / Would you condemn Me that you may be right?"

(Job 40:8). God's justice may be inscrutable, but for the Bible it is undeniable, a core characteristic of the divine.

God enforces His demands of justice. He hears the cry of those who suffer injustice and responds by punishing the perpetrators. Thus the Torah admonishes: "You shall not abuse a needy and destitute laborer, whether a fellow countryman or a stranger in one of the communities of your land. You must pay him his wages on the same day, before the sun sets, for he is needy and urgently depends on it; else he will cry to the LORD against you and you will incur guilt" (Deut. 24:14–15).

It is not enough, however, to be just from fear of punishment or hope for reward. Justice is necessary for holiness. All Israelites are obligated to aspire to a life of holiness: "You shall be holy, for I, the LORD your God, am holy" (Lev. 19:2). In the verses that follow that divine demand, the Torah specifies what holiness requires: providing for the poor and the stranger; eschewing theft and fraud; rendering fair and impartial decisions in court; treating the blind, the deaf, and the stranger fairly; and ensuring honest weights and measures. All of these are components of a society that has both procedural and substantive justice.

One other aspect of the biblical concept of justice derives from its theological foundations. God loves the people Israel for reasons having nothing to do with their number or power, the usual marks of a nation's greatness; and He promises the patriarchs to continue that relationship through the generations (Deut. 7:6–11). The Israelites, in turn, are to love God and "always keep His charge, His laws, His rules, and His commandments" (Deut. 11:1). The commandments of the Torah are thus not legalistic formalisms, totally divorced from human compassion, moral values, and a spiritual relationship with God—as some Christian writings portray them. Quite the contrary, the practice of justice is an extension of love, as demonstrated by commandments calling on all Israelites to "love your neighbor as yourself" (Lev. 19:18), to "love the stranger" (repeated 36 times in the Torah), and to "love God" (Deut. 6:5, 11:1).

In fact, one of the primary expressions of God's love is precisely that He provides human beings with rules of justice. Parents who love their children take the time and energy to insist on proper behavior because they know it will ultimately be in the children's best interests; in the same way, "the LORD commanded us to observe all these laws, to revere the LORD our God, for our lasting good and for our survival, as is now the case" (Deut. 6:24). Again, "Bear in mind that the LORD your God disciplines you just as a man disciplines his son. Therefore keep the commandments of the LORD your God: walk in His ways and revere Him" (Deut. 8:5–6).

The Torah itself, and the sages even more, appreciated the fact that justice, to become a reality in people's lives, could not be left as a general value to which one mouths allegiance, but must be translated into concrete terms. By presenting specific cases, both the biblical and the Rabbinic traditions make the demands of justice clear and binding. It was not enough to require a person who finds a lost object to return it (as in Deut. 22:1–3). What if not one, but several, people claim it? How shall you determine the real owner? What happens if you cannot? What should you do, on the other hand, if nobody comes forward to claim the object? Must you keep it? If so, for how long? To what extent must you go to publicize that you have it? If it requires care (e. g., if it is an animal), must you spend your own money to provide that care? To what extent? May you use the object in the interim? Returning a lost object is a relatively simple demand of justice; but as these questions demonstrate, even a straightforward requirement easily becomes complicated—and the sages, in fact, devoted an entire chapter of the Talmud to this issue (BM 2). Without that discussion, the Torah's imperative to return a lost object would remain imprecise and unworkable; demanding (in some understandings) too much or (in others) too little to make this aspect of justice part of the ongoing practice within Jewish communal life.

Justice in the Bible, then, is made a concrete reality by spelling out at least most of its demands in specific laws. The Torah and the later Rabbinic tradition insist, though, that we do the right and the good even when the details of the law would permit us to do otherwise. The Jewish tradition thus recognizes both that the legal framework is indispensable in making justice a reality and that the demands of justice extend beyond the law, however extensively it is defined. The Torah and the later Jewish tradition also place the demand for justice in a theological context, thereby affirming the authority of the demand for justice and giving it a rationale: We are to be just because God requires it of us and because it is one important way in which we can imitate God's ways.

These legal, moral, and theological parameters of the biblical and Rabbinic concepts of justice make it an ongoing, living component of a life lived in loving covenant with God.

Study Questions

1. How does Dorff distinguish between "substantive" and "procedural" justice?

2. Dorff discusses Plato's ideal of justice as "social harmony, which could be achieved only when everyone did what his or her station in society demanded." How is the biblical view "radically different" from this definition? How has the biblical view shaped our contemporary societies?

3. Dorff's essay asserts that human justice is, at best, imperfect, and that God's justice, though ultimately beyond our understanding, is a given. How, then, are human beings able to reshape the law in each age, the better to approximate God's demand of justice? How is this task further complicated in Jewish Law, which is presumed to be a reflection of God's covenantal will?

4. What external standards of justice or morality legitimately inform the process of reshaping divine law? What safeguards keep those who are "reshaping" the law in pursuit of justice from abusing their power for the purposes of self-interest or personal agendas? How does "reshaping" the law differ from "going beyond the letter of the law?"

5. Dorff notes that the pursuit of justice is associated with an ongoing quest for holiness and functions as an expression of a loving relationship with God. How might the commandment to "pursue" justice be expressed in our daily personal and communal lives, apart from court proceedings and the legislative process?

6. By biblical standards, is our contemporary society a "just" society? In what ways does it meet those standards better than in previous eras? Where does it fall short? Is the Jewish community adequately fulfilling its obligation to pursue a more just society?

Study material by *Joseph H. Prouser*

MARRIAGE AND FAMILY

Gilbert S. Rosenthal

Summary

In this essay, Rabbi Rosenthal demonstrates the centrality of the family in biblical literature. As evidence, he points out that 38 of the 50 chapters of Genesis—over three-quarters of the first book of Scripture—deal with family issues and relationships.

Biblical law permitted polygamy, yet biblical narrative seems to prefer monogamy. Thus, Rosenthal explains, Cain (who introduced murder—indeed, fratricide—to human society) was a polygamist, while his virtuous brother Seth initiated a monogamous family line. Monogamy was affirmed as an ideal by the Prophets, who used marital fidelity and exclusivity as a "touching" metaphor for God's covenantal bond with Israel.

While emphasizing the companionship, societal stability, and personal pleasures deriving from marriage, the Bible also deals with stresses and adversity in family life. The pain of infertility is a common motif, and divorce is seen as a function of the reality that "not all marriages succeed."

Even in the typically patriarchal family of biblical Israel, women wielded considerable influence and, over time, increasing rights. "The biblical family was an extended one"—more resembling a clan tied to tribal structures. The importance of family ties is also demonstrated by the Bible's emphasis on family burial plots.

Through its emphasis and affirmation of marriage and family, the Hebrew Bible has had a formative influence on Western thought, Christianity, and Islam, in addition to its critical impact on the evolution of the Jewish People.

In Judaism, creation of the universe and the creation of the first human relationships are interwoven in the Book of Genesis: The cosmogony includes the birth of the archetypal family unit. Of the 50 chapters of Genesis, 38 deal with the gamut of family relationships and tensions, ranging from love and courtship to lust and seduction, from sibling rivalry to fratricide, from sterility to domestic controversies, from marital stress to tender affection. These themes occur frequently throughout the Bible.

Although there is no systematically developed family structure in the Bible, we can sketch a fairly ample portrait of the biblical family. Unquestionably, the Bible views marriage as the norm and a divine imperative. "It is not good for man to be alone," states the Torah (Gen. 2:18), indicating that the first goal of marriage is companionship. The second is procreation: "Be fertile and increase, fill the earth" (Gen. 1:28). Subsequent Jewish tradition considered procreation to be the first *mitzvah* incumbent on the human species and more specifically on the Jewish people (M Eduy. 1:13). Adam and Eve are the primordial ancestors of all races and families.

The societal structure comprised three components: the tribe (*sheivet*), the largest unit, which was subdivided into the clan (*mishpaḥah*), which was further divided into the household (*beit av*). The Bible records detailed genealogic lists in which we may detect this triple division of Israelite society.

Details on marriage ceremonies and rituals are sketchy and must be pieced together from scattered clues. No marriage ritual is specified, nor is a document of marriage or marriage contract mentioned. The earliest reference to a writ of marriage is postbiblical and the oldest *k'tubbah* (marriage contract) thus far discovered by archaeologists is from Elephantine, a Jewish military colony in Egypt from the 6th and 5th centuries B. C. E. Because the Bible does mention a writ of divorce on several occasions, it seems logical that some form of marriage contract also was in use as early as biblical times (Deut. 24:1–4).

Invariably, fathers arranged matches or picked their children's future mates. In the absence of a father, this responsibility fell to a brother. Sometimes the steward of the household was charged with this mission, as with Abraham's steward (Gen. 24). It appears that a bride's consent was required (Gen. 24:57 ff.; Gen. R. 60:12). If a man seduced or raped a virgin, he paid the father 50 shekels and had to marry her—subject to the father's approval (Exod. 22:15–16; Deut. 22:28).

A dowry (*mohar*) and a gift (*matan*) such as jewelry were presented to the bride's family at a betrothal feast in anticipation of the marriage. The wedding itself was accompanied by feasting, singing, and dancing for seven days. The bride donned special attire, including a veil; the groom wore a turban to signify his new status. The marriage was consummated on the first night, possibly in a special bridal chamber.

Biblical law allowed polygamy (more than one wife) and polygyny (more than one woman). Often, when a man took a second wife or concubine it was because of infertility. Thus Abraham took Sarah's handmaid Hagar as his concubine when Sarah seemed hopelessly sterile.

Jacob was tricked by his unscrupulous father-in-law Laban into marrying Leah. He ultimately was able to marry his beloved Rachel, Leah's sister, so that he was married to two sisters—a practice later outlawed by the Torah. Kings of Israel were permitted by the Bible to marry several wives and maintain harems. Indeed, David and Solomon followed this pattern. However, the system of polygyny was fraught with tensions and jealousy, as is clearly seen in the conflicts between Sarah and Hagar, Rachel and Leah, Hannah and Peninah, and others. The ideal marriage is a monogamous union, as evidenced by the Adam and Eve story: "Hence a man leaves his father and mother and clings to his wife, so that they may become one flesh" (Gen. 2:24).

It is noteworthy that Adam and Eve's fratricidal son, Cain, begets a polygamous tradition through his son Lamech, whereas a virtuous son, Seth, is the antecedent of a monogamous line. Similarly, the outstanding judges were monogamous, and the dissolute ones were not (Gen. 4:19,26; Judg. 8:30 ff., 14:1 ff., 16:1 ff.). The prophetic ideal, which draws a touching comparison between God's relationship to Israel and a husband's relationship with his wife, is equally monogamous. *Kohelet* urges a man to enjoy life "with the woman you love" (Eccles. 9:9), while the authors of Proverbs never tire of warning young men to beware the wiles of "foreign women" and courtesans, urging them to seek fulfillment in a virtuous spouse in whom they could confidently trust (Prov. 31:11).

The Bible prescribed permitted marriages in great detail while proscribing prohibited unions with equal meticulousness. In patriarchal days, marriage with a half-sister was not a taboo, as evidenced by Abraham and Sarah. But the abhorrence of incest was so strong that eventually such unions were outlawed and the list of proscribed marriages was substantially expanded. Homosexuality and bestiality were branded as "abominations," and adultery is listed as one of the cardinal sins in the Ten Commandments. The abhorrence of out-marriage is as ancient as Abraham, even as the preference for mating with one's own clan or tribe goes back to the patriarchs and matriarchs. The bane of Abraham's and Isaac's lives were sons Ishmael and Esau, who took wives from non-Hebrew nations, marrying Egyptian and Canaanite women. Samson caused his parents grief by dallying with Philistine women and courtesans. A Hebrew woman was expected to be a virtuous virgin whose husband had to be a Hebrew, most often from the same tribe or clan.

Not all marriages succeeded. Fidelity and chastity were expected and adultery was a capital offense. Divorce was allowed, except when a rapist married his victim (Deut. 22:29). Although no specific grounds are enumerated in the Bible, immorality was the most obvious cause for a husband to "send his wife a bill of divorcement" (Deut. 24:1–4). A woman suspected of infidelity (*sotah*) was compelled to submit to a nerve-wracking ordeal. If she failed the test, she was liable to be executed. The ideal marriage is beautifully described by the psalmist (128:3): "Your wife shall be like a fruitful vine within your house; / your sons, like olive saplings around your table."

The biblical family was remarkable because of certain unique elements, many of which are still discernible today, namely, love and sexual joy, companionship, respect, fidelity, and abiding trust.

The family was endogamous; the preference was for marriage to relatives. In patriarchal times, as noted, that implied half-brother or half-sister, cousins, nieces, nephews, aunts, uncles, and members of the clan. Although marriage with neighboring nations was forbidden in later biblical law, Ezra the scribe was forced to battle out-marriages in the 5th century B.C.E. (Ezra 9–10). If a husband died leaving no issue, his widow was obligated to marry her brother-in-law (levirate marriage, or *yibbum*) to perpetuate the deceased's name and, presumably, to keep the property from leaving the clan. If the brother-in-law refused to marry his sister-in-law, he was subjected to a humiliating ritual, *halitzah* (Deut. 25:5 ff.).

The biblical family was also patrilineal in that the family traced its lineage or tribal affiliation to the father rather than the mother. If the father came from the tribe of Levi, his offspring were Levites no matter the mother's tribe. If he was a *kohen* (priest), the children were likewise. Male offspring were referred to as sons of their father: Isaac son of Abraham, Moses son of Amram, Jeremiah son of Hilkiyah, Jonah son of Amittai. Only on rare occasions is the mother's name used. Matrilineal descent later becomes the standard in the Mishnah for cases when a valid marriage could not take place (M Kid. 3:12).

The family was also patriarchal; father was LORD and master. He headed the family, owned the property, conveyed divine blessings to family members, and made critical decisions. He could sell children in marriage, although his right to sell them into slavery was limited and he was barred from selling them into prostitution. He could annul his unmarried daughter's vows, and he received the money for damages inflicted on children. He demanded and expected obedience, respect, and honor. When a man married, he brought his bride to his father's household. Evidently, widows and divorcees often returned to their father's residence.

Women were subordinate to men. Often the names of wives are not even mentioned in the Bible, as is the case with Noah's and Job's wives and the Shunammite woman who aided Elisha. Still, they did enjoy certain rights. A husband was obliged by law to provide his wife with "food, clothing, and conjugal rights" (Exod. 21:10; Ket. 47b). Women ultimately received the right to inherit in the absence of male heirs (Num. 27:1–11). They also exerted considerable influence, as may be deduced from the sagas of the matriarchs, Sarah, Rebekah, Leah, and Rachel, as well as Miriam, Hannah, and Deborah. Primarily, they were to bear children, name and educate them, and run the household. Some women engaged in commerce and real estate transactions. A handful became public figures, prophetesses, and judges, such as Miriam, Deborah, and Hulda. At least two queens ran the government (Jezebel and Athaliah), and Queen Esther exerted considerable influence over the king of Persia. The queen mother (*g'virah*) was a force to contend with in dealing with the monarchy.

Children, especially sons, were the crown and blessing of parents and grandparents and the goal of marriage. Sad, indeed, was the infertile couple. The barren woman was scorned; sterility was viewed as divine punishment (Gen. 16:5; 1 Sam. 1:6). Abraham's words still resonate: "What can You give me seeing that I shall die childless?" (Gen. 15:2). And Hannah's plaintive, silent prayer at Shiloh—that if God would but grant her a son she would apprentice him to the priests—moves us still. Both father and mother were expected to nurture and educate young children who were viewed as blessings from God. Still, children (young or old) were expected to honor and revere father and mother, and the biblical authors shuddered as they contemplated the loss of respect by children for parents. To disobey, curse, or hit a parent was a capital offense; to mock the older generation was both a sin and an outrage (Exod. 20:12).

The biblical family was an extended one whose modern analogue is the Bedouin family or urban Arab clan in today's Middle East. Grandparents or great-grandparents served as the head of the family, which consisted of husbands, wives, concubines, children, servants, and slaves. Counting everyone in the household, the family swelled to a veritable tribe. Uncles and cousins, nephews and nieces were part of the extended family. In fact, they were often referred to as "brothers," as in the relationship of Abraham and his nephew Lot. Sibling rivalry existed from Cain and Abel down to the last kings of Israel and Judah—often with lethal results. Yet, the family members worked together in common fields, tilled their ancestral patrimony, plied a common trade or craft, and came to the rescue of kinsmen in times of danger or trouble. Family members who married lived close to one another, often sharing meals as is typical of extended rather than nuclear families. Even in death, the cherished wish was to be buried with the family, preferably in a family plot or sepulcher (Gen. 23, 50).

Remarkably, the biblical elements in the Jewish family prevailed throughout the ages, crystallizing into law in Rabbinic times, shaping the nature of Christian and Muslim families as well. At the same time, these familial patterns fortified Jews and Judaism in dozens of lands, enabling them to survive stresses and storms, crises and calamities into the 21st century.

Study Questions

1. Rosenthal states, "The biblical family was remarkable because of certain unique elements, many of which are still discernible

today, namely love and sexual joy, companionship, respect, fidelity, and abiding trust." Does the essay provide good supporting evidence for this? Which relationships in the Bible live up to these standards? Which fall short? How well do the legal sections of the Torah, which support Rosenthal's vision, match up with the actual depictions of the biblical narratives?

2. Rosenthal notes the dominant role of family life in biblical narrative, while the Torah gives only "sketchy" details regarding the rituals of marriage and divorce. What principles of family life does Rosenthal infer from biblical narrative? What others might we add?

3. To the few details of biblical marriage law, the Rabbis added copious religious regulations. What contributions do you feel that contemporary Jews should make to the evolving understanding of family?

4. What does Scripture have to say about in-marriage and intermarriage—both in law and in narrative? How do biblical law and narrative continue to influence our understanding of these issues for Jews today?

5. How do biblical law and narrative view the physical intimacy and "tender affection" associated with marriage?

6. According to Rosenthal, "the bane of Abraham's and Isaac's lives were sons Ishmael and Esau, who took wives from non-Hebrew nations." Is this a fair depiction of the biblical text and of these fathers' relationships with their sons? Which biblical characters provide admirable parental role models for today's families? For husbands and wives?

Study materials by Joseph H. Prouser

WOMEN

Judith Hauptman

Summary

Judith Hauptman's essay argues that in the Bible women hold an inferior legal and social position relative to men. Rarely leaders, warriors, or prophets, women often go nameless and are not counted in the Israelite census. Using marriage, childbearing, and divorce law to support her claim, Hauptman asserts that in the Bible women participate in covenant only peripherally, as subordinates to men, who are full covenantal partners. She notes a few limited areas of legal equality, such as ritual vows, as well as several forceful female biblical personalities, but concludes that biblical women were subjugated to men. Hauptman asks how these unfair laws can be reconciled with the Torah's conception of social justice.

Using examples from the Talmud, Hauptman suggests that the Rabbinic sages gradually enacted laws to improve the position of women. Hauptman argues that it is not the Torah's treatment of women but evolving standards of talmudic law that indicate Judaism's progressive approach to the status of women. She advocates for continued change to ensure women's equality.

A candid look at biblical society, religion, and law reveals a system that favors men over women. Women, as a rule, did not play key political roles. They were not rulers, warriors, or prophets. Named women appear in the biblical narrative far less frequently than named men. The principal religious and social institutions placed women under the control of men. The Bible, in fact, seems to define society as being composed of men only. On at least three occasions (Exod. 30; Num. 1, 26) a census of men was taken. The women and the children were never counted.

This blatant gender imbalance jars contemporary sensibilities. Many wonder how the same treatise that campaigns so forcefully and persuasively for social justice can, at the same time, sanction discrimination against women.

167

To come to terms with biblical sexism, one must first grasp the broad contours of the biblical narrative and only then focus on the treatment of women. A major theme of the Torah is the covenantal bond that exists between the Israelites and their God. The first to enter into such an arrangement was Abraham. The terms of his covenant were simple: If he continued to believe in God, as he had done until that point, then God would bless him with progeny as numerous as the stars in the sky, and they, after a stay in Egypt, would come back to inherit the land of Israel (Gen. 15).

This covenant was renegotiated at Sinai with the masses of Israelites and others who left Egypt. God stipulated that if they would keep His commandments and pledge allegiance to Him alone, then He would not only lead them to the land of Israel but also provide them with the things that human beings, regardless of gender, want most—health, prosperity, children, and security.

For this new covenant, the ritual and social demands were substantial. To begin with, as set down in the Decalogue, one had to respect the integrity of another's life and property. Beyond that there was a vast array of ritual requirements, many of which related to holy times and places. In addition, as spelled out in *parashat Mishpatim* (Exod. 21–24) and elsewhere, Israelites were obligated by an extraordinary set of social justice requirements, involving issues that include poverty law, justice in the courtroom, bailments, torts, and decent treatment of slaves.

In considering the treatment of women, the reasonable question to ask now is: Since the terms of the covenant at Sinai are essentially gender neutral, does it follow that women were equal partners with men? The answer is no. Although women were present at Sinai, they do not seem to have been part of the covenantal process in the same way that men were. The basis for this observation is that the Torah, in many passages, addresses itself to men only. For example, the tenth commandment states that a man is not to covet his neighbor's wife, slave, animals, or anything else his neighbor owns.

Although women did not enter into the covenant directly, they did enter indirectly. The Torah, it seems, viewed each man as the head of a household responsible for the behavior of all individuals under his aegis, usually understood to be his wife (or wives), slaves, and children. It is as if each family stood at Sinai in a line, with the head of the household in front, and all members of his family standing behind him in single file. It thus became his responsibility to demand of them the same behavior that was being demanded of him.

This means that, in general terms, the covenant with God bound women in the same way that it bound men: Women were to pursue justice and champion the cause of the underdog, to observe *Shabbat,* the holidays, and the dietary laws—just like men. But, because the Bible was speaking to a society that viewed women as less than men, key biblical institutions regulating gender relationships and communal ritual performance treat women not as equal to men but as subordinate, even though significant. Surveying some of these rules will illustrate this point.

According to the Bible, marriage is the acquisition of a woman by a man. Fathers, as a rule, arranged marriages for their daughters at about the time that they reached puberty. A husband was required to provide his wife with the basic necessities of life, including conjugal relations (Exod. 21:10).

The Bible places a premium on female virginity. When a virgin was seduced, the offender was required to marry her. If her father refused to give her in marriage, however, the offender still had to pay him the bride-price of virgins (Exod. 22:15–16). The bridal payment is required in this instance because the marital value of a young woman plummets when she loses her virginity. This suggests that in the biblical period men viewed women for sexual, marital purposes as objects.

It was incumbent on a wife to bear children for her husband. Sometimes this male prerogative determined the course of a woman's life. If a man died childless, his widow was not free to remarry but was considered to be already betrothed to his brother (Deut. 25:5–10). The purpose of her marriage to her levir (husband's brother), was to produce an heir, presumably a male, who would continue the name and line of his father's deceased brother and inherit his property. In this situation, a woman glided from one marriage to the next, suffering no period of financial distress, but having no choice of life options or partners. The levir could choose to release his sister-in-law from the marital bond by undergoing a ceremony called *ḥalitzah,* but she could not refuse to live with him.

Fidelity to one's husband is a basic marriage rule for women. The seventh commandment understands adultery as sexual relations between a man and someone else's wife, not as sexual relations between a man and any woman other than his wife. Married women, but not married men, are limited to a single sexual partner. As a consequence of this rule, if a husband merely suspects his wife of behaving in a promiscuous manner, even though he has no evidence, he may bring her to the tabernacle (or later, the Temple) and subject her to the water ordeal, described by the Torah in gruesome detail (Num. 5:11 ff.).

As for divorce, it is the husband who sends the wife out of his house, with a writ of severance, if he finds her unseemly in some way (Deut. 24:1). Nowhere is provision made for a woman who finds her husband unacceptable or wishes to resist a divorce. Women, it seems, had no say in this matter.

Can this array of sexist rules be reconciled with the Torah's high-minded concept of social justice and its expressed concern for the vulnerable members of society? Yes, but only in the biblical period and not later. That is, it seems reasonable to say that women at that early time did not expect equality but protection. Just as children did not think that they should have a voice in family decision making or control over family financial assets, neither did married women. They apparently found marriage satisfactory if it supplied them with their basic needs, which it did.

Difficulties arise in the postbiblical period and later, when the Jewish understanding of marriage and social philosophy changed, and women came to be viewed as deserving of more rights and higher status. To ease the tension between the more enlightened social outlook and the Torah's sexist rules, the Rabbinic corpus, produced about 1,500 years after the Torah, made significant changes in laws affecting women. Although equity of women and men as a principle of law is not to be found in Rabbinic literature, and until the 20th century is not a feature of any of the major religious or even civil law codes, still, amelioration of women's status and an increase in their rights marks much of Rabbinic marital legislation.

According to the Talmud, marriage is not a purchase of a woman by a man but a living arrangement in which each has rights and responsibilities to the other, although he is dominant and she subordinate. The *k'tubbah,* or marriage document, drawn up by the groom and presented to the bride, was instituted for the protection of women: It stipulates a lump sum payment to the wife from the husband's estate in the event that he predeceases or divorces her. Although not written into the *k'tubbah* itself, a set of additional stipulations accompanies it, such as provisions for medical care, ransom money, and maintenance and domicile for the widow. The *k'tubbah* has often been called one of the Talmud's most socially progressive pieces of legislation. In reciprocal manner, the Talmud lists a wife's obligations to her husband, most of which lay in the domestic sphere.

Significant changes also took place in the area of divorce. The Talmud presents a wide variety of situations in which distress suffered by the wife would lead to divorce. Not that she may write her husband a *get,* a bill of divorce, but she would have recourse to the rabbinical courts that could petition her husband to issue a divorce. Even more important, the particulars of the *get*—its language, the material on which it is written, the ink with which it is written, the manner in which it is delivered—are all standardized so that no one would later be able to challenge the validity of the divorce proceedings and, therefore, a woman's second marriage. Because it is only she and not he who needs a document of divorce to remarry, these rules, although still patriarchal in nature, are designed with her welfare in mind.

According to the Torah, in economic matters women totally depended on men. Real estate, the most valued asset, was usually owned by men. Property in the land of Israel was to be distributed to men only (Num. 26:53, 27:6–11). Upon death, a man's parcel of land was to pass to his kin—sons, brothers, uncles, or other relatives on his father's side. In the event that he left no sons but only daughters, however, the daughters superseded all other relatives and inherited their father's land, sharing it among themselves. In such cases, women were required to remarry within the tribe so as not to reduce its land holdings. In the Rabbinic period, although women could not inherit per se, the institution of gifts in contemplation of death and generous marriage dowries moved in the direction of making it possible for fathers to pass on their accumulated wealth to their daughters.

In ritual areas men predominated. The males of the priestly class served as religious functionaries in the Temple, and lay Israelite men were bidden to make a pilgrimage to the Temple three times a year. Women, however, did take part in organized religious life. Women could bring voluntary offerings—and were even required to bring a purification offering after each birth (Lev. 12:6)—although their ability to enter the holy precincts of the Temple was impaired by their regular periods of ritual impurity owing to menstrual flow (Lev. 15:19–30). As for ritual restrictions in the home, such as ceasing to work on *Shabbat,* fasting on *Yom Kippur,* and avoiding leaven on *Pesah,* women were bound by these rules just like men.

The laws of vows (Num. 30:2–17) provide an important—but limited—exception to the general rule of women's subordinate status. It was standard behavior in the biblical period for people to take a vow to influence or implore God to grant a request. In return for engaging in some form of self-denial, the vowing individual hoped to gain healing for a sick family member or the safe return from war of a soldier husband or son. The main point of this section of Torah is to distinguish between men's and women's vows. If a man takes a vow, no matter what transpires, he must keep his word; if a woman takes a vow, her intentions may be subverted by either father or husband. There are two categories of women, however, whose vows may not be canceled by anyone at all—widows and divorcees (v. 10). Thus women as women are viewed as competent to maintain absolute control over their own affairs, religious and financial. But when under the control of a father or husband, their vows need approval.

The one area in a woman's life in which she achieved parity with men was her status as a parent. In the eyes of the Bible, the older generation, both males and females, had absolute authority over the younger. A child was to honor and fear both father and mother; a son or daughter who cursed or struck either parent was to be put to death (Exod. 21:15, 17). Both mother and father had to declare a son rebellious for him to be punished (Deut. 21:18–21). Children were obligated to fulfill the same rites of mourning for a deceased mother as for a deceased father (Lev. 21:2).

Did social realities in biblical times conform to the legal prescriptions? The narrative portions of the Bible suggest that women's position in society, although not equal to that of men, was not as subordinate and marginal as one might have expected, given the patriarchal configuration of society. The matriarchs, as well as other female characters in the Bible, exhibited independence of thought and action, and critically influenced the course of history, although differently from men. To mention a few examples: Rebekah behaved more like a patriarch than did her passive husband, Isaac—securing the patriarch's blessing for her favorite son, Jacob, to whom God wanted it to go, and thwarting Isaac's plan to bestow it on his favorite, Esau (Gen. 27). Tamar (Gen. 38) and Ruth, in different ways, each enticed a man to engage in marital or quasi-marital sexual relations to maintain the family's line. In reward for and acknowledgment of the merit of their actions, each of them became an ancestress of King David. These heroines, and scores of others who appear throughout the Bible, show that women, despite sociolegal limitations, could act resolutely to shape the future according to their own vision.

This limited survey indicates that, at least in its legislative sections, women are regarded by the Torah as dependent, not independent, beings. Such a view of women meshed well with that of most ancient Near Eastern societies, which also placed women under the control of men. The Bible thus prescribes a pattern of gender relationships that was acceptable for that era, even though by contemporary standards it would be found wanting.

The test of the Jewish tradition, however, is not how the Torah treated women at one point in time but how the Jewish tradition treated women with the passing of time, how it responded to evolving ethical insights. The references made earlier to Rabbinic changes in marital and inheritance law clearly show that not only does the Torah stake out a claim to moral behavior in its own day but, even more important, it intends for its abstract ethical teachings, which transcend time and place, to be upheld in every generation. This cleaving to general principles will guarantee that the specific rules do not, in the course of time, devolve from ethical to unethical.

The response to those who critique the sexism of the Jewish tradition is that the Torah's laws were prescribed for its own day and were not intended to remain as they were, but to be changed as necessary. The primary thrust of the Talmud and related Rabbinic writings is not, as many think, to codify the law, but to adjust the Torah's rules to changing circumstances and philosophical outlook. It follows that today, too, with equality for women and men a widely accepted social truth, more changes must be made to ensure full equality.

Study Questions

1. What examples from biblical law does Hauptman use to prove her assertion that women were subordinate to men in the biblical period? Do these laws seem right or fair? What historical or ethical principles would you use when evaluating these biblical attitudes?

2. How does Hauptman deal with the contradiction between the Torah's commitment to fairness and justice and its treatment of women? Does her argument resolve the contradiction?

3. How can Jews balance their reverence of the Bible with the modern ethic of egalitarianism? In what way is Hauptman's view of the evolution of Jewish law helpful in reconciling these two beliefs?

4. For you personally, in what ways does the treatment of women in the Torah increase or decrease the credibility or relevance of the Bible? Do you feel Jewish law has "evolved" enough on this issue? If not, which issues are still in need of attention?

5. Hauptman uses examples such as Rebekah and Tamar to suggest that, in spite of biblical law, individual women found ways to participate in shaping the future. In your opinion, why are these exceptions possible? Do they change your view of biblical women? Given the patriarchal nature of Israelite society, why do you think these stories were preserved in the literature, if they seem to undermine the Bible's value system?

Study materials by *Shoshana Jedwab*

EDUCATION

Hanan A. Alexander

Summary

Hanan Alexander reads between the lines of the biblical text and finds in it a coherent theory of education. He claims that a role for education arises because God wishes God's creation to be good, and people must serve as partners in this task, a task in which they must cooperate with each other as well. But once the notion of a community aimed at creating a good life gets started, there must be a conception of that good life (this is provided by God through revelation) and a means to transmit it to successive generations—hence the need for education. The biblical conception of education depends upon action, not simply study. Action, however, requires the intelligence to understand what is being transmitted, and re-enactment of good behavior helps to deepen the understanding. While the primary responsibility for educating the young falls upon parents (think of the passages in the Torah about instructing children about the Exodus), in other places in the Bible priests, prophets, and scribes also play a role in the education of both young and old.

The Bible views education spiritually, as embedded in a vision of the good life committed to a divine moral purpose. It is through this understanding of transcendent purpose that values are transmitted from generation to generation.

In the biblical narrative, God needs partners to bring good into the world, so He creates people in His image, with creative intelligence and the freedom of will to behave as they choose (Gen. 1:26–31; 2–3). People also need human partners with whom to share ethical insights and to check moral action, so man is given a wife as "a fitting helper for him" (2:18). Rashi understands the Hebrew *eizer k'negdo* as meaning "helper over against him," suggesting that she will help him if he is worthy and oppose him if he is not. Because man can serve in a similar capacity as a helper and friendly critic for his wife, the possibility of community—a collective based on mutual deliberation and decision making—is born.

As the Genesis narrative develops, it becomes clear that people will naturally be divided over issues of language, land, and lineage (4:1–16; 5; 6; 11:1–9). To communicate God's vision of the good, a community needs to be bound by a common moral creed. So God chooses Abraham and Sarah and their descendants and teaches them what is right and good (12:1–6).

The Jewish tradition calls this teaching *"torah,"* its specific legal path is called *"halakhah,"* and the specific steps along that path *"mitzvot."* The community that bears witness to God's message through *halakhah* and *mitzvot* is known as the *"edah."* What unites this community above all else is the enactment of God's moral vision by its members. Continuity depends on remaining committed to the vision of goodness on which the community is founded.

What is the substance of this vision, and by whom, how, and where is it communicated?

> When, in time to come, your children ask you, "What mean the decrees, laws, and rules that the LORD our God has enjoined upon you [in other versions: us]?" you shall say to your children, "We were slaves to Pharaoh in Egypt and the LORD freed us from Egypt with a mighty hand. The LORD wrought before our eyes marvelous and destructive signs and portents in Egypt, against Pharaoh and all his household; and us He freed from there, that He might take us and give us the land that He had promised on oath to our fathers. The LORD commanded us to observe all these laws, to reverence to the LORD our God, for our lasting good and for our survival, as is now the case. It will be therefore to our merit before the LORD our God to observe faithfully this whole Instruction, as He commanded us" (Deut. 6:20–25).

The way of life enjoined by God is not for slaves, but for people who are free to serve the LORD, who can choose the path they wish to follow. Freedom is a precondition of education, of initiation into a community committed to the good.

The child's question and the parent's response exemplify an approach to pedagogy delineated a few verses earlier in the *Sh'ma:* "Hear [*sh'ma*], O Israel! The LORD is our God, the LORD alone" (Deut. 6:4). The word *sh'ma* means "to hear, or heed, or consider"; to listen carefully so that the understanding that accompanies action can result. Intelligence—the capacity to understand—is a second prerequisite for education. How is this understanding achieved? "Impress them [*v'shinnantam*] upon your children. Recite them when you stay at home and when you are away, when you lie down and when you get up" (Deut. 6:7). The Hebrew *v'shinnantam* means "impress upon," by repetition or rote if necessary; recite these words even if at first they are not understood; that is, engage in training. Understanding can grow from repetition, as is evidenced if after all of this recounting of exhortations, laws, and norms, the child's curiosity is aroused—and he or she begins to inquire. Once the question is asked, the story can be retold, the commandments re-emphasized, the vision of the good rearticulated and re-enacted. The capacity for understanding is not only a prerequisite for education but part of the desired outcome as well.

One cannot achieve an understanding of goodness, however, through talking and thinking alone. Intelligent action is required. Repetition and explanation lead to more questions, which lead, in turn, to deeper understanding and more meaningful action. The classic response of the Israelites to receiving God's commandments, *na·aseh v'nishma*—we will faithfully do (Exod. 24:7), is often misunderstood as expressing a preference for action over understanding or sometimes even as rejecting the importance of understanding altogether. The literal translation is "we will do and we will hear" (in the sense of comprehending), which implies not that action is sufficient without understanding but that acting out God's will and understanding it go hand in hand. In fact, the order of the terms—action before hearing—suggests that religious observance leads to an understanding of divine instruction.

And what is to be repeated to the children? "You must love the LORD your God with all your heart and with all your soul and with all your might" (Deut. 6:5). This is stated as a command; but can love be forced on a person? Must it not be given freely, as a result of mutual understanding? Maimonides teaches that the very idea of commandment presupposes free agency (MT Repentance). Why have commandments in the first place, he asks, if people are not free to obey? "Freedom," he explains, does not refer to the license to follow one's most immediate desires, because that is a form of enslavement to caprice. Freedom requires choices made on the basis of understanding. Love of God as expressed in the observance of the *mitzvot* is evidence that a person has acquired an understanding of their meaning which is the key to genuine freedom. Not only are freedom and love of God preconditions of observance, like understanding the meaning of religious practice, but also their enhancement is a desired outcome.

This is why the Midrash (Mekh. Bo 18; JT Pes. 10:4) sees the questioner in Deut. 6:20–25 as wise; including himself among those who have been commanded and referring to the LORD God as his own. By stating the question in this way, the wise son demonstrates that he has not only participated in the rote repetition of the *Sh'ma* and the *mitzvot* but has also evidenced genuine understanding of their import and chosen to accept them of his own free will. He has not only been trained; he has been educated (the *Pesah Haggadah* also employs such a question and answer technique).

But why should such a person inquire about the meaning of these "decrees, laws, and rules"? He is already presumed to have had an education. Should he not, then, have knowledge of the answers? This is the significance of the response of the Midrash to the wise son. "Even he can be instructed in the laws of Passover." For example, he can be engaged in deciphering the passage concerning the ruling that there is to be no *afikoman*—a Greek term the meaning of which is obscure in the Mishnah—after the *pesah*. Spiritual education is not a means to achieve a predetermined end. It leads to ever-increasing meaning and fulfillment in pursuit of the good. There are always new interpretations to be mined.

What have we learned so far about the Bible's theory of education? When parents live in a community dedicated to a life of Torah, children will naturally inquire about that life. In response, they can be educated—initiated into the community—by being told the story of their people's liberation from bondage, by being trained in the practices enjoined on their ancestors and on succeeding generations, and by being taught to understand the meaning of those practices. Thus observance leads to the enhancement of their intelligence, freedom, and love of God. It constitutes the content, the method, and the purpose of instruction.

This path, however, is not always smooth. Errors are expected (Deut. 29:9–30:20). This is among the most radical and profound aspects of the Bible's educational theory. Because we are free agents, we are capable of making mistakes and straying from the right path. Here is the meaning of the biblical concept of *het* or "sin": to miss the mark, lose the way, abandon the good life. But because we are moral agents we can learn from our mistakes and return to the right path. The ability to return is a consequence of freedom; the capacity to learn is a consequence of intelligence. Here is the meaning of the concept of *t'shuvah,* or "returning to God's path."

But how are we to decide which course to choose and whether we have gone astray? This returns us to the concept of Torah, of God's moral teaching, the very purpose of which is to teach us which path is the right one. "See, I set before you this day life and prosperity [i. e., goodness], death and adversity [i. e., evil]. ... Choose life—if you and your offspring would live—by loving the LORD your God, heeding His commands, and holding fast to Him. For thereby you shall have life and shall long endure" (Deut. 30:15–20). Engagement with Torah does not produce Jewish identity or Jewish continuity, and the acquisition of knowledge on its own does not generate love of God or commitment to a life of Torah. On the contrary, identity and continuity are prerequisites for this very engagement to take place, and commitment to a vision of the good is required to determine what knowledge is worth acquiring. Studying, practicing, and celebrating Torah for its own sake is what leads to spiritual renewal, to a strengthened commitment to God's vision of the good life.

From this account, it is clear that parents have primary responsibility for the education of their children. Although vocational training is also valued (Prov. 24:27–34, 27:23–27) the most significant educational task is induction into a religious community with a particular moral point of view. This is accomplished through story, ritual, and liturgy; at home, in the place of worship, and in the life of the community as a whole. Although the Bible emphasizes the role of the father, we know that the mother also played a significant part in instructing the young. "My son, heed the discipline of your father, and do not forsake the instruction of your mother" (Prov. 1:8, see also 6:20, 23:22). Because of this responsibility, the child is enjoined to respect both parents: "Honor your father and your mother" (Exod. 20:12; Deut. 5:16; and also Prov. 15:20, 20:20). This is the earliest and most basic form of Jewish education.

In time, the role of the parents was supplemented by elders, priests, prophets, scribes, and teachers. The tribal elders were probably the earliest to supplement the parent's role, as in the case of a rebellious son: "If a man has a disloyal and defiant son, who does not heed his father or mother and does not obey them even after they discipline him, his father and mother shall take hold of him and bring him out to the elders of the town at the public place of his community" (Deut. 21:18–19, see also Exod. 21:17). The role of the elders as teachers of the law was a natural outgrowth of their role as judges in the city gates.

The priests of the *bamot* (altars; before the unification of the cult) and of Jerusalem also supplemented parental instruction. Already, the Deuteronomist enjoins families to come together to hear public recitations of the Torah on the *Sukkot* festival (Deut. 31:12) and other public feasts, such as covenant renewal ceremonies (Exod. 24:7). In some instances, fathers even served as or were identified with priests (Judg. 17:10; Prov. 6:20); and as in other ancient Near Eastern cultures, perhaps the earliest formal schools developed alongside the altars in such places as Shilo. It may be in these schools that the tradition emerged for children to begin the study of Torah with *Va-yikra* (Leviticus), which contains the Priestly Code. It is probably here too that psalms, which were an important part of the liturgies at these sites, became significant texts for instructing the young.

> Give ear, my people, to my teaching,
> turn your ear to what I say.
> I will expound a theme,
> hold forth on lessons of the past,
> things we have heard and known,
> that our fathers have told us.
> We will not withhold them from their children,
> telling the coming generation

the praises of the LORD
and His might, and the
wonders He performed
(Ps. 78:1–4; see also Pss. 15, 19, 119).

Prophets also played a role in educating the young. In prophetic circles, we find the first instances of masters and disciples that became so prominent among the rabbis (2 Kings 3:11). There are also allusions to "schools of the prophets" (1 Sam. 10:5), and it may be in these schools that the concept of *musar*, or moral instruction as independent from *mitzvot*, began to emerge as a key educational concept (Jer. 2:30, 7:28, 17:23, 32:33).

In the 5th century B.C.E., Ezra and Nehemiah placed the study and practice of Torah at the center of the curriculum by institutionalizing its public reading on Mondays, Thursdays, and *Shabbat* afternoons. They prepared scribes to preserve the text, and *meivinim min ha-l'vi·im* (learned Levites) to interpret its meaning. It was out of this circle of the learned scribes that the Pharisaic rabbis emerged as teachers of Torah par excellence. The Torah, joined by other books of the canon, became their textbooks.

Wisdom texts, for example, began to emerge as formal pedagogic tools under the influence of Hellenism. Many of them, such as Proverbs, Job, and Ecclesiastes, were composed as textbooks by and for wisdom teachers. Especially among the upper classes, they taught that intellectual and ethical enlightenment would awaken a fear of God and a desire to fulfill His commandments (Prov. 9:10; Job 28:28). Some of these texts are known to have been written on tablets, so their use in pedagogy corresponds to the emergence of literacy as a goal of instruction, along with the oral recitation of laws and narratives that preceded it and that continued well into the 3rd century C.E.

In the 1st century C.E., the high priest Yehoshua ben Gamla reformed and reorganized the educational system, appointing *m'lamdei tinokot* (teachers of children) in every province and town (BT BB 21a). The classical curriculum emerged: "At five years one is fit for scripture, at ten for Mishnah, at thirteen for *mitzvot*, at fifteen for Talmud" (M Avot 5:21).

In sum, the biblical conception of education is not instrumental, at least not in the strong sense in which education is used to achieve goals extrinsic to the practices, values, and beliefs being promoted. Rather, it is spiritual, in that it offers God's vision of the good life. Although education is essential to Jewish knowledge, identity, and continuity, when we view these as the ultimate ends, we lose sight of the very ideals to which such an education must be devoted if it is to renew our collective and individual commitment to them.

Study Questions

1. Alexander says that the Bible holds that freedom is a precondition for education to take place. Do you believe this is true? You may want to consider historical cases, such as Jewish education in the Soviet Union, or attempts to educate slaves in American history.

2. The author says that observance "constitutes the content, the method, and the purpose of instruction." Is a true understanding of the Bible impossible for those who were neither raised to practice nor those who currently practice? What does your own experience tell you about the role of observance in education?

3. If the Bible wants Jews both to act and to understand, what sort of Jews does the Bible hope to produce from this process?

4. Consider the passages Alexander cites as evidence for the theory he describes (particularly Deut. 6:20–25). Do the sources support his conclusions, or are other interpretations possible?

5. Alexander's essay stresses the role of education in the transmission of values and a way of life. Should this be the primary function of education? What about education as a method for creating new forms of understanding, practice, or ways of living? Is there support in the Bible for such a creative concept of education?

Study materials by Jacob Pinnolis

ECOLOGY

David M. Gordis

Summary

The word "ecology" comes from Greek and refers primarily to the relationship between organisms and their environment in the discipline of biology. Sociologists use the concept to describe the distribution of a population in relation to its material and social conditions, their causes and effects (*Oxford Universal Dictionary*).

In this beautifully written essay, David Gordis offers a very profound and more expansive view of the term "ecology." He examines narrative, legal, and poetic sections of the text, developing themes and principles through careful and original readings. Beyond the values he articulates, it is worthwhile to pay close attention to his interpretive method. As you read, can you begin to formulate your own statement of the biblical view of ecology?

Through narrative, poetry, law, and prayer, the Bible conditions its readers to feel reverence for nature, enjoins restraint in the exploitation of natural resources for human needs, elicits awe in response to the diversity and complexity of creation, and articulates the principle of human responsibility for faithful trusteeship over the natural world.

Beginning with the Creation narrative in Genesis, every component of the Hebrew Bible is a strand in the fabric that defines the biblical approach to issues of ecology. Human beings are commanded: "Be fertile and increase, fill the earth and master it; and rule the fish of the sea, the birds of the sky, and all the living things that creep on the earth" (Gen. 1:28). Although the creation of human beings is the high point of the creative process as depicted in Genesis, it is, however, only part of the process, which includes all the natural world. Flora and fauna, birds and fishes, forests and grasses are all parts of God's design. God reflects on creation at every successive stage and pronounces it "good." The sequence developed in the biblical narrative may lead up to the creation of human beings, but it does not suggest that what precedes their creation is peripheral or insignificant.

Later reflections on the Creation narrative in halakhic and midrashic literature are also relevant. The commandment to be fertile and master the earth is understood as directed primarily to the obligation to procreate, not to dominate or to exploit. Although the Midrash suggests that God was conflicted about creating human beings who would be capable of both good and evil, corollary readings imply that it is their potential moral capacity that places them at the pinnacle of creation. Yet the natural world is good in and of itself, implying that everything created by God before the emergence of humans represents a pure rather than an instrumental good. It follows quite naturally that human beings should appreciate this purity, respecting and using the natural world as the handiwork of God, but not exploiting it.

In this context, the story of Noah is most relevant to issues of ecology. In the face of the widespread destruction that God brings about because of human depravity, cruelty, and sinfulness, Noah is commanded to preserve the blameless animals two by two, alerting the reader to the reality of animals as sensing and feeling creatures, part of the life process, entering into relationships, procreating, and generating life themselves.

> And of all that lives, of all flesh, you shall take two of each into the ark to keep alive with you; they shall be male and female. From birds of every kind, cattle of every kind, every kind of creeping thing on earth, two of each shall come to you to stay alive (Gen. 6:19–20).

Every species is to be represented. Noah's obligation is to save endangered species and to promote life. No suggestion is put forward that the species are to be rescued for the benefit of Noah and his descendants. Quite the contrary: They are to be kept alive "with you" and not "for you." It is taken as self-evident that their existence enhances the world, that they are blameless and undeserving of the destruction facing humankind, and that they should be rescued in all their variety and diversity. A precious product of the divine creative process, they merit protection and nurture.

Legal passages in the Bible contribute substantially to the themes of human trusteeship for the natural world and restraint in the use of natural resources. Scholars have debated the sources and original functions of the laws of *kashrut*. Whatever their origin and other functions, the dietary laws, imposing limits on what may be eaten, establish the principle of restraint. In so doing, they continually remind us that to take this life for food represents a compromise, for it destroys a living, feeling creature. Meticulous regulation of the process of slaughtering animals for food, with a focus on limiting the suffering of the animal as much as possible, was a natural Rabbinic expansion of biblical principles. The case has been argued that a further legal embodiment of biblical principles would prohibit the killing of animals for human needs entirely and would suggest vegetarianism as a high form of *kashrut*. Be that as it may, the general principle of sensitivity to taking an animal's life is clear.

The biblically based and rabbinically articulated laws of *sh'hitah* express the principle of *tza·ar ba·alei hayyim,* "sensitivity to the pain of living creatures." This general principle is formulated in Rabbinic Judaism, but its foundations in biblical law are apparent. It underlies the inclusion of one's animals in the commandment to rest on *Shabbat*, the fourth commandment (Exod. 20:10; Deut. 5:14, Exod. 23:12). Similarly, the Bible prohibits muzzling an ox when it is treading out grain (Deut. 25:4) and plowing with an ox and a donkey yoked together (Deut. 22:10), because these practices would cause suffering to the hungry and to the weaker animal, respectively.

Restraint on exploitation and sensitivity to all living creatures are important biblical principles. An intriguing and eloquent example of biblical sensitivity training occurs in Deut. 22:6–7:

> If, along the road, you chance upon a bird's nest, in any tree or on the ground, with fledglings or eggs and the mother sitting over the fledglings or on the eggs, do not take the mother together with her young. Let the mother go, and take only the young, in order that you may fare well and have a long life.

Whatever the original context of this law may be, its poignant reminder of the existence of the sentient animal family moves the reader to a higher level of concern for living things and their pain and suffering.

Fundamental to the biblical view of the natural world and humankind's place in it is the principle that human ownership is temporary and illusory. The world belongs to God; people are its trustees and not its proprietors. This principle underlies the biblical laws relating to the jubilee and the sabbatical years. Regarding the sabbatical (seventh) year, Lev. 25:5–6 states:

> You shall not reap the aftergrowth of your harvest or gather the grapes of your untrimmed vines; it shall be a year of complete rest for the land. But you may eat whatever the land during its sabbath will produce—you, your male and female slaves, the hired and bound laborers who live with you.

Several themes come together here. The "seven" cycle recapitulates the Creation cycle and places the natural world into the context of divine creation. Human beings may use the natural world for their needs, but not without limitation. The land, too, requires and deserves rest. This is not simply a personal obligation, however; it carries with it principles of social justice and concern. The poor and the stranger were granted the privilege of eating the produce that grew as the result of earlier years' planting, just as they were granted access to unpicked harvest and the corners of the field during other years (Lev. 23:22). Limitation, obligation to others, and concern for the needs of the poor all express the fundamental value of the sabbatical: During the seventh year, God is reasserting proprietorship—and so human beings do not have access to the field. Human ownership is temporary.

This principle is explicit in providing the rationale for the law of the jubilee year. The jubilee was quite radical in its prescribing that on the 50th year—i.e., after the completion of seven sabbatical cycles, seven times seven, connecting again with the Creation motif—all land that had been sold during the preceding half century was to be returned to its original owner. Why? "The land must not be sold beyond reclaim, for the land is Mine; you are but strangers resident with Me" (Lev. 25:23).

An additional area of biblical legislation most relevant to this discussion occurs in Deut. 20:19–20:

> When in your war against a city you have to besiege it a long time in order to capture it, you must not destroy its trees,

wielding the ax against them. You may eat of them, but you must not cut them down. Are trees of the field human to withdraw before you into the besieged city? Only trees that you know do not yield food may be destroyed; you may cut them down for constructing siegeworks against the city that is waging war on you, until it has been reduced.

Even in time of war, when wanton destruction is common, biblical law imposes severe constraints. Once again, a contrast is made between human beings who may bring destruction on themselves through their behavior and the blameless natural world that deserves protection and nurturing. And though trees may be used within limits for the purposes of war, that use is severely limited and contained.

The principle implicit in this law and the term employed in this passage were expanded and articulated in the Rabbinic law of *bal tashḥit,* the prohibition against unnecessary and wanton destruction. Although the full development of the principle is Rabbinic, we again see the clear biblical foundation for a traditional value.

The biblical picture is rounded out in a number of other passages that contribute to the biblical ecologic perspective. One noteworthy passage concludes the Book of Jonah (4:9–11):

Then God said to Jonah: "Are you so deeply grieved about the plant?" "Yes," he replied, "so deeply that I want to die."

Then the Lord said: "You cared about the plant, which you did not work for and which you did not grow, which appeared overnight and perished overnight. And should I not care about Nineveh, that great city, in which there are more than a hundred and twenty thousand persons who do not yet know their right hand from their left, and many beasts as well!"

The coda of this passage is quite striking. Had the divine demonstration by comparative syllogism ended with mention of the 120,000 who lived in Nineveh, the argument would have been complete but not quite so jarring. The inclusion of "many beasts" implies a shift from a human-centered view of the world. Mercy for animals is as significant as concern for innocent people. Jonah was not wrong to be concerned for the plant, but his grief may have centered on the usefulness of the plant to himself as it provided him shelter and protection. In a world that is God's, the human perspective can be only partially true and, therefore, is necessarily distorted. The Bible reminds its readers of the limitations and the error of a human-centered perspective.

A striking text articulating the limitations of humankind's orientation toward the natural world is found in the Book of Job (38–40). Readers and scholars have debated the thrust of God's response to Job's challenge. Does God simply overwhelm Job with divine creative power and strength and thus silence Job? Is it suggested that Job simply cannot understand the justice of God's ways, which may be hidden from him? Perhaps elements of both are contained in God's responses. Doubtless also present is God's assertion that the world is not created to be comprehensible to human beings or to serve them. Examples adduced in the God speeches refer to a range of creatures that God has created as well as to divine power and creativity. The lioness, the mountain goat, the wild ass and wild ox, the ostrich and the crocodile are included, as are the hawk, the vulture, and the hippopotamus. As Robert Gordis pointed out, notable about this list of creatures is that virtually none of the animals is useful to human beings, nor do the animals generally represent creatures that people find beautiful or appealing. They are part of God's plan, which often is unfathomable to human beings. That is part of the thrust of God's reply to Job. It is certainly relevant to the Bible's ecologic stance. The bedrock of the biblical approach to the environment (and our place in it) demands the abandonment of a world-view that puts people at the center and evaluates all things in terms of their utility to people.

On the subject of ecology in the Bible, we can find no structured or systematic statement of principles. The Bible, by and large, does not teach by direction; it teaches by conditioning us to understand the nature of the world and the profound implications of the choices and decisions we make in our lives. It invites us to learn ethical and spiritual lessons by reflecting on the complex and never unflawed lives of its heroes. It urges us to search out the values underlying most of its legal admonitions. It entices us to be moved by the imagery of its poetry. The Bible allows us to weave a tapestry, to synthesize a perspective of the natural world, which can warn us about the dangers of excess, alert us to our responsibility, condition our thinking and our behavior, and sensitize us to the beauty and fragility of the natural environment around us.

Most of what has been pointed out articulates the principle of the psalmist (24:1): "The earth is the LORD's and all that it holds." Remember that human ownership is only temporary. Protect from destruction what God has entrusted to us. Ponder the enigmatic, bearing in mind that the world was not created from our point of view, so that not everything will be comprehensible to us. Strive for godliness by remembering and commemorating the creative process initiated by the ultimate creator, and by being responsible protectors of what God has created.

Study Questions

1. In the first two paragraphs of the essay, how does Gordis characterize the Bible's relationship between humankind and the natural world? Do you sense any connection between the realms of ethics and ecology? What does the word "commanded" in the second paragraph add to this characterization?

2. In citing the words "and God saw that it was good" that appear in Genesis, chapter 1 for each day of creation, what might Gordis be claiming about the "value" of the natural world in its own right? In its relationship to humankind?

3. In your opinion, does the story of Noah and the Flood in Genesis 6–9 reinforce the idea of the value of the earth and creation?

4. Gordis spends a substantial part of his essay focusing on the dietary laws (kashrut). How does he connect this very ritualistic and particular rite of the Jewish people to the issue of ecology? Do you agree?

5. The concept of the seventh year, during which the land is left fallow (*shemitah*) in Lev. 25:5–6, is particular to an agrarian society. Following Gordis's example, what are the general principles or values

involved in this mitzvah? How might these ideas translate into the complex industrial/ecological system of our modern world?

6. Why might the Bible have placed the law about the corner of the field being left for the poor (Lev. 23:22) in close proximity to the law of the *shemitah* year (Lev. 25:5–6)? Is there a relationship between ecology and ethics/morality? Some scholars suggest that these chapters of Leviticus are part of a special section of *Humash* called the "Holiness Code." In what ways does this lend additional significance to these passages?

7. For further study, you might take a look at two other significant biblical texts:

   • Deut. 11:13–21 is recited twice daily in the traditional liturgy as the middle paragraph of the *Shema* prayer. What does it affirm as the relationship between ecological health of the earth and obedience to the laws of Torah?

   • Look at Psalm 92, the psalm designated as the "Psalm for the *Sabbath*." What does this psalm assume poetically as the relationship between ecology and ethics?

8. Returning to the initial question in the introduction to these study questions: Can you now formulate a statement of the biblical view of the relationship among the natural world, divine commandment, ritual, morality, and human ethical conduct?

9. How would biblical religion rewrite the definition of the Greek term "ecology"?

Study materials by Sheldon Dorph

LAND OF ISRAEL

Benjamin J. Segal

Summary

In the biblical tradition, the Land of Israel is both worldly and other-worldly. God gifted the land to the forefathers, but the forefathers, in turn, possessed the land in mundane ways. After being redeemed from slavery in Egypt and wandering in the desert for 40 years, the Israelites conquered the Land of Israel and lived there like they might in any other land. However, according to the Torah, their prosperity was contingent upon their loyalty to God (which would yield rainfall). Additionally, the Israelites could work the land like they might work any other land, but their enjoyment of its produce was tied to obligations: resting on the seventh day and the seventh year, and leaving portions of their crops for the poor and the Priests. The Israelites were promised a long-term lease on the Land of Israel, but God remained the Landlord. If the tenants neglected their payments—moral and religious piety—they could be evicted, or more precisely, exiled.

Expulsion from territory is a dominant theme of the Torah's early world history (Gen. 1–11): Adam and Eve are expelled from Eden, Cain exiled from before the presence of the LORD, Noah's generation blotted out "from the earth" (6:7), and humanity scattered from (the tower of) Babel. With Abraham, God opts for a narrower channel of access to the world—through a people who will have a special relationship to Him and to a particular land.

Because this land exists in triangular relationship with the descendants of Abraham and with God, it forever straddles the transient and the eternal, the real and the ideal. It is both subject to human influence and unalterably divine; these diverse qualities form a grid on which the land is described in the Torah. The human and the divine seek to coexist in the land.

In tracing that relationship, one must note the nature of the Torah sources concerning the land. This home is not a subcategory of Israelite thought. It is axiomatic; a primary, defining category of the people's existence vis-à-vis its God. Observations are made from within, reflecting ultimate involvement and identification but lacking external perspective. References to the land should be understood as a nation's self-expression, not objective reflections on a subject of concern.

In this essay, I will explore the relationship of the people to the land in four of its expressions: the early struggle to establish human "ownership," even in total absence of political control; the attempts to define the land as both physical and divine entities; the matter of justifying ownership, with its implications for the giver and the recipients; and the land as seen on the eve of Israelite entry, from across the Jordan River.

GENESIS: HOMELESS AT HOME

In what sense did the forefathers "own" the land? Time and again, the forefathers are "given" this land (Gen. 13:15,17, 35:12 ff.), as part of the covenant. As we learn from ancient Near Eastern covenant terminology, the giving is more properly understood as "assignment": they are assigned the land of Israel.

In the forefathers' time, theirs was the promise, not the possession; the legal deed, not the control. Much later the Israelites would be told that they were to be only strangers in residence (Lev. 25:23). The forefathers needed no such message, for they lived that reality. Understanding that full ownership was God's promise for the future, they faced the first challenge of the land: establishing personal bonds symbolizing their connection. They, the people, had to gain possession of the divine land.

The first response lay in traversing the land. God told Abraham: "Up, walk about the land, through its length and breadth, for I give it to you" (Gen. 13:17). Centuries later, Joshua would still recall this tour as a basic step in establishing ownership (Josh. 24:3). As in Joseph's trip through Egypt (Gen. 41:46), physical contact sealed legal rights.

The second response reflected a religious attachment, accomplished by building altars throughout the land. In Shechem, Bethel, Mamre, and Beer-sheba, the forefathers erected places of worship (Gen. 12:6–7, 13:18, 26:25, 35:7).

Purchase was the third response. Refusing what seemed to be the gift of a burial site, Abraham insisted on purchasing the cave of Machpelah

(Gen. 23), which would become the family burial ground. Jacob later bought territory in Shechem (33:19). The first small, legal possessions were attained.

Fourth, the predominant theme of the forefathers' relationship to the land is the determination to be buried there; the Machpelah burial cave served all three generations. On his deathbed, Jacob insists that his body be returned to the land of Israel from Egypt (Gen. 49:29–32), and Joseph insists that his bones be reburied there (50:25).

Finally, one forefather established the precedent of residing there exclusively. When faced with a local famine, Isaac was told that he could not, like his father, Abraham, go to Egypt. Rather, he was to stay in the land (Gen. 26:2 ff.) all his life. Therefore Jacob, his son, on leaving the land (for what would be the last time), prayed in fear specifically to "the God of his father, Isaac" (46:1), the model of permanent residence. Only God's reassurance that the connection would not be severed and that Jacob's progeny would return allowed him to depart with his mind at ease.

The story of the forefathers in the land is one of ongoing struggle. Except for Abraham's successful foray against the kings who abducted Lot and his family (Gen. 14), the forefathers are depicted as relatively weak. They remained in the mountains, away from the strong centers of settlement on the coast. They were subject to harassment by their neighbors and they wandered from place to place, resorting to machinations to protect themselves and their households. Neither sovereign on the one hand nor powerless on the other, the forefathers struggled and maneuvered to establish ownership of their "home."

Genesis thus projects a striking aggregate picture, a depiction of the homeless at home. A young clan claims ownership, but not control, while forging nonpolitical ties to bind itself to the territory. It is of some fascination that for millennia these patterns of burial, traversal, and purchase remained active models for the Jewish people in maintaining their ties to the land.

DESCRIBING THE LAND:
DESTINATION AND DESTINY

After Genesis, the Israelites in the Torah are constantly directed toward the land. So Exodus begins, as God speaks to Moses in Midian:

"I have come down ... to bring them out of that land to a good and spacious land, a land flowing with milk and honey, the region of the Canaanites" (Exod. 3:8). So, too, Deuteronomy concludes with Moses allowed only to see the land, as the LORD says: "This is the land of which I swore to Abraham, Isaac, and Jacob, 'I will assign it to your offspring'" (Deut. 34:4). Because it is forever on the horizon, the land cried out for a double description: both in human terms (Who lives there? What are its borders?) and divine (In what ways is it so different?).

That land of future possession was then occupied by others. Most often titled the "land of Canaan," it was associated with as many as 10 peoples (Gen. 15:19 ff.), known in varying degrees from extrabiblical documents. Leviticus (18:24 ff.) provides a rationale for the eventual expulsion of the current residents: moral turpitude. Thereafter, God would give it to His chosen people.

Throughout, the Torah foresees interaction with neighbors resident in the land and the ensuing dangers. The Torah is acutely aware that the Israelites, although the conquering power, would be attracted to local pagan practices (Deut. 17:3), rooted in place and soil. Consistently, they are warned to distance themselves from the pagan cults of the Canaanites, who attributed the land's bounty to gods of nature. Rather, the land was to be seen as the assigned gift of the one God (Deut. 26:3–10).

The land's borders are variously defined in the Torah. They approximate neither the eventual settlement area of the tribes nor the eventual Davidic kingdom. Rather, they are either grand overviews of the entire territory between the great powers of Egypt and Assyria (as in Gen. 15:18, which speaks of "this land, from the river of Egypt to ... the river Euphrates") or an approximation of the borders of Canaan, relying heavily on settlement area, contiguity, and natural boundaries (Num. 34:1–12). The Torah's geographic definition is not an attempt to anticipate later developments but a reflection of preconquest general concepts of the land's parameters.

The territory on the horizon, of course, is also God's promised land. In articulating its divine qualities, the Torah describes the land's delights, dependency, and demands, as I now detail.

A Delightful Land

This is "a land flowing with milk and honey" (e. g., Exod. 3:8). Some commentators once held that this idealized picture, with its reference to natural gifts, reflected an early, preoccupation origin of the phrase, because the land is scarcely perfect. However, an Egyptian text provides a similar description of northern Israel: "It was a good land. ... Figs were in it, and grapes. ... Plentiful was its honey, abundant its olives. Every fruit was on its trees." The Torah's idealization should, therefore, be understood as an emphasis on the land's advantages. This is

> a good land, a land with streams and springs and fountains issuing from plain and hill; a land of wheat and barley, of vines, figs, and pomegranates, a land of olive trees and honey; a land where you may eat food without stint, where you will lack nothing; a land whose rocks are iron and from whose hills you can mine copper (Deut. 8:7–9).

The sin of the spies (Num. 13–14) was not in bearing a false report, but in choosing to emphasize the negative, thereby disheartening the people.

A Dependent Land

The land is also dependent. Unlike Egypt and Mesopotamia, which derive their water from significant rivers fed by distant sources, the land is a country of mountains, dependent on rain. For the Torah this meant dependency on God's mercy and justice.

> The land you are about to cross into and possess, a land of hills and valleys, soaks up its water from the rains of heaven. It is a land which the LORD, your God, looks after, on which the LORD, your God, always keeps His eye, from year's beginning to year's end. ...

> Take care not to be lured away to serve other gods and bow to them. For the LORD's anger will flare up against you, and He will shut up the skies so that there will be no rain and the ground will not yield its produce; and you will soon perish from the good land that the LORD is assigning to you (Deut. 11:11–12,16–17).

A Demanding Land

The land is central to all of the Torah's prescribed behaviors. So marked is the emphasis on observing God's law within the land, that Ramban, the 13th-century commentator, concluded that all laws of the Torah were intended for observance exclusively there. (Observance elsewhere would reflect empathy and constitute preparation for return.) Although this is an idiosyncratic view, the Torah text does see the land as the primary locus of observance. Furthermore, many of the demands are connected directly to the land, detailing when produce could be eaten, which products had to be brought to the Temple, which produce had to be left for the poor, etc.

The demands are not framed as an "object" (the land) being imposed on a living entity (the people). Rather, the land is almost personified. As humans must rest every seventh day, so every seventh year the land must lie unplanted to gain its rest. As humans must observe the 50th year, canceling all individual debts, so, too, the land returns by section to its original owners in the 50th year.

Personification reaches its apex in august moral terms. The land could not abide immoral behavior. The previous residents were expelled because of their disobedience to God's norms, and so would the land expel the Israelites were they to misbehave similarly. Expulsion might also follow abuse of the soil, through failure to grant the land its proper rest (Lev. 26:35). The land exhibits a living claim of its own, against which the Israelites had to measure and understand their presence. Otherwise, the land would expel them to gain its respite. The land's divinity was understood as posing a demand.

RIGHTS AND OBLIGATIONS

By what right would the Israelites possess the land? The nation's self-conception emphasized arrival from abroad. They were the descendants of Abraham's family who came to the land from without. As a people, they immigrated after a long stay in Egypt, which they celebrated in an annual holiday cycle. Each year they would recite that history when offering God the first fruits of the land, at the same time personalizing the gift: "I," each farmer would say, "have entered the land that the LORD swore to our fathers to assign us" (Deut. 26:3–10). They came from afar and constantly reminded themselves of that fact. That recalled "outsider" status demanded a justification of possession, and in the response lay the most complex reflection of the divine–human partnership in the land of Israel.

The basic right to the land was grounded in God's assignment, but that was scarcely an absolute claim. With possession came responsibilities. In the context of one of them, return of property to original owners every 50th year, a striking assertion is made: "The land must not be sold beyond reclaim, for the land is Mine; you are but strangers resident with Me" (Lev. 25:23). The assigning owner maintains His property rights! The claim of the people is tenuous indeed.

Further emphasizing the dependency of occupation on God's mercy and memory, the text states that the Israelites inherited the land by virtue of the original covenant God made with Abraham, Isaac, and Jacob—and not by merit of their deeds (Deut. 9:4 ff.). Ironically, the very question of rights to the land, then, leads to the possibility of exile! If this gift implied obligation, continued disobedience ultimately implied expulsion (Lev. 26:33 ff.; Deut. 28:63 ff.). No other ancient people so placed a moral qualification on its right to its territory. The Israelites thus extended their original understanding of a universal order that allowed God to expel humans from territory to apply to their own land.

The exile is described as torturous for both the land and the people. The land will be "desolate" (Lev. 26:32); it "shall become a desolation and your cities a ruin" (26:33). The Israelites in exile, for their part, will live in fear and suffer persecution:

> The sound of a driven leaf shall put them to flight. ... With
> no one pursuing, they shall stumble over one another as before
> the sword. You shall not be able to stand your ground before
> your enemies, but shall perish among the nations; and the land
> of your enemies shall consume you" (26:36–38).

But beyond exile lay a final and ultimate reunification. The land and the people, part of the same covenant, could never be fully separated. Following repentance and atonement, the people would return (26:41 ff.).

The Torah thus posits simultaneously the strongest and most fragile of relationships: A direct assignment from God but a connection that can be cut off because of human acts of omission or commission. Given this complexity, it is no surprise that the Torah at times attributes the land's holiness to an immanent, inherent quality (most often emphasized in Leviticus and Numbers) and at times emphasizes the holiness granted the land by the people's presence and deeds thereon (Deuteronomy). Sanctity is inherent in the land and, therefore, it is demanded of its residents; but simultaneously it is given to the land by the acts of those residents.

As later history unfolded, the complex interweave of the land's characteristics (permanently assigned yet potentially lost, bearing both obligations and opportunities, idealized yet fraught with dangers of contact) formed the basis of a complex relationship with the nation, permanent at its deepest level yet constantly volatile on the surface.

THE VIEW FROM ACROSS THE RIVER

Nowhere is the sense of immediate occupation felt more keenly than in Deuteronomy. Speaking to the Israelites in Transjordan, Moses recalls history and dream, commandment and dangers. The book opens with a recollection of God's order to go to the land (1:7) and concludes with Moses' ascent to Mount Nebo and his death, the Torah ending short of fulfillment, looking forward to imminent entrance into the land of Canaan.

So close to arrival, Deuteronomy focuses on the expected normal life on the nation's own soil. Exclusive to this book are the themes of kingship and centralized worship (the "chosen place") and a marked concentration on the court system, one of the bases of an organized society.

Deuteronomy, however, also constantly reminds the people that occupation requires obedience to God. The past is cited as testimony, the laws repeated as prescription. Reinforcing the divine–human partnership in the land, the book's framework is land centered: "Observe … that you may long remain in the land that the LORD your God is assigning to you for all time" (4:40), and "to the end that you and your children may endure, in the land … as long as there is a heaven over the earth" (11:21).

Although the possibilities of rebellion and loss are recalled, this final book of the Torah ends in anticipation, with the people poised to enter the land. The land and all its potential, for glory and failure remain untested and, therefore, untarnished. The dominant message presents the land as the locus of the potential ideal, a concept that would pervade Jewish history for millennia.

AND BEYOND

Many commentators tend to seek out reflections of later developments in the Torah text, which itself always sees the land of Israel as a category of the future. However, there remains significant dissonance between later reality and the Torah's combination of prescriptions and predictions. The Torah emphasizes aspirations. Thus it provides the building blocks for all future ideologies of the land. Deuteronomy's "chosen place," for example, is identified as David's Jerusalem, which develops its own centrality, absorbing and encompassing some earlier approaches to the land as a whole. The Torah's idealized hopes are strongly strained in light of reality. The dream of potential perfection is recast, with renewed emphasis on the future, attached to a new image of Jerusalem, expected at "the end of days" (e. g., Isa. 27:13; Zech. 2:14–16).

The Bible and Jewish literature throughout the ages, however, remain faithful to the primary relationships established in the Torah: an axiomatic connection between God, the people, and the land; a complex interaction of ownership, possession, and exile; an understanding of the land as delightful, dependent on God, and demanding of the people; and a view of the land as destiny, the locus of hope.

The relationship is sui generis. No other ancient nation had such a complex understanding of its territory, for whom it was "the Holy land" (Zech. 2:16). These vicissitudes reflected involvement, not ambivalence. The movement in and out—in the Bible and across the centuries—reflects not dissociation, but the centripetal and centrifugal forces created around a center. All this derives from the Torah, for which this land was assigned, the exclusive potential locus for human–divine harmony. The Torah traces a grand march toward that center, from the first command to Abram to go forward to the land, to the final scene of Moses looking on it from across the Jordan.

Study Questions

1. From information in the essay, name three ways in which the fore-fathers displayed active ownership over the Land of Israel. Why do you think God's promise of the land was not sufficient?

2. After Genesis, the Torah's narrative arc leads toward a return to the Land of Israel. Why do you think the Torah concludes before this arc is complete, before the Israelites enter the land?

3. Who lived in the Land of Israel before the Israelites? What reason does the Bible give for their expulsion from the land? How do you feel about this explanation?

4. Zech. 2:16 describes Israel as "the Holy Land." What makes the land holy? Is this holiness or sanctity innate or is it bestowed by its residents? Do you believe a piece of land can have spiritual significance? Can one land be holier than another?

5. How does the biblical promise of the Land of Israel relate to the modern State of Israel? Do you believe the Israelite right to the land detailed in the Torah has significance today?

Study materials by *Daniel Yechiel Septimus*

DEALING WITH STRANGERS: RELATIONS WITH GENTILES AT HOME AND ABROAD

Joel Rembaum

Summary

In this essay, Rabbi Rembaum points to a dynamic tension between attitudes of exclusivity and inclusivity regarding non-Israelites in the Bible, and how those orientations play out in postbiblical attitudes towards non-Jews and converts.

On the exclusive side, the gift of the Land of Israel to the descendants of Abraham and Sarah was linked to the sinfulness of the Canaanite nations. The settlement and survival of Israel in the land required separation from the native inhabitants. This led to the biblical command that some of these pagan people be exterminated or exiled. The inclusive orientation is seen in the Genesis narratives that emphasize the commonality of all people as creations of God. The *ger*, or alien, is to be treated with respect and special care, for we are to retain a historical memory that the Israelites were once strangers in Egypt. In prophetic imagery, Isaiah and Zechariah envision all people ascending to Jerusalem in the end of days.

Although the Bible does not have a concept of religious conversion, it does have the notion that women can join the people of Israel by marriage to Israelites. The inclusive perspective about joining the Jewish people is seen in the story of Ruth, while the exclusive orientation is evident in the Book of Ezra. The rabbis applied the biblical term for stranger or alien, *ger*, to proselytes and viewed their decision to choose Judaism as an important statement of faith. While the Rabbinic tradition has some negative ideas about converts, the overall thrust of Judaism toward conversion has been positive.

Postbiblical Jews were culturally connected to the Hellenistic world, yet the Talmud maintained that Greek, Roman, and Persian cultures were steeped in immorality. However, these same rabbis articulated the notion of the seven Noahide commandments (*sheva mitsvot b'nai Noaḥ*) which dignified non-Jews as moral beings and saw them as being subject to a covenant of "universal ethical monotheism." In turn, this laid the groundwork for the development of tolerant attitudes toward Christians in the Middle Ages and, ultimately, paved the way for the Jewish openness toward the gentile world in the modern era.

––––––––––

Although the Bible's focus is the unique relationship between the people Israel and God, relationships between Israel and the non-Israelite world constitute a significant element of the biblical traditions. Commentators on the Bible from Maimonides to contemporary scholars have noted that an important purpose of biblical law and narrative was to direct the ancient Israelites away from the beliefs and practices of the pagan nations that surrounded them. It should come as no surprise, therefore, that the overriding view of the non-Israelite world expressed in the Hebrew Bible is negative.

This attitude first represents itself in Gen. 15:16. After promising Abram that the land of Canaan will be given to his descendants as an inheritance, God tells the patriarch: "And they shall return here in the fourth generation, for the iniquity of the Amorites is not yet complete." Taking this idea one step further, Deut. 9:5 emphasizes that the Israelites will gain possession of the Land not because of their righteousness, but because of the sinfulness of the nations that had inhabited it; and thus God can fulfill the promise made to the patriarchs.

A further elaboration is presented in Exod. 23:31–33:

> I will deliver the inhabitants of the land into your hands, and you will drive them out before you. You shall make no covenant with them and their gods. They shall not remain in your land, lest they cause you to sin against Me; for you will serve their gods—and it will prove a snare to you.

The issue is laid out in very clear terms: The pagan nations must be eradicated from the Land because they pose a threat to Israelite belief in the one, true God. Because the removal of the pagans from Canaan will occur over a protracted period of time, the Israelites in the interim are prohibited from worshiping the gods of the nations, making any covenants with the nations, and giving their sons in marriage to the daughters of the nations (concerning the latter, see Exod. 34:16). If the Israelites are attracted by the paganism of the nations they, in turn, will be punished. Deut. 7:1–6 reiterates these points, including the prohibition against intermarriage, and adds yet another reason for this destruction of and separation from pagan society: "For you are a people consecrated to the LORD your God." Because of Israel's unique relationship with God, total separation from the pagan world is mandated. Deut. 23:4 adds that peoples not indigenous to the land of Israel, such as Ammonites and Moabites, are not to be "admitted into the congregation of the LORD ... even in the tenth generation." This is "because they did not meet you with food and water on your journey after you left Egypt, and because they hired Balaam son of Beor ... to curse you" (23:5). Rabbinic tradition interprets "the 10th generation" to mean forever (Sifrei Deut. Ki Tetzei 39). Accordingly, Ammonites and Moabites never could be welcomed into the nation of Israel.

Carrying the notion of Israel's uniqueness as a people even further, Leviticus adds another dimension to the idea of the sinfulness of the pagan world and the Israelites' need for separation. Leviticus 18 views Egypt and the nations of Canaan as engaging in sexual abominations, which result in serious defilement. The land of Israel, we are told, cannot tolerate such impurity and will vomit out any people thus defiled. The Israelites, to remain in the land, must avoid such activities.

Ezra and Nehemiah, interpreting these Torah traditions in the 5th century B.C.E., forced the Israelite men of Judea to send away non-Israelite women they had married. These leaders, confronted with Israelite intermarriage of sizable proportions, feared that the people and the land to which they had returned would be defiled through the forbidden marriages and that God would punish the people by sending them into exile once again (Ezra 9–10; Neh. 9:1–2, 10:31, 13:1–3, 23–28). Since the option to convert the women did not exist at that time, removal from society was the only resolution. Clearly, these and similar assessments of the pagans, and the emphasis of Israelite separation from the nations in whose midst they lived, cast the non-Israelites in a negative light.

Yet, despite the general antipathy of the Bible toward pagans, certain tolerant attitudes toward non-Israelites do emerge from the biblical traditions. The Torah begins with the assumption that Elohim/*YHVH*, as Creator, is the God of all humankind. In this vein, Maimonides conceives of humankind as being initially monotheistic and believing in the one true God, with idolatry developing only later as a result of human ideologic error (MT Idol Worship 1:1). After the Flood, during which most of humanity was destroyed, God rebuilds the human race with Noah and his children. *Elohim* enters into a covenant with Noah and his descendants and all the living creatures on earth (Gen. 9:8–17), thereby deepening God's relationship with humankind. All the nations of the world emerge from Noah's children (Gen. 10), and therefore, we can presume that the Torah considers all nations to be under God's kingship. The Rabbinic concept of the Noahide laws (discussed below) is rooted in these biblical traditions.

At one point, the Torah presents us with a rather surprising attitude toward pagan religious practice. In Deut. 4:19 we read:

> And when you look up to the sky, and behold the sun and the moon and the stars, the whole heavenly host, you must not be lured into bowing down to them or serving them. These the LORD your God allotted to other peoples everywhere under heaven.

God warns Israel not to worship the heavenly host while providing other nations with those luminaries as objects of worship. It would appear that God, according to Deuteronomy, cannot tolerate Israel's worshiping the stars, yet somehow can tolerate such practices among the other nations.

The prophet Amos, in his expressions of God's anger at a sinful Israel, comes close to placing Israel's neighbors on the same plane as Israel in its relationship with God. In the first two chapters of his book, the prophet, for rhetorical effect, enumerates the sins of various peoples, culminating with the sins of Judah and Israel. God, we discover, judges all the nations, Israelite and non-Israelite. Although the prophet recognizes Israel's special relationship with *YHVH*, according to him it serves only to allow God to judge Israel with even greater severity (Amos 3:2). Then, in 9:7, we read:

To Me, O Israelites, you are
Just like the Ethiopians—
declares the LORD.
True, I brought Israel up
From the land of Egypt,
But also the Philistines from Caphtor
And the Arameans from Kir.

Although this is undoubtedly a rhetorical flourish, underlying the prophet's rhetoric is the idea that *YHVH* maintains relations with all nations, with regard to whom God can act either as judge or as redeemer.

In their end-of-days prophecies, certain of the prophets see the nations turning to God. Isaiah, for example, looks forward to the pagans flocking to Jerusalem so that God can teach them how to walk in God's ways (Isa. 2:3). Zechariah adds yet another dimension to this idea. In his vision of "the day of the LORD" (Zech. 14), he foresees God defeating the nations that had attacked Jerusalem and then mandating: "All who survive of all those nations that came up against Jerusalem shall make a pilgrimage year by year to bow low to the King LORD of Hosts and to observe the Feast of Booths." If they disobey this edict they will have no rain, says Zechariah (14:16–17). Here the nations are held accountable for following the divine command to worship *YHVH* by celebrating an Israelite festival; and if they do not comply with the mandate, they are subject to a punishment that is similar to what Israel would face in the same circumstances (see Deut. 11:13–17). While not negating the unique covenant between God and Israel, these prophets foresee the nations coming closer to God at some point in the future. So it is that amid all the Bible's anti-paganism, seeds of tolerant attitudes toward idolaters can be found.

The non-Israelite in the biblical sources who most closely approaches the status of the Israelite is the *ger,* "the resident alien." Although originally from another nation, the *ger* chooses to live among the Israelites in their land. The *ger* is to be treated with loving kindness because Israel, having been strangers in a strange land (Egypt), understands the *ger*'s plight (Exod. 22:20, 23:9; Lev. 19:33–34; Deut. 10:19, 24:17–18).

According to the Torah, the *ger* is expected to follow the laws that are incumbent on the native-born Israelite (e.g., Lev. 10:1 ff., 16:29, 17:8 ff.; Num. 19:10). The admonition that there be one standard for the native born and the *ger* applies to both ritual and ethical laws (Lev. 24:22; Num. 15:16).

The Bible has no procedure by which a proselyte may become formally converted to Israelite religion and a full citizen in Israelite society. One element of the law, however, begins to move in this direction. A discussion of the law of the paschal lamb in Exodus includes the following: "If a stranger [*ger*] who dwells with you would offer the passover to the LORD, all his males must be circumcised; then he shall be admitted to offer it; he shall then be as a citizen of the country" (Exod. 12:48). Only those who have been circumcised may eat of the paschal lamb. Should a *ger* wish to partake of the *pesaḥ* sacrifice, he and the males of his household must be circumcised. They then become like citizens of the country. Not surprisingly, this verse serves as a proof-text for later Rabbinic traditions that formalize such procedures (see BT Yev. 46b).

In the most fully developed biblical story of an alien who with a full heart chooses to become a part of the household of Israel, the Book of Ruth, the term *ger* does not even appear. This may be because Ruth enters the land of Israel only after she had become a member of an Israelite household. In Moab she married Mahlon, son of Elimelech and Naomi. When Naomi returns to Bethlehem with Ruth, the latter is considered a member of Naomi's household, not a resident alien. Formal conversion, as the later Jewish sources will come to define it, has not taken place. In fact, Ruth's status is not clear. Even after she makes her now famous statement of commitment (Ruth 1:16–17) she is called "Ruth the Moabite," a "Moabite girl" (Ruth 1:22, 2:6,21, 4:5,10). She refers to herself as *nokhriyyah*, "a foreigner" (Ruth 2:10). The only recognition of the significance of Ruth's choosing to remain with Naomi and to become part of Naomi's people is Boaz's warm reply to Ruth's self-deprecating remark:

> I have been told of ... how you left your father and mother
> and the land of your birth and came to a people you had not
> known before. May the LORD reward your deeds. May you

have a full recompense from the LORD, the God of Israel, under whose wings you have sought refuge! (Ruth 2:11–12).

Boaz, however, does not indicate that Ruth has become an Israel-
ite. In taking her as his wife he does so as the redeemer of the estate of
Naomi's husband and sons, of which Ruth was a part (Ruth 4:9–10).
Perhaps the positive reaction of the crowd that witnessed Boaz's act of
redemption points to the community's enthusiastic acceptance of Ruth:
"May the LORD make the woman who is coming into your house like
Rachel and Leah, both of whom built up the House of Israel" (Ruth
4:11). This declaration would seem to hinge on Boaz's intent to marry
Ruth. That seems to be the act that brings her into the community, not
her prior espousal of commitment. After all, typically it was through
marriage to an Israelite man that a foreign woman entered into the
household of Israel. And so, the Book of Ruth really teaches us nothing about what we call conversion. It does, however, present a foreign
person in a positive light and opens the door to an attitude of acceptance of the *ger*-convert in later generations once the requirements for
conversions are more fully developed. (The reconciliation of the Book
of Ruth with the anti-Moabite legislation of Deut. 23:4–5 is subject to
much scholarly discussion.)

Attitudes toward non-Israelites continued largely unchanged in the
postbiblical era. Jewish assimilation into the Hellenized culture that
dominated their world notwithstanding, many Jews of the late Second Temple period (ca. 150 B.C.E.–70 C.E.) and the talmudic age (ca.
70–500 C.E.) maintained strongly negative views of pagans and pagan
society. Not only were the Jews heirs to the biblical traditions but their
experiences with the Greco-Roman and, later, Persian civilizations were
often bitter and antagonistic. Greeks, Romans, and Persians were, in the
eyes of many Jews, no different from the peoples whom the Bible paints
in negative colors. So, for example, in the Mishnah we read:

> Cattle may not be left in the inns of the gentiles since they are
> suspected of bestiality; nor may a woman remain alone with
> them since they are suspected of lewdness; nor may a man
> remain alone with them since they are suspected of shedding
> blood. The daughter of an Israelite may not assist a gentile

> woman in childbirth since she would be assisting to bring to
> birth a child of idolatry (Av. Zar. 2:1).

In a long midrashic account of the day of divine judgment at the end of time, the gentiles are depicted as having been unworthy of receiving the Torah (BT Av. Zar. 2bff.). Elsewhere, they are considered to be infected with lasciviousness (BT Shab. 145b–146a) and sexually immoral (BT Ket. 13b). Further we read: "All the charity and kindness done by the heathens is counted to them as sin, because they only do it to magnify themselves ... [and] to display haughtiness" (BT BB 10b). These statements reflect the attitudes of the Jews of the land of Israel in the generations after the destruction of the Second Temple when the land was under Roman rule and subject to the indecencies of an army of occupation and the corruption of local Roman officials. They also express attitudes of Babylonian Jews in the later talmudic period (250–600 C. E.), who suffered under increasingly repressive Persian regimes.

The negativity of the Sages' view of the pagan world was tempered, however, by a concept that introduced into Judaism a level of tolerance of non-Jews that would continue to operate for centuries: *sheva mitzvot b'nei No·aḥ*, the "seven commandments of the children of Noah." The term by which the Sages defined the gentile (non-Jew) was *ben No·aḥ*, literally "the son of Noah," a category different from *ben Avraham*, "the son of Abraham"—the Jew (BT Ned. 31a). Inasmuch as all humankind descended from Noah, all people (other than the Jews) were considered to be bound by the covenant God established with Noah after the flood (Gen. 9:8–17) and obligated to fulfill seven commandments. (Jews, through the covenant of Abraham as ratified by God and the Israelites at Sinai, were obliged to follow the Torah, with its 613 commandments.) According to Rabbinic tradition, six of the seven commandments of the children of Noah actually had been given to Adam: prohibitions against idolatry, blaspheming God's name, murder, incest, and stealing and the obligation to establish courts of law. At the time of Noah, when people were first allowed to eat animal meat, a seventh commandment was added: the prohibition against tearing a limb from a living animal (Gen. R. 16:6, 34:8,13; BT Sanh. 56a; see MT Kings 9:1). These commandments, for all intents and purposes, were the Sages' principles of universal ethical monotheism. Talmudic law articulated the ramifications of the Noahide commandments and set down the consequences for failure to observe them. The gentile who followed the seven commandments was called *ger toshav*, "a resident alien," and the tolerant biblical attitude toward the resident alien was transferred along with the terminology (BT Sanh. 56bff.; MT Kings 9–10).

On occasion, the Sages' critical view of the pagan world made them skeptical of the gentiles' ability to fulfill even these few, very basic obligations (BT BK 38a; Lev. R. 13:2). Nevertheless, with the notion of the Noahide laws in the background, tolerant feelings toward the non-Jewish world do emerge. Reality dictated a more open-minded perspective, given that the Jews, of necessity, had to maintain relations with the gentiles in whose empires they lived. The Talmud contains references by Sages to individual gentiles with whom cordial relations were maintained and even a recognition by certain Sages that gentiles whom they knew were not ideologically pagan but rather simply following the customs of their ancestors. This outlook opened the door for the development of tolerant attitudes toward Christians on the part of rabbis in the Middle Ages and, ultimately, paved the way for the Jewish openness toward the gentile world in the modern era (see *Tosafot* on BT Av. Zar. 2a). Building on the foundation laid in the Rabbinic sources, Maimonides writes that a gentile need not be coerced to accept the Torah and become a Jew; such a person must be made to accept the seven commandments of Noah (MT Kings 8:10). He is indicating that forced conversion to Judaism is not a necessary component of Jewish law and that there is a difference between an ethical monotheist and a pagan. The former must be accepted, whereas the latter cannot be tolerated. Given that Jews lived primarily among monotheistic people, this notion further reinforced the tolerant point of view that was set down in the earlier sources. A further significant contribution to Jewish toleration of the non-Jew is the statement: "The righteous among the pagans have a place in the world to come" (Tosef. Sanh. 13:1). Maimonides codified this concept in these words:

> Anyone who accepts the seven [Noahide] commandments
> and is careful to fulfill them is counted among the pious of

the nations of the world and has a place in the world to come, as long as that person accepts and fulfills them because God commanded them (MT Kings 8:10).

Building on these and other Maimonidean views of certain elements within the non-Jewish world, Menaḥem Meiri (ca. 1300) concluded that Christians and Muslims were "nations restricted by the ways of religion" (*Beit Ha-B'ḥirah* on BT Av. Zar. 20aff.). Meiri thus redefines Christians and Muslims as monotheists to whom the biblical and talmudic categories of idolaters do not apply. This "righteous gentile" notion echoed down through the generations and became a linchpin of Jewish tolerance.

During the late Second Temple period, interest in and conversion to Judaism became a widespread phenomenon. As a result, the term *ger*, which in biblical parlance referred to the resident alien, took on a new meaning: proselyte. The Sages of the postdestruction era (70–220 C. E.), the *Tanna·im*, began to formalize the procedure by which a gentile became a Jew, undoubtedly as a response to the gentile interest in Judaism. Although there was disagreement among Sages as to what was ritually required for conversion, the conclusion ultimately reached was circumcision and immersion for a male and immersion for a female, under the supervision of a rabbinical court of three. The court would also determine the nature of the proselyte's religious commitment and would instruct the *ger* in certain laws of the Torah (BT Yev. 46a–47a). Although certain legal differences between a born Jew and a *ger* remained, the thrust of the tradition was to equalize the status of the convert. "Scripture says: 'There shall be one law for the citizen and for the stranger' [Exod. 12:49]. This passage comes to declare the proselyte equal to the born Jew with respect to all the commandments of the Torah" (Mekh. Pisḥa 15).

Although the Rabbinic attitude toward the *ger* generally was positive and welcoming, there were rabbis who distrusted proselytes and discouraged their admittance into Jewish society. This perspective may have been a result of the actions of converts who left or betrayed the Jewish community during the period of heightened Roman oppression in Palestine in the first half of the 2nd century C. E. The dominant point of view, however, was expressed in the Rabbinic maxim: "When a proselyte comes to be converted one receives him with an open hand so as to bring him under the wings of the divine Presence" (Lev. R. 2:9). This remains the operative principle in our own day.

Study Questions

1 Does your sense of a covenant between God and the Jewish people lead to a negative image and relationship to the non-Jewish world?

2 How is your faith challenged when you read the biblical commandment to exterminate or exile non-Israelites and other negative views about non-Jews found in the Jewish tradition?

3. How did the idea of "*ger*" as "stranger" evolve into the concept of "*ger*" as "Jew-by-choice"?

4. What are the seven Noahide commandments? Why would they be considered an expression of universal ethical monotheism?

5. Do you think that Jews still feel some ambivalence about conversion to Judaism?

6. How does this essay side with exclusivity vs. inclusivity? Why?

7. How might you maintain a love for the covenantal uniqueness of Judaism and the Jewish people while still remaining open to and accepting of non-Jews and other religious traditions?

8. Is there a price to be paid for religious inclusiveness? For religious exclusiveness?

Study materials by *Baruch Frydman-Kohl*

WAR AND PEACE

Michael Graetz

Summary

In this essay, Rabbi Graetz makes it clear that even though war plays a major role in biblical literature and was a familiar reality of the biblical world, the Bible has no single view of war. "The primary justification" for war is "to eradicate evil." At times, this evil is identified among Israel's enemies; at times among Israelite wrongdoers. Rabbi Graetz identifies two views of war. According to one view, God wages war unilaterally, in order to bend humans to God's will. In an alternate view, God enters into partnership with human forces in the conduct of war, and both "partners" may hold the other morally accountable for the conduct of war.

Although God may achieve goals through warfare, war is generally depicted as undesirable. The war pitting four kings against five, in which Abraham commands a personal combatant force, "stresses the venal nature of war." Living and leading a congregation near Beer-sheba, Israel, Rabbi Graetz points out that the name of that city means "well of oath"—referring to the ideal of peaceful coexistence promised Abraham by God. The Rabbis understood the scriptural requirement that "your camp be holy" as a call for ethical behavior, particularly in the conduct of military affairs.

"The theme of peace as God's ultimate goal is reaffirmed in the Prophets and Writings." Prophets sharply criticize the cruelty of war. Chronicles, with which the Hebrew Bible concludes, "contains a constant criticism of the brutality of war." King David, who virtually embodies Israelite sovereignty, is not allowed to construct God's Temple. His history of war and bloodshed are deemed inconsistent with "bringing God's presence closer to humanity"—the manifest goal of the Temple. That task is reserved for Solomon—whose name means "Peace."

Issues of war and peace play major parts in the biblical narrative: in the historical books, as background to the prophetic books, in the laws, and in biblical theology. There is no one view of war in the Bible, rather there are various views. I shall confine myself largely to the Torah, but shall touch on other parts of the Bible and on Rabbinic Judaism. Both of these bodies of literature are influenced by the laws and instances of war in the Torah.

GOD AT WAR

The polytheistic myths of the ancient Near East take strife and war as inherent parts of nature. Polytheism explains the strife and animosity that exist in the world by assuming that gods are at war, or that the state of war or struggle is part of nature. Indeed, some biblical scholars explore how the themes of strife between gods are sublimated into oblique references in the biblical text (e. g., texts dealing with the creation of the universe).

In the Bible, it is clear that God is capable of waging war—and is indeed portrayed as a warrior in the Exodus story. The Ten Plagues and particularly the slaying of the firstborn are acts of war against Egypt (Exod. 13:14–15). Having unilateral power, God imposes His will on evildoers, and humans play no active part in this war. Only those who accepted God's sovereignty and are willing to submit to His power by sacrificing the paschal lamb are protected by God and removed from the war zone. However, some scholars view the paschal sacrifice as expressing another, different, view of war. This view claims that God's power is expressed in partnership with humans, and thus humans and God can be allies in war. I will return to this view shortly.

The defeat of Egypt's army and chariots at the Sea of Reeds is an act of war. The first time that the image of God as a warrior unequivocally appears is in the punishment of the Egyptians at the Sea of Reeds (perhaps because the Egyptians are soldiers). The Torah specifically tells us that God leads the people in the Exodus away from settled areas, lest they encounter war and return to Egypt (Exod. 13:17). From this verse, it is clear that the Israelites are not prepared to fight a war, even though the next verse tells us that they were armed with weapons when they left Egypt (13:18). Moses, indeed, tells the people that God will "battle for you" (14:14) against the Egyptian army.

In the Song of the Sea, God is thus portrayed as a warrior, fighting against the Egyptians (15:3). The phrase *ish milḥamah* describes God's power in destroying the Egyptians; it is also found in five other biblical verses, each of which refers to a soldier or warrior (Josh. 17:1; Judg. 20:17; 1 Sam. 17:33; 2 Sam. 17:8; Ezek. 39:20). Indeed, the messenger of God to Joshua appears as a soldier with drawn sword and proclaims that he is a general in God's army (Josh. 5:13–14). God exerts power over Pharaoh in a sort of conquest. God brings plagues against Pharaoh, and this leads to an ironic fulfillment of Pharaoh's own prediction that if a war occurs, Israel will join Egypt's enemies and fight against it to leave the land (Exod. 1:10). Indeed, Pharaoh has unwittingly predicted the future: Israel does join Egypt's enemy, God, and so becomes God's partner in His war against Egypt.

Pharaoh's prediction is alluded to in a double entendre in Exod. 14:31. Israel has seen God's hand (*yad*) in the fate of the Egyptians, and as a result they believe in God and in Moses. The word *yad* also means "sign" or "portent" in biblical Hebrew, thus indicating that God's fighting for Israel is both a sign of God's might and the culmination of the portent of Pharaoh's own mouth.

The core of the Exodus narrative, namely the plagues that culminate in the killing of the firstborn and the destruction of Pharaoh and the Egyptian army at the Sea of Reeds, portrays God's power as a kind that bends evildoers to the divine will by waging war against them. Hence, both Egypt and Israel seem to be nothing more than objects under the control of God's will. Indeed, Moses tells the Israelites at the sea: "The LORD will battle for you; you hold your peace" (Exod. 14:14). This clearly expresses the first view discussed above.

Yet there are passages in these chapters that express the second view. These passages exhibit a different view of God's power—that it is relational, an expression of partnership. In this view, Israel must take some action to be part of the battle against Pharaoh. The Israelites are to perform a ritual sacrifice, the paschal lamb, whose purpose is to protect them from the slaying of the firstborn (Exod. 12: 3–13). It is clear that in doing this they act in partnership with God in the war against Egypt. Furthermore, this action of Israel also displays properties of an act of faith, because it is a kind of self-selection or volunteering to be part of God's ally force.

At the sea—despite the view expressed in Exod. 14:14—God tells the Israelites that they must enter the sea before He uses His control over natural forces to destroy the Egyptians. Indeed, God seems upset at Moses' passivity. God says: "Why do you cry out to Me? Tell the Israelites to go forward" (14:15). These verses indicate a role for the Israelites in God's battle plan. Indeed, they seem to indicate that Israel needs to use its ability to fight wars to further God's plans for its salvation. It is ambiguous here whether this ability is God given or learned. Still, it becomes a given in the Torah that Israel must fight and that God's plan of salvation for Israel includes its being an active partner in destroying its enemies in battle. Indeed, the whole goal of the Exodus, namely establishing a sovereign kingdom under God's leadership in the land of Israel, can be achieved only by Israel creating an army.

HUMANS AT WAR

God does not seem to be much involved in the instances of war in the ancestral stories of Genesis. The first clear instance of a war in the Torah is the story of a battle of four kings against five kings in the Abraham narrative (Gen. 14). In this story, Abraham has men in his camp whom he can call on at a moment's notice to form an army; and he sets out to restore his nephew Lot, who has been taken captive in the war between the kings. This whole episode stresses the venal nature of war. It is about control of land, money, and people. Abraham, who had willingly divided the land with his nephew (13:8 ff.), aids the side of the Sodomites, because Lot is a captive from their side. He refuses, however, to take any spoils from the war or any captives. He does not want anyone to think that his wealth came from war (14:23), yet he does allow his partners, who helped him, to take their spoils. Another instance of war in Genesis is the example of Simeon and Levi, who trick the people of Shechem and are able to take the town (34). This is a type of war move that relies on "tricks," somewhat akin to the Trojan Horse. On the one hand, this story is a precursor of the later tales, as well as the laws concerning the conquest of the land of Israel by Joshua.

On the other hand, it is a story that is repudiated by other parts of the patriarchal narratives (49:5–7).

In the Exodus story, as we have seen, God does it all. Human involvement in this war is next to nothing. Surprisingly, the next instance of war comes shortly after the Israelites have crossed the Sea of Reeds. They are free of the Egyptians and can seemingly breathe easily in the barren desert on their way to the Promised Land. There are not too many people around to bother them, and they purposely avoid population centers so that they will not have to go to war. But then they are attacked by Amalek—a fierce desert tribe of bandits, whose whole life is built around robbing and killing. They are forced to fight. After the experience of the Sea of Reeds, where they witnessed God's power, they now have to experience war directly. We can thus discern a transition of views—from merely implied participation by God in the wars of the ancestral stories, to God being the only warrior in Egypt and at the sea, to an open partnership between God and humans in the wilderness and conquest of the Land stories.

Joshua is chosen to pick men to go out and fight (Exod. 17:9). But the people are still tied to the notion of God fighting for them, so Moses ascends a hill overlooking the battlefield and raises his hands to heaven. His hands become heavy; and whenever they fall, the Israelites lose the battle and when they are raised, they win. The solution is to prop up his hands. Here we see graphically the transference of part of the power and ability to make war from God to the nation. Formerly, God's hand did the work of war; and now it is Moses' hands, but it is also the hands of the soldiers whom Joshua chose. In the end, Israel is commanded to carry on a war against Amalek in each generation (17:16). It is an example of a holy mission against those who wish to rule over others by force. In this view, God's ability to carry out war against evildoers is, in some sense, transferred to humans. (For other instances of battles that combine God's acting as a warrior on behalf of Israel's warriors see Josh. 6:4–5 and 2 Chron. 20:27–29.) At the same time, the partnership model suggests God's willingness to absorb influence from human participation.

Other instances of war have to do with the punishment of evildoers in the midst of Israel itself. After the people made the Golden Calf,

Moses asks the tribe of Levi to kill everyone who took part in that re-volt against the LORD and the authority of Moses (Exod. 32:25–28). This incident demonstrates that, although war is a divine instrument that can help punish evil forces, it can be applied universally even to the Israelites themselves. That is, war can be justified when waged against evil, even in the camp of Israel itself and not just against foreign nations. There are other instances of this internal warfare, some of them being on par with the defeat of the Egyptians at the Sea of Reeds. For example, God fights against Korah and his group by causing the earth to swallow them up, almost a replay of the sea swallowing up the Egyptians (Num. 16 ff.).

Other instances of war in the Torah are waged against foreign nations as part of Israel's approach to the Promised Land. In all of these cases, God is part of the equation, and there is justification of the battles be-cause those nations, like Amalek, did evil to Israel or behaved immorally toward Israel (e. g., Num. 21:1–3,33–35). The Israelites even offer a vow to God, saying that if the Canaanites are delivered to them in war, they will proscribe their towns (21:2 ff.). Proscription or ban (*ḥeirem*) is part of Israel's ongoing effort to achieve a kind of ideal purity.

In the retelling of the battle against Og in Deut. 3:6–7, the vow of the Israelites is not mentioned. Victory and occupation are attributed to God alone (2:30–35). All of the people are killed under the law of proscription (see Lev. 27:28–29; Deut. 20:16–18), but booty is kept, which is not mentioned in Numbers. In Deut. 7, another rationale for the ban is spelled out, namely, that the existence of these peoples will lead to intermarriage, which will cause syncretism, resulting in aban-donment of God and the adopting of the idolatry and evil practices of the Canaanites (Deut. 2–8).

The justification for these wars is strengthened in Deut. 12:31 in the statement that the abhorrent acts of the Canaanites include the sacrifice of children in fire. The war against Israelites who lead the people astray after foreign gods is reformulated once again (13:2–19) and includes Is-raelite prophets or dreamers who preach disloyalty to God. These people are in the category of evil that is not to be tolerated in Israelite society and can be removed by force. This passage does demand a thorough in-vestigation of the allegations; but if the facts are established, there is to be no mercy shown and all are to be killed. This passage includes the possibility that a whole Israelite town may be placed under the ban (*ḥeirem*) if all of its inhabitants subvert the nation to idolatry (13:13 ff.).

The *ḥeirem* is a sweeping kind of "justification" for war and killing. It is put into the context of punishment for evil and in the context of Israel, or more properly, Israel's legitimate rulers, being partners of God in punishing evil, i. e., making war on them or executing them. The principle is to be applied to evildoers equally, whether foreign or Israelite.

ḤEIREM: THE BAN

Even though the ban is a central part of war in the Torah, the circumstances of applying the *ḥeirem* are unclear. As to male soldiers, one consistent rule applies: All are to be slain. But there is confusion about the women and children. Indeed, the very notion of having to wage a war of proscription (ban) against "all" inhabitants of Canaan is far from clear. Further lack of clarity will be apparent in the next section, when we consider the ambiguities surrounding the laws concerning women captives.

In Deut. 20 the whole notion of *ḥeirem* is made even more ambiguous by the statement that "when you approach a town to attack it, you shall offer it terms of peace" (20:10). If the town responds peaceably, its inhabitants are spared and made into laborers. This injunction seems to be, at the very least, a compromise with the command to destroy every town in Canaan and all of its men, women, and children—and, at the most, a direct contradiction. Indeed, the Midrash attributes this innovation to Moses (see Deut. R. 5:13), with God accepting his idea! Here the biblical texts that present the relational view of God's power—that Israel is a partner with God, and that each side absorbs influences from the other—are carried to their logical conclusion. Not only is Israel a partner with God but a human can also be an initiator of a law. In this case, God's command to first try the road of peace and to adopt war as a last resort is instigated by Israel's leader. God, according to this *midrash*, willingly accepts Moses' decree.

If, however, the town responds with war, then the ban is applied— i. e., all males are to be killed, but "You may, however, take as your booty the women, the children, the livestock, and everything in the town—all its spoil—and enjoy the use of the spoil of your enemy, which the LORD your God gives you" (20:14). Here there seems to be no distinction, even by hint, between women who have had sexual experience and those who have not (see below).

We are informed that this rule applies only to towns that are not part of the Canaanite nations. Because they are the ones that can lead Israel astray, they must be proscribed, and not a soul shall remain alive, including women and children. Presumably, this is part of the view that justifies the *ḥeirem,* because of the evil that the inhabitants of Canaan would do to Israel. But this view is undermined by the events of Josh. 9. The Gibeonites trick Israel into thinking that they are from a town far away and that they want peace. Up to this point, Joshua has enforced the ban as written (in Jericho and Ai; Josh. 6–8). According to the law of the ban, Joshua should kill all the Gibeonites, because they are residents of Canaan to whom the laws of the *ḥeirem* apply. It is true that he has already made peace with them, but there is no moral or legal reason for him to keep the agreement, because it was procured under false pretenses. On the other hand, there is a clear legal reason for him not to keep the agreement, namely, that is the law! Yet, Joshua decides to honor the agreement, and this signals a change in policy. From then on, in the Book of Joshua, the ban is not applied in an all-encompassing manner. A *midrash* explains this by interpreting the law of *ḥeirem* as applied by Joshua in a way that follows the law of Deut. 20 (Lev. R. 17:6). Indeed, this *midrash* assumes options not mentioned in the Torah, namely exile, or exchange for other land. By adding details and options to the application of *ḥeirem* by Joshua, it makes clear that war is not considered optimal.

So, ironically, within the ban literature itself, a way to make peace is hinted at, and it is this hint that is seized on and used by Joshua for his policy toward the Canaanites. Assuming that the laws in the Torah are meant for a theoretical situation, their actual implementation went not in the direction of war and total destruction but rather toward peace and accommodation. The implication seems to be that war is not an end in itself, but at best a means to the attainment of some other end.

How are we to understand the ban? In my view, the ban passages represent an attempt to think of war solely in terms of God's unilateral power and overall control. This kind of wishful thinking might have been popular at times when Israel was in fact powerless or weak and felt threatened by outside enemies. Unilateralism spawns the claim that the impetus for both war and the *ḥeirem* is a command of God, and that Israel is only "following God's will." Some thinkers view these passages as showing that, for the Torah, war is neutral—and whether a particular war is good or bad depends solely on whether it conforms to God's will. But the ethical weakness of the unilateral model is that its answer to the question of justification is facile.

Meanwhile, other passages make it clear that killing defiles—and that no partaking in war can be viewed as praiseworthy; rather it demands purification and atonement. These passages view God's power in the partnership model, for which moral questions are part and parcel of war. Here, both God and humans have mutual responsibility to justify any war. As has been shown, in biblical and, more strongly, in Rabbinic texts, either side of the partnership can initiate war and check-and-balance the other side. The partnership view cannot adopt an oversimple justification of war. Although it is also concerned with conforming to God's will, those adhering to it cannot merely say, "This war is God's will," because then the question must be raised, "Does the human partner agree to this decision?" In the partnership model, the human cannot appeal to powerlessness or the virtue of obedience as an argument for avoiding moral responsibility.

LAWS

Laws are central to the Torah, and there are laws concerning war and peace. These laws cover rules about armies, captives, booty, army bases, and the war that will be fought against the Canaanite peoples. These laws apply to different stages of war. Rabbinic literature introduces two basic terms to distinguish between wars, terms that are not found in the Bible: *"milḥemet r'shut"* (a war of discretion) and *"milḥemet mitzvah"* (a war of obligation) (M Sot. 8:7). In that same *mishnah*, Judah employs the terms *"milḥemet mitzvah"* and *"milḥemet ḥovah,"* respectively.

Maimonides uses the first set of terms exclusively and does not refer to Judah's usage at all. This confusion in terminology resounds throughout Rabbinic literature. However, it is also made clear that some wars are obligatory; because, like the war against the Canaanites or against Amalek, they are commanded, whereas others are discretionary, like David's wars to expand Israel's borders (MT Kings 5:1 ff.).

Numbers 31 is a major source for laws about war and soldiers; it includes rules about conscription of soldiers into an army. It is specified that the campaign is led by a priest, who takes sacred utensils and trumpets that serve as means of relaying messages to the troops and serve as instruments of victory. There are rules about how booty and captives are to be treated. In this narrative, the soldiers had slain every male but brought back all females and children as captives. Moses is angry when the expedition brings back all of the captives and booty of the war. He points out that the females were used to entice Israel to foreign gods (see Num. 25:1–2). Thus he instructs them to kill every woman who has had carnal relationships with men, and all the boys (who would otherwise grow up to be soldiers). Only women who have had no sexual experience are spared. Every soldier who had killed others or who had been in contact with the slain has to undergo ritual purification and bring a purification offering. It seems as if participating in a war and killing others, although justified by divine command, could nevertheless be viewed as "impure." There are also rules for dividing up the spoils of the booty. It should be noted that priests (who did not take part in the war) and those who stayed behind also received part of the spoils.

Other passages in the Torah contain different formulations of these same laws. For example, in Deut. 21:10–14, the law does not state that the spared women must be virgins as specified in Num. 31:18. The wording of the law in Deuteronomy makes the desire of the male the operative function. It assumes that the desire for this beautiful woman is to make her a wife (as polygamy is the norm). However, the Torah demands that she be made less beautiful by trimming her hair, etc., and that she be given a month to mourn her slain parents (hinting that an unmarried woman lived with her parents, as was the biblical custom). This woman cannot be enslaved, but is treated as a wife; and if the man tires of her, she must be divorced as a wife. In Num. 31 women captives seem to be on a par with booty, but the formulation in Deuteronomy attributes clear social status to women captives.

Another formulation for conscription exists. In Deut. 20:1–9 we find an exhortation to soldiers to be fearless. This general order has a specific ceremony of induction for soldiers and a specific list of reasons for exemption, at least for a year. Exemptions include the person who has built a new house and has not dedicated it, and one who has planted a new vineyard and has not had the first harvest, and the newlywed who has not yet lived with his wife. The list of exemptions is ceremonially read to those gathered for induction to the army. The closing reason for exemption ties up to the general beginning. Those who are faint of heart and afraid of battle may return home, because they may cause general weakness in the morale of the other soldiers. In Rabbinic literature these rules are thought to apply only to a nonobligatory war (*milḥemet r'shut*), whereas in an obligatory war (*milḥemet mitzvah*) even the bridegroom and bride must leave their bridal canopy to take part in the war (e. g., M Sot. 8:7).

Another law concerning war has to do with destruction of property during a battle. The Torah rules that when setting up a siege against a city, the army should not cut down fruit-bearing trees to build a siege camp. Only trees that are clearly not fruit bearing may be used for that purpose (Deut. 20:19–20). Although the context of this rule is the *ḥeirem,* the connection between this rule and the *ḥeirem* is not clear. Furthermore, there seems to be some tension between the two verses themselves. However one solves the exegetical problems, the rule itself seems to contain an unusual sensitivity to preventing wanton destruction.

Another set of rules has to do with the army camp or base itself. Deut. 23:10–15 states: "When you go out as a troop against your enemies, be on your guard against anything untoward. . . . Since the LORD your God moves about in your camp to protect you and to deliver your enemies to you, let your camp be holy." In the biblical context, these rules have to do with ritual purity and with hygiene and cleanliness. That is, the biblical laws of war include a section that emphasizes the importance of purity in any army camp, both religious purity and hygiene, such as the provision for keeping excrement outside of the camp and keeping it covered (23:13–14).

In the Talmud, this verse is cited in discussions of what is appropriate in terms of the performance of bodily functions in proximity to sacred space or sacred things (BT Ber. 25a, Shab. 23a,150a). This discussion thus preserves the original context of the verses, while widening the scope to places that are not necessarily an army camp. In the Midrash, the idea of a "holy camp" is widened to include the notion that the encampment of Israel at war must display general ethical behavior at all times (Lev. R. 24:7; Num. R. 2:4).

INSTANCES OF PEACE

Making peace—a formal cessation of war—occurs many times in the Torah. Abram, after the war between the kings, proposes peaceful relations with the king of Sodom. Even more central to the Torah narrative is the peace treaty between Abraham (and his descendants) and the Philistine king Abimelech (and his descendants) at Beer-sheba. Armed combat over rights to water is the background to many of the patriarchal stories. The fact that Abraham and Abimelech swear an oath to each other to share water and refrain from warring against each other, for all generations, is a striking contrast to the idea that Israel must conquer the land by exterminating all of the inhabitants. Indeed, the name of the place Beer-sheba means the "well of oath," and the oath referred to is the one for peaceful coexistence in the land that God had promised to Abraham (Gen. 21:22–34, esp. v. 31; see also 12:7 ff.).

Isaac also makes a covenant of cessation of war with Abimelech, after an incident of filling up wells (26:26–33). Apparently the pact made by Abraham was not holding up and so had to be renewed. Jacob seems to be interested in making such a covenant of peaceful relations with Shechem, but this intention is thwarted by his sons Simeon and Levi. This is made clear by Jacob's reaction to their deeds (34:30) and even more clearly by his final words on this subject (49:5–7). Jacob also intends to have peaceful relations with his brother, Esau (33:3–11).

God also insists that Israel is not to make war against the descendants of Lot, for God has given them directly the land they occupy

(Deut. 2:19 ff.). Israel is to refrain from war with any polity that treats them honorably and civilly. Since the primary justification is to eradicate evil, presumably, all of these cases concern nations that cannot be described as "evil" and war against them cannot be justified. The same principle can be applied internally. For instance, when the Israelite tribes of Reuben, Gad, and Manasseh seek to settle east of the Jordan (Num. 32), they appear at first to be abdicating their responsibility for participating in the war of conquest of the Land. This is presented as tantamount to blasphemy against God. Once it is clear that their intention is not to shirk their duties as soldiers, they are spared punishment (see also Josh. 22).

PEACE IN THE PROPHETS, WRITINGS, AND RABBINIC LITERATURE

The theme of peace as God's ultimate goal is reaffirmed in the Prophets and Writings of the Bible; and it finds expression in Rabbinic literature, examples of which were discussed above. It is fair to say that in the later books of the Bible, peace is seen as a major expression both of God's power and will (e. g., Isa. 2:1–4, 11:6, 45:7; Job 25:2; Micah 4:1–5), and justice seems to replace war as the major expression of God's power (e. g., Pss. 96, 98).

Prophets denounce war because of the cruel excesses that it brings about. The first two chapters of Amos criticize the brutality of war in a very direct way; and in some sense, Amos's words are a literary heir of the criticism of Simeon and Levi's actions (Gen. 34) by Jacob in Gen. 49. Both Isaiah (2:1–4) and Micah (4:1–5) envision a day when nations will abandon the making of war and turn the implements of war into productive vessels. This is considered by them to be the essence of God's Torah, the Torah that all the nations come to Zion to learn. This Torah of helping one another produce full lives for citizens of the world seems to be a contradiction to the idea of God at war in the earlier biblical works. Indeed, this aspect of these prophecies is the most striking. God's power is not used to subdue others but is used to eliminate the desire to make war. Indeed, Micah can even imagine that the worship of God is not the issue separating nations at all, for in his words (4:5):

Though all the peoples walk
Each in the names of its gods,
We will walk
In the name of the LORD our God.

Perhaps of all the books of the Bible, Chronicles contains a constant criticism of the brutality of war, and of war as a means to approach God. And even though it is seemingly a history paralleling Joshua through Kings, Chronicles hardly contains Canaan conquest stories at all. The peak of its critique is found toward the end of 1 Chronicles, where David (the ideal king of Israel in the books of Kings) is told specifically by God: "You have shed much blood and fought great battles; you shall not build a House for My name for you have shed much blood on the earth in My sight" (22:8). The task of building a house for God cannot be fulfilled by someone who has waged war almost his whole life. Bloodshed is antithetical to bringing God's presence closer to humankind. War, rather than promoting God's plan, ends up opposing it.

Thus later Judaism condemned war as a goal in favor of peace. War of self-defense is justified in Jewish religion, but war as a means of diplomacy or for any reason other than self-defense is to be resisted and very much limited, as seen above (M Sot. 8 ff.; MT Kings 5 ff.).

In conclusion, war is part of the biblical conception of God's power. It is fair to say that peace is also part of that same conception. Although later Jewish sources did not directly deal with such matters, it seems clear that the tendency was to interpret war as part of a relational view of God's power and to praise peace as the goal of God's plan of salvation.

Biblical theology does not present a univocal view of God's power and of war. One view is that God has unilateral power and wages war to bend humans to His will. In that view, God can command war, and humans have no choice but to carry out the commands. Thus carrying out such a war is morally sound, and no questions can possibly be raised about it.

The other view, which becomes stronger in the later biblical books and in Rabbinic Judaism, is that God's power is expressed through equal partnership with humans, with mutual influence. In that view, each side may raise moral questions about a given war at any time. Thus even if a war is justified, actually killing another person is not an act that should be praised excessively, and peace is preferable to war as the final expression of God's redemption.

Study Questions

1. What justifications for war does Graetz identify in the Bible?

2. How is God's conflict with Pharaoh, culminating in the Exodus (a crucial core of the Torah's narrative) portrayed as a war? What special moral challenges or obligations grow from the centrality of war to this founding of the Israelite nation?

3. What constitutes the "evil" that war is intended to "eradicate?" How do we distinguish what we believe to be evil from cultural differences? How do we determine the purity of our motives in going to war?

4. What is *ḥeirem* warfare? What are its limitations? How do today's ethics of war compare to the practice of *ḥeirem* warfare? How do we, as modern Jews, relate to this element of our past?

5. How can we (and how does Graetz) reconcile the Torah's statement that "God is a Man of War" with the Bible's preference for peace? Why was King David penalized for being a "man of war" if the Temple was to be built to honor a God described in the same way?

6. How do the biblical views of war—and the actual wars described in the Bible—relate to the experience of the modern State of Israel? In what ways might Graetz's role as an Israeli have influenced his essay?

7. Do the different views of war in the Bible make Scripture a more (or less) suitable resource for today's religious, moral, and national leaders?

Study materials by *Joseph H. Prouser*

Biblical Foundations: Prayer and Ritual Mitzvot

BIBLICAL PRAYER

Reuven Hammer

Summary

Reuven Hammer traces the development of prayer in the biblical period starting with the idea of sacrifice. Israelite sacrifice differed from pagan sacrifice in two main ways. God, unlike the pagan deities, did not require sacrifice for food, and so could not be controlled through the use of sacrifices. Furthermore, the Israelites conducted their sacrifices in near total silence in order to make it clear that no magic was being done. Hammer argues that this silence opened the door to a unique invention of ancient Judaism—personal, verbal prayer. Because prayer was not connected to ritual sacrifice, it could become varied and spontaneous, an expression of a personal connection to God. In the Torah, personal prayer, though devoid of ritual or fixed verbal formulas, does fall into the basic categories of later Rabbinic prayer: petition, praise, and thanksgiving. Although the Torah contains only one extended example of a formal, literary prayer (Song of the Sea), in the "First Prophets" spontaneity starts to give way to more of these poetic prayers. At the same time, the emphasis in prayer shifts away from sacrifice toward verbal prayer. Many of these prayers, especially psalms that were used in more ritual circumstances, began to be composed "professionally" (rather than by the person offering the prayer). Still, the Prophets themselves continued to use spontaneous prayer to intercede with God on behalf of the people. After the biblical period, the forms of prayer used in the Bible, as well as the wording of those prayers, were adapted by Judaism into the system of fixed prayers.

One of biblical Judaism's most important gifts to the world is personal prayer—prayer that is spontaneous, informal, and independent of sacrifices or magical rites. Such prayer was not to be found in the ancient world from which the Bible emerged. Pagan worship consisted of sacrificial rites tied to magical utterances, formulas that the participants believed would yield desirable results automatically. Such rites were performed for the benefit of the deities, not only for the benefit of human beings.

These pagan deities were believed to depend on humanity for food and drink; they were subject to forces outside themselves. This is not true for the God of Israel. Underlying biblical prayer is the Torah's concept of God as above nature, uncontrolled by other forces (including fate), and requiring neither physical gifts nor metaphysical aid to exist. In spite of its cultic significance, sacrifice in Israel became a means for human beings to express themselves and relate to God. In the Mesopotamian flood epic, the gods are described as anxiously waiting for the flood to be over so that humans can once again supply them with sacrificial food. "The gods smelled the pleasing odor. The gods crowded like flies about the sacrificer." All that remains of this in our flood story is the enigmatic phrase, "The LORD smelled the pleasing odor" (Gen. 8:21). If the will of God is supreme, sacrifices at most can be a method of persuading God of the sincerity of human intentions and thus bring about His acceptance of human desires.

Ritual sacrifices were offered in the sanctuary in the wilderness. Yet the Torah prescribes virtually no prayers, blessings, or verbal formulas for recitation during the sacrificial ritual—something unheard of in the pagan world—thus leading some scholars to speak of the sanctuary as "a realm of silence." The confession of sin on *Yom Kippur* (Lev. 16:21) constitutes an exception. When an individual is required to confess wrongdoing before bringing an offering (Lev. 5:5), it is not clear whether or not this is part of the sacrificial ritual. A verbal recitation of the history of Israel was made when presenting the first fruits (Deut. 26:4–10). The only words given priests to recite are those of the Priestly Blessing (Num. 6:22–26). They were uttered in the Temple but only after the ritual had been completed; thus they were not connected with the ritual. As Yehezkel Kaufmann pointed out, all of this can be explained as an indication of a desire to divorce sacrifices from the magic verbal formulas so common elsewhere. Eventually, however, probably after the

Temple had been established in Jerusalem, silence was overcome in ways that did not negate the original intent of avoiding pagan practices. The levitical singers filled the Temple with song. The pilgrims chanted their psalms there. Individuals came to pray, and at various occasions prayer gatherings were held within its precincts (Jer. 7). None of this, however, was linked to the sacrifices.

Verbal forms of worship developed at the same time that sacrificial rituals were practiced. Prayers became the sacrifices of our lips; sacrifices became nonverbal prayers. Neither was considered acceptable if the individual was insincere or had violated the basic moral demands of the deity. Thus the prophets could denounce them both with equal vehemence:

> If you offer Me burnt offerings—or your
> > grain offerings—
> I will not accept them;
> …
> Spare Me the sound of your hymns,
> And let Me not hear the music of your lutes.
> But let justice well up like water,
> Righteousness like an unfailing stream. (Amos 5:22–24)

Indeed, because it was divorced from sacrifice, prayer was now free to become a spontaneous utterance, a way of relating to and communicating with the Almighty, praising, thanking, and blessing God, pleading with God and asking that He heed our words. Although prayer in the Torah is relatively brief and simply formulated, it contains all of the elements of later, more fully developed prayer.

PRAYER IN THE TORAH

The Sages may have been exaggerating and anachronistic when they ascribed the three daily prayers of Judaism (evening, morning, and afternoon) to the three patriarchs: "Abraham ordained the morning prayer … Isaac ordained the afternoon prayer … Jacob ordained the evening prayer" (BT Ber. 26b). They were not wrong, however, in linking the origins of even later Rabbinic prayer to the stories of the patriarchs and of Moses. Their prayers fall into three categories: petition, praise, and thanksgiving, and confession and forgiveness.

In the case of Abraham himself, we find little that we would identify as prayer, because Abraham and God speak in open dialogue. It is the language of prayer, however, when Abraham says of his son, "Oh that Ishmael might live by Your favor!" (Gen. 17:18). His servant, who has less free access to God, utters a petition in Gen. 24:12–14. After he addresses God specifically as "O LORD, God of my master Abraham," he states his request, beginning "grant me good fortune this day." When his petition has been granted, he expresses his thanksgiving, "Blessed be the LORD, the God of my master Abraham, who has not withheld His steadfast kindness from my master" (Gen. 24:27). The use of the word "blessed" (*barukh*) is taken from expressions in which someone is said to be worthy of God's blessing—as in Melchizedek's blessing of Abraham: "Blessed be Abram of God Most High" (Gen. 14:19), which is followed by the proclamation "And blessed be God Most High" (v. 20). Although, as Greenberg has pointed out, *"barukh"* is not exactly appropriate when used in reference to God (as only God can bestow blessing), it came to be the most common expression of Jewish prayer, indicating our proclamation of God's greatness and our thankfulness to God. In Rabbinic times it became the basic formula of prayer, "Blessed are You, O LORD" (*Barukh Attah Adonai*). This is presaged in one late biblical passage: "Blessed are You, O LORD, God of Israel our father, from eternity to eternity" (1 Chron. 29:10).

We are told that "Isaac pleaded with the LORD on behalf of his wife because she was barren; and the LORD responded to his plea" (Gen. 25:21), but we are not given the words of his prayer. Later, Isaac blesses his son Jacob when mistaking him for Esau in another petitionary prayer, "May God give you of the dew of heaven" (Gen. 27:28). Note that none of these prayers is accompanied by a sacrifice.

Jacob prays when he leaves his home, asking for God's protection and help during his exile. Later he offers a more humble prayer expressing thanksgiving: "O God of my father Abraham and God of my father Isaac, O LORD ... I am unworthy of all the kindness that You have so steadfastly shown Your servant. ... Deliver me, I pray, from the hand of my brother" (Gen. 32:10–13). Note the similarity to the prayer of Abraham's servant, especially the way in which God is addressed.

The Book of Exodus is replete with prayer and references to prayer. The Israelites cry out because of their bondage (Exod. 2:23). The Sages remarked that "cry" always refers to prayer (Sifrei Deut. 26). Moses also speaks to God in the language of complaint, "O LORD, why did You bring harm upon this people" (Exod. 5:22–23). This questioning of God became a characteristic theme of the prophets and of the psalms (Pss. 10, 13). Particularly revealing of the Bible's understanding of the function of prayer is the incident of Miriam stricken with leprosy as a punishment by God. Moses prays for her in what the Sages called the shortest of all prayers—five Hebrew words: "O God, pray heal her!" (Num. 12:13). Moses does not perform any ritual action but simply implores God's help. And God remains free to answer his plea or not.

Prayers of confession and forgiveness are exemplified in the pleas of Moses on behalf of the people: "Stiff-necked though this people be, pardon our iniquity and our sin, and take us for Your own" (Exod. 34:9). "Pardon, I pray, the iniquity of this people according to Your great kindness, as You have forgiven this people ever since Egypt" (Num. 14:19).

The Torah has one magnificent example of formal, poetic prayer, which served as a pattern for other prayers thereafter: the Song of the Sea (Exod. 15:1–19). Quite different from other prayers in the Torah, it is unique in its formal literary structure. Most scholars believe it to be a later work stemming from the period of the kingdom (10th century B.C.E. or later).

This magnificent hymn of salvation served throughout the ages as the archetype of prayers of thanksgiving.

In summation, the prayers of the Torah are basically brief, spontaneous utterances of praise, petition, or thanksgiving, couched in simple language and devoid of ritual elements.

PRAYER IN THE PROPHETS

The historical books that form the section known as "First Prophets" continue the informal prayer found in the Torah. David confesses his sin in language much like that used by Moses in confessing the sin of the Israelites, "I have sinned grievously in what I have done. Please, O LORD, remit the guilt of Your servant, for I have acted foolishly" (2 Sam. 24:10). When attempting to revive a dead child, Elisha "prayed to the LORD" (2 Kings 4:33), probably much as Moses did for Miriam. Samson asks for strength using the petition formula of the Torah, "O LORD GOD! Please remember me, and give me strength just this once, O God" (Judg. 16:28). Hannah's vow (1 Sam. 1:11) is similar to that of Jacob. As a general rule, prayer in the books of early prophets is more highly developed than prayer commonly found in the Torah. The art of prayer developed greatly during the 10th century B.C.E., and this is reflected in these books. It is no longer the spontaneous outpouring of the heart, but rather the sophisticated literary expression of human feelings, needs, and desires. Consider Hannah's prayer of thanksgiving as an example. It is hardly that of a simple woman:

> My heart exults in the LORD;
> I have triumphed through the LORD.
> I gloat over my enemies;
> I rejoice in Your deliverance (1 Sam. 2:1).

As in the Torah's Song of the Sea, it seems probable that a literary psalm has been inserted here for dramatic effect. What a contrast it is to her simple petition: "O LORD of Hosts, if You will look upon the suffering of Your maidservant and will remember me and not forget your maidservant, and if you will grant Your maidservant a male child, I will dedicate him to the LORD for all the days of his life; and no razor shall ever touch his head" (1 Sam. 1:11). The further description of her prayer—"Now Hannah was praying in her heart; only her lips moved, but her voice could not be heard" (1 Sam. 1:13)—so impressed the Sages that they took it as the example of how all of us should pray (BT Ber. 31a–b).

Another example of literary expression is Solomon's prayer at the dedication of the First Temple. Although we cannot be certain that this is what Solomon actually said, we may assume that it reflects the attitudes common during the period of the First Temple. If we are hard pressed to find in the Torah a mention of prayer within the sanctuary, here we find prayer—not sacrifice—emphasized as the main activity of the Temple. Solomon emphasizes the words of prayer with little attention to sacrifice. A few lines from his long prayer (1 Kings 8:23–53) will suffice to indicate its tenor.

> Yet turn, O LORD, my God, to the prayer and supplication of your servant. ... May Your eyes be open day and night toward this House ... may You heed the prayers which Your servant will offer toward this place. And when You hear the supplications which Your servant and Your people Israel offer toward this place, give heed in Your heavenly abode—give heed and pardon (1 Kings 8:28–30).

Interestingly enough, this plea for God to hear prayers and supplications of Israel uttered in and toward this House is followed by a not insignificant offering of 22,000 oxen and 120,000 sheep! (v. 63). What is God's response? "I have heard the prayer and the supplication which you have offered to Me" (1 Kings 9:3). Not a word about the sacrificial offering.

Just as the later prophets could speak about the sacrifices as less significant, so here too they are a subsidiary issue. Yes, sacrifice was an integral part of Israel's worship. Israel could not do without it, but God certainly does not need it.

David, in opposition to all accumulated Israelite tradition, had conceived the idea of creating a permanent house for God, as opposed to the nomadic tent of the *mishkan*. King Solomon carried this out. The dedication of this Temple was seen as the capstone of the new order, as God's approval of the change and His choosing of David's line: David's city and now Solomon's Temple.

But what about the form of worship? Did Solomon bring about a change in what went on in the central shrine? That is a difficult question to answer with utter certitude—perhaps impossible—but it seems very likely that he did. As we have seen, to Solomon, the house was more important for prayer than for sacrifice. True, he follows the Torah's instructions. He does not introduce prayer into the sacrificial service itself. However, he does emphasize the singing of psalms to accompany pilgrims (Ps. 122), to greet them (Ps. 134), and to serve as hymns in the

Temple at the great gatherings for thanksgiving (Ps. 118) or at times of trouble (Ps. 115). Here too he may have followed the lead of his father who, according to 1 Chron. 16:7, had commissioned the writings of general psalms for recitation in the new tabernacle. The Torah makes no mention of singing or composition in the descriptions of the duties of the Levites, but David is said to have appointed a group of them "to invoke, to praise, and to extol the God of Israel ... with harps and lyres" (1 Chron. 16:4–5).

It seems quite likely then, that the development of "professional" prayer—of literary as opposed to spontaneous prayer utterance—was prompted by the institution of the Jerusalem Temple, and that such literary prayers as the Song of the Sea and Hannah's prayer also stem from that time.

No wonder the prophet of the exile, Isaiah, could bestow upon the Temple that was to be rebuilt the title "house of prayer for all people" (Isa. 56:7). Solomon's contribution was to ensure that prayer became the focus. The Temple of the LORD—the Temple of silence—became the House of Prayer.

Prayer plays a major role in the lives and words of the prophets who lived during this period of the kingdom. Following the example of the father of prophecy, Moses, they pray to God on behalf of the people, interceding with Him on its behalf. They go far beyond that, however, and use spontaneous prayer as their own method of communication with God. They complain to God, and ask Him to relieve them from their tasks. Jeremiah provides clear examples of this: "Ah, LORD GOD! Surely You have deceived this people and Jerusalem, saying: It shall be well with you—yet the sword threatens the very life!" (Jer. 4:10). The prophets' role as intermediary for the people is clear from God's message warning Jeremiah, "do not pray for this people, do not raise a cry of prayer on their behalf; for I will not listen when they call to Me on account of their disaster" (11:14). Daringly, Jeremiah challenges God, "You will win, O LORD, if I make claim against You, yet I shall present charges against you: Why does the way of the wicked prosper? Why are the workers of treachery at ease?" (12:1). See also his complaint in 15:15–18, including the brazen "You have been to me like a spring that fails, like waters that cannot be relied on." He asks God for help against his enemies in 18:19–23 in language strongly reminiscent of passages from Psalms.

THE BOOK OF PSALMS

The Sages ascribed the authorship of the Book of Psalms to David (BT BB 14b). They did not mean by this, however, that he wrote all 150 of them. Indeed, in the same passage they acknowledge that David included psalms written by others. Many psalms seem to have been composed by professional writers assigned to provide psalms for the Temple choirs. Scholars are divided over the dates of the psalms. All would agree that the vast majority stem from the time of the First Temple (ca. 960 B.C.E.) and reflect the practices of that period. In a sense, Psalms is the first Israelite prayer book. Unlike later prayer books, however, it lacks texts prescribed for specific services of prayer. With a few exceptions, the psalms are not intended for recitation at specific occasions. There seems little doubt that some of them were written for historical events now lost to memory. Some may have been written to accompany specific rituals. Many believe that Pss. 93 and 97, for example, were written for the New Year. The psalms are presented as a collection of prayer and meditation that can be used in a variety of moods and situations by individuals and by the community. Many of them, such as Pss. 95–99, 113–118, 145–150, have been incorporated into the liturgy. As models for prayer, they express cries from the heart and whispers from the soul.

The psalms reflect three major modes of prayer: thankful acknowledgment (*hodu*), blessing (*bar'khu*), and praise (*hall'lu*). An examples of *hodu* can be seen in Ps. 136. When celebrating great victories or recalling wondrous deeds of the past, the people Israel used these formulas to thank and acknowledge God. The use of *bar'khu* can be seen in Ps. 135, proclaiming God's greatness and faithfulness to the people Israel. The *hall'lu* form can be seen in Pss. 148 and 150. These are songs of ecstatic praise, driven by powerful emotion.

Jewish prayer, as it developed during the Second Temple period and after its destruction (200 B.C.E.–200 C.E.), used the insights of biblical prayer, its various forms, and its terminology. Almost every prayer is built of biblical phrases. Large sections of the service consist of passages from Psalms and other sections of the Bible. Most of all, Jewish worship—as well as that of Judaism's daughter religions—has been shaped by two biblical insights: that prayer and sacrifice are independent, and that prayer can be uttered by anyone, at any time, and in any place. As the Sages taught, prayer is "service of the heart" (BT Taan. 2a).

Biblical prayer transformed what had been stilted and stylized ritual utterances into a method of communication in which all human beings can freely voice their deepest emotions before God. Though He may be "enthroned on high" (Ps. 113:5), God listens to the words of His creatures on Earth.

Study Questions

1. In what ways are sacrifices like verbal prayers and in what ways are they different? How did the two forms of worship complement one another in the biblical period?

2. Why does Greenberg think the term *barukh* does not make sense when referring to God? Can you think of other ways to understand the use of this term in our blessings?

3. What are the advantages and disadvantages of spontaneous personal prayer as opposed to formal prayer with a fixed text?

4. Locate one of the examples of prayer mentioned by Hammer (such as Hannah's in 1 Samuel, or Jacob's in Gen. 32:10–13). What sort of prayer is it? Is it highly literary or more spontaneous? Does it remind you of any prayers in our siddur (prayer book)?

Study materials by *Jacob Pinnolis*

SHABBAT AND THE HOLIDAYS

Joel Roth

Summary

The Sabbath, festivals, and High Holy Days are ancient institutions, which, over the course of Jewish history, have undergone an extensive evolution. In this essay, Rabbi Roth demonstrates how the dates, the central themes, the locus of celebration, and even the very names of these holidays have shifted in response to changing historical circumstances and needs.

Shabbat, for example, is distinguished as the only holiday observance mentioned among the Ten Commandments. However, while the version of the Decalogue in the Book of Exodus relates the Sabbath to Creation, Deuteronomy bases the Fourth Commandment on the Exodus from Egypt, emphasizing the social rather than the theological value of the Day of Rest. Both versions emphasize the preeminent sanctity of *Shabbat* and its expression through the prohibition of *m'lakhah*—constructive acts forbidden on the Sabbath. Roth points out how these acts are later defined extensively by the rabbis.

In the Torah, the descriptions of the three holidays of *Pesaḥ, Shavuot*, and *Sukkot*—collectively termed "pilgrimage festivals"—are "the pieces of a puzzle" that are "probably impossible to complete with certainty." Just as the Rabbis provided a thoroughly detailed guide to forbidden acts of *m'lakhah*, Roth emphasizes that Rabbinic literature crystallized the pilgrimage festivals into a coherent system.

The High Holy Days are given scant attention in Scripture. As Roth points out, "The Torah knows of no holiday called *Rosh ha-Shanah*." Nevertheless, these observances have become high points of the liturgical year, with a hold on the Jewish communal imagination disproportionate to their modest biblical origins. Observance of the High Holy Days in the seventh month (of the biblical calendar) actually reprises the centrality of the Sabbath, the uniquely sanctified seventh day—a day of heightened sanctity and spiritual focus.

SHABBAT

Shabbat is a unique institution in the Torah. All other holidays and festivals, among the Israelites and other ancient peoples, are linked to cycles of the moon or to the seasons of the sun's movement. Only *Shabbat,* as many scholars have noted, is completely severed from such a linkage. In Gen. 2:1–3, *Shabbat* is the culmination of Creation, marking God's rest from creative work. If Creation establishes God's supremacy over space, *Shabbat* establishes God's supremacy over time. Between the two, the essence of biblical theology is established: God is entirely free from any constraints of nature. God is the sovereign of space and time, and *Shabbat* is the symbol of that divine transcendence.

The Exodus version of the Decalogue (Exod. 20:8–11) links *Shabbat* directly to Creation. Israel is commanded to rest because God rested. The connection between *Shabbat* and Creation is also found explicitly in Exod. 31:16–17 and seems most consonant with Lev. 23:3. The Deuteronomic version of the Decalogue (Deut. 5:12–15), on the other hand, while retaining the prohibition against *m'lakhah,* predicates it on the liberation from Egypt. This version's emphasis seems to be far more ethically oriented than that of Exodus, which focuses on the sanctity of the day itself rather than on its social value. The two emphases are not mutually exclusive, although it is admittedly somewhat difficult to see the connection between the view of Deuteronomy and the holiness of *Shabbat,* which is its essence, according to both versions of the Decalogue.

The prohibition against *m'lakhah* stands at the core of *Shabbat.* Yet the Torah gives no definition of *m'lakhah.* Several activities are forbidden in the Torah and the rest of the Bible: gathering from the field (Num. 15:32–36), traveling (Exod. 16:29–30), kindling fire (Exod. 35:2–3), doing business and carrying (Isa. 58:13, Jer. 17:22, Amos 8:5), agricultural activity (Exod. 34:21), treading in winepresses, and loading animals (Neh. 13:15–18). However, there is no definitive list or definition. Not surprisingly, in subsequent eras much time has been devoted to clarifying this central factor of *Shabbat* observance.

The Talmud defines 39 basic categories of forbidden activity, called *avot m'lakhah.* All *Shabbat* prohibitions are included within these *avot.* Each one of them (*av*) has derivative prohibitions, called *toladot.* The

Sages themselves promulgated additional prohibitions called *sh'vut,* which are designed to prevent inadvertent violation of *avot* and *toladot* and to protect the spirit of *Shabbat* rest. The Talmud deduces these basic categories from the activities involved in the construction of the tabernacle, which are delineated in Exod. 35 in close proximity to the commandment to observe *Shabbat.* But even the Talmud does not provide an abstract definition of the concept of *m'lakhah.*

Nonetheless, there is near unanimity among modern scholars that *m'lakhah* is correctly defined as: "A constructive human act, initiated on the Sabbath, demonstrating supremacy over nature." Advocates of this definition include S. R. Hirsch, M. M. Kaplan, and A. J. Heschel. It is a reasonable thesis that makes sense of *Shabbat* prohibitions as they are delineated in the Talmud and the post-talmudic codes and responsa. Even more, it is supported by the biblical account of Gen. 1 and 2, in which God's work of creation is defined as *m'lakhah* (2:2–3). The definition encapsulates the rationale underlying *Shabbat* prohibitions: Humans desist from controlling nature on *Shabbat* to give concrete expression to their recognition that human mastery over nature and human creative abilities are divine gifts. Knowledge of the definition allows the details of *Shabbat* prohibitions to be seen and understood in better perspective.

Shabbat observance has been perceived as a source of pleasure and delight since the biblical period. Isaiah especially calls it a day of delight (Isa. 58:13). For the Sages, *Shabbat* is a precious gift (BT Betz. 16a) and its observance is a taste of the world to come (BT Ber. 57b). If all Jews would observe one *Shabbat* as it ought to be observed, the Messiah would come (Exod. R. 25:12). It becomes the focus of the week's attention, and full appreciation of it is truly possible only for those who observe it (BT Shab. 119a).

It was Ahad ha-Am who said that more than the Jews have preserved *Shabbat* observance, *Shabbat* has preserved the Jews. His words remain true.

THE HOLIDAYS

The Pilgrimage Festivals

The holidays known best as *Pesah, Shavuot,* and *Sukkot* are the pilgrimage festivals on which, by law of the Torah, one was obligated to present oneself at God's shrine. They are called *shalosh r'galim* in Hebrew.

The Torah lists the cycle of annual holidays in several places: Exod. 23:12–19, 34:18–23; Lev. 23; Num. 28–29; and Deut. 16. Some of them are more complete than others. *Pesaḥ* is also mentioned in Exod. 13:6–8. The details of these various listings constitute the pieces to a puzzle; and it is difficult, probably impossible, to complete the puzzle with certainty.

Some facts, though, are clearer than others. The holidays that are called *ḥag* in the Torah are pilgrimage festivals. In Exodus, the pilgrimages are as follows:

- *Ḥag ha-matzot:* festival of the unleavened bread (in Exod. 12:14, Lev. 23:6, and Num. 28:17, only the first day is a pilgrimage day; in Exod. 13:6, it is the last day that is the pilgrimage; and in Ezra 6:22, all seven days are pilgrimage days).
- *Ḥag ha-katzir:* festival of the reaping of harvest (although in Exod. 34:22 this holiday is called *ḥag shavu·ot,* the festival of weeks).
- *Ḥag ha-asif:* festival of the ingathering.

Exodus does not give specific dates for these festivals. Rather, the first is defined as being "at the set time in the month of Abib." Perhaps the phrase should be translated as "at the advent of the new moon of the season of soft-seeded grain ears." That timing is linked to the fact that Israel had been redeemed from Egypt in that season. The second is defined as occurring at the time of the harvest of "the first fruits of your work" (Exod. 23:16) and at the time of the "first fruits of the harvest of the wheat" (34:22). (Do these define each other? Does the latter define the former? A puzzle!) And the third is defined as occurring "at the end of the year, when you gather all of your work in from the field."

Leviticus 23 distinguishes between *Pesaḥ,* which occurs on the 14th of the first month, and *ḥag ha-matzot,* which begins on the 15th. The second holiday of Exodus is not named at all in Leviticus. Rather, it mandates a counting period of 50 days, at the conclusion of which an offering of new grain (wheat) is brought. This holiday is not called a *ḥag* in Leviticus, implying that no pilgrimage to the shrine was necessary. In Leviticus, the third pilgrimage of Exodus is called *ḥag ha-sukkot* (the festival of the booths), which lasts for 7 days, beginning on the 15th of the seventh month and culminating in a final (8th) day called *atzeret* (concluding assembly).

The Book of Numbers presents the distinction between *Pesaḥ* and the *ḥag ha-matzot*. The first occurs on the 14th of the seventh month and the second begins on the 15th with that day a pilgrimage. The second holiday is called *yom ha-bikkurim* (day of first fruits), which is defined as "your Feast of Weeks." However, like Leviticus, Numbers does not declare it a pilgrimage and defines the third pilgrimage as a nameless festival that lasts 7 days, beginning on the 15th day of the seventh month and culminating on an 8th day on which an *atzeret* (solemn assembly) is to take place.

Deuteronomy 16 does not distinguish clearly between *Pesaḥ* and the Feast of the Unleavened Bread. Instead it seems to combine the two together, stating in verse 1 that the people should "offer a Passover sacrifice," yet calling the pilgrimage by the name *ḥag ha-matzot* in verse 16. The second pilgrimage is called *ḥag (ha-)shavu·ot* by Deuteronomy and is defined as occurring after a count of "seven weeks from the time the sickle is first put to the standing grain." The third pilgrimage, called *ḥag ha-sukkot,* is celebrated for seven days "after the ingathering from your threshing floor and your vat." Regarding each of the three pilgrimages, Deuteronomy emphasizes that the celebration of the festival must take place "in the place where the LORD will choose to establish His name."

Of the three pilgrimage festivals, *Pesaḥ* is most clearly a historical holiday. Exod. 23:15 specifically links its observance with the Exodus: "You shall observe the Feast of unleavened bread . . . for it was then that you went out of Egypt." None of the listings of the holidays in the Torah calls this pilgrimage by any name that is linked to agricultural matters. Indeed, it would be difficult to do so, because *Pesaḥ* occurs just before the ripening of the grain in the spring. Yet, *Pesaḥ* appears in all of the listings in the Torah, even those that exclude the holidays now called *Rosh ha-Shanah* and *Yom Kippur,* and its inclusion in those lists indicates that it was also an agricultural holiday. One must say, therefore, that it had an agricultural element to serve as a counterpoint to *Sukkot. Pesaḥ* was the pilgrimage that preceded the harvest, and *Sukkot* was the pilgrimage that followed the end of the harvest.

Ginsberg hypothesized that the festival of the unleavened bread was originally celebrated at the time of the new moon of *Nisan,* just before the hardening of the barley. (This hypothesis is summarized by Baruch Levine in his commentary to Leviticus.) It was a seven-day festival, with the pilgrimage occurring on the seventh day. A separate sacrifice, the *pesaḥ* offering, was to take place near the home of each person on the eve of the first day of the festival. The second pilgrimage festival, originally known exclusively as *ḥag ha-katzir,* the pilgrimage of the reaping, was observed as a one-day pilgrimage on the full moon of the month of ingathering, *Tishrei* (September). All of these observances are predicated on the possibility of making the required pilgrimage to a shrine near home. Deuteronomy, with its newly ordained requirement to observe all pilgrimages in one central shrine, made the earlier calendar of festival observances difficult and impractical, if not impossible. Changes had to be made to accommodate the new requirement. The second pilgrimage could no longer take place at the beginning of the harvest because no one could afford to be away from the fields for the length of time needed to make a pilgrimage to the central shrine. So the festival was moved by seven weeks, from the beginning of the harvest to its end. The name of the pilgrimage was changed from *ḥag ha-katzir* (pilgrimage of reaping), which was no longer appropriate, to *ḥag ha-shavu·ot* (pilgrimage of weeks), marked by a period of counting of those weeks. The third pilgrimage was also moved so that it would not occur too close to the second. It is no longer called *ḥag ha-asif* (the pilgrimage of ingathering), because it now takes place after the produce has been processed. Its name is changed to *ḥag ha-sukkot* (the pilgrimage of booths). That name refers to the booths set up to accommodate the pilgrims who now ascend to the central shrine in a pilgrimage that has been extended to seven days, from its original one day.

By far the greatest changes necessitated by the Deuteronomic mandate occur in the celebration of *Pesaḥ* and the pilgrimage of *matzot.* Originally, the *pesaḥ* offering was made near one's home on the eve of the festival, and the actual pilgrimage to a shrine took place on the seventh day of the festival. This had become an impossible arrangement. The *pesaḥ* could now be offered only at the central shrine, and another pilgrimage offering was required seven days later at the same central shrine. People would have to arrive before the *pesaḥ* offering day and remain for the entire seven days, because there might well not be time to travel back and forth to home in that short span of time. So Deuteronomy mandates that the *pesaḥ* offering be made immediately before the onset of the pilgrimage of unleavened bread—serving also as the pilgrimage offering. And the pilgrimage now takes place on the first day of the festival instead of on the last day. After that first day, people can go home, although the requirement to refrain from eating leavened bread continues for an additional six days.

As *Pesaḥ* has no clear agricultural component in the Torah, *Shavu·ot* has no clear historical component in the Torah. Nonetheless, since Second Temple days, it carries a historical dimension as well, as the festival commemorating the revelation at Sinai—*z'man mattan torateinu,* the time of the giving of our Torah. This attribution is based on the dating of that revelation, intimated by Exodus 19, and seems to reflect an ancient tradition with echoes in 2 Chron. 15:10–13 and in some of the sectarian literature. Through this act, *Shavu·ot* acquires a historical dimension to accompany its agricultural dimension. The period of counting the seven weeks between *Pesaḥ* and *Shavu·ot* becomes not merely the counting of the period of the harvest, but the counting of the period between our liberation from Egyptian bondage to the beginning of nationhood through the act of revelation.

Deuteronomy and Leviticus call the third pilgrimage festival *ḥag ha-sukkot.* Deuteronomy gives no explanation of the name (although Ginsberg's explanation for it was offered above). Leviticus, however, does offer an explanation, stating in 23:42–43 that we are to dwell in booths for these seven days to remember that God "made the Israelite people live in booths when [God] brought them out of the land of Egypt." The explanation of Leviticus is replete with difficulties, not least of which is that the Israelites lived in tents during the wandering in the wilderness. The most likely explanation of the name is that the Torah is here imbuing with historical significance the practice of living in booths during the period of gathering in the grapes and fruits. It thus makes the third pilgrimage parallel to the other two pilgrimages in having both an agricultural and a historical significance.

Whatever the problems of putting together the pieces of the puzzle of the pilgrimage festivals in the Bible, the Rabbinic-halakhic tradition leveled the field. It made the festivals into a coherent system that incorporated the demands and the explanations of all the biblical passages. In addition to the names I have already referred to for the holidays, the Rabbinic tradition also refers to *Pesah* as *zman heruteinu*, the period of our liberation, and to *Sukkot* as *zman simhateinu*, the time of our joy. For the Rabbinic tradition, *Shavu·ot*, which marks the giving of the Decalogue, becomes the culmination of *Pesah* and is known simply as *atzeret*, the concluding assembly. *Sukkot* is called simply *he-hag*, the holiday.

The High Holy Days

The Torah knows of no holiday called *Rosh ha-Shanah*, New Year's Day. It does ordain the first day of the seventh month (*Tishrei*) as a day on which the horn is to be sounded (Num. 29:1) or commemorated with blasts (Lev. 23:24). Jacob Milgrom noted that the choice of the new moon of the seventh month preserves the sabbatical cycle in the lunar calendar. Just as the seventh day is unique among days, the seventh new moon is unique among new moons. Neither of the biblical passages that mention this holiday explains the significance of the horn to be sounded. Most probably, it was to indicate the advent of the pilgrimage of *Sukkot*, which began exactly two weeks later. The day is defined as one of cessation from labor and for sacred assembly. But it is not a pilgrimage holiday.

Rabbinic tradition, reflecting the view that the world was created by God in the autumn, recasts this holiday as commemorating the world's creation and, more important, as a day when human beings are judged by God. The sounding of the *shofar* remains central to its observance but takes on a totally different significance. It becomes the impetus to self-reflection and repentance and a reminder to God of the test of Abraham's faith at the binding of Isaac, on the basis of which his descendants seek God's forgiveness. *Rosh ha-Shanah* inaugurates a period of 10 days, culminating in the final judgment of *Yom Kippur*.

Yom Kippur, the Day of Atonement, is mentioned in the festival listings of Leviticus and Numbers (although it is not called by that name in Numbers) and also at the end of Lev. 16. The latter chapter contains the detailed account of the purification ceremonies ordained for cleansing the sanctuary from the defilements of humans during the year (see vv. 16,19). The term *kippurim* refers to this cleansing and purging of the sanctuary. Leviticus 16:29–34 establishes the date of the purification as the 10th day of the seventh month and mandates that the purification ritual is to be accompanied by fasting and total cessation of labor. From Lev. 16 it is clear that the purification rites of *Yom Kippur* were a priestly matter, and that the people were not present at the sanctuary. That fact is sufficient to explain why neither Num. 29 nor Lev. 23 makes any mention of the purification rites of the sanctuary in their descriptions of the holiday that occurs on the 10th of the seventh month. Both include the requirements of fasting and refraining from all labor. Probably, the timing of purification of the sanctuary was intended to ensure that it was pure just before the advent of the masses of pilgrims on the 7-day pilgrimage that would follow in five days.

Rabbinic tradition, of course, personalized the atonement of the biblical holiday and made *Yom Kippur* into the culmination of a 10-day period of judgment by God of all human beings. Intimations of personal atonement can be read fairly easily into parts of Lev. 23. Thus the two nonpilgrimage holidays of the seventh month became in Rabbinic tradition, and in subsequent Jewish practice, the most personal of holidays, focused on individual responsibility for one's actions and for ultimate accountability before God's judgment.

Study Questions

1. Rabbi Roth asserts that it is "somewhat difficult to see the connection" between the holiness of *Shabbat* and Deuteronomy's linkage of the observance to the liberation from Egypt. How might the emphasis on the Exodus be understood as strengthening the sanctity of the Sabbath?

2. Traditional Sabbath observance is often maligned as archaic. Roth emphasizes "near unanimity among modern scholars" in defining *m'lakhah* as "a constructive human act, initiated on the Sabbath, demonstrating supremacy over nature." How could this

contribute to the renewed importance of *Shabbat*? How might we affect "increased knowledge of the definition," as called for by Roth?

3. How do the festivals and High Holy Days balance communal observances and the individual (or household) spiritual experience?

4. What makes the High Holy Days—in which Jewish communities assemble in unrivalled numbers—"the most personal of holidays?"

5. The dramatic changes in the history of holiday observances suggest that their modern celebrants do not merely preserve ancient rites, but bear responsibility for keeping *Shabbat* and the holidays relevant, meaningful, and practicable. How did our ancestors meet this dual responsibility? How has this process been continued in the 20th and 21st centuries? What steps might individual Jews, families, and congregations take to contribute to this effort?

6. How is the approach to the holidays presented in Roth's essay characteristic of the Conservative Movement's understanding of the development of Jewish law and practice?

Study materials by *Joseph H. Prouser*

DIETARY LAWS

Edward L. Greenstein

Summary

The food regulations and dietary prohibitions of the Torah are ways in which the Jewish people articulate their special relationship to God and reaffirm their unique sense of peoplehood. The seemingly mundane act of eating becomes a primary means of illustrating "our covenantal obligations to God" and our recognition of the sanctity of life. In this essay, Greenstein explores the variety of specific "ethical and theological commitments" expressed through the Bible's many dietary laws.

In the biblical view, the taking of animal life is, ideally, the exclusive purview of God. The moral compromise by which God permits human consumption of meat is prescribed in Israel's covenantal framework. Blood is forbidden and must be purged and discarded, or ritually "returned to God," the source of the life it symbolizes.

The original significance of the permitted and forbidden species enumerated in the Torah ("pure" and "tainted," as Greenstein renders the biblical terms) is "somewhat obscure" and elusive, and he reviews several possible explanations. He also emphasizes the connection between these laws and other major themes (creation, holiness, making distinctions) in the Torah.

The manifold meanings to be found in the dietary laws of the Torah, and the elaborate system that has evolved around them, indicate the central significance they have long played in the religious life of Israel. These laws, as Greenstein notes, continue to serve as reminders "of who we are and from whom we are descended."

Virtually all cultures contain rules that regulate eating. We do not always notice these rules because they tend to be only implicit, but these rules encode cultural meaning. The Torah has an abundance of specific guidelines concerning what must be eaten on certain occasions and, in particular, what must not be eaten. These regulations carry ethical, cultural, and/or theological significance.

FOODS FOR SPECIAL OCCASIONS

Judaism is rich in symbolic food traditions. Thus, for example, on *Shabbat* and on festivals we say a blessing over not one but two loaves of *hallah*, recalling the Torah's instruction to the Israelites to collect two portions of manna on Friday because it was forbidden to gather food on *Shabbat* (Exod. 16:29). On *Rosh ha-Shanah* we eat honey, praying for a sweet New Year; on *Hanukkah* we eat foods fried in oil, commemorating the miracle of the *m'norah* that burned eight nights on one night's measure of oil; on *Purim* we eat pastries that represent the three-cornered hat ascribed by tradition to Haman (Yiddish: *hamentashen*).

The model for attaching symbolic significance to food is set by the Torah in its laws of *Pesah*. The three foods that are central to the *Seider*—paschal lamb, *matzah,* and bitter herbs (*maror*)—may have their historical origins in the rites of spring among shepherds and farmers. In the Torah, however, and in the developing Jewish tradition, each of the three foods is connected with the *Pesah* story. The paschal lamb was eaten by the Israelites in Egypt as God "skipped" (Hebrew: *pasah*) over their homes when bringing the 10th plague (Exod. 12:13). As in many types of sacrifice, the animal's life substitutes for the offerer's life. Hence, the paschal lamb symbolizes the sparing of our lives. The *matzah* is bread baked on the run (12:34), symbolizing more narrowly the haste of the Exodus and more broadly the Exodus itself. The bitter herbs recall how the Egyptians embittered the lives of the Hebrew slaves (1:14).

Bearing in mind the Torah's tendency to attach symbolic meaning to food, let us turn now to the area of generally permissible and forbidden foods.

FOODS PERMITTED AND FORBIDDEN
ON ANY OCCASION

The Torah is distinguished from all other law collections of the ancient Near East in delineating an entire system of eating rules. Although the Torah is remarkably systematic in the two passages that present most of the dietary laws (Lev. 11; Deut. 14), a number of diverse eating rules are spread throughout the Torah. Jewish tradition refers to food that is "fit" for eating—*kasher*, "kosher"—and food that is unfit—*tareif*, literally, "torn by an animal" and not properly slaughtered. The Torah's own terminology, as we shall see, relates to ritual purity and holiness.

The Ban on the Thigh Tendon

The symbolic significance of the eating rules is most evident in the ban on eating the "thigh muscle," or tendon or nerve, that was injured in Jacob's struggle with the divine being (Gen. 32:33). Because all Jacob's immediate descendants are called literally, "those issuing from his thigh" (a euphemism for his genitals; Gen. 46:26; Exod. 1:5), the ban draws attention to the ongoing condition of Israel as a people: impaired but surviving. The impaired thigh tendon signifies the people Israel; and because of that symbolism, the Israelites and their descendants are not to eat the part of the animal with which they are taught to identify themselves. The eating rule reminds us of who we are and from whom we are descended.

Life Belongs to God

The most fundamental eating rules seem designed to instill the idea that life belongs to God and may be taken for food only after acknowledgment of that paramount fact. In the beginning, both humanity and other animal life are allowed only vegetation for food (Gen. 1:29–30). Domestic animals are appropriate offerings to God (4:4, 8:20) but are forbidden for human consumption. This is one of several ways the Torah teaches that humans may not take for themselves the prerogatives of God. When the boundary between God and humanity begins to break down, however, leading God to bring the great Flood (6:1 ff.), God at once liberalizes and specifies the eating rules. Humans may eat animal meat, but not with the life still in it and not before removing the blood, which represents life and, accordingly, belongs to God who created it (9:4). God regards the unauthorized taking of life by humans and by animals as a cardinal sin (9:5–6). Because blood is God's alone, it is the most sacred substance, the one the Torah prescribes for the most serious purification rituals.

The Ban on Eating Blood

The ban on eating blood is the most basic eating rule in the Torah, a notion expressed in diverse ways. First, an animal that dies naturally (*n'velah*) or at the hands of another beast (*t'refah*) may not be eaten, for its blood cannot be properly removed. Second, the blood of sacrificed animals must be either collected for purification rites or drained beside the altar. Third, the blood of an animal that is slaughtered for eating must be returned to God. Killing an animal is taking a life and may be done only by acknowledging the severity of taking an animal's life by doing it in God's way. Leviticus (17:6) has the blood dashed on the altar or, in the case of an animal killed in the hunt, poured onto the ground (17:13). Deuteronomy (12:16) would have the blood of all animals killed for food poured onto the ground.

In later Jewish tradition, hunting will be permitted only in the case of trapping an animal with the intention of preparing it for food. All animals must be ritually slaughtered. Removal of the blood remains the most important dietary rule. All kosher meat is drained of blood in the slaughterhouse and then soaked and salted after butchering. Broiling also fulfills the requirement.

A fourth way in which the Torah bans blood is in forbidding the consumption of all those animals that themselves ingest blood. This fact goes far in explaining which species of animal the Torah defines as edible and inedible (discussed further below).

Milk and Meat

Reverence for life is reflected as well in the prohibition against boiling a kid in its mother's milk. This law first appears in connection with the spring ritual (Exod. 23:19, 34:26). Maimonides sensibly supposes that boiling a kid in its mother's milk was a seasonal fertility practice that the Torah forbids. Israelites are not to copy the pagan ritual; they are to express appreciation of the spring's renewed fertility by presenting first fruits to God. But Deuteronomy (14:21) incorporates the prohibition against boiling the kid in milk into the regular eating rules. In that context, the prohibition takes on symbolic significance: Milk, which is meant to sustain life, may not be turned into a means of preparing an animal for eating. A clear distinction must be made between life, which is godly, and death. The postbiblical Jewish tradition underscores the distinction by broadening it: Not only milk, but all dairy products and the utensils used for serving them must be kept apart from meat products and utensils.

Permitted and Prohibited Species

Most of the Torah's dietary rules elaborate the species of animals that one may and may not eat. Edible animals are "pure" (*tahor,* often translated "clean") and inedible animals are "tainted" (*tamei,* often translated "unclean"). In general, things are pure when they signify life and conform to the way that God created the world, and things are tainted when they signify death and blur the distinctions God has established in nature.

Why the inedible animals were originally tabooed is somewhat obscure. Anthropologists have suggested diverse reasons. One reason was mentioned earlier: Predators among land animals and birds, who ingest blood, are forbidden. Also scavengers, like dogs, pigs, and mice, who pick up dead meat and refuse, are taboo. Many animals who travel close to the ground were also probably regarded as scavengers. Beasts of burden, like asses, horses, and camels, are not raised for food and tend not to be eaten. Nor are people inclined to eat animals resembling themselves, like those with paws rather than hooves. Pigs need a damp environment and favor the kinds of food that humans eat. Thus in addition to being scavengers, pigs actually compete for food with humans. It is, therefore, not surprising that archaeological research has shown pig raising to have diminished in the land of Israel in the biblical period, thriving mainly in certain Philistine cities.

The general observation can be made that most of the animals prohibited as food by the Torah are those that would not have been eaten by Israelites anyway. The same can be said for the Torah's ban on eating the hard fat that covers the entrails of many permitted animals. Though inedible, it is allocated to God. The fat when burned in a sacrifice makes heavy smoke, signifying the rise of the offering to God in heaven. As in the case of the fat, the Torah often legislates behavior that would be practiced ordinarily; but, as with the fat, it adds to such behavior a covenantal meaning. Keeping the dietary rules is not something we do for our own—practical or aesthetic—reasons. We do it as part of our covenantal obligations to God, symbolizing Godly values and sanctifying our lives.

Hallowing Our Lives

Most of the eating rules are detailed in a tightly organized form in Lev. 11, and they are repeated in a modified fashion in Deut. 14. One express purpose of the dietary system is to make us holy, like God (Lev. 11:45). As B'khor Shor put it: "It befits the Holy One that those who serve Him be holy, removed from the tainted, and pure." Originally, the special restrictions fell only on those who ministered to God in the sanctuaries—the priests and the Levites. Other individuals would take on the restrictions only to fulfill a vow or a sacred duty. Thus the parents of Samson were instructed by an angel to raise their son as a nazirite. In addition to not cutting his hair, he would have to abstain from intoxicating beverages and from tainted food (Judg. 13:4,14). Abstention from tainted, or impure, food is understood in that story as an extraordinary observance. Leviticus and Deuteronomy, however, address their dietary laws to all Israelites; thereby a process begins to evolve by which the holiness originally expected only of priests—and only in the sanctuary—falls on all members of the covenant community.

Especially following the destruction of the Jerusalem Temple in 70 c. e., rituals that were attached only to the priestly service were transformed by tradition to make them the province of all Jews. When the Temple service was discontinued, the table of every Jew was seen as an altar—a locale of divine–human encounter, where the Jew would enjoy and acknowledge God's blessing of food to eat. And, because the Temple sacrifices were salted, the meal is lent a sacred sense by salting the bread over which a blessing is recited.

Basically two principles give the Torah's eating rules their sense of purity. The first was discussed above: Animals that ingest blood or pick up carrion are tainted and, therefore, inedible. We are to associate life with the godly and death with the ungodly. The second principle is an appreciation of God's role as Creator and of the created world and a recognition of our limitations as creatures in that world.

Categories of Creation

The creation story in Genesis presents the acts of creation as a series of divisions—between light and dark, water above and water below, land and water, different species of vegetation, different species of animal, male and female, the six days of the work week and the holy *Shabbat*. The pattern of creation is reflected in the *Havdalah* (division) ceremony marking the transition from the holy *Shabbat* day to weekdays (discussed further below).

In creating animals, God divided them into four groups: fish, fowl, crawlers, and land animals. The animals are all associated with three domains in which they may live: water, sky, and land. The Torah, as the anthropologist Mary Douglas has shown, highlights God's creation of the world by classifying animals as edible and inedible according to how well each is suited to the domain in which it was placed in Creation. The Torah stipulates that animals that perfectly reflect the domain in which they live by moving about in it in the most appropriate fashion are pure, whereas those animals that move about in a manner that is inappropriate to their domain are tainted. The idea is that only creatures that are relatively perfect representatives of their kind are fit for eating. Just so, only priests who are fully sound may serve, only Israelites who are in a ritually pure state may enter the sanctuary, and only animals that have never been worked and have no blemish may be offered.

Accordingly, Leviticus, in defining the traits of pure and tainted animals, pays special attention to the limbs by which they move. Land animals, which are the ones who lived in the closest proximity to biblical Israel, are classified by two traits. They must chew their cud and have a proper hoof. They must walk and graze on the land. The dual requirement removes animals such as the pig, which does not chew its cud, and the camel, whose padded foot does not pass as a proper hoof, from the category of pure land creatures. Crawling and slithering creatures, which would not likely be eaten under any circumstances, are eliminated by the grazing requirements. The system of classification, therefore, explains those animals that the Israelites would ordinarily tend to eat or avoid eating in a theological fashion, tying the diet laws to an appreciation of Creation.

As for fish, they are meant ideally to swim in the water; pure fish must, therefore, possess fins and scales. Animals such as shellfish that live in the water but move about like land animals cross categories, so to speak, and do not set a model of the created order; they are tainted. Fowl are enumerated according to the species that are forbidden. Most of these prey on other animals or feed on carrion; others, like the ostrich, may walk on land more than fly. Although birds are not classified anatomically, insects are differentiated by whether their legs seem built more for jumping or walking. Jumping insects "fly" and so are edible. But walking insects are anomalous; their wings define them as creatures of the air, while their legs identify them with the land. (Rabbinic tradition suggests anatomical traits for birds, too: Those that are unfit are those whose claw seems made for grasping other animals [M Ḥul. 3:6].)

MAKING DISTINCTIONS

The system may appear artificial and arbitrary. But, as in setting a table, what is important is not so much how the system is organized but the fact that it is organized. The Torah has the community make distinctions, just as God did in creating the world. Observance of the eating rules shows not only an appreciation of God's creation; those who observe them practice a form of *imitatio dei* (Latin: "the imitation of God"), making the sorts of distinctions God makes. Following in God's footsteps, so to speak, conveys holiness, just as following God's lead in ceasing from work on *Shabbat* does.

It is nevertheless important to bear in mind that the distinctions that are observed are those made by God, just as the values by which the created world is to be cared for are God's. In this vein, Sforno interpreted the command to be holy: "Always acknowledge your Creator and walk in His ways." The dietary laws are explicitly meant to serve these functions.

Shoring Up Ethnic Identity

A passage in Lev. 20 adds yet another meaning to the eating rules. The Israelites are to "set apart the pure beast from the impure, the impure bird from the pure" because God has "set you apart from other peoples" (see vv. 22–26; cf. Deut. 14:2). The theme is evoked in the *Havdalah* ceremony mentioned above. Among its divisions between light and darkness and between the holy and the profane is the division between the people Israel and the other nations. The former are obligated to fulfill the covenantal duties; the latter are responsible for only the seven universal Noahide commandments, which include one law of eating: a prohibition against eating live flesh.

The notion that a people maintains its ethnic identity by eating differently appears first in the story of Joseph, when the Egyptians refuse to dine together with their Hebrew visitors (Gen. 43:32). In the late biblical period, the heroes of Jewish narrative display their loyalty to their religious tradition and to their people by observing the dietary laws. Thus the young Daniel in the Babylonian court "resolved not to defile himself with the king's food or the wine he drank"; he made do on a spare vegetarian diet (Dan. 1:8,12). The heroic Judith brought her own food so that she might dine with a Babylonian general (Judith 12:2). In the Maccabean period (ca. 165 B. C. E.) obedience to the dietary laws became a touchstone of Jewish loyalty. Thus, 2 Maccabees 6–7 relates two stories in a row in which the faithful—an old man named Eleazar, and the seven sons of an anonymous woman—refuse to eat pig meat on pain of torture and death and thereby choose martyrdom.

In the Christian scriptures, some early followers of Jesus still adhere to the dietary restrictions (Acts 10:9 ff.). But several texts abrogate the rules precisely because they tend to reinforce ethnic boundaries. Jesus is said to have argued that food cannot defile because it enters the belly, not the heart (Mark 7:18–19). A separation is assumed between the physical and the spiritual. The Torah takes a different view: The heart is entered through the belly as well as through other organs and limbs. That is, the spiritual in this world does not exist in the abstract; it is always concretized in what we say and do. The behaviors associated with eating may be expressed through the body; but the many meanings that are encoded within those behaviors are meant to act on and cultivate the ethical and spiritual dimensions of those who observe them. Eating may seem purely physical, but the questions of what is eaten and how one eats are entirely bound up in ethical and theological commitments.

Study Questions

1. Greenstein observes that "when the Temple service was discontinued, the table of every Jew was seen as an altar." What specific aspects of the dietary laws contribute to this "new" reality? What other religious observances reinforce this dynamic? How else is the Jewish home transformed into a sanctuary?

2. This essay emphasizes how kashrut elevates a mundane physical act into a concrete medium for expressing sacred values. How else does Jewish practice seek to sanctify the potentially profane? How does this approach to spirituality distinguish Judaism from other religious and cultural traditions?

3. In the course of his essay, Greenstein provides several justifications and opportunities for finding meaning associated with these laws. Which of these explanations speak most strongly to you?

4. The Bible seems to suggest vegetarianism as the ideal human condition. Do vegetarians achieve a "higher" form of kashrut?

5. To what extent is awareness of the meanings conveyed by the dietary laws essential to their fulfillment? If the practitioner of kashrut is already aware of its meanings, why are the rituals necessary?

6. Greenstein relates the dietary laws to the exclusionary Egyptian food taboo mentioned in Gen. 43:32 in conjunction with Joseph's reunion with his brothers. What are the limitations of this comparison? How does the strengthening of ethnic identity differ from encouraging insularity?

Study materials by *Joseph H. Prouser*

T'FILLIN AND M'ZUZOT

Jeffrey H. Tigay

Summary

In this essay, Jeffrey Tigay carefully reviews the biblical texts that serve as sources for the practice of wearing *t'fillin* (leather boxes containing texts from the Torah bound to the arm and head with leather straps) and affixing *m'zuzot* (containers with selected passages from the Torah that are affixed to a doorpost). He also provides comparable examples of these practices from surrounding contemporaneous cultures. He notes that the literary and historical evidence seems to indicate that the commandment to write words of Torah on one's doorposts was interpreted literally from earliest times. However, in ancient Israel there was debate as to whether the commandment to "bind them as a sign upon your hand and let them serve as a frontlet on your forehead" was meant literally (resulting in *t'fillin*) or as a metaphor. Through his historical analysis, Tigay reminds us that our own encounter with these ritual objects has ancient roots.

Before delving into Dr. Tigay's essay, read the passages he cites in the first paragraph of the essay: Exod. 13:1–16 and Deut. 6:8 and 11:18. While it is difficult to read these passages without assuming they refer to *t'fillin* as we know them today, try doing so with no assumptions in mind.

T'FILLIN

Exodus 13 contains the commands beginning with the words "And this shall serve you as a sign on your hand and as a reminder on your forehead ..." (13:9) and "it shall be as a sign on your hand and as a frontlet [i. e., headband—not "symbol" as in the translation] on your forehead ..." (13:16). Similar commands appear in Deuteronomy: "Bind them as a sign on your hand and let them serve as a frontlet on your forehead" (6:8, 11:18). At least since later Second Temple times (2nd century B. C. E.) and perhaps already in Deuteronomy (7th century B. C. E.), these verses have been understood to be a commandment

257

to wear objects that enable certain words of God to be fastened to the arm and the forehead. For this purpose, Jewish law adopted the expedient of having a scribe write the requisite words—passages from the Torah—on slips of parchment inserted in small leather capsules that the Sages called *t'fillin*. One capsule is fastened to the forehead, suspended from a leather headband knotted in the back of the head, with its loose ends hanging down like streamers, as in some of the headbands seen in ancient Near Eastern art. The other capsule is fastened to the upper arm by another leather strap.

Such capsules, in the form of amulets, were a common device in antiquity for attaching inscriptions to the body. The physical similarity of *t'fillin* to amulets was clear to the ancients. Two of the ancient terms for *t'fillin* (Hebrew: *kami·a;* Greek: *phylakterion,* or "phylactery") literally mean "amulet," and talmudic sources frequently mention *t'fillin* and amulets together and note the possibility of confusing them with each other. However, *t'fillin* resemble amulets only in their external form, not in their contents. They contain biblical passages about the Exodus and God's instructions and thus serve an educational purpose; amulets typically contain magical inscriptions, or materials, to protect the wearer from evil.

Initially, there was some disagreement about which biblical passages should be placed in the *t'fillin*. Since talmudic times, they have been limited to the four passages that contain the verses that serve as the basis for the practice of wearing *t'fillin:* Exod. 13:1–10 and 13:11–16 and Deut. 6:4–9 and 11:13–21. The *t'fillin* found with the Dead Sea Scrolls at Qumran included these passages as well as others, most notably the Decalogue. Josephus seems to imply that they contain texts that record God's benefactions, power, and goodwill.

The words "bind them" and especially "let them serve as a frontlet" (headband) may imply that the written texts were to be worn directly and visibly on the arm and forehead, instead of being placed in containers affixed to those spots. This would be similar to inscribed armbands known from Egypt and to the inscribed gems and frontlet worn by the Israelite high priest (Exod. 28:9–12,21,29,36–37). There is evidence that some Jews in talmudic times may have worn the texts this way; some of the Church Fathers quote reports that certain Jews wrapped the parchment strips around their heads like crowns. In any case, the *halakhah*, Jewish law, did not accept this interpretation but required that the texts be placed in containers.

In talmudic times, *t'fillin* were worn throughout the day on weekdays. Since the Middle Ages the practice has usually been to wear them only during weekday morning prayers.

The oldest *t'fillin* found by archaeologists have come from the caves of Qumran and antedate the destruction of that settlement in 70 C.E. Others were found among the remains of Bar Kokhba's forces (132–135 C.E.).

Not all Jews agreed that the biblical texts in question meant to ordain a concrete practice. Although the Pharisees, the Qumran sect, and other Jewish groups did agree, some of the ancient Greek translations of the Torah take the verses metaphorically to mean that God's teaching should be kept constantly in mind. The Samaritans also did not accept the precept of *t'fillin*. This suggests that before the Jewish–Samaritan schism the literal interpretation of the verses was not universally accepted. Similarly, the reference in the Mishnah to "whoever says 'there are no *t'fillin*'" (M Sanh. 11:3) must refer to a denial that the biblical verses have *t'fillin* in mind. The neglect of the precept reported in some talmudic passages may also reflect a rejection of the literal interpretation.

In the Middle Ages, the meaning of these verses was debated by Rabbanites and Karaites. The latter stressed a metaphoric interpretation—that God's commandments and teachings should be remembered well, as if they were bound to our bodies, like a string tied around the finger as a reminder. In favor of this interpretation, they cited similar Hebrew metaphors, including "binding" to the body for remembering teachings (Prov. 1:9, 3:3, 4:9, 6:21, 7:3). Most Rabbanite commentators rejected this argument on the grounds that analogies from Proverbs, which is explicitly metaphoric in style, have no bearing on the Torah, which is not metaphoric (Ibn Ezra on Exod. 13:9). Still, no less a Rabbanite authority than Rashbam conceded that the plain sense of the text is metaphoric, meaning "let it be remembered always, as if written on your hand," comparing it to a similar metaphor in Song 8:6.

The divergence of interpretations since Second Temple times may go back to different meanings in the biblical texts themselves. It seems that Exod. 13:9 and 13:16 used "sign," "memorial," and "headband" metaphorically, whereas Deut. 6:8 and 11:18 may have intended them literally. Consider that in Exod. 13:9 and 13:16 the grammatical subject of "shall be a sign on your hand and a memorial/headband on your forehead" cannot be the biblical passages themselves, for they are not mentioned. As metaphors these terms indicate that something is to be kept close at hand and remembered well. (For the metaphoric use of apparel and ornaments that are close or dear to their wearers, see the Proverbs passages cited above and Isa. 62:3; Jer. 2:32, 13:11, 22:24; Hag. 2:23; Job 29:14.) And the verb's subject must be either (a) the fact "that the LORD brought the Israelites out of Egypt" (Exod. 13:9b,16b); or (b) the grammatical antecedents of "shall be"—namely "this day" or "this practice" or the festival of unleavened bread (vv. 1–8,10) and the sacrifice/redemption of the first-born (vv. 11–16). What then must be remembered well? In the former case: the LORD's mighty deeds. In the latter case: this day and these rites—so that God's teaching will be remembered well. In neither case does "it shall be a sign" represent an observance beyond those mentioned in verses 2–8 and 12–15. ("This institution" in v. 10 refers to an annual practice, the eating of unleavened bread in vv. 3–8, not to a daily rite such as *t'fillin*.)

On the other hand, the injunction to "bind" these words in Deut. 6 and 11 seems to be meant literally. Here the reference is to words—which, unlike events and ceremonies, can literally be bound to the body; and the following command (to write these words on the doorposts and gates; Deut. 6:9, 11:20) suggests that something concrete is intended. It is true that even Proverbs speaks of binding teachings and commandments to one's body and refers to writing them on "the tablet of your heart [i.e., mind]" (Prov. 7:3). Writing words on the heart, however, is a known metaphor, while writing them on doorposts and gates is not; it is a concrete practice (see Deut. 6:9). Hence it is plausible that the accompanying injunction to bind God's words as a sign on the hand and as a band on the forehead is also meant literally. Thus, what began as a metaphor in Exod. 13 may have been interpreted or recast literally as early as the time of Deuteronomy.

At first glance it might seem surprising for Deuteronomy to give a literal, ceremonial interpretation to something that Exodus means metaphorically. Deuteronomy normally presents a more abstract approach to religion than do the other books of the Torah. The nature of

Deuteronomy's "abstractness," however, may help explain why it might have been the book to ordain the practice of wearing *t'fillin*. Deuteronomy's abstractness is aimed primarily at combating an overly anthropomorphic conception of God and sacrificial worship, and it must have had the effect of reducing the role of sacrifice in daily life, especially in the provinces. In its struggle against idolatry Deuteronomy even outlaws religious artifacts that once had been considered unobjectionable, such as sacred pillars and trees (16:21–22; note also its silence about the cherubim when describing the Ark in 10:1–9). But Deuteronomy does not indiscriminately oppose religious symbols per se. It ordains the precept of *m'zuzah* (6:9; discussed below), and it preserves the injunction to wear fringes on one's garments (22:12; cf. Num. 15:37–41). It opposes only symbols that were too anthropomorphic or that had actual or potential idolatrous associations. The Deuteronomic reformers may well have realized that their reformation would deplete an already small stock of religious symbols in Israelite religion. Concrete, visible symbols are important, and it may be that just as Deuteronomy advocated the precepts of fringes and *m'zuzah,* which serve as reminders of God's commandments, it advanced the precept of *t'fillin* for the same purpose. Given the current state of evidence, this suggestion is speculative, and whether the precept of *t'fillin* goes back to Deuteronomy or only to Second Temple times remains an open question.

M'ZUZOT

In contrast to the question of *t'fillin,* it is certain that Deut. 6:9 literally ordains the writing of God's teachings on doorposts and city gates. The verse was understood that way even by the Samaritans, who rejected the precept of *t'fillin,* and the practice is attested at Qumran and in literary sources of the late Second Temple period.

It was not unusual for inscriptions to be written on the doors, lintels, and doorposts of private houses. Inscriptions of various types have been found at the entrances to ancient Egyptian houses; and to this day invocations, proverbs, and verses from the Qur'an are commonly inscribed on or over doors in the Muslim world. No examples of this practice have been found in ancient Israelite houses, but inscriptions on the entrances to tombs, identifying those buried in them, suggest that writing on entrances was known in Israel. In the Sinai Peninsula, the sanctuary at Kuntilat'Ajrud had inscriptions of religious character written in Hebrew and Phoenician script on its walls and doorposts. In Mesopotamia, Syria, and Hatti, royal inscriptions celebrating the accomplishments of the kings and charters guaranteeing the privileges of certain cities were sometimes inscribed at city gates.

The closest parallel to what Deuteronomy prescribes—writing God's teachings on the doorposts and gates—is the ancient Egyptian practice of writing instructions at the entrances of temples, enumerating moral and cultic prerequisites for entering the temple. The prescription in Deuteronomy differs in that it is not stating prerequisites for entering the sanctuary but seeking to make people aware of God's teachings at all times and places.

The text in Deut. 6:9 implies that the words are to be written visibly on the doorposts and gates. This is what the Samaritans did, writing on the stone of the building or on stone slabs affixed to it. For an unknown reason, at some point in the late Second Temple period Jewish law modified this practice, ruling that the inscription was to be written on parchment, rolled up, and inserted in a case. The *m'zuzah* texts found at Qumran are of this type. The inscription is known as a *m'zuzah* (plural: *m'zuzot*), from the word for "doorpost" in Deut. 6:9. A *m'zuzah* case is affixed, with the top slanting inward, to the upper third of the right-hand doorpost at the entrance of the house and of each residential room in a house.

According to the *halakhah*, the texts to be written in the *m'zuzah* are the two passages that contain the commandment (Deut. 6:4–9, 11:13–21). As in the case of *t'fillin*, there originally was some variation in this practice. The *m'zuzah* texts from Qumran (if all of them are really *m'zuzot*) include these two passages, but some also include the Decalogue and Deut. 10:12–11:12; others include parts of Exod. 13, which is also contained in *t'fillin*. The Samaritan *m'zuzot* contain the Decalogue, and a few add the poem of the Ark from Num. 10:35–36.

Like many other religious objects, *m'zuzot* lent themselves to use as amulets. This use was facilitated by their location on doorposts and gates, which suggested that they could serve as amulets to protect the house or city within. No less a figure than R. Judah the Prince sent a *m'zuzah* to the Parthian king Ardavan, explaining that it would protect him. To enhance their use for this purpose, other names of God and the names of angels were sometimes added to *m'zuzot*. Maimonides forbade this practice, declaring that this not only disqualified the *m'zuzah* but turned the instrument of unifying God's name into a mere charm for personal benefit. He concisely summed up the intention of the precepts of *t'fillin* and *m'zuzah,* and of *tzitzit* (fringes), as follows:

> The ancient sages said, "Those who have *t'fillin* on their head and arm, *tzitzit* on their garment, and a *m'zuzah* on their door may be presumed not to sin," for they have many reminders—and these are the "angels" that save them from sinning, as it is said, "The angel of the LORD camps around those who revere Him and rescues them" (Ps. 34:8) (MT *T'fillin* and *M'zuzah* 6:13).

Study Questions

T'FILLIN

1. Go back and review Exod. 13:1–16 and Deut. 6:8 and 11:18. What do they suggest to you in their simplest meaning? What do you think the Torah is requiring? Do you see a difference between the Exodus and Deuteronomy texts? How would you characterize the difference?

2. How do you react to the idea that *t'fillin* were physically similar to ancient amulets used by other Near Eastern peoples to protect the wearer from evil? Can you think of any other Jewish ceremonies and rites that are similar to those of other cultures, but have been transformed by Jewish tradition to carry different meanings?

3. Note that the four passages that mention "sign on your arm and remembrance on your forehead" are those placed inside the *t'fillin* (Exod. 13:1–10 and 13:11–16; Deut. 6:4–9 and 11:13–21). Can you identify other common ideas or themes in these four texts?

4. Were you aware of other groups mentioned in the essay who interpreted these passages quite differently, such as the Samaritans or

Karaites (you might find resources to explore these groups further)? What makes the rabbinic interpretations more authoritative?

5. Dr. Tigay makes a strong distinction between the Exodus sources and those in Deuteronomy. In doing so, he hints at the fact that he believes, as do most biblical scholars, that Deuteronomy represents a later scroll, dating from the time of King Josiah in the 6th century B.C.E., in the land of Judah. The Exodus sources are drawn from an earlier period, probably about 1200–1100 B.C.E. How does this compare with ideas explored in the essays in the section on Revelation in this volume?

M'ZUZOT

1. If Tigay is sure that Deut. 6:9 involves the actual inscribing of words on the doorposts (m'zuzot) of one's house and the community's gates, does it help you to decide if the commandment about t'fillin is meant as an actual inscription or as a "reminder"?

2. Look at the passage in Exod. 12:1–13. Tigay mentions the inscriptions found on the entrances to Egyptian homes and temples. In light of this fact, how do you think the smearing of the blood on the doorposts—m'zuzot—was understood by the Egyptians at the time of the slaying of the first born? What feelings would this sight arouse in them?

3. Examine the various biblical passages that the Samaritans and Qumran sects put in their m'zuzot. Why might these groups have added these particular passages? What picture of the development of law and practice in the early centuries of Rabbinic Judaism does such variation give you?

4. The next-to-last paragraph of the essay points to the fact that historically, in the popular view, the m'zuzah was seen as an amulet, protecting the home from evil. The last paragraph points to an alternate view of the m'zuzah and its purpose. Which of these two views has the most meaning to you personally? Which would you teach to your children? To teenagers? To adults? Why?

Study materials by *Sheldon Dorph*

TZITZIT (TASSELS)

Jacob Milgrom

Summary

Jacob Milgrom introduces *tzitzit*, or ritual fringes on the four corners of a garment known as a *tallit*, in the context of ancient Near Eastern costume, law, and ritual. Milgrom indicates that men and women in the ancient Near East declared their identity, power, and social status through the embroidery on the hems of their garments. *Tzizit* (fringes that hang from the corners of a garment) are essentially hem tassels, an ornament worn by the aristocracy of ancient Near Eastern society. Important people would sign documents by pressing their hems into clay tablets, and a husband could divorce his wife by cutting off her hem.

Biblically, the *tzitzit* required a thread of a shade of blue known as *t'kheilet*. Milgrom points out that the blue dye necessary for this color was expensive, and was the symbol of a noble costume. Only after the blue dye became scarce did the rabbis suspend the requirement of *t'kheilet*. *Tzitzit* also symbolized the priesthood: the Talmud requires the *tallit* garment to contain *sha'atnez*, a combination of wool and linen, which is forbidden by biblical law except for priestly garments. In the Rabbinic period, *tzitzit* were worn throughout the day by Jewish men, and by women as well, though their use changed somewhat over time. They were meant to visually spark the wearer to religious consciousness, inspired action, and restraint. For Milgrom, the biblical commandment to the Israelites to wear *tzitzit*, a symbol of priesthood and nobility, encourages all Israel to aspire to holiness and integrity.

In his commentary on *tzitzit* (tassels; Num. 15:37–41), Ibn Ezra writes: "In my opinion one is more obligated to wear the *tzitzit* when not in prayer [than during prayer]—so that one will remember not to go astray in sin at any time, for in the time of prayer one surely will not sin." Ibn Ezra's comment is a reminder that the *tzitzit* commandment enjoins—

and early practice attests—the attaching of the *tzitzit* to the outer garment. They were worn all day long. Indeed, the term *tallit*—the prayer shawl bearing the *tzitzit*, which Jews wrap about themselves each morning in prayer—is actually the Rabbinic term for outer garment, again alluding to the fact that *tzitzit* were worn throughout the day.

The nature of *tzitzit* is illuminated by the literature and art of the ancient Near East, which shows that the hem of the outer robe was ornate compared to the rest of it. The more important the individual, the more elaborate the hem's embroidery. Its significance lies not in its artistry but in its symbolism, as an extension of its owner's person and authority. Its use is best illustrated by the Akkadian *sissikta bat'qu,* "to cut off the hem." For example, an exorcist pronounces an incantation over the detached hem of his patient's garment; a husband who cuts off a piece of the hem of his wife's robe thereby divorces her.

A reflex of this practice is found in the Bible in what heretofore was a puzzling dialogue. King Saul has pursued David into the Judean hills. Saul enters a cave and removes his cloak to relieve himself, unaware that David and his men are hiding in the cave. David sneaks up on the unsuspecting Saul and cuts off the hem from his cloak. The text then relates that "afterward David reproached himself for cutting off part of the hem of Saul's cloak." He said to his men, "The LORD forbid that I should do such a thing." When Saul realizes what David has done, he responds: "I know now that you will become king" (1 Sam. 24:6,21). What was the reason for David's remorse and for Saul's response? The answer rests in the meaning of the hem: It was an extension of Saul's person and authority. David felt remorse for taking it because God had not so ordered. Saul, however, regarded it as a sign from God that his authority had been transferred to David; Saul was now cut off from the throne.

The legal force of the hem in ancient Mesopotamia is evidenced in other ways. In ancient Mari, a professional prophet or dreamer would enclose with his report to the king a lock of his hair and a piece of his hem. They served both as his identification and, more important, as a guarantee that his prediction was true. In effect, these articles gave the king legal control over their owner. Another legal context of the hem is illustrated by clay documents, on which the impression of a hem replaces a signature. Today a nonliterate might sign with a fingerprint; in ancient Mesopotamia, however, it was the upper class that might use the hem.

Ephraim Speiser suggested that the practice in the synagogue to this day of pressing the edge of the *tallit* to the Torah scroll is a vestige of the ancient custom. This act, followed by the recital of blessings, may well have originated as a dramatic reaffirmation of the participant's commitment to the Torah. One thereby pledges both in words (blessing) and in deed (impressing a "signature" on the scroll) to live by the Torah's commandments.

That *tzitzit* are an extension of the hem is profusely illustrated in ancient Near Eastern art. In one picture, a pendant *tzitzit* is clearly evident, taking the form of a flower head or tassel, thus supporting the rendering "tassel" for *tzitzit*. The biblical text, moreover, enjoins that *tzitzit* be attached to the corners of the garment. But how can a closed robe or skirt have corners? There are two possibilities. One figure shows that the *tzitzit* are only the extended threads of the embroidered vertical bands that, instead of being cut off at the hem, are allowed to hang free. These bands terminate at quarter points of the hem, thereby forming four "corners." Another figure illustrates a second possibility: The skirts are scalloped and the tassels are suspended where the scallops meet. The biblical text validates this mode of dress. It prescribes that the *tzitzit* be attached to the *kanaf,* a term that does not mean "corner" but "extremity" or "wing." Strikingly, a scalloped hem is the winged extremity of the garment. Thus the significance of the *tzitzit* (as well as of the elaborate hem) lies in this: It was worn by those who counted; it was the identification tag of nobility.

The requirement of the *t'kheilet,* the blue cord, gives further support to the notion that *tzitzit* signified nobility. The blue dye was extracted from the gland of the murex snail (*ḥillazon;* see Sifrei Deut. 354; BT Shab. 26a; BT Men. 42b) in a painstaking process. Though the snails were plentiful, the amount of dye yielded from each was infinitesimal and consequently expensive. Only the wealthy could afford large quantities of this dye.

Following the two Roman wars, the Jewish community was so impoverished that many could not afford even the one blue-dyed cord required for each *tzitzit*. Moreover, the dye industry was shut down by Rome, which declared it a state monopoly; and the *t'kheilet* became scarce (BT Men. 42b). To be sure, a cheap counterfeit blue had been developed from the indigo plant, but the Sages disqualified it as *t'kheilet* (Sifrei Num. 115; BT Men. 42b–43a). These factors contributed to the suspension of the blue cord requirement, and since then *tzitzit* have been totally white.

Another historical fact revealed by early Rabbinic sources is that *tzitzit* were worn by women. In fact, some Sages actually affirmed that *"af ha-nashim b'mashma,"* i. e., women are required to wear *tzitzit* (Sifrei Num. 115; BT Men. 43a) because it falls into the category of a commandment whose observance is not limited to a fixed time (*she-ein ha-z'man g'rama;* Tosef. Kid. 1:10).

Finally, because the *tzitzit* marked their wearers as Jews and because, as members of a powerless minority within a hostile majority, it might single them out for persecution, it was ordained that the *tzitzit* should be transferred to an inner garment (*tallit katan*). Nevertheless, among pious *Ashk'nazim* to this day the *tzitzit* are still visible, in fulfillment of the commandment "look at it [namely, the blue cord]" (Num. 15:39).

The purpose of the *tzitzit* is set out by a series of verbs: "look ... recall ... observe" (Num. 15:39). These three verbs effectively summarize and define the pedagogic technique of the ritual system of the Torah: Sight (i. e., the senses) combined with memory (i. e., the intellect) is translated into action (i. e., good deeds). Thus the experience of rituals and the comprehension of their values lead to loftier ethical behavior. The text also adds a negative purpose: to bridle the passions (v. 39) and thereby, according to the Sages, prevent heresy and harlotry (Sifrei Num. 115).

The final purpose of the *tzitzit* is indicated in verse 40, the conclusion of the pericope: "Thus you shall be reminded to observe all My commandments and to be holy to your God." The ultimate goal of seeing the *tzitzit,* reminding oneself of God's commandments and fulfilling them, is to attain holiness. The nobility to which Israel belongs is not like other power structures characterized by corruption and self-indulgence. Israel is commanded to be "a kingdom of priests and a holy nation" (Exod. 19:6).

But what is there about *tzitzit* that would remind its wearer of holiness? The earliest Rabbinic sources, perhaps dating back to biblical days, taught that the *tzitzit* are *sha·atnez,* a mixture of wool and linen (Septuagint; Targ. Jon. to Deut. 22:12; cf. Rashi; Ibn Ezra on this verse; Men. 39b–40a,43a; Lev. R. 22:10). In fact, white linen cords and dyed woolen cords were found in the Bar Kokhba caves, proving that the Rabbinic teaching was actually observed. The wearing of *sha·atnez* is forbidden to the Israelite (Lev. 19:19; Deut. 22:11), patently because it would resemble some of the priestly garments made from a blend of linen and wool (e. g., Exod. 28:6, 39:29). In fact, the high priest's linen turban is bound by a *p'til t'kheilet,* a blue woolen cord (Exodus 28:37,39). Thus *sha·atnez* is forbidden because it is a holy mixture, reserved exclusively for priests. That *sha·atnez* is forbidden because it is holy can be derived from the injunction: "You shall not sow your vineyard with a second kind of seed, else the crop—from the seed you have sown—and the yield of the vineyard may not be used [*yikdash;* literally: will become sanctified]" (Deut. 22:9). In other words, the produce will belong not to you but to the sanctuary. However, early in the Rabbinic period it was taught—perhaps stemming from a biblical practice—that every Israelite should wear *tzitzit* made of *sha·atnez* (cf. Tosafot on BT Men. 39b,40a). Thus the *tzitzit,* according to the Sages, are modeled after a priestly garment that is taboo for the rest of Israel!

The *tzitzit* are then an exception to the Torah's general injunction against wearing garments of mixed seed. In actuality, however, inherent in this paradox is its ultimate purpose. The resemblance to the high priest's turban and other priestly clothing can be no accident. It is a conscious attempt to encourage all Israel to aspire to a degree of holiness comparable to that of the priests. Indeed, holiness itself is enjoined on Israel: "You shall be holy, for I, the LORD your God, am holy" (Lev. 19:2; cf. 11:44, 20:26). True, Israelites who are not of the seed of Aaron may not serve as priests (cf. Num. 17:5), but they may—indeed, must—strive for a life of holiness by obeying God's commandments. Hence, to their garments they are to attach tassels containing one blue cord—a woolen thread among the threads of linen. Indeed, the use of mixed seed in the prescribed garments reveals a gradation in holiness. The outer garments of the high priest are *sha·atnez,* the belt of the ordinary priest is *sha·atnez* (Exod. 39:29; cf. BT Yoma 12b)—and the fringes of the Israelite are *sha·atnez* by virtue of one blue woolen thread. The fact that the cord is woolen and blue marks it as a symbol of both priesthood and royalty, thereby epitomizing the divine imperative that Israel become "a kingdom of priests and a holy nation."

Study Questions

1. What examples does Milgrom use to support the connection between *tzitzit* and hems in Near Eastern aristocratic society?

2. How has the use of *tzitzit* changed over time according to Milgrom?

3. Milgrom describes *tzitzit* as attired signs of caste, personal power, and identification. What are the appareled signs of social group, power, and personal identification in your society?

4. What do we do today to create physical representations of our commitments to ideals such as faith, honesty, national allegiance, and fidelity to friends and partners?

5. Do you know someone who wears *tzitzit* (*tallit katan*) today as an undergarment throughout the day? If so, why do you think that individual does so? Is it something you would consider making a part of your Jewish observance?

Study materials by *Shoshana Jedwab*

Biblical Models of Character and Leadership

MATRIARCHS AND PATRIARCHS

Debra R. Orenstein

Summary

Debra Orenstein explores the matriarchs and patriarchs of Gene-sis—early biblical ancestors such as Abraham, Sarah, Rebekah, and Jacob—as exemplars of a nation. She particularly notes the repetition of specific narrative elements in these stories: the barren matriarch, the conflict between brothers, the favorite son of the patriarch. Oren-stein argues that these repeated patterns show that the stories are not primarily about individuals, but about a covenant with a people.

Though the roles of patriarchs and matriarchs have considerable differences, Orenstein observes that there are three crucial life pas-sages for matriarchs and patriarchs in Genesis: leaving one's home; facing difficulties in the outside world; and returning to family and land. She suggests that in the Genesis narratives, spiritual maturity requires facing repeated challenges, and each successive genera-tion faces different aspects of similar problems. In Genesis, "repeti-tion is not a loop but a spiral upward." Ultimately, Orenstein asserts, these ancestral stories can shed light on our own lives.

The Book of Genesis addresses the primal and profound questions that children ask: Who am I? Where did I come from? Why am I here? What is this family I have been born into? In the Bible, these questions extend beyond the nuclear family to the primordial origins of humanity and the ancestral origins of our nation and faith. Who are we in the "family of man"? Who are we as a people?

In Genesis, these ideas are framed in the language of two other ques-tions: the first question God ever asked, and the first question posed by a being created in God's image. God called out to a guilty Adam, who was trying to hide in the Garden of Eden: "*Ayyeka*—Where are you?" (3:9). Later, Cain asked about Abel, the brother he had murdered: "Am I my brother's keeper?" (4:9). Both questions may appear to be rhetorical, but they reverberate throughout Genesis as profoundly serious inquiries. The family narratives serve as a discursive, exploratory, and open-ended response. Matriarchs and patriarchs continually struggle with where they are—in terms of birth order, family and gender roles, spiritual development, the chain of covenantal heritage, and (more literally) locale. Sibling rivalry regularly threatens to turn fratricidal. In the story of Joseph, brothers finally mature to the point of becoming each other's guardians and keepers. Indeed, they come to see such mutual care as the divine plan and the ultimate human purpose (43:8–9, 50:20). Finally, four generations after Abraham, the sons of both Judah and Joseph avoid conflict in the first place and accept their respective roles in the family.

The dilemmas faced by our ancestors communally, as well as personally, endure as struggles and boundary issues. We are still making our peace with Ishmael and his descendants. Within the "immediate family," division over who is a proper heir to the covenant—or, "who is a Jew"—threatens both our genealogic and our religious integrity. The matriarchs and patriarchs favored in-marriage, promoted connection to the Promised Land, and feared the lure of foreign temptations. Physical survival and continuity of heritage—difficult propositions throughout Genesis—absorb us today as well.

The terms "matriarch" and "patriarch" can be variously interpreted. They might well include such guarantors of continuity as Bilhah, Zilpah, Tamar, Judah, and Joseph. The terminology can be confusing, too, because patriarchy, in contemporary usage, refers to a broad institutionalized system of rigid sex roles, through which men retain authority over women. Of course, such a cultural system neither began nor ended with the patriarchs of Genesis. Reclaiming and relating to our male ancestors neither requires nor condones patriarchy.

In this essay and in Jewish tradition generally, the titles "matriarch" and "patriarch" are reserved for the *avot*, key figures of the first three generations: Abraham and Sarah; Isaac and Rebekah; Jacob, Leah, and Rachel. These exemplars are valued above all others and are considered the purest representatives of a meritorious ancestry (BT Ber. 16b). More-over, it is in these first three generations that a single family prepares to become a tribe and a nation. During these years—roughly the first half of the 2nd millennium B. C. E.—it is still debatable who the next rightful heir will and should be. Yet, the covenant is firmly established.

It is significant that there are seven early ancestors, because that num-ber connotes a perfect completion in the Bible. The world was created in seven days, and the *avot*—a whole and perfect set—are said to fulfill, and even to cause, Creation (Lev. R. 36:4). The early chapters of Gen-esis record false starts and second chances—attempts by God to begin (and begin again) a positive partnership with humanity. Ten generations after Adam and Eve are driven from the Garden, God takes Noah as a new "first" being and initiates the covenant of the rainbow. A parallel 10 generations after the Flood, God chooses and builds a more par-ticipatory covenant with Abraham. Several genealogies link the various players in these dramas (5, 10, 11:10–32). Abraham's call marks both closure for Creation and the opening of a new era for the future people Israel and humanity.

Although a "whole and perfect set," our seven famous ancestors cer-tainly had faults and weaknesses. Their development within Genesis can be seen as a template for personal growth; as a study in family dynam-ics; or, even more broadly, as a paradigm for the nation's history and destiny. Matriarchs and patriarchs represent the promise of a people as well as the fulfillment of Creation.

REPETITION PAINTS A COMPOSITE PICTURE

The themes that run throughout the stories of the patriarchs and matri-archs are so often repeated that one could almost conceive a composite couple. The tales of the patriarchs are especially easy to conflate. Excep-tions and nuances aside, a patriarch chosen by God finds a wife within the clan, who gives him a special son. The son chosen for succession resembles his father in several crucial respects: He will have a stormy relationship with a brother (or brother figure), leave his father's house, marry a "barren" woman, benefit from divine communication and in-tercession, retain and gain a firmer foothold in the land he inherits.

Possessed of neither firstborn status nor extraordinary merit, he is nevertheless destined to receive the blessing of the firstborn. He may well be called by a new name, indicating a spiritual evolution. The composite patriarch will play favorites among his children, settle disputes with neighbors, build an altar, leave (or have his sons leave) the immediate area in time of famine, trick a man more wealthy and powerful than he, return with even greater wealth to where he started, and receive God's promise of chosen and numerous progeny living in a sacred homeland. God will reiterate this promise, but not (yet) fulfill it. The patriarch will become estranged from family members over the course of his lifetime, and he will heal the breaches—at least to some degree. He will offer blessings to family members, receive God's blessing, and ultimately be a blessing himself.

Even the vocabulary of the stories recurs across the generations. When called to make a change that will initiate a higher calling and connection to God, the patriarchs are told or tell the next generation to "go" (*lekh*) and "take" (*kaḥ*). "Going forth" from one's roots and habits is a necessary step on the road to spiritual growth and independence. According to Hasidic commentary, it enables the patriarch to "go unto himself" (Gen. 12:1)—i.e., his best self. That inner journey prepares him to unite with family and land and to receive God's blessing.

Duplications in language and behavior specifically connect Jacob back to Abraham. Abraham's name is changed upon his circumcision; Jacob's name is changed at the point when he receives a wound on the thigh. Jacob repeatedly refers to the covenant and God of "my father Abraham" as well as "my father Isaac." On their deathbeds, Abraham and Jacob both extract oaths from trusted men for the care of future generations.

The (conflated) matriarch is chosen for a man whom God has chosen. With even greater consistency than her male counterpart, she leaves her father's house and homeland. Probably discovered near a well, she journeys with her husband and serves the mission to which he has been called. The matriarch suffers various trials and tribulations with him, including dangers she must face because of his apparent greed or self-protection, such as when he passes her off as his sister.

Most likely, the woman is barren and prays for children. In response, God blesses her with a son and a divine message about his birth. If the matriarch is fertile, her life still appears to be "barren" with respect to affection and social station. Regardless, she, and the household generally, struggle with procreation and sexuality. Although infertility is the matriarch's ultimate source of grief, motherhood may well be her ultimate source of rivalry and pain. Perhaps because her power is so limited in the male-dominated world, she is fierce in attaining and defending her status as a mother and will compete with other women in this arena. She gains prestige, security, and personal fulfillment by becoming a mother and may well form impressive connections with God along the way. The matriarch exercises significant control over domestic and sexual issues, e.g., assigning a handmaid to her husband, setting the schedule for conjugal relations, dispatching members from the household, naming children.

The matriarch, more than the patriarch, understands and shapes the destiny of their progeny. She plays a major role in managing the transition from one generation to the next, championing the proper son for inheritance. Her voice is generally in synch with God's voice and often out of synch with that of her husband (Gen. 21:12, 25:23, 31:16). Yet, when God remembers the matriarch, it is for fertility, not covenant. Her ability to bear children secures the covenant for the patriarch. The miraculous birth of a son confers upon the child—not his mother—the status of a divinely chosen leader. In biblical literature and society, the matriarch remains a secondary character, with major ellipses in her biography. Inheritance is neither hers to give nor hers to receive. The primary focus is on brothers' rivalries, male lineage, and God's covenants with and through men.

Literary and psychological patterns cross gender as well as generational lines. For example, while the matriarchal and patriarchal figures prove complex in their own right, they also serve as foils to one another. Sarah is the aggressor on behalf of the passive Isaac; Hagar is helpless and retreats from action in defending her aggressive son, Ishmael. In the next generation, favored sons seem to live out the repressed side of their parents. Isaac's favorite, the outdoorsman Esau, resembles Ishmael and Rebekah more than Isaac. Rebekah's favorite, the domestic Jacob, has his father's temperament. Similarly, Jacob will reject the wife who resembles his youthful self (Leah) and favor her more aggressive sister (Rachel). In an extended struggle toward maturation and balance, he lives out both hyperaggression (25:29 ff.) and extreme passivity (34:5–30).

The last scene of the archetypal ancestral marriage is one of silent betrayal regarding a beloved child and prospective heir. Abraham goes off to slay Isaac without speaking to Sarah, whose death is reported just after Abraham returns. Rebekah guides Jacob to make a fool of Isaac and steal Esau's blessing. Dialogues between parents and children move the story forward, but Rebekah and Isaac do not speak until the trick is done—when Rebekah addresses Isaac briefly, gruffly, and for the last time in their lives (27:46). With her dying breath, Rachel names her son *Ben-oni* (son of my suffering, son of my strength). Perhaps Jacob never hears, or perhaps he doesn't listen; he renames the boy *Ben-ya-min* (which roughly repeats Rachel's "son of my strength," but ignores her suffering).

Already in the first generation, we are alerted to the significance of repetition, as it is too consistent and relentless to be coincidental. Hagar is driven from the household twice; both Isaac's parents laugh at the thought of his impending birth; and Isaac's name is announced twice. Twice Abraham identifies (or perhaps misidentifies) Sarah as his sister, separates from Lot, encounters Abimelech, enters into covenant with God, is told "get yourself out ... to a place that I will show you" (12:1, 22:2). Abraham has two potential heirs and is willing to sacrifice both.

Why all the repetition? Recurrent patterns show that the trials and promises we have come to associate with our ancestors were not their individual concerns. This family was passing on a vision and a covenant. In response to that—then and now—certain foibles and resistance typically arise: We laugh (17:17, 18:12), we doubt (28:15 vs. 28:20 ff.), we banish others (21:14), we rob them of their blessings (27:19 ff.), we act superior (21:10), we offer up human sacrifices (22:10), we favor one heir over another (25:28, 37:3). Victory in Genesis depends on three crucial passages: leaving one's parental home; confronting trials and lessons in the wider world; and returning, a changed person, back to family and land. The final third of that journey is male dominated and directed. Nevertheless, the lives of both the matriarchs and the patriarchs become a paradigm of being and becoming, of how to—and how not to (BT

Shab. 10b). As heirs to the covenant and as heirs to Western culture, we owe a debt to these Genesis narratives for the very notion that spiritual maturity has something to do with repeated exposures to a challenge and more to do with noticing and transcending the patterns, than with resolving or escaping the situations.

NOTING THE ELEMENTS OF CHANGE

While it is useful to notice repetition, differences and nuances are also instructive. Variations in a known, archetypal story yield lessons about the uniqueness of a particular matriarch's character, patriarch's mission, or generation's dilemma.

Virtually every action Isaac takes re-enacts some episode from his father's life. Gen. 26:18 can be read as a summary of Isaac's biography: "And Isaac dug anew the wells which had been dug in the days of his father, Abraham." Yet Isaac differs from both his father and his son, in that he tends to react, rather than initiate action. In fact, biblical scholars have quipped that—based on commonalties in leadership, risk taking, deception, travel, and aggression—the patriarchs might more accurately be listed as "Abraham, Rebekah, and Jacob." Rebekah exercises a degree of power initiative unmatched by the other matriarchs. The contrast between Isaac and Rebekah is more than temperamental. It represents differing approaches to managing a sacred inheritance. Isaac models persistence, even without the allure of innovation or the glory of completion. Rebekah models aggressive and zealous commitment to a divinely approved end.

Social and genealogic developments in Genesis profoundly affect both women's status and the transmission of the covenant. Early on, matrilineal and patrilineal descent are not wholly separable. Abraham and Sarah may actually have been (half-) brother and sister (20:2,12). That would explain why Sarah's genealogy is omitted. (Alternatively, the couple may have been related by means other than blood. Adopting one's wife as a sister was a known way of elevating her status.) Rebekah the matriarch is part of the patriarchal family, being Abraham's grandniece and Isaac's cousin once removed. Laban was Jacob's uncle on his mother's side, living in what was also the land of Jacob's "fathers"

(24:38). Yet Paddan-aram comes to be associated exclusively with his mother's house (28:2). Women are allied with Paddan-aram, and men, of a related genealogy, with Canaan. Continuity, kinship, and the Promised Land are general family interests that come to be dominated by men. Despite women's place on the family tree and their role in promoting the proper heir, covenant and blessing are ultimately passed down from father to son.

Disputes over the Land, doubt over succession, and rivalry within the family are recurrent problems. Yet, each generation faces a higher order of the dilemma. For example, Jacob's concern over brutality against his neighbors indicates a far more secure and settled position in the Land than do Abraham's tussles with neighbors over the wells, or his beholden position in bargaining for the cave of Mach-pelah. The matriarchs and patriarchs face the same questions, more than once, in relation to transmission: Will there be an heir? Which son will be chosen to inherit the covenant? Will the sons make peace with one another? All three questions are relevant in each generation, but the first is dominant for Abraham and Sarah, the second for Isaac and Rebekah, and the third for Jacob, Rachel, and (to a lesser extent) Leah.

Repetition in Genesis is not an endless loop, but an upward spiral. In the first generation of a revolutionary new faith, Abraham must leave his father's house and establish ownership and presence in the Land; in the second generation, Isaac must stake claim to that still insecure inheritance; in the third generation, Jacob must learn the ways of the world and his own heart, before returning home to greet his brother and father and resettle the Land. In the fourth generation, the family reconciliation is more complete, as Joseph remains in contact with his father and brothers over time. Yet Joseph asserts love and responsibility for his brothers outside Canaan. Genesis is working its way toward complete redemption: peace and communication among siblings united by a covenant and living in their own land. Devora Steinmetz has pointed out that the narrative progresses toward this dream, achieving pieces of the vision without full realization: Genesis—indeed, the entire Torah—ends on the cusp of completion. The text thus invites the reader to continue, and fulfill, the story.

WHERE IS THE FAMILY HEADED?

As rabbinic tradition teaches, beginning with Abraham "the deeds of the ancestors are a sign for the descendants" (*ma·asei avot siman l'vanim*; see Ramban at Gen. 12:6). The patriarchs and matriarchs not only give rise to a nation but also embody it and portend its future. God predicts that the nation will sojourn in a foreign land and emerge with great property. The covenant through which God reveals this to Abraham clearly refers to the exodus from Egypt. At the same time, the terms of that covenant are fulfilled, albeit on a smaller scale, in the lives of Abraham, Isaac, Jacob, and Joseph—who each leave home, best a wealthy and powerful man, and return with some of his riches. To Abraham, as to the Israelites at Sinai, God declares: "I am the God who took you out" (Gen. 15:7; Exod. 20:2).

Jacob, renamed Israel, is father, namesake, and symbol of the Israelite nation. His children are sometimes textured and complex characters, but they are also eponymous stand-ins for the tribes. The Israelites are called "the people of the God of Abraham" (Ps. 47:10), "the House of Isaac" (Amos 7:16), and most popularly the "Children of Israel." Rachel becomes mother to the entire nation (Jer. 31:14). Procreation from the womb of a "barren" mother represents not just a hope, but a paradigm, for Jerusalem's rebirth (Isa. 54:1–3).

Stories of the matriarchs and patriarchs are linked to the Israelite's national destiny. Like Rebekah and Rachel before her, Zipporah, Moses' wife, is discovered and chosen at a well. Miriam, too, will be associated with wells and water, symbols of women's power to mother, nurture, manage danger, and redeem. Later biblical books regularly invoke God's promises to the patriarchs in relation to the divine covenant with subsequent generations (Exod. 2:24; Lev. 26:42; 2 Kings 13:23). We now take it for granted that the covenant made at Sinai is one with the covenant established with the patriarchs. Deuteronomy, in particular, makes that link.

The Midrash further connects the ancestral family with subsequent generations. Abraham was understood to have observed all the commandments, even though the revelation at Sinai would happen centuries later (BT Yoma 28b). Similarly, Sarah and Rebekah are said to have practiced extraordinary hospitality, set dough aside during baking, and enjoyed the distinction of a holy cloud above their tent; in these ways, the matriarchs both presaged and modeled conventions that would govern the Tabernacle and Temple (Gen. R. 60:16).

An important principle that motivates our continuing connection to the ancestors is *z'khut avot,* their merit. In deference to the merit of matriarchs and patriarchs, we were delivered from Egypt (Exod. 2:24), forgiveness was granted for building a Golden Calf (BT Shab. 30a), and our sins are pardoned on the Day of Atonement (PdRE 29).

Avot can be translated as "ancestors" or, using a gender-specific reading, as "fathers" or "patriarchs." In relation to ancestral merit, it is probable that "fathers" was generally meant, because Rabbinic sources also attribute God's mercy on later generations to *z'khut imahot,* the merit of the mothers. However, Hebrew grammar permits us to interpret most texts about *avot* as inclusive of *imahot,* in that one male among myriad women will alter the feminine plural to the masculine. Where the context is ambiguous, counting matriarchs among the *avot* has the effect of enfranchising women and reading them into the texts and tales of our ancestors. For that reason, many feminists prefer to call all the ancestors *avot,* rather than distinguishing Sarah, Rebekah, Leah, and Rachel as *imahot.* Traditional liturgy sometimes invokes mothers along with fathers, e. g., in relation to healing and the birth of baby girls. Following a responsum by the CJLS, many Conservative synagogues have added the matriarchs to the *Avot* blessing in the *Amidah.*

THE LIVING HERITAGE

Using our earliest ancestors as models in liturgy and ritual communicates essential values, even as it connects us intimately with our past. This process began within the Bible itself. In the Book of Ruth, Boaz is blessed: "May the LORD make the woman who is coming into your house like Rachel and Leah, both of whom built up the house of Israel" (4:11). In a prewedding ritual still practiced today, we invoke Leah, Rachel, and Rebekah. As the groom veils the bride (making sure he is getting the correct sister!), he quotes the bridal blessing given to Rebekah:

"may you grow into thousands and myriads" (Gen. 24:60). Today, as in the ancient world, we wish our daughters progeny and power. At the Friday night dinner table, parents bless their daughters: "May you be like Sarah, Rebekah, Rachel, and Leah." To their sons they say, "May you be like Ephraim and Manasseh."

By using scripture and its characters as a guide for contemporary living, we create an interchange between a fixed text and the changing, subjective contexts in which it is read. Reading ourselves backward into biblical text and our ancestors forward into contemporary situations is nothing new. During the time of the Crusades, Isaac, bound to the altar, became not only a hero but a tragic role model as well. For the philosopher Maimonides, Abraham exemplified the highest level of faith because he used reason to verify God's existence. Today, feminists read the experience of the matriarchs in light of the women's movement.

From a purely historical point of view, "our God and God of our ancestors" should be rendered as two different phrases and ideas—separated by time, experience, and theology. Yet, however we re-engage and reinterpret God and scripture over time, our relationship to them and to ourselves is influenced and nurtured by the *avot* of old. In the words of Isaiah, "Look back to Abraham your father / And to Sarah who brought you forth" (51:2).

Study Questions

1. What meanings does Orenstein assign to the patterns that continue to reappear in the stories of the patriarchs and matriarchs? How does she understand the unique aspects of individuals such as Isaac, Rebekah, or Rachel?

2. How does Orenstein distinguish between patriarchal and matriarchal roles?

3. Orenstein quotes a rabbinic tradition that "the deeds of the ancestors are a sign for the descendents." How would you interpret this statement? Is it still relevant today?

4. At the end of her essay, Orenstein notes that we still use the names of the patriarchs and matriarchs to bless our children on the Sabbath. Would you want to bless a child to be like the patriarchs and matriarchs?

Study materials by *Shoshana Jedwab*

MOSES: MAN OF ISRAEL, MAN OF GOD

Stephen P. Garfinkel

Summary

In Stephen Garfinkel's essay on the character and symbolism of Moses, he argues that the life of Moses parallels the life and fate of the Jewish people. Moses is a national "alter ego" whose life begins as the life of the nation begins, and whose life ends as they move on into a settled life. He establishes the political, religious, and judicial systems of the Israelite people, and he stands between God and Israel when God threatens to destroy the people. His roles as liberator, law giver, nourisher, provoker, and redeemer will guide the Israelites from slavery in Egypt to residence in their own land.

The two markers that surround Moses, Garfinkel argues, are water and the mountain. In his early life he is saved from water (the Nile) and later water becomes his instrument of redemption as he parts the Sea of Reeds and brings the people through. Similarly, he is first called by God to the service of the Israelites at a mountain, and it is at a mountain that he mediates the covenant between God and Israel. His poignant death occurs before the entry into the Promised Land, for the newly settled people will have new needs and will require a new leader. Garfinkel suggests that the story of Moses is not meant as history but as a theological teaching about the nature and fate of Israel.

The Torah mirrors the life of Israel in the life of Moses. The Book of Genesis presents the patriarchs as the progenitors and spiritual forebears of the Israelites, even culminating in Jacob's renaming to become the eponymous Israel. Yet it is Moses—not Abraham, Isaac, Jacob, or even Joseph—whose life parallels the life of the Israelite people and whose actions determine their destiny. The nation is first formed in the opening chapter of Exodus (in contrast to the Genesis narratives about families and clans), and Moses' birth and the role he is destined to fulfill are announced in the following chapter. The nation of Israel will have many leaders after Moses, but he is replaced by none of them. The life of the Israelite people from national birth to possession of a permanent territory is coterminous with the life of Moses. He is in effect the national alter ego. That characterization, however, is never articulated explicitly; it can be inferred from the many diverse roles Moses serves. His assignments range from liberator to law giver, from guide to goad, from castigator to collaborator. He is scapegoat and strategist, provoker and protector, referee, resource, and redeemer.

As noted in the commentary, Exodus begins with the fulfillment of the often-reiterated promise made to the patriarchs that they will have countless descendants. Ironically, however, the growing attainment of that very blessing increases the Egyptian ruler's fear of Israel, leading to his intention to dominate or annihilate them. After several pharaonic schemes to weaken Israel, the nation's fate appears bleak by the end of chapter 1. But just a few verses later, the narrative of Moses' birth furnishes provocative hints in which the meticulous reader can discern Moses' future redemptive role. Moses will survive his near drowning at birth to save Israel, and water (in this instance, the Nile) becomes one of two central markers throughout Moses' career. What might have been the location of his death will become the site of his great success. When Pharaoh's daughter names the child found in the water "Moses" (possibly using or mimicking an Egyptian term for "son"), she formally adopts him and bequeaths much more than a bilingual pun. Exodus interprets the name "Moses" to mean that he is "drawn out" of the water (2:10); but a more precise grammatical analysis of the Hebrew term *mosheh* confers a richer, predictive message. Moses is destined to be the one who draws out the people of Israel (even as the prophet Isaiah suggestively refers to God as *mosheh ammo*, "the One who draws out His people"; Isa. 63:11). Moses will save them by drawing them out through the water of the Sea of Reeds. Because Israel is the "new humanity" and cosmic fortune is reflected in the nation's fate, Moses' calling takes on an even greater significance. For the Torah, redeeming this nation redeems the world.

The other major marker in the life of Moses is the mountain. When God appears to Moses, announcing from the Burning Bush (Exod. 3) that he is the person designated to bring the suffering Israelites out of Egypt, Moses is incredulous. However, God reassures Moses with a fittingly enigmatic sign intended to authenticate this revelation of Moses' commission: the mountain (later called *Har ha-Elohim,* "the Mountain of God"), or possibly the people's returning to the mountain to worship once they are freed, will somehow become the sign, even if in the future. I shall examine both the water and the mountain at several stages later in Moses' life, after considering the historical setting the Torah provides.

When did Moses live? Many scholars assign the time of the Exodus (and, by implication, the life of Moses) to either the early 13th century or the middle of the 15th century B. C. E. (In part, their uncertainty results from contradictory or inconsistent verses found elsewhere in the *Tanakh.*) Some scholars draw further support for these dates by interpreting statements in Exod. 1 or by drawing on archaeological artifacts and extrabiblical inscriptions, none of which mentions the Exodus or Moses. However, even for those who accept either of the proposed dates for the Exodus (and Moses' birth 80 years earlier and his death 40 years later), it is appropriate to ask about the reliability of the biblical information used to calculate that chronology. The dates are not likely to be precise; they are, in fact, more likely to be schematic. Accuracy is pertinent only to a historical or a scientific document; another approach is appropriate for a theological, or religious, work. Once we understand that the Torah is a theological text dressed in historical garb, focusing on the date of the Exodus (or on the dates of other events in the Torah) misdirects our attention.

The search for historical context is of more than antiquarian interest and can sometimes provide a framework to enrich exegesis by providing entire sets of clues for interpreting biblical material. However, the primary concern for communities of faith must be the search for meaning of the Exodus narrative and its implications. We must always be aware that whatever we "know" about Moses is extrapolated from religious literary sources. So the question to ask in understanding the Torah on its own terms is not when, or even if, Moses lived, but what his life conveys in Israel's saga. How does God's redemption of the people unfold in the human arena, and what function does Moses serve in that national redemption? Irrespective of the chronologic background,

Moses is presented as a model of leadership—with strengths and weaknesses—for future generations.

Typical of the folkloristic, national hero, Moses successfully withstands trials to prove himself early in his career and continues his mission by undertaking a variety of specific roles. While the Israelites are still in Egypt, he is their chief negotiator to Pharaoh (admittedly sometimes against their wishes). During the ensuing 40 years, he coaxes them to mature as a nation. As God's spokesman, Moses helps institute a legal system; a judicial structure; and a cultic infrastructure for worship, forgiveness, and purification. He creates, or supervises the formation of, institutions that the nascent nation requires during its period of wandering and the administrative structures upon which they can rely and build even after their permanent settlement. Occasionally he needs advice or guidance to initiate these projects, but his leadership ensures their establishment. Throughout his calling, Moses is the people's guide—in geographic, military, socio-political, and moral senses, as necessary—and he nourishes them when food, water, or morale is in short supply.

Despite his initial reluctance, Moses is not only compelled to take on the next challenges confronting him; he is ready. Moses' most dramatic successes and the highlight of his career must be seen at the next confluence of water and mountain. Typical of the hero in many ancient epics, Moses crosses over the water—in this case miraculously traversing the Sea of Reeds—and he takes with him the entire nation in formation. Almost immediately thereafter, Moses reaches the pinnacle of his unique status, sharing God's own aura at the mountain (Sinai), after which he brings back God's word to the people. Here, in what becomes the keystone of the national identity, the nation assumes and accepts its special charge, and Moses reaches his most spectacular grandeur. He has succeeded in bringing Israel out of Egypt; he has gone beyond that at Sinai, forging the people's eternal contract with God.

The mountain experience at Sinai is not without its own complications. Here Moses must take to new heights the role of prophet as intercessor, first undertaken in the Torah by Abraham (Gen. 20:7,17). In the words of Ps. 106:23, Moses "stands in the breach" between God and Israel. Later prophets will follow the Mosaic model, delivering

God's message to Israel, warning, threatening, cajoling, and chastising as warranted. With equal fervor, however, Moses at Sinai takes the side of the people against God's wrath, conveying their plea to God and even compelling God to rescind the divine plan to destroy them after their apostasy in worshiping the Golden Calf. Moses puts his own life on the line for the future of the nation: "Erase me from your Book [of Life]," he tells God, if his future is separate from that of the people (Exod. 32:32). God relents, recognizing that Moses is an extension of the people and the people, an extension of Moses.

Over his extensive career, Moses retains and expands his heroic posture—notwithstanding increasingly severe challenges to his leadership: by his siblings, Miriam and Aaron (Num. 12); by his first cousin, Korah, and many of the community leaders (Num. 16); and by the nation as a whole (Num. 20, in which the people for the second time demand water to drink). Rabbinic tradition realized in the latter episode that Moses' death was, in fact, brought about by water, but it was the water springing from the rock at Massah and Meribah, not the Nile in which he was placed at birth. After the trials, the dangers, and the triumphs, Moses' life will end by means of water after all.

Although Moses is larger than life in the narrative of the Torah, he exhibits human shortcomings, sometimes in private dealings with his family, occasionally in public displays of anger, and even in an apparent growing sense of hubris (notwithstanding the description of him as the most humble of all people). However, one may speculate that Moses, like great leaders in other cultures, was raised to superhuman stature by many of those he led. It is not possible to know if the ancient Israelites perceived Moses in this same heroic category, but later Jewish tradition aggrandizes Moses even more. Rabbinic texts glorify Moses, referring to him as *Mosheh rabbeinu* (Moses our teacher) or *Mosheh ha-tzaddik* (Moses the righteous one, or saint) (BT Ned. 31b), and even appear to raise his status from transmitter of God's law to source of the law. One example of this is found in the formula of betrothal used during the Jewish wedding ceremony, "according to the law of Moses and Israel." By contrast, for fear of attributing Israel's redemption to Moses rather than to God, the *Pesaḥ Haggadah* all but eliminates Moses from the picture!

Even the structure of the Torah from Exodus through Deuteronomy revolves around Moses' centrality. In Exodus, Leviticus, and Numbers, Moses presents God's word; Deuteronomy is the (re)presentation from Moses' perspective. It is his version of the past that has final pride of place, in his speeches to the nation on the eve of their conquest and as the final word transmitted to readers of the Torah. Yet, at the very end of Moses' saga, God takes back the center stage to bid farewell to Moses, God's partner of the past 40 years. In one of the most poignant scenes of any literature, the narrative describes Moses' death. In simple majesty, despite his unique status, despite his Herculean efforts and accomplishments, Moses shares the fate of all mortals. Here, at the mountain—Mount Nebo—he and the nation part ways. They will cross the water—the Jordan River—to journey onward, leaving him behind. As the people were about to leave Egypt (Exod. 13), Moses took Joseph's bones for burial in Canaan, but now no one will take Moses' bones into the Land. He has devoted one third of his life to bringing the Israelites here, but he cannot participate in their inheritance. His allotted 120 years—the ideal limit given to human beings (Gen. 6:3)—are completed. His time of glory and burden is over. His tenure of leadership has expired, and his burial place must not become a shrine. It is in Transjordan, and no mortal can know its location. Moses moves into the people's past as they conquer Canaan. They move forward (past the end of the Torah), although he must remain on the distant side of the river. The Torah begins Israel's chronicle with Abraham, the one "from the other side," and it ends this stage of Israel's national saga with Moses remaining "on the other side." Settled people have new and different needs, and it will be up to Joshua (true, wearing Moses' mantle) to pick up the staff. Yet, later Rabbinic tradition recognizes that Moses is a vibrant force in the psyche of the people, claiming the date of his birth to be *Adar* 7, the exact same date it ascribes as the date of his death. One cannot memorialize his death without simultaneously recalling his birth. He remains an eternal watchman for Israel, as the saying has it: Zeus never lived, but Moses never died.

At the outset of his career, Moses tried to dissuade God from selecting him for the mission that ultimately became his. One of his ploys was to claim a deficiency in speech. How fortunate were the Israelites, and how fortunate are those who continue to read *Torat Mosheh* (the Torah of Moses), that the one time he was unable to make a convincing argument was in that initial dialogue with God. Consider the masterful narratives and instructions, the expressive rituals, the eloquent soliloquies, and the ennobling poetry of which we would have been deprived, had it been otherwise.

Study Questions

1. According to Garfinkel, in what ways do the events of Moses' life mirror the life of the Jewish people?

2. What are some of the roles Moses plays in relationship to the Jewish people? What are the roles he plays in relationship to God? In your view, does he succeed in these roles?

3. How does Garfinkel characterize Moses' human flaws? Do they enhance or take away from Moses' stature?

4. What does the manner of Moses' death teach us about how the Bible views prophets and leaders?

5. Garfinkel posits that water and the mountain are the two repeating themes in Moses' life. Why do you think this is? What do these images call to mind for you?

Study materials by *Shoshana Jedwab*

PRIESTS AND LEVITES IN THE BIBLE AND JEWISH LIFE

Baruch Frydman-Kohl

Summary

In this essay, Rabbi Frydman-Kohl outlines the history of the priestly castes in ancient times. He details the specific tasks assigned by Scripture to the priests (in Hebrew, *kohanim*) and to the Levites, and then goes on to discuss other related issues: the level of anatomical perfection required of priests who would serve at the altar; the special role of the High Priest (in Hebrew, *kohen gadol*); the relationship of the priestly castes to the royal house in biblical times; the laws that governed the marriage of priests in ancient times; and the latter-day evolution of the laws that pertain to both priests and Levites in our own day.

Readers trained from childhood to esteem democratic values (and to hold the equality of all citizens of any country to be wholly self-evident) will find it challenging to accept the validity, let alone the sanctity, of a caste system specifically designed with reference neither to merit nor actual achievement. Indeed, the essay causes us to focus on one of the cardinal issues of all ethical debate: what constitutes merit, and how should society relate to people whose place in the world is a function of family status (or family wealth) rather than personal accomplishment?

Although the collective people Israel was intended to be a "kingdom of priests and a holy nation" (Exod. 19:6), the *kohanim* (priests) from the tribe of Levi were singled out as the bearers of unique sacred status. They were the primary religious actors in the biblical pattern of worship, both in the wilderness tabernacle and in the Jerusalem Temple.

The word *kohen* occurs more than 800 times in the Bible, but there are far fewer references to the Levites (*L'viyyim*), whether as individuals, a clan, or the tribe of Levi. The religious status of *L'viyyim* was secondary to that of the *kohanim*. The root לוה came to mean "escort" or "accompany." It apparently refers to the Levites' role of assistants to the priests in the sanctuary to whom they were assigned (*n'tunim;* Num. 3:9, 8:19). They may have served as a human barrier between the *kohanim,* restricted by rules of purity, and the people as a whole.

The Levites were noted for their loyalty to God during the crisis of the Golden Calf. The Torah stipulates that they were responsible for guard duty (*mishmeret*) and porterage (*avodah*) for the portable tabernacle of the wilderness (Num. 3). The levitical role as guardians of the sacred sanctuary was a lifelong duty that continued throughout the Temple period. The Books of Chronicles describe the Levites as being responsible for the care of the Temple's courts and chambers, the cleaning of the *k'lei kodesh* (ritual materials), the preparation of *matzot* and the *minḥah* offering, and the supervision of the Temple measures; they were also the singers or choir in the Temple (1 Chron. 23:26–32). They assisted the *kohanim* as magistrates and judges (1 Chron. 23:4, 26:29) and in overseeing the Temple treasury (1 Chron. 26:20). And they appear to have had a role as teachers and interpreters of Torah (Neh. 8:7; 2 Chron. 17:7–9).

Although the Levites were dedicated to God when substituted for firstborn sons (Num. 3) and were consecrated in a special ceremony (Num. 8), they did not have a distinctive dress, possess any ritual "power," or have a specific role in the sacrificial system.

The Levites did have a minor degree of sanctity and were sustained by tithes from the people (Lev. 27:32–33; Num. 18:21), because they possessed no ancestral land. Their landless position contributed to a precarious social and economic status, often associated with the alien, the orphan, and the widow. They were assigned to live in 48 cities scattered throughout the territory of the various tribes (Num. 35:1–8; Josh. 21:1–41).

In later Jewish tradition, the *L'viyyim* were accorded the honor of being called to the Torah for the second *aliyah* (after the *kohanim*). The historic levitical task of assisting the *kohanim* was preserved in the tradition of the Levites' washing the hands of the priests before their formal blessing of the congregation. Funerary art has symbolized *kohanim* by two hands in the position assumed during the traditional priestly blessing; and many gravestones designate *L'viyyim* with the symbol of a pitcher of water in recognition of their role in this ritual. Children of Levites were exempt from the commandment of redemption of the first born, because the *L'viyyim* were originally designated as replacements for the firstborn.

The institution of the priesthood was widespread in the ancient Near East. Non-Israelite priests are mentioned in the Bible (e. g., Melchizedek in Gen. 14:18; priests of Dagon in 1 Sam. 5:5). The qualifications and functions of non-Israelite priests were not necessarily the same as those of the Israelite *kohanim*. For example, in Canaanite religion, there were female priests, but the Israelite priesthood was limited to males, initially the firstborn and later the male descendants of Aaron from within the tribe of Levi.

During a certain period, all *L'viyyim* appear to have been eligible to serve as *kohanim*. This is clear from phrases that make no distinction between the two groups, such as "the priests the Levites" (*ha-kohanim ha-L'viyyim*) in Deut. 17:18 (see also 10:8–9, 33:8–10). Eventually, however, the specific designation of the *kohanim* as members of one family within the tribe of Levi came to be accepted as the basic "history" of priestly appointment.

In the biblical period, the tasks of the *kohanim* included the following:

- Officiation at rituals connected to the sacrificial system.
- Blessing the people (Num. 6:22–26).
- Sounding the trumpets on festivals and new moons (Num. 10:10).
- Blowing the *shofar* on *Yom Kippur* of the jubilee year (Lev. 25:9).
- Ascertaining the will of God through oracular means, such as the Urim and Thummim (Exod. 28:30; Num. 27:21).
- Determining the fate of a woman suspected of adultery (Num. 5:11–31).
- Ascertaining and treating impurities and various eruptions on the skin, clothing, and buildings (Lev. 11, 13–15).
- Judging the people along with the elders (Deut. 21:5; 1 Sam. 4:18; Ezek. 44:24).
- Preserving traditions and instructing the people (Deut. 31:9–13, 33:10; Mal. 2:7) and the king (Deut. 17:18–19).

The Torah continually stresses the twin ideals of holiness and purity (*k'dushah* and *tohorah*) in relation to the Israelites, the portable wilderness camp, and the sanctuary. The *kohanim* served as the symbolic exemplars of those spiritual paradigms and consequently lived with strict personal requirements of purity and holiness. The core of biblical information about these obligations is found in Lev. 21–22. The priests were enjoined to have contact with the dead of only their immediate family (Lev. 21:1–4,10–12) and were limited in their marital relationships (Lev. 21:7–8,13–15).

Kohanim were prohibited from marriage to a prostitute, divorcée, or *halalah* (someone born of a parent from a priestly family and a mate from a category of people forbidden to *kohanim*). The rationale for these forbidden marriages apparently was linked to the notion that sexual relations for a *kohen* must be limited to those untainted by problematic lineage or unsuspected of immoral behavior. The *halalah* had a blemished lineage, the prostitute engaged in immoral sexual behavior that may have been linked to Canaanite religious practices, and the divorcée was associated with sexual infidelity (via interpretation of Deut. 24:1: *ervat davar,* "unseemliness").

The Talmud added two categories to the list of prohibited relations. The first was the convert, because gentile women were considered to have lived in a licentious society in which they were presumed to have had illicit sexual relations. The second was the *halutzah,* a woman who after her first husband's death had been married to her husband's brother and later was compelled to divorce him. The *kohen gadol* was subject to a more restrictive standard of purity and prohibited from marriage even to a widow.

Just as animals offered as sacrifices had to be physically sound (Lev. 22:18–25), so *kohanim* had to be free of disabilities or deformities (Lev. 21:16–24). *Kohanim* were not to be exposed to working in society at large. Therefore, they were to be supported by donations and by designated portions of some of the sacrificial offerings (Lev. 6:16,29, 22:10–16). To be allowed to consume this designated (sacred) food, the *kohanim* had to fulfill special obligations that included ritual washing of hands and feet (Exod. 30:17–21), refraining from alcohol (Lev. 10:8–9), and maintaining a state of ritual purity. Like all other Israelites, *kohanim* also were prohibited from consuming meat that came from animals that had not been properly slaughtered (Lev. 22:8; Ezek. 44:31).

The *kohen gadol*—probably a shortened version of the phrase *ha-kohen ha-gadol me-eḥav* (the priest who is superior to his brothers, Lev. 21:10)—was a hereditary position from the descendants of Phinehas, Aaron's grandson (Num. 25:10–13). The investiture and clothing of the high priest resembled that of ancient Near Eastern royalty. He was anointed with oil (1 Sam. 10:1; 2 Kings 9:6), he wore special clothing (Exod. 28:2–4) made with gold and a special purple dye (*t'kheilet*), and wore a unique headdress (*mitznefet*) with a frontlet (*tzitz,* Exod. 28:36–39) and a diadem (*nezer,* Exod. 29:6, 39:30, Lev. 8:9). The *mitznefet* was compared to a crown (Ezek. 21:31; Isa. 62:3). Other priests also were anointed, as were the sacred vessels and utensils (Exod. 30:26–30; 40:9–15), in ceremonies that paralleled the construction and the dedication of the tabernacle (Exod. 29; Lev. 8).

The Bible differentiates between the roles of priest, prophet, and sovereign, although the *kohanim* were linked to the royal court because of the close connection between political and divine authority (1 Kings 1:32). Thus the appointment of a new cadre of priests was an essential element in the rebellion of Jeroboam (1 Kings 12:31). They were identified as central to the recovery or discovery of the book of the Torah and the subsequent revolution under King Josiah (2 Kings 22–23). *Kohanim* were among the elite of the kingdom of Judah taken into exile by the Babylonians (2 Kings 25:18–20).

The prophet Ezekiel, a *kohen,* provided spiritual support to the exiles in Babylon, as well as a vision of a rebuilt Jerusalem Temple. The *kohen* Ezra led the return of the exiles from Babylon and the rebuilding of the Temple. Under Ezra's leadership, *kohanim* began the public reading and interpretation of the Torah on a regular basis outside of the Temple walls, thus lending authority and prestige to a new expression of religious life (Neh. 8:5–11). In the absence of a Davidic king, the *kohen gadol* became the head of the Jewish community.

During the days of Antiochus IV in the 2nd century B.C.E., many priestly families actively supported the Seleucid monarch's efforts to impose Hellenistic customs in Jewish life. In this way, the spiritual stature of the *kohanim* was degraded to a concern for wealth, power, and influence. Other priestly families opposed this moral and ritual disgrace, especially the family of Mattityahu, the Hasmoneans. This is one of the factors that led to the Maccabean revolt, led by the Hasmoneans.

After the Hasmonean victory, Mattityahu's son Simon assumed the role of *kohen gadol.* This was a departure from the tradition of designating the *kohen gadol* by direct lineage. The disregard for that tradition, as well as eventual moral corruption of the priesthood under the Hasmoneans, led to the rise of the Pharisees as the primary teachers of Torah in place of the *kohanim,* the hereditary teachers of Torah.

After the destruction of the Temple, the role of the *kohanim* was significantly altered. The presence of the *kohanim* was not necessary for public worship, which now consisted of prayer, not sacrifice. Other activities clearly linked to the Temple ritual (sanctified food and determination of purity) were no longer in practice. Nonetheless, the social and legal distinctiveness of the *kohanim* was preserved, and certain rituals were instituted to recall the sacrificial service.

The most solemn and significant ritual of ancient Judaism was the *Yom Kippur* rite of the high priest. It fused three aspects of sanctity: the holiest individual, the holiest time, and the holiest space. It was the moment when forgiveness and atonement for sin could be achieved. Since the destruction of the Temple, the ritual of the *kohen gadol* has been re-enacted during the *Musaf* service of *Yom Kippur,* through the recitation of the *Avodah* service. Incorporating poetry and the Mishnah's description of the *Yom Kippur* ritual, the *Avodah* service serves as a substitute for the Temple practices. The recollection of the service of the high priest is the focal point of the *Yom Kippur* liturgy.

The Sages assumed that the holiness of the *kohanim* did not end with the destruction of the Temple. The biblical command to sanctify the priest (Lev. 21:8: *v'kiddashto*) was interpreted as applying to the ritual prerequisites of blessing the people and being called first to the Torah. The Talmud (BT Git. 59b) justified this as a biblical law and to ensure the "ways of peace"—to prevent arguments about who should receive the initial *aliyah.* Prohibitions against marrying converts or divorcées (BT Yev. 94a) and the prohibition of contact with the dead (BT Sanh. 5b) continued, as did the obligation of redeeming firstborn sons.

The marriage of a *kohen* with one of the women prohibited by the Torah is still forbidden according to the most restrictive understanding of Jewish law. Consequently, a *kohen* may not marry a divorcée or convert in the Orthodox community and in the State of Israel. Since the 1950s, the Conservative Movement, through the CJLS, has maintained a different approach to this biblical prohibition. The Talmud recognizes these marriages as having legal standing, for although such marriages violate strict rules of biblical purity for the *kohen,* they do not transgress laws of holiness (which would be violated by an adulterous or incestuous relationship). Following this precedent, the Conservative rabbinate came to view such marriages as permitted.

This development illustrates the general approach of Conservative Judaism to Jewish law. In 1947, the chairman of the CJLS indicated that a "*kohen* who married a divorcée should be barred from being called up to the Torah first." But by 1954, the reconstituted CJLS had accepted a responsum by Ben Zion Bokser and Theodore Friedman that validates such a marriage. This decision was based on four considerations: (a) although prohibited by biblical law, such a marriage has legal standing, (b) priestly lineage in modern times is doubtful, (c) the status of the *kohen* in the community has changed, and (d) the status of the divorcée is no longer stigmatized. Nonetheless, in recognition of the violation of a biblical commandment, the *kohen* is required to relinquish his status and the marriage ceremony is to be consciously modest and private.

A similar process of legal development took place regarding the rabbinical prohibition of marriage between a *kohen* and a convert. In 1946, the CJLS approved the instruction of a convert engaged to marry a *kohen,* stipulated that the rabbi should not solemnize the marriage ceremony, but reluctantly permitted such a marriage if the *kohen* were determined to marry the woman. The committee ruled that because such a marriage would have legal status it would be preferable to an interfaith marriage with an unconverted woman. In 1968, Isaac Klein permitted such a marriage, arguing that (a) although prohibited by rabbinical enactment, such a marriage has legal standing; (b) priestly status today is questionable; (c) the status of the *kohen* in the community has changed; and (d) non-Jews should not be considered licentious. Klein contended that to maintain the traditional prohibition would be a *ḥil-*

lul ha-shem. Unlike the earlier decision of the committee regarding the divorcée, because this prohibition is of rabbinical origin, the *kohen* is not required to renounce any priestly prerogatives.

In 1997, the CJLS approved a responsum by Arnold Goodman that contends that no stigma should be attached to marriage to divorcées or converts because in our time divorce and conversion are commonplace. Moreover, given the high rate of intermarriage, everything should be done to encourage endogamy. The biblical prohibition was abrogated, no restrictions were placed on the marriage ceremony, and the status of the *kohen* remained unchanged. Conservative rabbis, because of the variety of responsa adopted by the CJLS, may legitimately act in accordance with any one of three halakhically sanctioned decisions. They may maintain the biblical prohibition of marriage between a *kohen* and a divorcée as well as the rabbinical prohibition of marriage between a *kohen* and a convert; they may follow the responsum that allows the marriage to take place (placing limits on the subsequent status of the *kohen*); or they may follow the 1997 decision that allows such marriages to take place without restriction.

Some Conservative rabbis, influenced by 20th-century democratic trends, have argued that it is possible to disregard the priestly privilege of being called first to the Torah. This was legitimated in a responsum by Mayer Rabinowitz and adopted by the CJLS in 1990, based on the unreliability of family traditions about priestly lineage.

The ritual in which *kohanim* formally bless the congregation during the *Musaf* service on festivals (Hebrew: *oleh l'dukhan;* Yiddish: *dukhenen*) also fell out of favor in most synagogues. A number of Conservative congregations, however, have restored this traditional practice, attaching renewed significance to the spiritual dimension of this public ritual and desiring to preserve its religious significance for the families who treasure maintaining their tradition of being *kohanim.*

Although all the Temple rituals were performed by male *kohanim,* wives of *kohanim* were permitted to partake of the food designated for priestly families, unless they were divorced or widowed. This permission also extended to unmarried daughters of *kohanim.* In 1989, based on a responsum by Joel Roth, the CJLS permitted daughters of *kohanim* to receive *aliyot* as *b'not kohen.* However, the status of being in the family of *kohanim* is still transmitted through the father, not the mother, even though she is the daughter of a *kohen.*

The historic prohibition against priestly contact with the dead may have had its origins in an abhorrence of the Egyptian cult of the dead. The Israelite *kohen,* elected to serve the living God, was forbidden contact with the dead except for his immediate family. Historically, *kohanim* avoided entering cemeteries and did not serve on burial societies. Conservative Judaism has officially retained these practices. However, in 1929, the CJLS approved a responsum by Louis Epstein that argues that all *kohanim* in post-Temple Judaism are already ritually impure, cannot become further defiled, and thus are no longer subject to possible impurity by contact with the dead. Although not explicitly permitting a *kohen* to enter a cemetery, the responsum recognizes that there are grounds for leniency.

The *kohen* and the *Levi* symbolize two types of religious behavior. *Kohanim* represent the structure and order of Jewish ritual, whereas the Levites—with their service, song, and celebration—reflect the ideal of divine inspiration. Both are essential to the nurturing of a spiritual life.

The main institutions of biblical religion—prophets, kings, and a central temple—no longer exist in their original form. Prophecy has ended. The monarchy is no more. Sacrifice has ceased. Yet Jews have been able to sustain a religious culture by adapting and developing the core biblical traditions. The *kohen* and *Levi* symbolically serve as a living remnant of the earliest strata of biblical religion and as testimony to the creative power of that adaptive process.

Study Questions

1. Consider the personal obligations Scripture places on the *kohanim* and separate them into categories: the idea that a priest must be blemish-free; that a priest's allegiance to the laws of purity and impurity must be dramatically more intense than an average Israelite's; the specific ways a *kohen* must conduct himself in public or in private; and the rules that pertain to a priest's choice

of a wife. What are the core values Scripture seems to wish that *kohanim* embody? Do these values agree with what you know of biblical ethics? Can you find a common thread that seems to link all the values you have identified?

2. Frydman-Kohl offers a list of nine specific tasks that were assigned to priests in ancient times by biblical legislation. Look at the elaborate investiture ceremony described in Leviticus chapters 8 and 9. What are the specific details of the ceremony that make it an appropriate rite for the investiture of officials soon to be charged with these tasks?

3. Rabbi Frydman-Kohl's essay also features information about the Levites, members of the lesser sacerdotal caste in ancient Israel. Locate the details regarding their investiture ceremony in Numbers 8 and compare it to the priestly investiture ceremony in Leviticus 8–9. Compare what the levitical ceremony says about the place of the Levites in ancient Israel with the parallel message that the investiture ceremony of the priests says about the status of the *kohanim* in Israelite society.

4. In our day, Jewish communities vary widely in terms of the degree to which they are willing to grant *kohanim* (and, to a lesser extent, Levites) any special status in synagogue life or to insist that they remain faithful to the strictures Scripture places on their daily activities. What may be the reason behind the gradual resurgence of the practice of inviting *kohanim* (and, in some communities, the daughters of *kohanim*) to ascend to the *bimah* to bless the people that Frydman-Kohl mentions in his essay? Is it a desire to hold on to the *concept* of a priestly caste without feeling any concomitant obligation to force its members to adhere to ancient rules? Or does it seem more like an effort to use an archaic feature of traditional worship to dress up modern worship with a cloak of authenticity?

5. The *kohanim* and Levites of ancient times were all men. Does this gender specificity make the institution inappropriate for us to embrace today? If the point of retaining the special status of priests and Levites is to hearken back to the practices that existed in the

Temple in ancient Jerusalem, is there any benefit to making the institution *less* like its ancient model by revising its details in light of modern sensitivities? Or is there something reasonable, even noble, in building on this biblical foundation to create something reminiscent of an ancient practice without having to duplicate all of its less appealing aspects?

Study material by *Martin S. Cohen*

PROPHECY AND PROPHETS

Shalom M. Paul

Summary

In the Bible, God called upon prophets to deliver divine messages to the people. The prophets received the word of God, but in passing it on, they presented the divine will in their own unique styles. The prophets employed oracles, hymns, parables, and other stylistic forms to convey their messages. At times the people heeded these calls and at other times they did not. The preclassical prophets in the books of Joshua, Judges, Samuel, and Kings were also consulted by the people for advice and insight into the divine will. Sometimes they were political leaders as well, particularly in the premonarchic period. Some of these prophets had supernatural powers, such as the ability to predict the future and raise the dead. Figures with these characteristics are found in other ancient Near Eastern cultures as well.

The classical prophets, who arose during the rule of the Assyrians, Babylonians, and Persians, lived during a very different Israelite reality, one marked by calamity, instability, and exile. These latter prophets, such as Isaiah and Jeremiah, explained why this state of affairs had befallen the people and what they could do to rectify the situation. They urged repentance and focused on the need to correct ethical postures. They foresaw a day when the people would indeed return to God, and peace and prosperity would abound.

The phenomenon of prophecy is predicated on the premise that God reveals His will, by means of visions and oral communications, to individuals of His own choosing. The prophets are selected by God and irresistibly compelled to deliver His message, at times even against their own will and regardless of whether the people wish to hear it (Ezek. 3:11). Prophecy is neither a science nor an art that one may learn or master. One does not elect to prophesy, nor does one become a prophet by dint of any inherent or acquired faculty. There is no striving to be one with

God—no mystical union. Prophets are God's messengers. Standing in God's presence (Jer. 15:1,19) and being privy to the divine council (Isa. 6, Jer. 23:18; Amos 3:7), they translate their revelatory experiences into the idiom of the people. The divine message, refracted through the prism of their own personalities, is conveyed through the media of oracles, prayers, hymns, parables, indictments, dirges, letters, satirical tirades, and legal pronouncements. They act as covenantal mediators between God and the nation. Armed solely with the divine word, "word-possessed," they attempt to help shape the future by reforming the present. Their encounter with the deity affords them knowledge not of His being or essence but of His presence and designs in history. By experiencing God's word, they view the world from the divine perspective.

The Hebrew term for a prophet, *navi,* is a cognate of Akkadian *nabû,* "to call," and literally means "one who has been called by God." The prophet par excellence is Moses, who, at the revelation at Sinai, declares to the Israelites, "I stood between the LORD and you at that time to convey the LORD's words to you, for you were afraid of the fire and did not go up the mountain" (Deut. 5:5). The prophet thus is the spokesperson of God, His mouthpiece, to whom God speaks and who, in turn, speaks forth to the people on His behalf. The prophet is God's forthteller as well as foreteller (Exod. 14:15–16; Deut. 18:18; Jer. 15:19). Moses is distinguished from all other prophets by God's revealing Himself directly to him, "mouth to mouth, plainly and not in riddles" (Num. 12:8); whereas to the others, revelation came only in visions or dreams. Although dreams were originally considered as an authentic conduit for the reception of the divine message (Gen. 20:3, 31:10–13; 1 Sam. 28:6; 1 Kings 3:5–14) and would be so again (Joel 3:1), they fell into disrepute and were frowned on by some prophets (Jer. 23:28, 27:9; Zech. 10:2).

The preclassical prophets (i.e., those preceding the first classical prophet, Amos) are called "seer" (*hozeh* and *ro·eh*) and "man of God" (*ish ha-Elohim*) (e.g., 1 Sam. 9:6, 9; 1 Kings 17:18,24; 2 Kings 1:10, 4:7, 9, 21). Several narratives concerning these and other early prophets mention their being banded together in groups (1 Sam. 10:5, 10, 19:18–24; 1 Kings 18:3–4, 13, 22:22–23; 2 Kings 2:3, 5, 7, 4:38–44) and report the ecstatic nature of their behavior (Num. 11:25; 1 Sam.

10:6, 18:10, 19:18–24; 1 Kings 18:46; 2 Kings 9:11) induced by the "spirit of God," which came upon them. They played a prominent role in the society, being consulted for advice and requested to make known the will of God, for which they were occasionally remunerated (1 Sam. 9:8; 1 Kings 14:3; 2 Kings 8:9). These preclassical prophets also had a predominant role in influencing the political destiny of Israel, e.g., Samuel chose both Saul (1 Sam. 9) and David (1 Sam. 16) for kingship. Nathan severely reprimanded David for his affair with Bathsheba and for causing the death of her husband, Uriah (2 Sam. 12:7 ff.) and later instigated the scheme to persuade David to recognize Bathsheba's son Solomon as the next king (1 Kings 1:8 ff.). Ahijah proclaimed both the election and the rejection of Jeroboam I as king of northern Israel (1 Kings 11:29–39, 14:1–8, 15:29), Elijah foretold the eventual defeat of Moab by kings Jehoshaphat and Jehoram (2 Kings 3:16 ff.), and Elisha sent one of his coterie to anoint Jehu as king of Israel and inspired the latter's rebellion against Jehoram (2 Kings 9).

They were capable of foreseeing future events. For example, Elijah foretold both a drought (1 Kings 17:1) and the death of Ahaziah (2 Kings 1:4); Elisha foretold a famine that would last for seven years (2 Kings 8:1) and the harm that Hazael, king of Aram, would cause Israel (2 Kings 8:11 ff.). Even if some of these predictions were actually prophecies after the events themselves, the narratives clearly indicate that the people believed in the prophets' abilities to foresee what was about to occur.

These prophets also dramatized and concretized their prophetic word by performing symbolic acts, which were charged with the power to initiate the process of actualizing the event itself. Ahijah tore his robe into 12 pieces and commanded Jeroboam I to take 10 of them, "For thus says the LORD, the God of Israel: I am about to tear the kingdom out of Solomon's hands, and I will give you ten tribes. But one tribe shall remain his—for the sake of My servant David'" (1 Kings 11:31–32). In his contest with the Canaanite prophets of Baal and Asherah, Elijah succeeded in bringing fire down from heaven (1 Kings 18) and later split the Jordan River with his own mantle (2 Kings 2:8). Elisha, his successor, also split the Jordan with Elijah's mantle (2 Kings 2:13–14), made a single jug of oil fill many larger vessels (2 Kings 4:1–7), and revivified the son of a Shunammite woman (2 Kings 4:8 ff.), similar to Elijah's bringing back to life the son of the widow in Zarephath of Sidon (1 Kings 17:17–24). Elisha also ordered Joash to take a bow and arrow, open the window eastward, and shoot: "An arrow of victory for the LORD. An arrow of victory over Aram!" (2 Kings 13:17). Nevertheless, all these feats are based on the will of God and are ultimately ascribed directly to Him.

In all of these phenomena, the preclassical prophets of Israel closely resemble their earlier counterparts, known from early-18th-century B. C. E. Akkadian documents from the city of Mari, located on the Euphrates River in Syria. They also refer to charismatic professional and lay individuals who appear spontaneously before the king, deliver an oral message in the name of their god who "sent" them, and occasionally supplement their pronouncements with a symbolic act. These prophets include males and females (for the latter, compare Miriam, Deborah, Huldah, and Noadiah—called prophetesses in Exod. 15:20, Judg. 4:4, 2 Kings 22:14, and Neh. 6:14, respectively). Groups of such prophets are also mentioned in the Mari records.

Although the cuneiform documents contain the closest known parallels to early biblical prophecy, there are some salient differences between them. Both address themselves primarily to their respective kings, but the prophets at Mari are mainly concerned with cultic and political affairs and only rarely, in one extraordinary case, do they confront their king with an ethical demand. Contrast this to the prophet Nathan's condemnation of David for adultery and homicide (2 Sam. 12:1 ff.) and Elijah's taking Ahab to task over being an accessory in the appropriation of Naboth's vineyard and in the latter's death sentence (1 Kings 21:1 ff.). Furthermore, at Mari, in several instances the prophet's word was not considered absolutely authoritative (as it always is in the Bible), and the final decision on how to act was left to the discretion of the king. At times these prophets would even send a lock of their hair or a fringe of their garment as a personal identity check and as a guarantee of the veracity of their pronouncement. Even with these additional signs of authentication of their word, the Mari prophets do not commend unqualified acceptance, because their oracles were sometimes submitted for further verification by divinatory means. In the Bible, on the other hand, the prophetic word is the sole and absolute mark of attestation.

The Mari documents, although attested for only the final decade of Mari's existence, do, however, provide an analogue to the later biblical phenomena, as do the small corpus of 28 neo-Assyrian oracles from the 7th century B. C. E., uttered primarily in the name of the goddess Ishtar to the Assyrian kings Esarhaddon and Ashurbanipal.

Classical prophecy, which makes its first appearance during the middle of the 8th century B. C. E., was indebted in many ways to the spiritual and ethical heritage of its preclassical biblical predecessors. Nevertheless, commencing with the oracles of Amos and extending for the next 300 years, these inspired spokespeople of God introduced many new concepts and ideas into Israelite religion. The classical prophets arose and reached their zenith during the rise and fall of three great world empires: Assyria, Babylonia, and Persia. Isaiah, Micah, and Zephaniah prophesied at the time of Assyria's ascendancy ("Ha! / Assyria, rod of My anger," Isa. 10:5). Jeremiah (25:8 ff.), in turn, viewed Nebuchadrezzar as God's "servant" and Babylonia as God's "nation from the north," which was destined to bring about the destruction of Jerusalem and the Temple. The anonymous prophet of the Exile, Second Isaiah, called the Persian king Cyrus His "anointed one," who would release the nation from captivity and allow them to return to Israel and rebuild the Temple (Isa. 44:28, 45:1 ff.). The last three prophets, Haggai, Zechariah, and Malachi, were active during the Persian rule in the postexilic period. Thus the age of these great world empires also witnessed the unique religious phenomena of the appearance of classical prophets, who interpreted these world-shaking events in the light of an entirely new theological viewpoint. They provided the answer to the "why" of the destruction of both the northern (Israel) and southern (Judah) kingdoms and the "how" of future restoration.

Several of these prophets were reluctant to accept their calling (Exod. 3:11, 4:10; Isa. 6:5; Jer. 1:6; Jon. 1), because their task was unenviable and burdensome. These messengers of God were often rejected by their audience, who constantly and consistently refused to listen to their words and thereby reform their recalcitrant ways. The prophets' emotional experience upon receiving God's "stern vision" was overwhelmingly frightening (Isa. 21:3–4; Jer. 4:9, 6:11, 15:17; Hab. 3:16), and they became isolated individuals marked by loneliness and bitterness

(Jer. 9:1, 15:10, 20:14,18). Their lives were replete with anguish, fear, ridicule, and occasionally even imprisonment (Isa. 28:9–10; Jer. 11:18–23, 12:1 ff., 15:10,15, 17:14–18, 18:18–23, 20:7–10, 37:12–21; Ezek. 21:11–12; Hos. 9:8; Amos 7:12–13; Mic. 2:6), because they were primarily harbingers of doom and destruction. Although they bemoaned their nation's imminent tragedy (Isa. 6:11, 22:4; Jer. 8:23; Mic. 1:8–9), they did not shrink from their divine call but persisted to remonstrate against their people, even at the price of great personal danger.

There is, moreover, another dimension to the prophetic mission. They not only served as God's "district attorney" but also acted as the "defense attorney" for their people. Herein lies one of the most distinguishing characteristics of true prophets—their roles as intercessors. In fulfilling this task, they attempted through prayer to defend their people against their impending doom. The first individual in the Bible to be called a *navi* is Abraham; the term is applied to him not because he delivered oracles in the name of God, but because he interceded for Abimelech when the latter had taken Sarah into his household: "Since he is a prophet, he will intercede for you—to save your life" (Gen. 20:7). Abraham, with unbridled daring, also challenged God in a futile attempt to save the twin cities of evil, Sodom and Gomorrah: "Shall not the Judge of all the earth deal justly?" (Gen. 18:25). Moses, the paragon of the prophets, eloquently exemplified this intercessory role after both the construction of the Golden Calf (Exod. 32:11–14) and the pessimistic report of 10 of the 12 spies who were dispatched to scout out the possibility of entering Canaan (Num. 14:13–20). In both cases, God renounced His resolve to destroy the people immediately. (Cf. the incident at Taberah in Num. 11:1–3.) Samuel, too, prayed on behalf of his people after their defeat by the Philistines (1 Sam. 7:5–9), when their request for a king so embittered God (1 Sam. 12:19,23); and he even intervened on behalf of Saul, whom God had rejected as king of Israel (1 Sam. 15:11).

Moses and Samuel are singled out as the paradigmatic exemplars of intercessors on behalf of their people in the Book of Jeremiah (15:1). Jeremiah himself—unlike Amos, who successfully mediated twice for his people (Amos 7:13–6)—proved a worthy but unsuccessful successor in this role. Often he pleaded and prayed for the nation's salvation from the imminent Babylonian invasion (cf. Jer. 18:20: "Remember how I stood before You / To plead in their behalf, / To turn Your anger away from them"). Once the die had been cast, however, and the nation's doom became irrevocable, God prohibited any further intercession (Jer. 7:16, 11:14, 14:11–12).

The true prophet, as intercessor, was ready to risk a confrontation with God, in contrast to his counterpart, the false prophet. The problem of distinguishing between them was indeed perplexing, as is shown by two separate passages in Deuteronomy. According to Deut. 13:2 ff., if a prophet delivers an oracle (even if it is subsequently confirmed by an external sign) to worship other gods, he obviously is a false prophet. In turn, Deut. 18:20–22 raises the question, "How can we know that the oracle [uttered in God's name] was not spoken by the LORD?" The answer given is that if the "oracle does not come true, that oracle was not spoken by the LORD; the prophet uttered it presumptuously." This, however, cannot serve as an infallible criterion, because there are several occasions when an oracle delivered by a true prophet did not materialize even in his own lifetime. Such unfulfilled prophecies include Jeremiah's prediction of the ignominious fate of king Jehoiakim (Jer. 22:19), which was belied by 2 Kings 24:6, and Ezekiel's foretelling the destruction of Tyre by Nebuchadrezzar (Ezek. 26:7–21), which later was admitted to have failed but was to be compensated by the Babylonian king's attack on Egypt (29:17–20). Jeremiah provided yet another criterion for determining a true prophecy in his dramatic confrontation with the false prophet Hananiah. The latter predicted that the LORD was to break the yoke of the Babylonian oppressor in 2 years and the exiled community would henceforth return to Israel (as opposed to Jeremiah's oracle of 70 years of captivity). Jeremiah (28:9) declared that "if a prophet prophesies good fortune, then only when the word of the prophet comes true can it be known that the LORD really sent him." Jeremiah himself was in continual combat with several types of false prophets, three of whom he attacks in chapter 23. Against those who constantly uttered: "Peace, peace," he responded, "There is no peace" (6:14, 8:11). Ultimately, the falsity or veracity of prophecies could not be determined by context alone but could be judged solely by the one who truly had been granted divine revelation and stood in the LORD's council (23:18). For only a prophet "who has received My word, [can]

report My word faithfully! How can straw be compared to grain? ...
Behold My word is like fire—declares the LORD—and like a hammer
that shatters rock!" (23:28–29).

Although some of the false prophets did claim the gift of revelation
and imparted oracles (Jer. 23:31) in the LORD's name (14:14, 29:9),
they nevertheless did not intercede with God on behalf of the people
(27:18), as Ezekiel remonstrates: "Your prophets, O Israel, have been
like jackals among ruins. You did not enter the breaches and repair the
walls for the House of Israel, that they may stand up in battle on the
day of the LORD" (Ezek. 13:4–5). And as he explicitly states in God's
name: "I sought a man among them to repair the wall or to stand in
the breach before Me in behalf of this land, that I might not destroy it;
but I found none. I have therefore poured out My indignation upon
them; I will consume them with the fire of My fury" (22:30– 31; cf.
Ps. 106:23). For only the true prophet stood in the breach, even against
God, to defend Israel.

God's universal will was revealed to the prophets in the panoramic
language of history, but only Israel was His elected and selected covenantal partner. The consequence of such chosenness was not a bona
fide guarantee of immunity but rather a heightened responsibility. All
the nations of the world stand in judgment before God and are held
culpable for gross violations of the established order (Amos 1:3–2:3; Isa.
13–23; Jer. 46–51; Ezek. 25–32), but only Israel was taken to task for
every infringement of its moral and ethical code of behavior: "You alone
have I singled out / Of all the families of the earth—/ That is why I will
call you to account / For all your iniquities" (Amos 3:2). The prophets
condemned and castigated juridical corruption, violence, cruelty, dis-
honesty, greed, oppression, exploitation, bribery, harlotry, debauchery,
infidelity, arrogance, luxury, apathy, lust for power, and militarism, because all these were ultimately a blatant rejection of God. So, too, they
severely attacked the absolutization of the cult, because in their eyes the
essence and quintessence of God's demand was not to be found in cultic practices but in the moral and ethical spheres of life. They thereby
introduced the novel concept of the primacy of morality (Isa. 1:11–
17, 66:1 ff.; Jer. 6:20, 7:21–23, 14:12; Hos. 6:6; Amos 5:21–25; Mic.
6:6–8). For them, worship and its accompanying ritual were means to

draw closer to God; whereas justice and righteousness were ends unto themselves. God demanded primarily right, not rite, and when the cult became a substitute for moral behavior, it was condemned. Henceforth, any cultic act performed by a worshiper whose moral probity was not beyond reproach was considered abominable to the deity. Ritual now became, for the first time, contingent on the individual's personal behavior. The prophets, moreover, declared that morality not only was of absolute importance but also was the decisive factor in determining the national destiny of Israel, rather than idolatry or the desecration of *Shabbat*, as stated in the Torah. (The prophets did not repudiate the cult per se but only its becoming a surrogate for ethical behavior. This is shown by the later prophets' positive attitude toward the ritual, as evidenced in Ezek. 40–44; Hag. 1:4; Zech. 4:9; and Mal. 1:6–10.)

The prophets demanded wholehearted faithfulness to the covenant between God and Israel; they threatened inexorable punishment, embedded in the covenantal curses, for all those who were disloyal to it. Their ultimate purpose, however, was to achieve the desired goal of repentance, which demanded a change of heart and conduct. They censured, threatened, and admonished to evoke a change in the hearts and behavior of the people so as to avoid the imminent destruction. "Maybe" God would relent (Hos. 11:8–9; Joel 2:14; Amos 5:15; Jon. 3:9; Zeph. 2:3), because His plans are at times revocable, predicated on the people's actions (Jer. 18:7–10; Ezek. 3:17–21, 33:7–20). The frustration, however, of waiting for the nation's return to God ultimately led to yet another prophetic theological innovation: the "new covenant." Because the Sinaitic covenant had been broken, God, despairing of the futility of punishment to evoke a change in their hearts, would eventually implant His will directly on their hearts by a divine "grafting." Their "heart of stone" would be circumcised, and their entire being would be filled with the "knowledge of God." This new covenant would be unbreakable and would presage final redemption (Isa. 55:3; Jer. 24:7, 31:30–33, 32:38–41; Ezek. 16:60, 34:25 ff., 37:26 ff.; cf. Deut. 30:6; Isa. 11:9, 54:13). With the covenant renewed, the "remnant of Israel" (Isa. 4:3–4, 10:20–22; Jer. 31:31 ff.; Amos 9:8 ff.; Mic. 4:7; Zeph. 2:9), who will have survived the "Day of the LORD," would be restored and would live in peace, no longer troubled by oppression, injustice, or war

(Isa. 2:1–4, 10:27, 11:1–9, 60:5–16, 61:4– 9; Hos. 2:21 ff.; Mic. 4:3–4). God's ineffable presence would manifest itself to all humankind (Isa. 40:5), and the nations would come to reject their polytheistic worship and revere the God of Israel alone (Isa. 19:18–25, 45:22 ff.; Jer. 3:17, 12:16; Ezek. 17:24; Mic. 7:16 ff.; Hab. 2:14; Zech. 2:15, 8:20–23, 14:16–19). Jerusalem would become the spiritual and juridical center of the world, from which God's instruction would be disseminated to the entire world (Isa. 2:2). Israel itself, according to the anonymous prophet of the exile, Second Isaiah, would become a prophet nation (49:2–3, 51:16, 59:21) and a "light unto the nations" (42:6, 49:6), recounting God's glory (43:21) and bringing His blessing and beneficence to the ends of the earth (45:22–24).

Study Questions

1. How does the Hebrew word *navi* reflect the nature of prophecy?

2. Which prophet reached the highest level of prophecy? What distinguishes his prophecies from those of other prophets?

3. Some prophets, such as Moses, were skeptical of their calling, while others, such as Jonah, rejected God's mission outright. What do you think the Bible is telling us about prophecy and prophets when it tells us about these recalcitrant prophets? Does it change your perception of what a prophet is or should be?

4. According to the essay, how can one identify a false prophet? Who might today's false prophets be?

5. In contemporary society, are there figures—political, religious, social—who fulfill the role of the biblical prophets? Are they more accepted/successful than the prophets of the Bible?

Study materials by *Daniel Yechiel Septimus*

Understanding the Bible in Its Historical Context

ISRAELITE SOCIETY IN TRANSITION

Gordon Freeman

Summary

Reading the Bible as a history book is a challenging endeavor; it reports history through a moral and theological prism. Thus, to discover the social, political, and cultural roots of Judaism, one needs to read the Bible with a very different set of intellectual glasses. In this essay, Gordon Freeman offers a distinct set of social, cultural, and political lenses that help us draw a picture of ancient Israelite society and its evolution over time. It makes us more attentive to the geography, land, weather, and surrounding cultures that affect and shape the emergent Israelite culture and ritual.

While there are occasional digressions, this essay traces the chronological development of Israelite society, moving smoothly through the time of the Patriarchs, settlement in the Land of Israel, the period of the monarchy, the period surrounding the Babylonian exile, and the return to Israel under Ezra and Nehemiah. In each period, it is helpful to focus on the economic, social, cultural, and political trends that Freeman describes.

The narratives and teachings of the Bible develop in the context of the social, political, and economic realities of its time. Because the Bible includes literature written and compiled over many centuries, it should not be surprising that the reality of its context changed many times. These changes led to tensions that influenced biblical recordings of events and teachings. Those who decided what would be included in the biblical canon lived after the recorded events. Their decisions were influenced by their own perceptions of reality.

The Book of Genesis sets the scene for many of the issues repeated throughout biblical literature. We immediately confront the tension between agricultural and pastoral economies. The story of Cain, the farmer, and Abel, the shepherd, may be understood in terms of the rivalry over land use. Anthropologists teach that this tension occurred in primitive societies and is reflected in the settlement of the American West. The difference between agricultural and pastoral societies has profound consequences for relationships, political systems, and social concerns. People living in pastoral societies move constantly from place to place. The reality of pastoral life requires work by both men and women, thus affecting gender roles. Political models use pastoral language to describe leadership (see especially Ps. 23). Later literature tends to idealize the shepherd/leader.

People who till the soil, unlike shepherds, usually regard change as a potential threat to their well-being. The descendants of Cain, whose agricultural offering was not favored, become artisans and technicians. These tasks are based on life settled in one place, on teachings and learning skills that require a stable society. Territory becomes a major concern of law and politics; power is based on ownership.

We do not have any record of rituals or liturgy during this early period, but we know that the pastoral reality affects the superstructure (the symbols, rituals, myths, stories, and religion) of the culture. People on the move are constantly dealing with change. Given the constant state of uncertainty that comes with leading flocks from place to place, stories about divine messages that speak of promise and destiny might have been driven by a search for meaning.

The weather patterns provide us with a background for biblical stories. Lack of rainfall, a constant problem recorded in Genesis, and the subsequent famines caused people to leave their land to find new sources of food. Abraham and Sarah left for Egypt because of famine. Because the rainfall in the land of Canaan was not consistent, people came and went.

Scarce food supply, caused by weather conditions, led Jacob and his family to leave the Land, but a decline in the hegemony of the Egyptian Empire made it possible for Israelites to return and spread their area of settlement. The newly settled population was concentrated in the hill country, away from the Canaanite settlements in the western plain and the Philistines along the coast. The hill country, the north-south range just west of the Jordan Valley, offered a defensive position but was a challenge to agricultural development. Fields, orchards, and vineyards had to be carved out of the terrain through an intricate system of terracing. The infrastructure (population size, work patterns, geographic distribution, production of food in relation to the environment) during this time was based on a labor-intensive economy made possible by a large concentration of laborers. People apparently had no alternative places to settle; it would have been counterproductive to relocate. We also learn from this that the demography was stable, for the intensive type of work required would not have been possible otherwise.

Terracing techniques were similar in various places and were not the work of individual farmers. From these techniques, we can begin to describe the social structure. A group effort reflects the willingness to make a long-term investment without immediate gain. This in turn tells us that strong relationships existed within and between communities whose members were willing to be involved in mutual help to create the terraces.

Evidence of the construction of individual grain pits demonstrates that the family was the center of life. There is no evidence of an elaborate administrative establishment or of a professional bureaucracy, except for the existence of a small priestly bureaucracy.

The biblical text presents a picture of women occupying a significant place in this predominantly patriarchal society. The matriarchs exhibited strong personalities and wielded great influence on family life and the raising of children. This picture seems to reflect premonarchic Israel during the late Bronze Age. The economy was labor intensive; many hands were required to clear the land of trees and build cisterns and terraces. Because there was no military class or standing army, men were often called to military service. These realities led to the need for women's labor in every aspect of life. The worth of women was enhanced by utility, leading to higher social status. The text in Gen. 2–3 depicts nonhierarchical gender relationships.

By the time of the period of the monarchy, the household-based economy was no longer dominant. In describing a time when the Land was settled, the Torah reflects significant participation of women in the festivals (Deut. 12:18, 16:10–13 ff.). Women were fully obligated and accountable in covenant observance (Deut. 13:7, 17:2–5, 29:10–13, 31:12), which continued into postexilic Jewish life (2 Chron. 15:12 ff.; Neh. 8:2). Although women were excluded from the priesthood, the role of *nazir* was open to them (Num. 6:2). Women like Miriam, Deborah, and Hulda also were among the prophets.

The biblical woman experienced legal disadvantages (e. g., she passed from the authority of her father to that of her husband). Yet she was entitled to make legally binding agreements. The significant inheritance reform described in the Book of Numbers dealing with women's disadvantage in matters of inheritance was instituted because of the claims made by the daughters of Zelophehad.

Women maintained a strong place in society and in the family (see Prov. 31:10–31 for a description of the ideal woman). The Bible recognized that the relationship between husband and wife should be not one of dominance but of partnership (e. g., Hos. 2:18). A wife could not be treated as a slave; if she had been a maidservant and subsequently married her owner, she could not be sold (Exod. 21:7).

The Torah declares the primary equality of women and men, because both were created in the divine image (Gen. 1:27), i. e., both symbolize God's presence, according to Nahum Sarna's understanding of *tzelem* (image). This teaching must have been in constant tension with social reality. The text may be attempting to find the legal means to relieve the perceived social disability.

The economic reality needs to be placed in the context of the geopolitics of the day. The extent of Egyptian power had a direct effect on Israel's ability to control land area. While Israelites were languishing in Egyptian servitude, Egypt had control over the land of Canaan. The great story that eventually became the master story of the Bible, the Exodus from Egypt, is a dramatic reflection of the Egyptian Empire's loss of power. The change in the cultural superstructure is reflected in Moses, the pastoral leader, confronting the landed, agricultural Pharaoh. This at once takes us back to the original pastoral–agricultural tension and points us forward to the eventual break between the agricultural northern tribes called Israel and the southern pastoral tribes called Judah.

Around the time of early Israelite settlement in the highlands, the Egyptian Empire was in further decline. Archaeological evidence demonstrates that during the period between the early 13th and middle 12th centuries B.C.E., the Egyptian Empire began to withdraw from the area. Consequently, the Hittites left, probably owing to a famine, and the Assyrians began incursions against the Egyptian Empire. The Canaanite city-states under the control of the Egyptian Empire were losing their power base by the time of Deborah (12th century B.C.E.). Their breakdown marked the effective end of Egyptian sovereignty in the area. Philistine incursions on the western shore also challenged Canaanite hegemony. All these factors led to the spread of Israelite population westward.

At the same time, hardly any Israelite cities existed; Israelite tribes were rural/pastoral. The Canaanite settlements on the western plain and the coastal Philistine area threatened the Israelites during the time of the Judges. Israelite tribes were largely confined to the north-south hilly spine, between the Jordan River on the east and the coastal plain in the west.

Tribal and clan-based polities were led by inherited leadership, with occasional ad hoc charismatic leaders, such as Gideon and Jephthah, who defended the people from various external threats (including Philistines, Moabites, and Canaanites). This type of leadership was replaced by a centralized monarchy but was not without tension between central rule and tribal fiefdoms. Although rural Israel was decentralized (a refrain in Judg. 17:6, 18:1, 21:25 declares, "There was no king in Israel, everyone did what was right in his own eyes"), a strong sense of ethnic identity existed. Premonarchic institutions were established based on this identity. These included the *shofet,* a national magistrate, and *sheivet,* the tribe as a constituent unit of the *edah,* the entire people as a constituted polity.

Before the monarchy (from the late 13th to the 11th centuries B.C.E.), governance was local and controlled by tribal leaders. A loose intertribal assembly, much in the sense of a confederation without any transcending political power, might have existed. The tribes were not willing to give up any hegemony, except during times of external threat.

Even then, not all of the tribes would heed the call to contribute troops to the effort.

By the 10th century B.C.E., the eclipse of Egypt and the Canaanite city-states and the introduction of iron usage among Israelites posed a new situation. The Israelites were willing to recognize the centralized authority of a king who could increase territory and secure the borders. As their enemies collapsed, they came to control larger areas of arable land. Although artisans still had to be imported to aid the vast Solomonic building projects, in time Israel developed native trade and artisan classes. By the destruction of the First Temple (586 B.C.E.) the economy was a sophisticated mix of pastoral and agricultural, trade and crafts.

By the time of the monarchy (10th century B.C.E.), urbanization increased because of landless peasants looking for opportunities in the growing cities developed by the kings. Competing social groups constantly realigned themselves. The peasantry and the urban poor were defended by the prophets. The wealthy landowners were supported by the court. The central priesthood in Jerusalem competed with the local shrines and ritual centers led by itinerant priests and Levites.

Saul, the first king of Israel, had great difficulty maintaining the tribal alliance. The tribes were unwilling to support his court or maintain a standing military force to discourage Israel's enemies from attacking. David's successful rise to power was based on his skill at carefully building alliances. The rise of the Davidic monarchy was also owing to the power vacuum left by the declining Canaanite city-states.

A strong central power was needed to balance various economic, political, and social power centers that were in tension with each other. Eventually, they yielded power to David because of his skill. As the empire expanded and conquered territories and helped maintain the court and the military, the power concentrated in the monarchy was not challenged. However, those territories began to break away at the end of David's reign. Solomon had to increase taxes to support an expensive court. The tensions between royal power in Judah and tribal power centers in the north increased to the breaking point, and the northern tribes of Israel split from Judah. Ironically, the revolt was led by Jeroboam of the tribe of Ephraim, who had been appointed to oversee the forced labor and collection of taxes from the northern tribes (1 Kings 11:26 ff.).

King Solomon was the first king to attempt to consolidate his power by creating administrative districts that ignored tribal territories, thus marginalizing local leadership and replacing it with governors appointed by (and loyal to) the king. By transferring authority from local clan and tribal leaders to their own agents, the kings hoped to gain compliance to their rule. This tactic backfired: Loyalty to the kings decreased. The people preferred the traditional tribal authorities who were native to their localities.

Another example of the tension between local authority and central rule is found in the biblical assertion that all cultic activity should be limited to the centralized Temple in Jerusalem. It should be remembered that David had brought the Ark to Jerusalem and that his son Solomon built the First Temple there, perhaps to demonstrate that God legitimized their monarchy. Any alternatives—local shrines, for example—were denounced. Nevertheless, local shrines continued to compete with Jerusalem for loyalty, just as the rebellions by the local authorities against David and Solomon showed that old tribal loyalties were strong. It was almost as if the monarchy/central priesthood had been plastered onto a tribal confederacy. When taxes were required from localities to support the center, the fragile structure of centralized government in Jerusalem began to crumble.

After the death of Solomon, when the kingdom split between Judah and Israel, the tribal memories began to fade. These two small and weakened polities realized that to survive they needed to withstand the growing threat of expanding Assyrian and Babylonian empires by consolidating their power around their respective monarchies. The family/tribal origins of Israel, now shrouded in myth, became a distant memory. Northern Israel was organized around the dominant Ephraimite territory. The other nine tribes were hardly mentioned. Benjaminite territory became integrated into the kingdom of Judah located in Jerusalem.

The prophets Jeremiah and Isaiah spoke in the context of deep social and economic cleavage. Whereas they supported the central government, they decried its corruption and asserted that the monarchy had to act with righteousness and justice to deserve the loyalty of the people. For example, Jeremiah decries the advantages of wealthy landowners who had the means to increase their power at the expense of the peasantry, whose small plots of land were unable to sustain them over time (Jer. 34:8–20). Social legislation found in the Torah obligating people to support the poor dealt with providing food, correcting economic and social dislocation through sabbatical and jubilee laws, and regulating the laws of indentured servitude (see Lev. 25:25 ff.). These laws reflect social cleavage between the wealthy, landed gentry and the impoverished peasantry. Peasants, losing land because of debt, eventually fled to urban areas searching for ways to feed themselves and their families. Whether or not these laws were ever fulfilled, they became the model for prophecies, especially of Amos and Jeremiah (see Amos 2:6–8; 4:1–3; 5:11– 12; 8:4–8).

The prophets not only responded to growing social cleavage but also to changing geo-political reality. Jeremiah understood that there was a relationship between these two factors. He claimed that the growing distance between the wealthy and the impoverished was a direct result of moral failure on the part of leadership. He counseled submission to the looming threat of the Babylonian Empire, which he explained as the inevitable punishment for social injustice and corruption. During his time, the king and his advisers believed that Judah could depend on the Egyptian Empire to come to its defense against a Babylonian attack. He analyzed the dependence on the political alliance with Egypt and saw it as a failure. Egypt, Jeremiah realized, was using Judah to soften the blow of a Babylonian incursion against it. Judean society had failed; it was indefensible because of its injustice and lack of compassion. It could choose to suffer submission or fight and lose everything.

But the cultural superstructure had experienced a change with the advent of the Temple cult. The master story before the monarchy was the Exodus. Solomon's Temple competed with the Exodus as a source of salvation. The Temple became the purpose and fulfillment of the Exodus promise. The master story had been slowly transformed from the distant events of the Exodus to the concept of the Temple as the place to experience God's presence. Worship in the Temple epitomized salvation.

The prophets at the end of the First Temple period introduced an alternative master story: the Sinai event, the giving of the Torah, which replaced the Temple as the fulfillment of the Exodus. This transformation began to prepare the people for the tragedy of destruction and exile. Although the Temple had been destroyed, God's word became the source for salvation.

We know very little about Jewish life in Babylonia after the exile in 586 B.C.E., but the Jewish community must have experienced stability and some degree of political and economic success. With the Persian conquest of Babylonia in the 6th century B.C.E., we find Jews in high political positions. Nehemiah has the ear of the Persian emperor, and is able to persuade him that it was advisable to establish a loyal colony in the western outpost of the empire. The majority of Jews decide against returning to their ancestral land, despite the attempts by Ezra and Nehemiah to persuade them. This demonstrates that although their Jewish identity was maintained, they enjoyed their apparent comfort in their new land. The community as a whole was accountable to the king. Yet the distinctions between Jews and Persians were often permeable and Jews participated in Persian society.

The Book of Esther indicates that Jews quickly assimilated. Aware of their difference, they attempted to blend quietly into the general population. The choice of Babylonian names, for example, Mordecai (a form of Marduk) and Esther (a form of Astarte) demonstrates this social reality.

When Ezra and Nehemiah led a small group back to Judah in the middle of the fifth century B.C.E. to re-establish Jewish life, they were confronted by a native Judean population that had also assimilated, though in a different way. Remaining on the land must have provided some sense of cultural identity, but many married "foreign" wives.

Ezra decided to make an ethnic distinction regarding personal identity and attempted to reinforce Jewish life by forcing the native Jews to divorce their foreign wives. The Book of Ruth may have been a response to this issue. The practice of formal conversion was introduced only in the early Roman period when a corpus of Jewish law regarding conversion began to evolve.

Ezra faced a jurisdictional requirement to establish the identity of a citizenry that would be regarded as part of this Persian colony. His preliminary solution (banning foreign wives) threatened the shared identity of the native Judean population and the returning exiles. Before a complete social break occurred, a new definition of Jewish identity had to be articulated. The books of Chronicles now defined Israelites as those following the Jerusalem Temple ritual and included natives (not only Persian Jewish returnees).

Following the teachings established by the prophets, Ezra, the religious leader of the colony, who was a priest and scribe, reinterpreted the master story. The meaning of the Exodus had to be applied to changing circumstances. The study of Torah now became the key to Jewish identity and survival. Now every Israelite could participate in redemption through his or her own observance and study of Torah. With Jewish communities in Egypt and Babylonia as well as in the ancient homeland, Judaism was no longer geographically bound. The Exile and return forced a rereading of the ancient stories to emphasize individual responsibility and participation in God's covenant with Israel.

Study Questions

1. In the first paragraph, Gordon Freeman hints at theories concerning the authorship of the Bible and the relationship of ancient literature to political and social reality. What is his view, and do you agree?

2. Freeman points to the tension in the Bible between an agrarian/farming culture and that of a nomadic/shepherding society. Which does he claim came first in the Bible? How does he view the mindsets of these two social orders in relation to change? How do you think these mindsets might influence the development of religion and law?

3. We have been conditioned to think that the enhancement of the status of women is a very recent phenomenon. How do you react to the picture Freeman portrays of women in the Bible? Do you agree? Is power and influence always synonymous with equality? Do you think that Freeman's evidence is sufficient to alter the commonly held notion that women in the Bible have inferior status? How does his view compare to that of Judith Hauptman's essay found elsewhere in this volume?

4. Freeman describes the transition from a wandering nomadic desert tribal existence to a settled shepherd/farmer collection of independent Israelite tribes, each with its own tribal leaders and land allotments. How does he account for the willingness of these tribes to give up a measure of autonomy and accept a king? Do you agree with his assessment? How did the United States deal with the question of local/state autonomy verses a centralized government?

5. Freemen describes the government of Israel under David and Solomon as an "empire" (albeit short-lived). It is interesting to read the books of Joshua, Judges, Samuel, and Kings with an eye toward the issues facing the State of Israel today. Does centralized power always corrupt? What checks and balances exist in a monarchy, if any? Does Freeman indicate what served as a check against the emergent monarchies of David, Solomon, and their successor kings?

6. What happened when Solomon disregarded old traditions and tribal loyalties as he reorganized the Davidic Empire? How "wise" was Solomon? Could he have handled things differently? Would a united Israel that was more aligned with tribal loyalties have been better able to withstand the Assyrian and Babylonian assaults?

7. What was the role of the classical prophets in relation to the political life and realities of Israelite society? What should be the role of religion and visionary thinking in society? In shaping governmental policy? Does the intertwining of religion and government cleanse or corrupt?

8. Freeman points to two "master stories" of the Jewish people: the Exodus from Egyptian slavery and Sinai and the giving of Torah. For the priestly and ruling classes of ancient Israel, freedom from Egyptian slavery is fully realized in the power of Temple worship and sacrifice, the right and power to serve and sacrifice to our own god in our own Temple. For the prophets, Sinai and the law were the fulfillment of the freedom from slavery. Which master story do you feel characterizes Judaism today? Which story is the most compelling to you personally as a Jew?

9. Consider the Rabbinic statement, "The world's existence rests upon three pillars: on the (giving and/or study of) Torah; on *avodah* (the sacrificial temple worship and/or prayer); and on deeds of lovingkindness (*gemilut hasadim*)." How does this dictum deal with the two master stories cited in this essay?

10. Freeman closes his essay by remarking that new "master stories" created after the exile emphasized "individual responsibility" and "covenant." As you read Bible, can you discern another master story of Judaism—one that might include a universal dimension?

Study materials by *Sheldon Dorph*

BIBLICAL ARCHAEOLOGY

Lee I. Levine

Summary

The history of biblical archaeology is mired in controversy and debate. Archaeology reveals new information that sometimes confirms the biblical narrative, but often it either fails to confirm the narrative or provides evidence that conflicts with the biblical account. For example, sites of destruction dating from the 13th century B.C.E. may attest to Joshua's conquest of Canaan, while coins, weapons, city remains, and other objects of everyday living from the middle of the first millennium B.C.E. are witness to the existence of an ancient Israelite society. At the same time, there are no Egyptian sources that attest to a period of Israelite slavery, and sometimes archaeological scholarship seems to deny not only the biblical narrative, but other archaeological evidence as well. Though we have evidence that seems to confirm Joshua's conquest of Canaan, we have no archaeological data from some places—such as Jericho—that are featured prominently in the Joshua tale.

Traditionally, religious leaders have appealed to archaeology to prove the veracity of the Bible, while skeptics have cited archaeological findings for the opposite purpose. Some sort of middle ground is, perhaps, the most honest response to biblical archaeology, and in recent years, the dichotomy between "religious" responses and "skeptical" ones has, to a large extent, been deconstructed.

Archaeological remains have been a source of fascination for centuries. Since the 17th and 18th centuries, travelers have braved difficult physical conditions and the hostility of the local inhabitants to bring home news of the remarkable remains of ancient civilizations. By the 19th century, many European countries had established societies to promote the exploration and sponsorship of archaeological excavations in the Middle East. The political realities of the time prompted Western powers to increase their presence in the region to fill the power vacuum that would be left by the impending disintegration of the Ottoman Empire. The almost immediate success of the archaeological excavations—which included sensational discoveries from Troy, Babylon, Susa, and Egypt—led to heightened public interest and support.

Interest in the archaeology of the Holy Land was generated in part by these developments, and in part by the role of the country as the historical backdrop in the biblical narrative for events ranging from Abraham to Jesus. Verifying the Bible became a pivotal motivating factor for many archaeologists, most of whom were, not coincidentally, clergymen, and one of the covert, and sometimes explicitly stated, goals of many of these expeditions was to prove the historicity and accuracy of the Bible. In the first half of the 20th century, Jewish archaeologists from the *Yishuv* (the emerging Zionist presence in Palestine) joined the exploration of ancient Israel with a similarly tendentious agenda. Academic and cultural institutions in the *Yishuv* that sponsored such initiatives sought to unearth the country's Jewish roots by uncovering the major sites of Israelite settlement in the biblical and postbiblical periods.

This picture changed dramatically during the second half of the 20th century. Religious motivation and the need to demonstrate the existence of Jewish roots in the country became less central, although understanding the Hebrew and Christian Bibles, as well as Jewish history in antiquity, remained a key motivating factor in these explorations. Archaeologists increasingly have questioned accepted assumptions about biblical history and the biblical narrative, owing to a revisionist and skeptical mode that characterizes some archaeological circles—a not uncommon phenomenon in scholarship generally in the latter 20th century. Thus, the beginning of the 21st century finds biblical archaeology in a state of flux. Although new material is brought to light almost every year and our knowledge of the material culture of the period increases geometrically, fundamental questions of interpretation and the resultant reconstructions of history have remained pivital issues.

Archaeological evidence has substantially impacted our knowledge and understanding of the Bible and of biblical history in the following ways.

REVEALING NEW INFORMATION

Archaeology has brought to light an enormous amount of information regarding the material culture of the times. Vessels, tools, weapons, seals, and coins (from the Restoration, or Persian, period; 538–332 B.C.E.), as well as names and official titles mentioned in inscriptions, all attest to various aspects of daily life in Israelite culture. Moreover, the discovery of residential quarters, city walls, and urban settlements reveals dimensions of biblical society that add immeasurably to our understanding of the written sources.

CONFIRMING THE BIBLICAL NARRATIVE

Many discoveries have a direct bearing on information appearing in the Bible. For instance, several archaeological sites such as Hazor bear witness to Joshua's alleged conquest of Canaan by showing massive destruction toward the end of the 13th century B.C.E. Other examples include the shaft (*tzinnor*) allegedly used by David to conquer Jerusalem, an inscription noting the "House of David," the plan and layout of biblical city gates, which are mentioned frequently in the biblical text, the discovery of local Israelite altars and shrines (presumably the high places, or *bamot,* referred to by the prophets), the appearance of hundreds of new settlements in the hill country from the 13th to 11th centuries B.C.E., evidence of royal building activities (e.g., Hezekiah's tunnel), and discoveries at other sites in Israel's neighboring countries (Syria, Jordan, and Iraq) that shed light on the patriarchal era. All of this material concretizes and contextualizes the biblical narrative. Such has been the case with documents from Mari (Syria) and Nuzi (Iraq), the Mesha inscription (Jordan), and the Merneptah stele (commemorative stone pillar) from late 13th-century Egypt noting the destruction of Israel.

REVOLUTIONIZING OUR UNDERSTANDING

Archaeological finds, however, at times call into question the historicity of the biblical narrative. For instance, some archaeological sites seem to deny Joshua's alleged conquest of Canaan by showing neither a destruction layer nor traces of walls nor even settlement from that era (e. g., Jericho, Ai). Realizing the highly theological and literary character of the Book of Joshua, some scholars have concluded that its accounts are selective and biased, having minimal historical value in reconstructing the events of the past.

The chronological factor is often used to determine the value of archaeology to the biblical account. The later the period in question, the greater the contribution of archaeology to illuminating the biblical text. With this in mind, we will survey the effect that archaeology has on our understanding of the various stages of biblical history: the patriarchal age, the Exodus and wilderness era, the settlement of Canaan, and the period of the monarchy. The information in this regard resembles an inverse pyramid. It is negligible for the first two stages, and we have somewhat more data for the settlement period (i. e., parallel to the narrative in the Books of Joshua, Judges, and 1 Samuel). Only for the period of the monarchy—particularly toward its end, in the 8th and 7th centuries B. C. E.—do we have a significant amount of reliable information that richly supplements the biblical account.

Patriarchal Age

Scholarly assessment of the historicity of the biblical narratives differs significantly. As early as the 19th century, J. Wellhausen had assumed that nothing historical could be derived from these accounts, calling them a "glorified mirage." This assessment changed radically in the first part of the 20th century with the counterclaim of W. F. Albright and E. Speiser, among others, for a large degree of historicity on the basis of comparative archaeological finds from sites outside of Canaan. Although Albright's approach finds many adherents to this day, a revisionist school centered in Copenhagen has reverted to regarding the patriarchal narratives, as well as the entire Bible, as devoid of historical accuracy. Most scholars, however, have taken the middle road between credence and rejection.

One problem in assessing the historical accuracy of these biblical traditions is that they relate largely to the private affairs of Abraham's family. The texts rarely refer to public events (such as the war of the kings in Gen. 14) that at least have the possibility of being corroborated by external sources. Assuming that patriarchal figures lived some time in the first half of the 2nd millennium and that the traditions as we have them in the Book of Genesis were composed about a millennium later, the historical reliability of such material would seem to be questionable. Nevertheless, what has propelled some scholars to assume a historical kernel of truth in these accounts is the remarkable similarity in detail between some of these stories and documents discovered at 2nd-millennium sites, such as Nuzi, Mari, and Emar. In the words of Albright:

> Abraham, Isaac, and Jacob no longer seem isolated figures, much less reflections of later Israelite history; they now appear as true children of their age, bearing the same names, moving about over the same territory, visiting the same towns, practicing the same customs as their contemporaries.

Personal names (Abram, Jacob), social customs, and legal practices (e. g., the wife-sister episodes in Gen. 12, 20, and 26) seem to correspond to information transmitted in documents from the aforementioned sites. Although many scholars have subsequently taken a more sceptical position, the tendency to ascribe some sort of historical value to these narratives remains strong. How much is history and not tradition? And how many details can be considered authentic and reflective of these early times? Since these customs are attested over centuries, their chronological value for dating the patriarchal era is severly mitigated. An attempt to formulate a more nuanced assessment—between assuming a historical patriarchal period on the one hand and relegating the entire Genesis corpus to the status of late literary traditions—has been attempted by G. E. Wright:

> We shall probably never be able to prove that Abram really existed, that he did this or that, said thus and so, but what we can prove is that his life and time, as reflected in the stories about him, fit perfectly within the early second millennium (B. C. E.), but imperfectly with any late period.

Exodus and Wilderness Era

The contribution of archaeology to the biblical narratives in the last four books of the Torah is likewise limited. There is no reference in Egyptian sources to Israel's sojourn in that country, and the evidence that does exist is circumstantial and indirect. A period of servitude that entailed building the cities of Pithom and Rameses seems to fit best the reign of Rameses II, who ruled in the 13th century B. C. E. By the end of that century, an entity called Israel was already in Canaan, as evidenced by a reference to it on a stele of Pharaoh Merneptah (ca. 1207 B. C. E.), which noted its total destruction (sic!).

Indications of an Egyptian sojourn may likewise be indicated by the names that appear in the Joseph narrative at the end of Genesis: Joseph's wife, Asenath, and that of his master, Potiphar, are Egyptian; and Joseph himself had an Egyptian name, Zaphenath-paneah. Moreover, the Hyksos period in Egypt, when the country was ruled by Asiatic princes, dates to the 17th and 16th centuries B. C. E., and some scholars regard this as the setting of the Joseph narrative. The land of Goshen, the region of Israelite settlement in Egypt, was probably in the eastern Nile delta where the Hyksos capital, Avaris, was likewise located; and the expulsion of the Hyksos may be related to the beginning of Israel's troubles in the country ("A new king arose over Egypt who did not know Joseph"; Exod. 1:8).

The 14th-century-B. C. E. el-Amarna letters point to the collapse of Egyptian rule in Canaan and the resultant warfare and insecurity that became endemic throughout the country. One of the causes of these disturbances was the presence of marauders called Habiru, who took advantage of the political and military vacuum to pillage the cities and the countryside. Such historical circumstances may well have provided the context for the one or more waves of invasion and settlement by Israelite (or proto-Israelite) tribes.

These circumstantial pieces of evidence are probably insufficient to corroborate the historicity of the biblical account, but they do suggest a contextual background for the Egyptian servitude (if not for all the people, then at least some of the people who later became Israelites). Nevertheless, it also has been maintained that here too, as in the patriarchal era, later writers used earlier material to present an account of what in reality was a folk tradition with little or no historical basis.

Conquest and Settlement of Canaan

The period of the conquest and settlement of Canaan is arguably the most controversial issue in biblical history. The Book of Joshua appears to offer a straightforward description of a united and complete conquest, but the Book of Judges relates a different story: Rather than conquest followed by an allotment of the Land, Judges speaks of a reverse process, whereby the Land was first divided up and then each tribe, or several tribes together, proceeded to conquer their respective territories. In contrast to the picture of a total and immediate conquest in Josh. 11:16–20, Judges acknowledges that many cities were not subdued (Judg. 1:21,27–33), that the period of conquest lasted a long time, and that the acquisition was carried out in various ways, including by peaceful settlement.

The not inconsiderable amount of archaeological evidence for this period is likewise ambiguous. Remains of a violent conquest in the 13th century B. C. E. are evident at Hazor, thus corroborating the biblical account; but the unwalled and uninhabited Jericho and Ai, respectively, clearly seem to contradict the violent and complete conquest portrayed in the Book of Joshua. Although Hazor may well be tied to events recorded in the Bible, it is also possible that its destruction was the result of other factors, such as the 13th-century-B. C. E. conquest by the Sea Peoples, a population that migrated from Greece and the Aegean islands and wrought havoc throughout the eastern Mediterranean. The degree to which Joshua and Judges can be culled for kernels of historical truth or simply considered as theologically motivated accounts using a historical framework for their purposes is a basic controversy in academic circles.

The archaeological material for the early Iron Age patterns of settlement (i. e., post-1200 B. C. E., the period of Joshua and Judges) is ambiguous in yet another vein. Do the hundreds of small settlements in the hill country (especially Judea and Samaria) date from this period? If so, were they inhabited by the local Canaanite population? Or are the finds (ceramic remains and domestic architecture [the four-room house]) from these settlements so different as to warrant the assumption of there being another population? In other words, do they reflect a new and different group (a proto-Israelite population) that invaded the country from the east? Finally, does the material culture of the hill country share enough common traits (e. g., plastered water cisterns and terracing) to justify referring to them as one type, or are regional variations so considerable as to point to other ethnic or social groupings, and perhaps even to other periods of settlement?

Such ambiguities and the inherent fascination of the conquest have generated four main approaches to explain Israelite settlement:

1. The "traditional" approach generally adopts the biblical outlook, especially that of the Book of Joshua, albeit with some modifications. A conquest did take place, as attested by the Book of Joshua and some archaeological sites, although the biblical account clearly exaggerates the extent and intensity of this phenomenon.

2. Israelite settlement in the highlands was a gradual process of infiltration over the course of centuries. A number of archaeological excavations seem to confirm this picture, indicating that large tracts of hill country became inhabited during the 13th and 12th centuries B. C. E.

A variation of this second approach views this settlement pattern as part of the general dislocation and migration of populations throughout the eastern Mediterranean at the time; those known as the Israelites eventually included peoples of diverse backgrounds: nomads and seminomads of Semitic and non-Semitic origins, former urban populations, those from within Canaan, and others who had migrated. An Israelite identity emerged only after a long process that required forging a political and religious unity from a plethora of regional variations within the country.

3. Israel came into being after a peasants' revolt against the Canaanite cities. This revolutionary liberation movement was thus a "Canaanite" phenomenon, with the victorious revolutionaries being led by Hebrews whose God was identified with the Exodus. The Habiru revolts of the previous century serve as a model for this view.

4. A combination of some (or all) of these theories accounts for the emergence of Israel, assuming that there was an incursion that attracted local groups, creating a new socio-religious identity known as Israel.

Period of the Monarchy

A significant amount of archaeological material has been recovered from the 400-year period (ca. 1000–586 B. C. E.) of the monarchy, which has illuminated many facets of First Temple history and culture. Many of these data supplement what is known from the biblical narrative and relate to the daily life and material culture of the society. Owing to the extensive excavations in numerous cities and towns, the subject of urbanization has received much attention. City plans, fortifications, and streets have been amply documented, and various types of royal buildings (palatial, storage, and administrative complexes) have been uncovered—from those of capital cities such as Samaria to those located in provincial centers such as Megiddo. Residential buildings of a variety of sizes have been discovered, most characteristically the four-room house, featuring one or two rows of pillars, a central courtyard, and surrounding rooms. Industrial installations are also well documented, the best known being small household workshops for producing wine and oil. Water-supply systems were ubiquitous in Israelite settlements, ranging from tunnels and shafts, either leading to sources outside the settlement or for bringing water to another location, to large-scale cisterns for storing water. Tombs and burial caves also shed a great deal of light on the funerary customs of the period. Finally, the discovery of a variety of city gates and city-gate complexes attests to the centrality of these areas for a wide range of communal activities that find expression throughout biblical literature.

Inscriptions constitute another type of archaeological find relating directly to the biblical text, illustrating and corroborating the descriptions contained therein. An inscription from Tel Dan in the Upper Galilee mentioning the "House of David" is a case in point. We have here, for the first time, a clear-cut reference to David and his dynasty from a source outside the Bible. The Bible's allusions to King Hezekiah's remarkable building activity in his kingdom are confirmed by the remarkable archaeological finds of the Siloam water tunnel and the "Broad Wall," marking the greatly expanded boundaries of Jerusalem to the west. Moreover, Hezekiah's administrative and fiscal reforms appear to be reflected in the *la-melekh* ("[belonging] to the king") seal impressions on jar handles, of which more than 1,000 specimens have been discovered. Opinion is divided as to the purpose of these inscriptions. Did these jars contain produce from royal estates intended as revenue for the king, or did they contain provisions for his army?

Nevertheless, archaeological material or the lack there of has raised questions regarding certain assumptions and claims based on biblical literature. At times this evidence has been interpreted as contradicting the biblical narrative; on other occasions, data that might have corroborated the literary account are judged as inadequate and the resultant absence of evidence is then regarded as conclusive. An example of the latter is the almost total absence of archaeological evidence from Davidic and Solomonic Jerusalem. The Bible devotes an inordinate amount of space to the reigns of these two kings who purportedly developed their new capital city in many directions. Yet, some archaeologists find it hard to identify any building, wall remains, or other installation as belonging to this period. In their minds, the absence of evidence is evidence of absence, i.e., Jerusalem was not a capital city, but at best only a small village. As these minimalists would have it, Davidic-Solominic rule and its grandiose description in Kings I and II was intended to serve the public relations agenda of the later, seventh-century Davidic dynasty. However, other archaeologists dispute this assertion of absence of evidence, claiming that remains from the era of David and Solomon do, in fact, attest to the importance of Jerusalem in the 10th century.

Disparity between the written word and archaeological material is also evident in other areas. The Bible praises Solomon's building of a number of royal cities throughout the country, while King Ahab, whose reputation in the Bible is sullied, is portrayed as a far inferior ruler. Yet, some scholars attribute the major urban building projects of Megiddo and Hazor to Ahab and not to Solomon.

No less striking, however, are indications of religious syncretism (the absorption of pagan rites, beliefs, and customs) in Israelite religion. Little is known about this from the biblical text other than the general condemnation of idolatry. Seen through the eyes of the Bible, this phenomenon is thoroughly rejected. Whatever the case, an ostracon (a pottery shard with writing on it) from Samaria bears the name

Egelyau, which is probably to be translated "the calf of *YHVH*" (or possibly "*YHVH* is a calf"!). However, the most sensational find in this regard comes from the wilderness settlement of Kuntilat'Ajrud, located between Beer-sheba and Elat and near a road leading into the Sinai Desert, where many votive offerings were found. The most intriguing of these finds were inscriptions and drawings on wall plaster and jars. The inscriptions are generally blessings, one of which reads "May you be blessed by *YHVH* of Samaria (or Teman) and his *Asherah*" (a Canaanite deity described here as *YHVH*'s female consort). Below this inscription is the drawing of three figures, two of which may represent *YHVH* and *Asherah*. Such finds are an expression of one type of popular religion against which many biblical authors, particularly the prophets, fought vigorously.

Archaeology thus plays a major role in illuminating the biblical text. It often highlights the complexity and diversity of Israelite society and the extent of foreign influences on aspects of its daily life. Archaeological material also questions the historical accuracy of the biblical text, forcing us to realize that the Bible is not an objective, historical document. The Bible's value lies not in its historical accuracy, but rather in the religious and theological truths that it conveys through the use of narratives, laws, wisdom literature, and prophecy.

Archaeology can rarely stand alone, especially when it comes to historical, social, and religious issues. The stone installation on Mount Ebal, for example, has often been referred to as the altar erected by Joshua on entering the Land (Deut. 27; Josh. 24). However, this claim is far from clear, because neither the purpose of this stone installation nor its date has been convincingly demonstrated, thus precluding any facile identification of the stone platform with the biblical story. Both archaeology and the biblical text are fragmentary when it comes to reconstructing early Israelite history. While each type of source might highlight the limitations of the other, they also can play a mutually positive role. Taken together, they enrich our knowledge of the period, at times offering vastly different perspectives and thereby affording us a much fuller and more comprehensive picture of biblical society than heretofore known.

Study Questions

1. According to Levine, we have no archaeological evidence that is linked to the Patriarchs and Matriarchs. Is it important to you that these characters lived as real people? Why or why not?

2. Find examples from the essay that confirm a biblical historical account and some that disagree with the biblical record. What could have caused the biblical text to disagree with the archaeological record? Do you think the Bible is concerned with historical truth, or some other kind of "truth?"

3. Levine examines, in some detail, the controversy surrounding the settlement of Canaan by the Israelites and presents four main approaches. Are you surprised that such controversy exists? What weight does each seem to give to the archaeological account versus the biblical account?

4. In 2001, Rabbi David Wolpe, rabbi of one of the largest Conservative congregations in North America, ignited a public debate over biblical archaeology when, in a sermon, he accepted the conclusions of scholars who suggest that "the way the Bible describes the Exodus is not the way it happened, if it happened at all." Rabbi Wolpe was not advocating the abrogation of tradition. Rather, he was asserting that the religious truth of the Bible is not contingent on its historical truth. Still, for many American Jews, this seemed heretical. As Dennis Prager put it, "If the Exodus did not occur, there is no Judaism." What do you think?

Study materials by *Daniel Yechiel Septimus*

ANCIENT NEAR EASTERN MYTHOLOGY

Robert Wexler

Summary

In this essay Robert Wexler explores the similarities between mono-theistic biblical narratives and ancient Near Eastern polytheistic myths. He notes that both the story of Noah and the flood and the Near Eastern myth of Gilgamesh describe a hero chosen by a divine source to survive the flood.

The two tales contain similar elements, such as a dove sent out from a boat to discover the extent of the floodwaters. After analyzing the evidence using a comparative approach, Wexler concludes that Genesis narratives such as Noah and the Flood, the tower of Babel, and the Garden of Eden draw from earlier Mesopotamian myths. Although Wexler concludes that Israelite faith had a unique character, and acknowledges that the Torah condemned other religions of the time, he argues that both Israelite and pagan religions of the ancient Near East were products of a cultural context that sought to explore the mysteries of human experience. His essay helps us think plu-ralistically about religious traditions, and encourages us to read our sacred texts as part of a larger body of spiritual literature imagining solutions to life's questions.

Among the most fascinating and famous stories of Genesis is the story of Noah. After torrential rains inundated the entire world, Noah's ark remained afloat until it came to rest atop Mount Ararat. To determine if the waters had begun to recede, Noah sent forth first a raven and then a dove. The following passage suggests that the dove could not find a place to alight and so returned to the ark.

> I sent forth and set free a dove.
> The dove went forth, but she came back again. But, since no resting-place for her was visible, she simply returned.

This passage is not from the Book of Genesis but from a very popular Sumero-Babylonian myth known as the *Gilgamesh* epic. Regarding the dove, the parallel text in Genesis (8:8–9) reads:

> Then he sent out the dove to see whether the waters had decreased from the surface of the ground. But the dove could not find a resting place for its foot, and returned to him to the ark.

How can we account for this obvious similarity to the *Gilgamesh* myth? We do know that fabled reports of catastrophic floods were not unique to the Levant. From Iraq to the South Seas, these stories are part of a genre of myths that recount the cataclysmic destruction of the known world. Among them, the flood motif is the most typical and represents a dramatic, mythic response to an almost universal danger. Still, even the nonscholar senses that Genesis and *Gilgamesh* have more in common than a shared theme. Both stories describe a hero chosen by a divine source to survive the flood (Noah in the Bible, and Utnapishtim in the Babylonian source). Each hero saved not only his family but many species of animals as well. In each case, the flood covered the earth, wiping out all forms of life except for those found on the boat. Both boats came to rest on the top of a mountain, and both heroes used the strategy of sending out birds to look for dry land.

If we claim that these two stories are related in some way, how do we go about discovering the nature of their relationship? Perhaps by examining these questions, we can also learn something about the techniques that scholars use to evaluate the relationship between any two literary texts.

Our first challenge is to make a case for some contact between the two cultures that would allow borrowing to occur. That case is easily made. The Book of Genesis itself relates that the Hebrew patriarch Abraham hailed from Ur, a site most commonly identified with the prominent Sumerian city-state of the same name. Furthermore, both biblical and extrabiblical sources confirm that sustained interaction did occur between Syro-Palestine (the geographic neighborhood of Israel) and Mesopotamia during the first three millennia of recorded history.

Given what we know about the geography of the two regions in question, it is unlikely that the Genesis story originated in Palestine.

Ancient Mesopotamia, which included virtually all of modern-day Iraq and much of modern-day Syria, was dominated by at least two major rivers: the Tigris and Euphrates. In fact, the name "Mesopotamia" itself derives from a Greek term meaning "between the rivers." Agricultural life in this area depended largely on the ebb and flow of the two rivers. Heavy rains caused the rivers to swell and spill over their banks, inundating the nearby fields. If these inundations could be contained and channeled, the harvest was good. If the flood-waters became uncontrollable, there could be crop loss, famine, and substantial destruction of life and property. Inundations were known in Palestine, but they usually were limited to localized flash flooding. In other words, the possibility of a catastrophic deluge was much more a concern for the Mesopotamian peoples than it was for the early inhabitants of pre-Israelite Palestine. In the Mesopotamian imagination, a disastrous flood had the potential of wiping out the entire known world.

Because myths routinely reflect the anxieties of a particular culture, we conclude that the Flood story portrayed in Genesis is more likely of Mesopotamian than Palestinian origin. This Mesopotamian influence is evident not only in the Flood story but throughout the first 11 chapters of Genesis. Perhaps these narratives were part of a cultural legacy transported by the patriarch Abraham and his clan as they made their way from Ur to Haran and eventually to the Land of Canaan.

The question of whether *Gilgamesh* influenced the Genesis account or vice versa is more complex. Once we rule out coincidence, there appear to be at least three logical possibilities: (a) Genesis drew its material from *Gilgamesh,* (b) *Gilgamesh* drew its material from Genesis, or (c) both stories were based on a common earlier source. How can we conceivably know which of the two stories—Genesis or *Gilgamesh*—is older? How can we discover whether the author of one was familiar with the other work?

What we can assume is that the *Gilgamesh* story was probably very well known in the ancient Near East. Archaeologists have found many clay tablets with fragments of this epic written in different time periods and representing a wide geologic area. The Genesis story, however, is known to us only through the biblical account, and perhaps this argues in favor of *Gilgamesh* being the original source of the two stories. Still, even if this were true, then we still would need to explain why so many discrepancies developed in the two related narratives.

The most likely assumption we can make is that both Genesis and *Gilgamesh* drew their material from a common tradition about the flood that existed in Mesopotamia. The stories then diverged in the retelling. Each account was shaped and refined by a specific religious message and embellished by the imagination of those who transmitted it through the generations.

The strong literary affinity that exists between *Gilgamesh* and the biblical Flood narrative has no equal among the other mythic texts of Mesopotamia. We do, however, encounter some distinct motifs and existential preoccupations that characterize both narrative traditions. The Garden of Eden story, for example, has some clear thematic parallels among the Mesopotamia myths.

According to the biblical text, Adam and Eve were given the opportunity to obtain immortality. God placed them in a garden, east of Eden, and provided them with a variety of trees from which they could eat, including the tree of knowledge and the tree of life (i. e., immortality). There was one proviso, however: "Of every tree of the garden you are free to eat; but as for the tree of knowledge of good and bad, you must not eat of it; for as soon as you eat of it, you shall die" (Gen. 2:16–17). Overcome by curiosity and a desire to be God-like, the man and the woman ate of the tree of knowledge, were banished from the garden, and forfeited their opportunity to live forever.

The lost promise of immortality was a key theme of several ancient Near Eastern myths, including the legend of Adapa and the South Wind, and the *Gilgamesh* epic. Adapa was a fabled hero who broke the wing of the god of the South Wind, risking the wrath of his fellow deities. He was summoned to appear before the high god, Anu, to receive his punishment. The god Ea, who often served as a divine advocate for human beings, gave Adapa specific information about how to win over the hostile gods who guarded the entrance to heaven. All of the gods were so impressed with Adapa that Anu offered him the waters of life, i. e., the gift of immortality. In an ironic conclusion to the story, the trusted Ea deliberately misled Adapa by counseling him that the waters contained death and not eternal life. Adapa followed Ea's advice, refused to drink the waters of life, and squandered the chance for humanity to become immortal.

Just as Utnapishtim is often called the Babylonian Noah, Adapa is occasionally referred to as the Babylonian Adam. Such a comparison does not really do justice to the much clearer parallels that exist between the stories of Noah and Gilgamesh. All we can reasonably say about the sagas of Adam and Adapa is that they both explain why human beings did not achieve immortality.

The *Gilgamesh* epic also has as its theme the quest for immortality. It begins by describing the exploits of the superhero for whom the myth is named. Accompanied by his equally impressive friend, Enkidu, Gilgamesh performs a number of courageous feats. Along the way he attracts the unwanted attention of the female goddess Ishtar whose love he spurns. Angered by his rejection of her, Ishtar resolves to kill Gilgamesh, but her plans are thwarted by Enkidu. Ultimately, Ishtar manages to end the life of Enkidu by afflicting him with a fatal disease. Gilgamesh is completely unnerved by the death of his friend. For the first time, he recognizes the possibility of his own mortality. No longer able to function as a hero, he devotes all of his time to the unsuccessful pursuit of eternal life. During his journey, Gilgamesh encounters an alewife who explains to him why his quest is doomed to failure.

> Gilgamesh, where do you roam?
> You will not find the [eternal] life you seek.
> When the gods appointed death for mankind,
> They kept [eternal] life in their own hands.
> (tab. X, col. iii)

In this statement we find a powerful echo of the words uttered by God at the precise moment Adam and Eve were expelled from the garden: "Now that man has become like one of us, knowing good and bad, what if he should stretch out his hand and take also from the tree of life and eat, and live forever!" (Gen. 3:22). God then banishes humanity from the garden and places a sword at its entrance to prevent their return.

The Garden of Eden story indicates that divinity consists of two primary elements: knowledge and immortality. Through an act of disobedience, human beings acquired the former, but they could not be allowed to attain the latter, lest they become like God. Similarly, the alewife observes that the gods are jealous of their own supremacy. The boundary between the human and the divine may not be traversed, and immortality must remain the sole province of the gods.

Despite the appealing nature of the evidence, we must resist drawing any conclusions about the specific influence that the Adapa or *Gilgamesh* texts might have had on the Garden of Eden narrative. We can say that the motif of immortality denied occupied a prominent place in the religious perspectives of both Mesopotamia and Israel. At the very least, the extrabiblical sources give us another insight into the powerful psychological and spiritual yearnings expressed in the drama of Adam and Eve.

Babylonian influence on biblical material is particularly evident in the brief account of the tower of Babel (Gen. 11). The story relates how human beings banded together after the Flood to build a tower that would reach to the sky. The declared motive for the construction was "to make a name for ourselves; else we shall be scattered all over the world" (Gen. 11:4). God responds to this effort by treating it as an act of rebellion. "If, as one people with one language for all, this is how they have begun to act, then nothing that they may propose to do will be out of their reach" (Gen. 11:6). Certain descriptive aspects of this story reflect a Mesopotamian cultural background. The offending tower, for example, recalls the ziggurats—the pyramidal, brick temple structures central to Sumero-Babylonian religion.

The biblical theme of rebellion against God has parallels in each of the two best-known Babylonian creation stories: Enuma Elish and Atrahasis. In these myths, the rebellion is not that of human beings against God but rather of one set of gods against another. In each case, the gods who mutiny strive to supplant other, more powerful gods to free themselves and secure their own hegemony.

The affinity between biblical and Mesopotamian literature in no way diminishes the special character of Israelite religion. By introducing the concept of monotheism into the ancient Near East, Israelite religion made a unique contribution to human civilization. However, we should also appreciate the depth and intensity of the religious sentiments expressed in the works of Mesopotamian mythology. The faiths of ancient Israel and Mesopotamia were ultimately the products of a similar cultural context, occasionally exhibiting parallel themes and religious metaphors.

Understandably, the Torah attempted to trivialize pagan religions as a means of securing loyalty to the God of Israel. Pervasive polytheism represented a threat to the belief in one God and required a strong rejection if monotheism were to take root. Yet despite the anti-pagan polemic of the Bible, the mythic tradition of the ancient Near East was a serious, complex, and profound attempt to comprehend both the natural and the supernatural. The impact of this tradition was felt far beyond the borders of Mesopotamia, and it had a fundamental influence on the formation of Israelite religion and some of the literary traditions of the Bible.

Study Questions

1. How does Wexler arrive at his conclusion that biblical stories and ancient Near Eastern myths come from a common source? Do you agree with his conclusion?

2. The great medieval commentator Rashi, in his first commentary on the Torah, wonders why the Torah does not begin with the first commandment to the Jewish people. He questions what purpose the narratives of Genesis serve. How do you think Wexler would respond to Rashi's question? How would you respond?

3. Wexler states: "The affinity between biblical and Mesopotamian literature in no way diminishes the special character of Israelite religion." Do you feel that this is true or untrue? How would you explain this statement to a Jewish child?

4. Does Wexler's analysis cause you to feel differently about the sacredness of the Torah? Why or why not?

5. How might you use Wexler's essay to appreciate the sacred myths of traditions that your neighbors practice?

Study materials by *Shoshana Jedwab*

BIBLICAL AND ANCIENT NEAR EASTERN LAW

Nahum M. Sarna

Summary

Professor Sarna sets biblical law in its ancient Near Eastern context. He begins by describing six different collections of laws—two written in Sumerian and four in Akkadian. After describing each of the collections, Sarna notes some features they have in common with one another and with the biblical legal code. Given the structure and incomplete nature of all of these codes, "there existed in Israel a body of unwritten common law, orally transmitted from generation to generation, knowledge of which is assumed" by the Torah. As must have been the case for these other codes, "what is prescribed in the Torah is a series of innovations to existing laws."

Sarna also emphasizes important differences that exist between the two legal sources. Unlike Mesopotamian law, biblical law ascribes its authority to God, not to the wisdom of a king in whom a god has invested authority. Instead, it structures a covenantal relationship between the people and God. Several crucial results flow from this, causing the Bible to differ from the Mesopotamian collections described at the beginning. First, there is an important relationship between the legal sections of the Torah and the narrative portions that outline the relationship between God and the Israelites. Second, the covenant requires that the laws will be "eternally binding on both the individual and society as a whole." Therefore, the population as a whole, rather than just the elite, must be able to study the law, and such study has both civic and religious significance. Third, law is intimately connected to morality. Fourth, the Torah demands "equal justice" for all, regardless of social status. And, finally, the Torah places prime importance on the sacredness of human life, not property.

If, as the Sages frequently stated, God employed the everyday language of human beings to communicate His will, then there is no section of the Torah in which this principle is more patently manifest than in the collections of legal ordinances. Extant corpora of laws, records of court proceedings and judicial decisions provide ample evidence to prove that in its external form—in legal draftsmanship, in its terminology and phraseology—the Torah followed long-established, widespread, standardized patterns of Mesopotamian law.

Documents from the practice of law run into the many tens of thousands, uncovered at several widely dispersed sites in the Near East. Collections of laws recovered number no more than six.

Two such collections have survived in the non-Semitic Sumerian language spoken in southern Mesopotamia during the 3rd and early 2nd millenniums B. C. E., written in cuneiform script. The older one is that of King Ur-Nammu of the city-state of Ur, founder of the Third Dynasty of that city in the 21st century B. C. E. The original has not been found, only a fragmentary copy from Nippur, a city about 100 miles (ca. 160 km) south of Baghdad. This has been supplemented by two broken tablets from Ur itself, both of which are much older. The extant materials preserve the prologue to the collection, together with 29 stipulations, probably less than half of the original number. The prologue refers to "principles of equity and truth" and describes social abuses that the king sought to correct "to establish equity in the land" by standardizing weights and measures and by protecting the orphan, the widow, and the poor. The stipulations cover sexual offenses, support of divorcées, false accusations, the return of runaway slaves, bodily injuries, the case of an arrogant slave woman, perjured testimony, and encroachment of another's private property. The laws are formulated in "casuistic" style; i. e., they are conditional, the opening statement beginning with "if" followed by the hypothetical, concrete case, and the concluding statement giving the prescribed penalty.

The second Sumerian collection of laws comes from Lipit-Ishter, king of the city of Isin, in central lower Mesopotamia, in the 19th century B. C. E. Although an Amorite, he wrote his laws in Sumerian. There may also once have existed an Akkadian version, now lost. The laws, of which about 38 remain, are estimated to have numbered about 200 originally. They are framed by a prologue and an epilogue. In the former, the king writes that his god had commissioned him "to establish justice in the land" and "to promote the welfare" of his people. In the latter, he declares that he has restored domestic tranquility and established righteousness and truth. The extant laws, which belong to the concluding part of the corpus, deal with a variety of civil cases: the hiring of a boat; horticulture; the institution of slavery; house ownership; and family laws such as marriage, divorce, polygamy, and inheritance; and responsibility for injury to a rented animal. In these laws, too, the casuistic formulation is the rule.

The other law collections from Mesopotamia are all written in Akkadian. The earliest in this language derives from the city of Eshnunna, situated about 26 miles (42 km) northeast of Baghdad, on a tributary of the Tigris River. Its author is unknown, and its date is uncertain. These were copied in the time of a contemporary of Hammurabi, but the original is believed to be considerably older. Neither prologue nor epilogue, if there was one, has been preserved. The legislation concerns the prices of various commodities, the cost of hiring a wagon and a boat, negligence on the part of the hirer, and the wages of laborers as well as laws pertaining to marriage, loans, slavery, property, personal injury, a goring ox, a vicious dog, and divorce. As before, the casuistic formulation is predominant. A peculiarity is that the application of the laws may vary according to the social status of the persons involved.

Mesopotamian jurisprudence reached its zenith in the 17th or 18th century B.C.E., with the promulgation of Hammurabi's great collection. These were inscribed on an eight-foot-high (2½ m) black diorite stele that was originally placed in the temple of Esagila in Babylon. In the early part of the 12th century B.C.E. it was looted by the Elamite king Shutruk-Nah and carried off to Susa (Hebrew: *Shushan*), capital of his kingdom, where French excavators discovered it in 1902. It now resides in the Louvre in Paris.

The upper front part of the stele bears a relief that features King Hammurabi standing before a seated deity, either the sun god, Shamash, or the chief god of Babylon, Marduk. The scene is often misinterpreted in popular books as Hammurabi receiving the laws from the god, but it is nothing of the kind. The god is really investing the king with the ring and the staff, which are the symbols of sovereignty. He thereby endows him with the authority, and perhaps also the wisdom, to promulgate the laws. The text makes it perfectly clear that Hammurabi himself is the sole source of the legislation.

Written in cuneiformed Akkadian in 51 columns, the stele now contains what is calculated to be 282 legal paragraphs. About 35 to 40 paragraphs were erased by the Elamite king; a few of these have been restored from other tablets. An extensive literary prologue and a lengthy epilogue frame the legal section. The prologue abounds in lofty sentiments about the purpose of the legislation, which is to further public welfare, to promote the cause of justice, to protect the interests of the weak, and to ensure the rule of law. The epilogue repeats these noble ideals and adds that the statutes are there so that anyone may know the law in case of need and that a future ruler may be guided by Hammurabi's ordinances. It closes with a series of blessings invoked on those who are faithful to the laws, and heaps fearful curses on anyone who is perfidious. Both prologue and epilogue are unabashedly replete with Hammurabi's copious and effusive self-praise and with massive hyperbole extolling his own greatness and mighty deeds.

The corpus of the laws, mostly styled casuistically, includes a large variety of legal topics. The first 41 paragraphs deal mainly with matters of public order; the rest belong overwhelmingly to the domain of private law, matters that affect the individual citizen. Distinctive features of the laws are the extraordinarily large numbers of capital offenses (some 30 in all), the penal mutilation of the body, vicarious punishment, the principle of talion (or legal retaliation in kind), intense concern with the protection of private property, and an innovative approach to several areas of private wrong that are now recognized as issues of public welfare to be regulated by the state. Finally, as in the laws of Eshnunna, Hammurabi's reflect a stratified society; as mentioned above, the penalties and judgments may vary according to the social standing of the litigants.

Considerably different from the collections hitherto described is the body of legislation that has come to be known as the Middle Assyrian Laws. Uncovered at the ancient city of Asshur on the Tigris River, about 250 miles (563 km) north of Babylon, the several clay tablets on which these are inscribed come from the 12th century B.C.E., but the legislation itself may well go back three centuries earlier. Although they conform to the casuistic pattern, the legal formulations and terminology as well as the prescribed penalties suggest influences, presently unknown, other than the standard Mesopotamian traditions. A total of 116 paragraphs are preserved in full or in part. An extraordinarily large number deal with matters relating to the status of women and to family law. Peculiarly characteristic of these Assyrian laws are the savagery and severity of the punishments they mete out: numerous instances of the death penalty, even for offenses against property; mutilation of the body; flogging, even to the infliction of 100 lashes; pouring pitch over the head; tearing out the eyes; subjection to the water ordeal; forced labor; and the exaction of grievously heavy fines. There are also instances of multiple punishments imposed for a single offense.

Greatly under the influence of Mesopotamian legal traditions but deriving from quite a different cultural and linguistic milieu and geographic region are 200 Hittite laws that have survived from the Old Hittite kingdom of Asia Minor, now central Turkey. The extant tablets date from about 1250 B.C.E., but they go back to a much larger corpus of laws, apparently promulgated or collected for the use of jurists about five centuries earlier. A unique feature of this compilation is the clear references to earlier laws that have been revised. Capital punishment has been restricted to but a few offenses and has been replaced by restitution. The casuistic style is extensively employed.

At this point it should be emphasized that none of the collections discussed can be considered to be a legal code in the usually understood sense of the term. First, one and all, they omit important spheres of legal practice, and none comes close to being a comprehensive regulation of the citizens' lives. Second, not one of the compilations decrees that it is henceforth to be binding on judges and magistrates. Third, none is ever invoked as the basis of a legal decision in all the thousands of extant documents from the actual practice of law in the courts. For these reasons, the various collections are to be regarded as recording emendations and additions to bodies of existing unwritten common law that are seen to be in need of reform.

This conclusion applies equally to the corpus of laws embedded in the Torah. It is silent on matters of commercial law, on such indispensable practices as sales and contracts, the transfer of ownership, the legalization of marriage, the regulation of professions, and on most aspects of inheritance. Clearly, there existed in Israel a body of unwritten common law, orally transmitted from generation to generation, knowledge of which is assumed. What is prescribed in the Torah is a series of innovations to existing laws.

It should be further emphasized that the review of the legal corpora of the ancient Near East given above unquestionably establishes that when the people of Israel first appear on the scene of history, their world was already heir to the widely diffused common legal culture of long standing. No wonder, then, that Israelite laws exhibit so many points of contact with the earlier collections. Like them, the Torah expresses itself in terms of concrete, real-life cases; and, like them, the underlying legal principles are not abstractly stated but are to be deduced from the resolutions of those cases.

Another feature that is common to both ancient Near Eastern law collections and their Torah counterpart is the difficulty in uncovering the organizing principle that determines the arrangement and sequence of legal topics, although modern scholars have made some progress in this regard.

The affinities and analogues that abound between the Israelite and the other Near Eastern law collections tend to obscure the fundamental distinctions that exist between the two, a subject that must now be addressed. First and foremost is the essential fact that biblical law is the expression of the covenant between God and Israel. Several important consequences flow from this. The legal sections of the Torah cohere with the Exodus narratives and cannot be separated from them without losing their integrity and identity. Their sole source and sanction is divine will, not the wisdom and power of a human monarch. As imperatives of a transcendent, sovereign God who freely entered into a covenanted relationship with His people, the laws are eternally binding on both the individual and society as a whole. Hence the public nature of the law. There can be no monopoly on the knowledge of the law, and the study of it is a religious obligation. Further, there can be no differentiation between the branches of public and private law and between both of them and religion and morality. All topics that fall under any of these rubrics are equally binding. Law is not severed from morality and religion.

As to the law's substance, the Torah forbids vicarious punishments and multiple penalties. Apart from the special category of the slave, it demands equal justice for all, irrespective of social status. Finally, whereas the Near Eastern laws place great stress on the importance of property, the Torah's value system favors the paramount sacredness of human life.

Study Questions

1. What is the connection between ethics and religion in Mesopotamian sources as opposed to biblical sources?

2. The ancient Rabbis articulated a concept of "Torah" that includes both a written and an oral law. How does ancient Near Eastern law provide an historical basis for this important Rabbinic theological belief?

3. Do the recorded similarities between biblical and nonbiblical legal sources diminish the religious significance and authority of the Torah?

4. How would a person who believes in the divine nature of the Torah reconcile this belief with the similarities Sarna describes? What do you think the significance of these similarities is?

5. Why does Sarna say that the covenantal framework for the law makes it available to the entire community? How well has Judaism maintained the original spirit of the "public nature" of Jewish law throughout its history? How is it manifested in today's Jewish world? What do you think about the other implications that flow from this idea of covenant?

Study materials by *Dov Lerea*

SACRIFICES

Gordon Tucker

Summary

Other than the laws relating to purity and impurity, there is probably no area of biblical law that modern students of Scripture find more difficult to admire than the rules and regulations that surround animal sacrifice. And it is, therefore, with a distinct lack of enthusiasm that many Jews, including some rabbis, anticipate the annual winter weeks during which the public lessons read aloud from the Torah present an endless sea of details concerning the sacrifices Scripture ordains as a response to sin or unintentional wrongdoing. The fact that these rituals are presented as meaningfully emblematic of Israel's willingness to worship God in as profound a way as possible makes us recognize that the sacrificial tradition must be taken seriously. But doing so is not at all simple, and, by organizing the laws into a cogent whole within their historical context, Rabbi Tucker has provided his readers with a framework for considering these laws, *not* as they might strike us today, but rather as they must have struck the ancient people who observed and preserved them.

IN BIBLICAL NARRATIVE

Throughout the ancient world, human beings connected with their gods in part through sacrifice. Altars abounded and received gifts of all manner of animals and, in some cases, of human beings as well. It is, therefore, not surprising that the narratives in the Hebrew Bible, including the Torah itself, are full of instances in which altars are built as vehicles of sacrifice and communication.

It begins when Cain and Abel, the first sons of the first couple, bring offerings to God, the former a gift of produce, and the latter a gift of "the choicest of the firstlings of his flock" (Gen. 4:3–4). Only Abel's sacrifice is accepted (how this was manifest is not made clear), and the reader is left with the unmistakable impression that sacrifice of animal life, with the life-sustaining blood and suet being offered to the Creator, is preferable to God. True, the Torah will later set forth rules for grain offerings (*minḥah,* see Lev. 2); and from the prominence it gives to the *minḥah* the Sages will centuries later extract the homiletical lesson that "the one who can give much is equal to the one who can give little, as long as their thoughts are directed to Heaven" (M Men. 13:11). But the simple narrative of Cain and Abel does not betray such sentiments.

The next sacrifice of which we hear is the one that Noah offered after surviving the Flood. Here our impression from the story of Cain and Abel is reinforced with a striking anthropomorphism. Noah presented "burnt offerings" (*olot*), i. e., animals turned entirely to ash and ascending smoke. Indeed, the word for "altar" (*mizbei·aḥ*) means "a place of slaughter." The text continues: "The LORD smelled the pleasing odor [*rei·aḥ ha-niḥo·aḥ*], and the LORD said to Himself: 'Never again will I doom the earth because of man'" (Gen. 8:21). The smoke of these burnt animals has created a sensation (literally!) in heaven, and the aroma of these sacrificial gifts has moved God to temper the anger that humanity is prone to ignite through its inevitable sins. There is no mistaking the message here about the power and efficacy of animal sacrifice in creating peace between God and humanity.

The patriarchs come on the scene next; and throughout their lives and many travels, their peak moments of communicating with God are invariably marked by the creation of altars and the offering of animal sacrifices. A few examples will establish the pattern:

- The LORD appeared to Abram and said, "I will assign this land to your offspring." And he built an altar there to the LORD who had appeared to him (Gen. 12:7).
- And the LORD said to Abram ... "Raise your eyes and look out from where you are, to the north and south, to the east and west, for I give all the land that you see to you and your offspring forever." ... And Abram moved his tent, and came to dwell at the terebinths of Mamre, which are in Hebron; and he built an altar there to the LORD (Gen. 13:14–18).
- That night the LORD appeared to him and said, "I am the God of your father Abraham. Fear not, for I am with you, and I will bless

you and increase your offspring for the sake of My servant Abraham."
So he built an altar there and invoked the LORD by name (Gen.
26:24–25).

- Thus Jacob came to Luz—that is, Bethel—in the land of Canaan,
  he and all the people that were with him. There he built an altar and
  named the site El-bethel, for it was there that God had revealed Himself to him when he was fleeing from his brother (Gen. 35:6–7).
- So Israel set out with all that was his, and he came to Beer-sheba,
  where he offered sacrifices to the God of his father Isaac. God called to
  Israel in a vision by night: "Jacob! Jacob!" He answered, "Here." And
  He said, "I am God, the God of your father. Fear not to go down to
  Egypt, for I will make you there into a great nation" (Gen. 46:1–3).

Over and over, the evidence of God's providence is accompanied by
a gift on an altar, the column of smoke symbolizing the link between
heaven and earth.

The motif of individuals offering animals to God in times of intense
joy or stress or in personal revelatory moments continues throughout
the Hebrew Bible. Sometimes those who offer the sacrifices are not
Israelites at all. Jethro, Moses' Midianite father-in-law, makes such an
offering (Exod. 18:12) when he learns of God's awesome victory over
the Egyptians. The somewhat less sympathetic characters Balak and
Balaam do likewise when they attempt (in vain) to invoke the power
of God against Israel (Num. 23:1–2,14–15,29–30). And Saul, the first
king of Israel, both celebrated a crucial victory over the Philistines and
attempted to divert divine displeasure over his soldiers' ravenous eating
of the spoils without offering the blood, by setting up an ad hoc altar
and offering on it the blood (and presumably the suet and entrails) of
all the animals to be eaten (1 Sam. 14:31–35).

The Torah's narrative takes another critical turn with respect to sacrifices in the second book of the Pentateuch. With the Exodus from Egypt,
sacrifice takes on, for the first time, the dimension that will ultimately
define it as a legal category, i. e., the public, communal dimension. The
paschal sacrifice that marks the Exodus, and is to commemorate it in
each subsequent year (see Exod. 12, esp. vv. 24–27), is no individual
expression of thanksgiving, as was Jacob's offering at Bethel when he

returned safely home after many years of exile. This was a community rite, one that bound the members of the community to one another as much as it bound each individual to God, whom the sacrifice addressed. (The *Pesaḥ Haggadah,* composed centuries later, captured this function perfectly when it noted that the "wicked" son's reference to "your service" meant that he was removing himself from the community and thereby striking at the very heart of the rite.) The paschal lamb was the first communal, or public, sacrificial rite. Significantly, it became the most central rite for an Israelite to perform (or, equivalently, the most serious rite to neglect to perform; see Num. 9:13).

Two months after the Exodus, the Israelites reached the wilderness of Sinai, and there they had their next great group experience—this time not one of liberation—but of law giving. And at Sinai as well, sacrifices were offered on behalf of the community. Significantly, they were offered in the presence of 12 pillars representing the 12 tribes. Here was another public sacrificial ritual intended once again to unite not only heaven and earth (both the smoke and the pillars pointed heavenward) but the people themselves through the sprinkling of blood on them (Exod. 24:4–8).

One more communal sacrifice marked this formative period of the nation. When they completed the construction of their tabernacle in the desert and the Presence of God appeared to inaugurate the new sacred space, the community was instructed to bring "a he-goat for a purification offering; a calf and a lamb, yearlings without blemish, for a burnt offering; and an ox and a ram for an offering of well-being to sacrifice before the Lord ... for today the Lord will appear to you" (Lev. 9:3–4). From that moment on, the altar was a public instrument, designed to receive the offerings of the community. To be sure, individual sacrifices would still be offered there, but they were voluntary by and large. (Purification offerings had as their primary purpose permitting individuals with ritual impurities to regain eligibility to enter the sacred precincts; if such individuals were content to stay away, they would have very few obligatory gifts to bring.) This was a major turning point, a departure from the notion that individuals would sacrifice at any place they chose (witness Saul's ad hoc call for a rock to be provided for this purpose, in the passage cited above from 1 Sam. 14). And this is a central focus of the central book of the Torah, Leviticus. The Torah largely reflects a priestly ideology, and Leviticus does so more than any other book. Sacrifice, as the Torah conceives it, is to be made public, regulated, and kept in the control of the priesthood. For the Torah, in other words, sacrifice is not properly the stuff of narrative, but rather of the law.

IN BIBLICAL LAW

The legal parts of the Torah introduce various restrictions and regulations into the practice of animal slaughter and into sacrificial slaughter in particular. The story of Saul's ad hoc sacrifice in 1 Sam. 14 makes it clear that there was already a deeply entrenched understanding among the people that the blood belonged to God and could not be eaten without committing sacrilege. Thus it is not at all surprising that one of the Torah's chief restrictions is that, even among sacrifices that were to be eaten, both the blood and the suet had to be dashed or turned into smoke on the altar, i. e., returned to God (Lev. 7:22–27). But there were more restrictions to be imposed by the Torah, and several among these almost certainly were not already known or practiced by the folk.

The very institution of the priesthood meant that the personnel involved in sacrifice were being both restricted and professionalized. This is a strong kind of regulation, for it creates uniformity, guards against syncretistic influences, and imposes an inevitable conservatism on forms of worship. Even if a sacrifice were to be brought by an individual, or a family or a clan, only the officially designated priest determined how it would be offered, not the owners of the sacrifice.

Moreover, the place of offering was no longer wide open. Sacrifice must be offered at an official altar: "This is in order that the Israelites may bring the sacrifices which they have been making in the open— that they may bring them ... to the ... entrance of the Tent of Meeting ... that the priest may dash the blood against the altar of the LORD ... and that they may offer their sacrifices no more to the goat-demons after whom they stray" (Lev. 17:5–7). This passage makes several things plain: (a) sacrifice, when left to individuals, is prone to absorb idolatrous practices; (b) one way to avoid this is to create a priestly monopoly on sacrificial rites; and (c) another way to complete this regulatory process is to restrict the number of altars that have official status and confine sacrifice to those. Later, in Deut. 12, the Torah would go further: It would insist that there not be even a limited number of official altars, but rather one single altar, at the central shrine that would be the only legitimate place of sacrifice. No greater regulatory scheme than this could be envisaged.

Thus we have regulation of personnel and place and, through them, regulation of practice. Here we must mention one other great concern that the Torah exhibits with respect to sacrifices.

It was noted that in the ancient world, altars received all manner of animals as sacrifices and, in some cases, human beings as well. Ancient Israel was not an exception to this phenomenon: "They have built the shrines of Topheth in the Valley of Ben-Hinnom to burn their sons and daughters in fire—which I never commanded, which never came to My mind" (Jer. 7:31; see also 19:5–6; Ezek. 20:31). Indeed, when Exod. 13:12 speaks of the obligation to dedicate firstborns to God in gratitude for the Exodus, it uses the same language that the Torah uses to describe the abomination of child sacrifice, in Lev. 18:21 and Deut. 18:10. (The term rendered in this translation as "you shall set apart" literally means "to pass," as through fire.) Apparently, the vocabulary of dedication was unalterably affected even by the ancient practices that the Torah meant to sweep away. And its method for sweeping it away included not only the legal prohibitions on child sacrifice given in Lev. 18 and 20 and in Deut. 18 but also the most powerful and gripping narrative to be found in the Torah. Genesis 22 tells the tale of Abraham receiving a command to sacrifice his son Isaac, only to be told as he demonstrates his piety and willingness to offer even this to God that God does not want him to carry out the offering. A ram is offered in Isaac's place, and thus does the Torah both acknowledge the existence of this practice in Israel and instruct us that its strict regulation of sacrifice would, first and foremost, preclude the offering of such frightful gifts.

What all of the elaborate biblical regulation produced, then, was this array of authorized sacrifices:

1. *Olah* (burnt offering; also called "holocaust" in the scholarly literature): brought from males of the herds or flocks, or from birds, with the entire carcass of the animal (but for the hide) turned into smoke on the altar. These could be individual donations, but primarily included all of the public offerings for daily, *Shabbat,* and festival worship (Lev. 1; Num. 28–29).

2. *Minḥah* (grain offering): brought from flour, generally functioning as an accompaniment to *olot,* although standing by itself at certain key agricultural observances and other rites (Lev. 2, 23; Num. 5:15).

3. *Sh'lamim* (sacrifice of "well-being"): brought from males or females of the herds or flocks; individual "shared meals" in which the owner of the animal receives the flesh to eat after the blood is dashed and other vital parts are turned to smoke on the altar (Lev. 3), except for two instances (Lev. 9:4, 23:19). This category includes offerings brought for thanksgiving and offerings of firstborn or tithed animals (Lev. 7:12–15, 27:32; Num. 18:17–18).

4. *Ḥattat* (purification offering): brought by individuals or public officials for inadvertent sins of a grave nature, sometimes from the herd (male), and sometimes from the flock (male or female). In the most grave cases, the entire carcass is burnt outside the Temple; but in most cases, the sacrificial animal is shared with the altar, but the flesh is eaten by priests, rather than by the sinner (Lev. 4).

5. *Asham* (reparation offering): brought to expiate trespasses against sacred things, for fraud against others, for false oaths, and in a variety of other special cases (Lev. 5:14ff., 14:1–32; Num. 5:5–10, 6:13–21). Its procedure matches that of the *ḥattat* (Lev. 7:7), although it is often accompanied by a monetary fine.

6. *Pesaḥ* (the paschal lamb): offered annually by every Israelite household and eaten by them in commemoration of the Exodus (Exod. 12; Num. 9).

IN BIBLICAL PROPHECY AND LATER THOUGHT

Although this essay is meant to treat the subject of the sacrifices primarily from the Torah's point of view, a few closing comments are in order with respect to the prophetic traditions in the Hebrew Bible. As we have seen, priestly traditions strove to harness and regulate sacrificial modes of worship that predated biblical law. Prophetic traditions, meanwhile, often contrasted the mediated, and frequently mechanical, nature of priestly worship with the immediate, passion-driven goal of heeding

God's words and fulfilling the divine mandate for justice. Thus both Amos and Jeremiah offered reminiscences of Israel's early and formative encounters with God as being devoid of sacrifice (Amos 5:22–25; Jer. 7:21–23). Micah, not going quite that far, nevertheless asserted a clear hierarchy of values in which sacrifice is subordinate to justice and goodness (Mic. 6:6–8). The notion that God needs our sacrifices was particularly offensive to the circles, prophetic or otherwise, that promoted the idea of a universal, all-powerful God (this is expressed, for example, in Isa. 40:15–17, 66:1–4; Ps. 50:7–15). Hosea, for his part, advanced (according to the compelling interpretation of H. L. Ginsberg) the idea that easy access to sacrifice (e. g., through a multiplicity of altars) could actually remove disincentives to sin by providing ready-at-hand expiation:

> For Ephraim has multiplied altars—for guilt;
> His altars have redounded to his guilt:
> The many teachings I wrote for him
> Have been treated as something alien.
> (Hos. 8:11–12)

The oft-expressed prophetic coolness for sacrifice as a pillar of worship found expression later in Rabbinic Judaism as well. A whole school of thought claimed (contrary to biblical chronology) that Israel's first official altar was established in the wilderness only as a reaction to the Golden Calf (Tanḥ. T'rumah 8). In other words, it was needed to regulate urges that could lead to idolatry. In the Middle Ages, Maimonides followed this reasoning to its logical conclusion and claimed that the sacrificial laws of the Bible were a divine technique to wean the Israelites away from idolatrous practices (*Guide* III:32). And as for contemporary Conservative liturgy, it has made a striking substitution in the daily prayer service; in lieu of the traditional recitation of texts related to sacrificial laws, it recalls Yoḥanan ben Zakkai's saying (in the wake of the Temple's destruction in 70 c.e.) that the atonement formerly provided by the altar can be gained at least as well from acts of kindness. Study of texts exhorting us to such acts follows. As a climax, the contemporary liturgy has us ask God to make us into true successors of Aaron the high priest. It is not, however, his priestly functions that are invoked but rather the characteristics by which the tradition remembers him, as an exemplar of love of humanity and the pursuit of peace (see *Siddur Sim Shalom,* pp. 14–19, and *Siddur Sim Shalom for Shabbat and Festivals,* pp. 68–70).

Study Questions

1. Tucker singles out five distinct scriptural passages (Gen. 12:7, 13:14–18, 26:24–25, 35:6–7, and 46:1–3), three about Abraham and two about Jacob, which can be read as narrative rationalizations of the practice of worshiping God through sacrifice. After reading these passages, consider the following issues. To what extent do they present a unified sense of why the sacrifice of animals should be considered reasonable? Taken together, what do these stories suggest about the way an ancient Israelite might have answered the simple question, "Why do we worship God by slaughtering animals and incinerating their carcasses?"

2. In his survey of the different kinds of animal sacrifice, Tucker identifies two kinds of sacrifice that were brought as a response to wrongdoing: the *hattat* ("purification offering") and the *asham* ("reparation offering"). Consider the scriptural passages that relate to both kinds of sacrifice and compare the laws you find to create a kind of classification of wrongdoing in ancient Israel. (Material about the *hattat* is covered in Leviticus 4 and 7; material about the *asham* in Leviticus 5 and 7, and Numbers 5 and 6.) Scripture places sinful behavior into at least two large categories that require expiation in different ways. In Leviticus 4–7, which material pertains to which kind of sacrifice? Considering the specific reasons for which these sacrifices are to be brought, how would you label those categories? How do you think the people of that time understood sin?

3. Rabbi Tucker refers to passages in other books of the Bible that appear to take issue with the sacrificial system. Read Psalms 50 and 51 and then compare them with the so-called "Temple Sermon" in the seventh chapter of Jeremiah and the first chapter of Isaiah. While these chapters appear to take a dim view of the

sacrificial system, their underlying intent has been endlessly debated. Are they challenging the very legitimacy of sacrificial worship, or do they merely reflect their authors' righteous indignation regarding the way sacrificial worship was abused by their contemporaries? The books of Isaiah and Jeremiah also preserve passages in which their authors spoke with less hostility about Temple worship. Compare, for example, the chapter from Isaiah mentioned above with the messianic vision of the second chapter of that same book that includes a Temple "that all nations gaze on with joy" (Isa. 2:2.). Can these passages be reconciled, or do you feel that they merely reflect the conflicts that must have existed for prophets unsure whether to seek their people's spiritual renewal through revolution or reform?

4. Biblical texts relating to the sacrificial system generally reflect a total lack of interest in the fate of the animals. In a text like 1 Kings 8, for example, where King Solomon is said personally to have presided over the slaughter of 120,000 sheep and 22,000 oxen in a single day, this act appears to our modern thinking more as a pointless waste of animal life than a praiseworthy act of piety. Given the widely held opinion that the laws prohibiting cruelty to animals (the so-called *tza'ar ba'lei chayyim* laws) have their origin in Torah legislation, how can our tradition maintain both views?

5. Many Jews all over the world pray daily for the restoration of the Temple in Jerusalem. In many prayer books, these prayers include the specific wish that the sacrificial system be re-established and that the Temple in Jerusalem be rededicated as a site of sacrifice. How do you relate to these prayers? After reading Tucker's essay, do you find yourself more or less able to imagine a restored Temple cult that would include animal sacrifice as the central act of worship? Do you think that would be a positive or a negative development in terms of the evolution of Jewish life? What alternatives could there be?

Study materials by *Martin S. Cohen*

Writing and Ritual: Preserving and Perpetuating Torah

THE TORAH SCROLL

Stuart Kelman

Summary

In this essay, Rabbi Kellman, who is himself a *sofer*, covers a number of the aspects involved in the "creation" of a Torah scroll:

- A short summary of the evolution in transmitting the words of the Torah—from stone tablets to parchment to a printed "book."
- The qualities and preparation of the *sofer* himself.
- Parchment, pen, and ink—the tools of the *sofer* and their proper preparation.
- The calligraphic and artistic skills of the *sofer.*
- The procedures for correcting errors.
- The procedure for physically assembling a *seifer Torah.*

In its earliest transmission, the words of the Torah were etched onto stone tablets. Later, the words were written on papyrus and animal skins. To maintain this sacred tradition, Jews observe the *mitzvah* of writing the words of the Torah on specially prepared parchment, which is sewn together and rolled onto two wooden rollers. When Torah is read publicly, it is read from a Torah scroll (*seifer Torah*). When the Torah text is studied, it is read from a book like this one (*ḥumash*).

In Deut. 31:19, it is written: "Therefore, write down this poem and teach it to the people of Israel." This verse, according to the Sages, prescribes the responsibility of each Jew to write a *seifer Torah*. To fulfill this *mitzvah,* one can personally write a Torah scroll, have it written by a professional scribe (*sofer*), or help purchase one for a community.

The word *sofer* is a shortened form of the title *sofer stam;* the last word is an acronym for *"seifer Torah, t'fillin,* and *m'zuzot,"* the three items containing texts that a *sofer stam* writes.

A *sofer*'s work is a sacred calling. The practice of *safrut* (the art that a *sofer* practices) is not akin to calligraphy: It requires the mastery of many halakhic details, and it is transmitted through an apprenticeship with a master *sofer*.

Kavvanah (intentionality) is required for every step of the process. The *sofer*'s day begins with immersion in a *mikveh* (ritual bath), which is an act of spiritual purification that declares readiness to accept the obligation of the holy act of *safrut*. (If a *sofer* is unable to attend the *mikveh* for the day, a space for God's name is left, postponing the writing of God's name for a day on which the *sofer* could immerse in a *mikveh*. On that day, a special "God quill" and special bottle of ink may be used.)

The *sofer* commences work by writing the name of Amalek (the ancient enemy of the Jewish people) on a scrap of parchment. The name is then crossed out to fulfill the *mitzvah* of "blotting out the memory of Amalek from under the heaven" (Deut. 25:19). The *sofer* then writes a statement that translates as: "I am writing this Torah in the name of its sanctity and the name of God's sanctity."

The *sofer*'s tools—parchment, pen, and inkwell—are referred to as "articles of honor." The parchment (*k'laf*) is made from specified sections of the hide of a kosher animal (not necessarily slaughtered according to Jewish ritual). The hide consists of three layers, but only the flesh side of the inner layer and the outer side of the hairy layer may be used for Torah parchment (BT Shab. 79b). The method of cleaning and softening the hide has changed throughout the centuries. During talmudic times, salt and barley flour were sprinkled on the skins, which were then soaked in the juice of gallnuts (BT Meg. 19a). In modern times, the skins are softened by soaking them in clear water for two days, after which the hair is removed by soaking the hides in limewater for nine days. Finally, the skins are rinsed and dried and the creases ironed out with presses, in a process similar to the curing of leather. In keeping with the sanctity of processing material for a *seifer Torah,* the person handling the skins must make a verbal declaration of intent, acknowledging that all actions are being performed for the holiness of the *seifer Torah*.

Due to the scarcity and high cost of parchment, a single *k'laf* was used more than once by rubbing out the writing with stone and super-imposing new writing. This palimpsest is referred to in the dictum of Elisha ben Abuyah, who compares learning as a child to "ink written on clean paper" and learning in one's old age to "ink written on erased paper" (M Avot 4:20; Git. 2:4).

Although reeds were used as pens in the days of the Talmud, quills are used today; and the sturdy, durable turkey feather is preferred. The *sofer* cuts the point of the feather to give it a flat surface, which is desirable for forming the square letters, and then slits it lengthwise.

The ink used in writing a *seifer Torah* must be black and durable, but not indelible. During talmudic times a viscous ink was made by heating a vessel with the flame of olive oil; the soot thus produced on the sides of the vessel was scraped off and mixed with oil, honey, and gallnuts (BT Shab. 23a). Today, ink is produced from a mixture of gallnuts, gum arabic, and copper sulfate crystals. Some scribes also add vinegar and alcohol to render it glossy.

The actual printing of the letters follows one of three styles of script: The Ashkenazic resembles the script described in the Talmud (BT Shab. 104a). The Sephardic is identical with the printed letters of the Hebrew alphabet currently used in sacred texts. The Lurianic is the third style. The *sofer* must shape each letter precisely as pictured, and each must be written from left to right, with the initial stroke being (generally) a curved line produced by using just the point of the quill. Next, using the entire surface of the pen, the *sofer* draws the letter. The thickness of each letter varies and it is often necessary for the *sofer* to make several strokes to form a letter.

Tagin (an Aramaic word meaning "crowns") are specific ornamental designs placed at the upper left-hand corner of seven of the 22 letters of the Hebrew alphabet. Composed of three strokes, these crowns and their letters form the source of many mystical interpretations found in kabbalistic literature. There is a tradition that the *tagin* and the letters contain spiritual essences that emanate from God. According to Maimonides, if the *tagin* are omitted from the *seifer Torah,* the scroll is not considered to be invalid, because the *tagin* are an "exceptionally beautiful fulfillment of the *mitzvah*" (MT Torah Scroll 7:9). Ashkenazic custom, however, maintains that the scrolls are invalid without the appropriate *tagin* (*Magen Avraham* and *Ba·er Heitev* on S.A. O.Ḥ. 36:3).

There are precise specifications concerning the number of sheets of columns a Torah must have on each piece of *k'laf*, as well as the size of the columns, the space between individual letters, and the size of the gap between *parashiyyot* (portions). Although guidelines are incised for the top of a line of Torah text, there are none for the bottom of each letter. This is often given as one meaning of the *midrash* that the Torah has 70 faces (Num. R. 13:15). If a *sofer* makes a mistake in writing the *seifer Torah*, the ink can be erased with a knife or pumice stone or piece of broken glass. However, base metals are generally not used to correct or even touch a Torah scroll, as these metals are used to make weapons, which render them unfit to touch a *seifer Torah*, which is an instrument of peace.

Any mistakes in the spelling of any of the names of God cannot be corrected, as the name of God cannot be erased. If a *seifer Torah* has extensive corrections, it is considered unsightly and, therefore, invalid. When invalid or beyond repair, a *seifer Torah* is buried in a *g'nizah* (place where holy objects are buried). In talmudic times, it was customary to bury such scrolls alongside the grave of a prominent rabbi (BT Meg. 26b).

Once the writing of *seifer Torah* is carefully checked and approved, the individual sheets of parchment are sewn together with *giddin*, a special thread made of tendon tissue taken from the foot muscles of a kosher animal. These sections of parchment are sewn on the outer side of the parchment, with one inch left unsewn both at the very top and bottom. To reinforce the *giddin*, thin strips of parchment are often pasted on the top and bottom of the page. After connecting the sheets, the ends are tied to *atzei ḥayyim* (trees of life), which is the name for the wooden rollers that hold the scroll. Each *etz ḥayyim* consists of a center pole, with handles of wood and flat circular rollers to support the rolled-up scroll. In addition to providing a means to roll the scroll, the *atzei ḥayyim* prevent people from touching the holy parchment with their hands. (In some Sephardic communities, flat rollers are not employed, because the Torah scrolls are kept in a *tik*, an upright ornamental wooden or metal case.) When reading from a *seifer Torah*, one does not touch the Torah with one's hands, but uses a *yad* (pointer; literally: "hand") to follow the letters.

The Talmud teaches that one who corrects even one letter in a *seifer Torah* is considered to have the merit of one who has written the entire scroll (BT Men. 30a). Many *sof'rim* outline the letters at the end of the Torah, leaving them to be filled in by individuals in a ceremony called *siyyum ha-Torah* (completion of a Torah scroll). In many congregations, this ceremony also includes a processional of other Torah scrolls, and the new *seifer Torah* is accompanied to the Ark with great joy and pageantry.

Study Questions

1. Have you ever looked at a Torah up close, perhaps when you took an aliyah? What do you remember seeing that was discussed by this essay? What will you look for next time you see one?

2. The Torah scroll is considered one of our holiest objects. In fact, the tradition is that a congregation must fast for 40 days if it is dropped (or do some other form of *teshuvah*—atonement—such as give *tzedakah*). In what ways does the scribe prepare himself so he can undertake to "bring a new Torah into the world?" In what ways do you consider these preparations "spiritual" or "holy?"

3. Why do you think the tools of the *sofer* are called "articles of honor"? What or whom is being honored?

4. In our tradition, Judaism is concerned about "*tza'ar ba'lei hayyim*—cruelty to animals." It is interesting that the rabbis require the use of animal skin to write a Torah. The Egyptians, for example, generally used papyrus (from plants). Why do you think some of our most sacred objects, such as the *seifer Torah*, mezuzah parchments, and *t'fillin* are made out of the hides of a kosher animal?

5. As we return the *seifer Torah* to the Ark after the Torah reading we recite, " I have given you good teachings; don't forsake my Torah; for it is a tree of life (*etz chayim*) to those who take hold of it and

those who uphold it are happily blessed" (from *Sim Shalom for Shabbat and Holidays*). In light of this passage, why is it appropriate to call the wooden rollers of the *seifer Torah atzei chayim* (trees of life)? How is the Torah a "tree of life"? Why do you think the Conservative Movement decided to call its *Humash* (synagogue edition of the Torah) *Etz Hayim*?

Study materials by *Sheldon Dorph*

TORAH READING

Lionel Moses

Summary

The public reading of Torah is mentioned in the Bible on four occasions: for Sukkot as the culmination of a seven-year cycle (Deut. 31:10–3); in conjunction with a covenantal ceremony during the time of Joshua (8:30–35); in relation to the discovery of the "Book of the Covenant" under King Josiah (2 Kings 22–23); and following the return of the exiles from Babylonia under Ezra's leadership (Neh. 8:1–8).

There is no internal biblical evidence that the Sukkot reading ever occurred as described in Deuteronomy, and the readings during the days of Joshua and Ezra probably referred only to the Book of Deuteronomy. Thus, the first public reading that involved "a prototype" of the Torah, took place in the mid-5th century when Ezra undertook the initial reading on Rosh Hashanah, followed by a daily reading during the festival of Sukkot.

According to literary references and archaeological evidence, by the time of the Second Temple, the public reading of Torah was a regular feature of the synagogue service. The Mishnah tells of the reading of the Torah (probably the Book of Deuteronomy) by the king as part of the seven-year sabbatical cycle. It also regulates the number of people called to the Torah and the minimum number of verses read for each *aliyah*. The Talmud stipulates the minimum number of verses to be read, who is eligible to read or be called to the Torah, and assigns specific passages for special *Shabbatot*.

The custom of *Eretz Yisra'el* was to complete the reading of the Torah once every three years; in Babylonia it was completed annually. In the Babylonian cycle, the reading began on the *Shabbat* following Simchat Torah and concluded the next year on that festival. In the triennial cycle, Simchat Torah was a moveable festival, occurring at various times during the year. However, by the twelfth century C.E., the influence of Babylonian Jewry was virtually universal and the annual cycle became the norm for most communities. In the modern era, Conservative synagogues that have adopted the triennial cycle have tried—with moderate success—to develop a uniform pattern for this custom.

The Torah is chanted using a series of accents developed by 9th and 10th century Tiberias-based scholars known as Masoretes (those who preserve the *masorah*, tradition). These notes are known as *ta'amim* or *trope*. In addition to indicating the motifs for cantillation, the *ta'amim* also designate the relationship between words, specify the stressed syllable in each word, and provide syntactical and grammatical direction to help understand the meaning of a verse. The Masoretes also preserved the accuracy of the biblical text, developed vowel signs to aid in vocalization, and enumerated the letters, words, and sections of the Torah.

Rabbinic traditions attribute the origin of the Torah reading to Moses, but there is no historical evidence to validate such an ancient genesis for this practice. These traditions of the Sages reflect an awareness that public instruction predates their era and acknowledge that they could not accurately date when the regular reading of the Torah began.

Internal biblical evidence about the public reading of the Torah is scarce. Deuteronomy legislates a public ceremony to be held every seven years during the *Sukkot* festival at which the Torah would be read to the assembled community (31:10–13). However, even as late as the end of the monarchy (587 B.C.E.) there is no evidence in the Bible indicating that such a ceremony and public reading actually occurred with the type of regularity anticipated in Deuteronomy. Moreover, many biblical scholars believe that this Deuteronomic legislation originally was part of a ceremony at which the covenantal relationship between God and the people Israel was ratified. Although the Bible recounts such covenant renewal ceremonies (Exod. 20; Josh. 8:30 ff., 24; 2 Kings 22–23), public readings of the text of the covenant are mentioned in only two of these passages.

One of these covenant renewal ceremonies in which the Torah was read publicly describes how King Josiah (639–609 B.C.E.) assembled all the people of Judah in Jerusalem during the 18th year of his reign. He read to them the "Book of the Covenant" that had been discovered in the Temple by the high priest Hilkiah (2 Kings 22:8–9, 23:2–3). Most contemporary biblical scholars agree that this "Book of the Covenant" was the Book of Deuteronomy, not the entire Torah.

The only other biblical example of a public reading of the covenant before the destruction of the First Temple in 587 B.C.E. comes from the period of the conquest of the land of Israel (1200–1050 B.C.E.). After the conquest of the Canaanite fortress of Ai, Joshua built an altar to God on Mount Ebal and inscribed on the stones of the altar a copy of the Torah of Moses. Then, in a ceremony reminiscent of the instructions given by Moses in Deut. 27:1–13, Joshua read "all the words of the Torah, the blessings and the curses," before the Israelites who stood facing Mount Gerizim and Mount Ebal in the Valley of Shechem (Josh. 8:30–35). Once again, most contemporary biblical scholars identify the Book of the Teaching referred to in this passage with the Book of Deuteronomy, not with the entire Torah as we know it today.

Not until the Persian period (5th century B.C.E.) does the term *Torah* apply to all five books of the Pentateuch. This transition in which the term the "Book of the Torah" came to encompass the entire Pentateuch is connected with the process of editing and redaction of the source material of the Pentateuch. Biblical scholars argue that this change took place during the 6th century B.C.E., after the destruction of the First Temple (587 B.C.E.).

On that basis, a scholarly consensus has formed that when Ezra the Scribe read the Torah publicly to the exiles who had returned to Jerusalem in the mid-5th century (Neh. 8:1–8), he read a prototype of the five books of the Torah that we know today. Despite the prescription in Deuteronomy that the Torah be read every seven years, the practice apparently had lapsed, if it had even been instituted at all. Nehemiah 8:9 records that when Ezra first began to read publicly from the Book of the Torah on *Rosh ha-Shanah,* the people began to cry. Perhaps this was because they had never heard the Torah read and expounded so forcefully. Perhaps it was because they had forgotten the Torah's demands and, through this public reading, became aware of their failure to observe the law. They began to weep and mourn because they knew the consequences for the previous generations who had failed to observe the laws of the Torah.

The narrative in Nehemiah subsequently recounts how the heads of the families of all the people, as well as the priests and Levites, continued to study the Torah with Ezra on the second day of *Rosh ha-Shanah,* learning about the festival of *Sukkot.* These leaders issued a proclamation to all the returned exiles living in the environs of Jerusalem to celebrate and observe *Sukkot.* During this seven-day celebration, Ezra read the Torah publicly every day, fulfilling the injunction of Deut. 31:10–13 that the Torah be read once in seven years on *Sukkot* (Neh. 8:18).

During the Second Temple period, both Philo and Josephus refer to the public reading and teaching of Torah in the synagogue. A Greek inscription found in Jerusalem in the remains of an ancient synagogue, whose ruins predate the destruction of the Second Temple (70 c.e.), declares that the synagogue was dedicated "to the reading of the Law and the teaching of the commandments." The septennial reading of the Torah on *Sukkot,* as prescribed by Deuteronomy, is recorded in the Mishnah (Sot. 7:8). The Mishnah calls this septennial reading the "Pericope of the King" and describes the procedure for this public reading of the Torah that occurred during the reign of King Agrippa (41–44 c.e.). The content of what Agrippa actually read during this ceremony, however, seems to be limited to the Book of Deuteronomy.

It is not known how the Torah was read during the period of the Mishnah and the early talmudic period (2nd and 3rd centuries c.e.). The Mishnah does not state whether the Torah was to be read consecutively from Genesis to Deuteronomy or whether the choice of each weekly reading was to be left to a local synagogue functionary. It is quite likely that in ancient Palestine there was far less uniformity than in Babylonia, even during the period of the Mishnah and the Talmud. From the post-talmudic era (5th to 11th centuries c.e.), however, we do have more detailed information about how the Torah was read in Palestine. The evidence indicates that there was no uniformity among the Palestinian Jewish communities on how the Torah was divided into weekly portions for reading.

The Mishnah, however, does present a number of regulations regarding the public reading of the Torah. Thus, for example, the number of people called to the Torah (*olim;* singular: *oleh*) on specific occasions is established: three on weekdays and for *Shabbat Minḥah;* four on *Rosh Hodesh* and on the intermediate days of festivals; five on festivals; six on *Yom Kippur;* and seven on *Shabbat* morning (M Meg. 4:1–2). The Mishnah implies that the required number of *olim* may be exceeded except on weekdays, at *Shabbat Minḥah,* on *Rosh Hodesh,* and on the intermediate days of a festival. The Talmud and the medieval codes, however, limit the addition of extra readers to *Shabbat* (BT Meg. 23a; Tur O. Ḥ. 282:1; S.A. O. Ḥ. 282:1).

The Mishnah further states that each of the *olim* must read a minimum of 3 verses (M Meg. 4:4). The Talmud adds that a public reading of the Torah must have a minimum of 10 verses (BT Meg. 21b; MT Prayer 12:3; S.A. O. Ḥ. 137:1–2). The only exceptions, apparently, are the reading for *Purim* morning (Exod. 17:8–16) and the weekday reading for the section of *Va-yeilekh* (Deut. 31:1–9), when a total of 9 verses are read. (Tosafot Meg. 21b, s.v. *ein*, justifies the abbreviated reading for *Purim,* but makes no mention of *Va-yeilekh.*)

The Talmud rules that women and children can be included among the seven *olim*, but the Sages ruled that women may not read from the Torah because of *k'vod ha-tzibbur*, a technical term that in this context appears to mean "the dignity of the congregation" (BT Meg. 23a). This talmudic text, which originates in the Tosefta (Meg. 3:11 with variations) is the source that teaches that the *olim* were expected to read their own portion from the Torah. Indeed, according to the Tosefta, if only one person was competent to read from the Torah, he was to be given all seven *aliyot*. This tradition of the *oleh* reading his own portion from the Torah continues through the medieval period, when it is codified as the norm in the *Shulḥan Arukh* (O. Ḥ. 139:1–2). The same passage of *Shulḥan Arukh* is already aware that a person who is unable to read his own portion might be needed as an *oleh* because he is the only *kohen* or *Levi* present; that code, therefore, permits a properly prepared reader to read the Torah for the *oleh*, who must repeat the passage word by word. By the end of the 19th century, however, the prevailing custom had changed. Those who could not read from the Torah—or even follow an expert reader—were given *aliyot,* on the premise that a person who hears the reading is like one who is able to repeat what he has heard (*Arukh Ha-Shulḥan* O. Ḥ. 139:3).

Another rule introduced by the Mishnah prohibits skipping verses when reading the Torah (M Meg. 4:4). This regulation means that a reading must be consecutive, so that the reader will not become confused. The Talmud provides one exception to this rule. On *Yom Kippur,* the high priest read Lev. 16 and then was permitted to skip to Num. 29. In the Talmud, Abbaye justifies this exception because both passages deal with the same topic: the rituals of *Yom Kippur* (BT Meg. 24a). The only other exception occurs on public fast days, when the Torah reading skips from Exod. 32:14 to 34:1 from the first to the second *aliyah.* The justification for this exception is that the time required to roll the Torah from one section to the next is no longer than the time required for a translator to render the biblical verse in an Aramaic translation (BT Meg. 24a).

By the 3rd century c. e., the Sages had assigned specific passages of the Torah for festivals and special Sabbaths (M Meg. 3:4–6). Many of these passages are still read today. Torah readings for special fast days are also recorded in the Mishnah (Taan. 4:2–3). Concerning which passages are to be read on *Shabbat* on a weekly basis, the Mishnah is silent. An oblique reference to the weekly Torah readings in the Talmud states that in Palestine the public reading of the Torah was completed once in three years (BT Meg. 29b). This implies that a different custom for reading the Torah on *Shabbat* prevailed in Babylonia.

In Babylonia, it was customary to complete the reading of the Torah in just one year, a practice that was established by 600 c. e. and probably even earlier. This annual cycle began on the last *Shabbat* of *Tishrei* (the *Shabbat* after *Simḥat Torah*). The Torah was then read consecutively each *Shabbat* until it was completed on the next *Simḥat Torah* (the 23rd day of *Tishrei*). The Torah text was divided into 54 sections, known as pericopes or *parashiyyot* (singular: *parashah*), so that the reading cycle could be completed in one year. This number of *parashiyyot* exceeded the number of Sabbaths in the annual calendar and provided the necessary flexibility for a Jewish leap year, which adds four weeks to the calendar. Thus in some years, certain *parashiyyot* were combined to ensure that the entire Torah was completed by *Simḥat Torah,* whereas during a leap year (which has four extra Sabbaths) each *parashah* was read on a separate week. The flexibility that allowed for combining and separating certain *parashiyyot* could also accommodate the special readings for festivals, when these festivals occurred on *Shabbat* (M Meg. 3:4–6).

In Palestine, an alternate cycle of reading the Torah was followed until the 12th century C. E. Like the annual cycle, it was also consecutive, beginning with Genesis and concluding with Deuteronomy. This alternative system divided the Torah into small units called *s'darim,* but this division was not uniform. Different manuscripts of the Torah divide the text into as few as 148 *s'darim* and as many as 175 *s'darim,* indicating that the divisions varied from one location to another in Palestine. This alternative system meant that in Palestine the reading of the Torah was completed in three or three and a half years, assuming that only one or two *s'darim* were read on each *Shabbat.*

The system of reading the Torah in approximately three years is referred to as the triennial cycle. The range in the number of *s'darim* suggests that there was greater flexibility and less uniformity among congregations of the Levant that followed this custom. And in the Palestinian triennial system, *Simḥat Torah* could not be a fixed date on the festival calendar as it was in Babylonia, because it coincided with the *Shabbat* on which the Torah reading was completed. The fluidity of the dates for *Simḥat Torah* in Palestine is indicated by some of the liturgical poems (*piyyutim*) written there during the 5th and 6th centuries C. E., some of which include a prayer for dew. This suggests that the poem was recited on a *Simḥat Torah* that occurred during the summer. *Simḥat Torah* poems of Babylonian origin, on the other hand, always include a prayer for rain, because the festival in Babylonia always occurred at the end of *Tishrei,* after the harvest was completed.

By the 12th century C. E., the Babylonian rabbinate and their heirs in North Africa had extended their religious hegemony over all of rabbinic Jewry, including the surviving Jewish communities of Palestine. In 1170 C. E., the Jewish traveler Benjamin of Tudela reported that he had visited synagogues in both Cairo and Palestine that still followed the triennial cycle. By the end of that century, Maimonides could state categorically that the annual cycle was virtually universal (MT Prayer 13:1).

The annual cycle instituted in Babylonia has remained the universal custom for reading the Torah since the 12th century. An attempt to reintroduce the triennial cycle during the 19th century met with little success. One London synagogue, the West End Congregation, was discouraged from reintroducing the practice by Adolph Buechler, who argued that following a triennial cycle would separate the congregation from the rest of normative Judaism.

Nonetheless, many American Conservative congregations (seeking ways to modernize the service and to increase Torah study on *Shabbat*) attempted to modify the annual cycle as early as the late 1940s by reinstituting the triennial cycle. These attempts, which increased over the following three decades for other practical considerations as well, lacked uniformity and consistency. Thus, even though every synagogue was reading the same *parashah*, very likely they were not reading the same sections of that *parashah*. Another attempt to reintroduce the triennial cycle of Palestine to the Conservative Movement was rejected in 1987 by the CJLS on the basis of arguments strikingly similar to those of Adolph Buechler, almost 100 years earlier.

In place of the ancient triennial cycle of Palestine, a new American triennial cycle was adopted in 1988 by the CJLS. This cycle takes each of its weekly portions from the corresponding *parashah* of the annual cycle, although generally the reading from the triennial cycle is shorter. This cycle also incorporates the festival calendar, so that the entire Torah is read every three years in such a way that the reading is completed on *Simḥat Torah* (23 *Tishrei*). Although this system attempts to follow the literary units of the Torah when dividing each *parashah* into thirds, the American triennial cycle has a distinct disadvantage. By reading only one third of each *parashah* each year, the Torah is no longer read consecutively, so that narratives and bodies of biblical legislation are interrupted from week to week. Nonetheless, the new cycle has become increasingly popular in Conservative congregations and has introduced a greater order of uniformity in the Torah reading among the congregations that have adopted it. [*Editor's note*: The CJLS triennial cycle, edited by Richard Eisenberg, is available from the Rabbinical Assembly.]

The Torah is not literally read. It is chanted in a musical mode according to a system of special markings that are found in printed versions of the Hebrew Bible, but not in the Torah scroll. Each of these marks designates a series of musical notes called Masoretic accents (*ta·amei ha-mikra* or *ta·amim*). As early as the 3rd century C.E., the talmudic sage Yoḥanan noted that the Bible should be read and studied with a pleasant melody (BT Meg. 32a). Over the centuries, different Jewish communities have developed distinctive musical notes for the Masoretic accents. Currently there are five musical modalities for reading the Torah, and within each of these modalities there are regional and local variations.

The system of *ta·amim* that appears in printed texts of the Hebrew Bible was developed by biblical scholars known as Masoretes who lived in Tiberias (in northern Israel) during the 9th and 10th centuries C.E. The development of the *ta·amim* is only one aspect of their work. Their main goal was to preserve the text of the Hebrew Bible with the utmost accuracy. To this end, they developed the system of vowel signs still in use today to ensure that each word in the Torah would always be read the same way. They also counted the number of words and letters in the Torah and compiled a list of even the most insignificant deviations from what they had established as the authentic text of the Hebrew Bible.

The *ta·amim* have three distinct functions—musical, syntactical, and grammatical. Primarily they indicate the musical motifs in which the biblical text is chanted. Each accent represents a group of notes (tropes) that the reader fits to each word. The accents identify the stressed syllable in each word by being placed above or below the syllable that receives the stress. Knowing which syllable receives the stress helps provide meaning to the text, because often the only distinction between two words that sound the same but have different meanings (homophones) is the syllable that receives the stress. The musical motif of the accents produces a chant that adds an aesthetic dimension to the public reading, as recommended in the Talmud.

All the *ta·amim* are classified into two groups—disjunctive *ta·amim* (called *m'lakhim,* "kings") and conjunctive *ta·amim* (called *m'shar'tim,* "servants"). They are arranged in patterns that help make the meaning of the text clear and intelligible by pointing to the interrelationship of words.

Most contemporary Jewish musicologists assume that the variety of musical modes or melodies for reading the Torah and other books of the Hebrew Bible developed independently in different places over a long period of time. Each of these musical modalities was equally legitimate at the time in which the forms of synagogue worship began to be stabilized. Later, some of these modes were accepted as normative by one community or by several communities.

The five current musical modes are: Yemenite; Ashkenazic; Middle Eastern and North African; Jerusalem Sephardic; and northern Mediterranean. Some of these have developed substyles. For example, the Middle Eastern and North African tradition developed distinctive musical motifs for Morocco and for Syria and Iraq. Similarly, the Ashkenazic style can be divided into western and eastern sub-styles. The former is still preserved by Jewish communities from Frankfurt and Hanover and is popular in Great Britain. The eastern Ashkenazic style developed in the Polish-Lithuanian communities, and it remains the most common system of musical motifs in North American Ashkenazic synagogues today.

Study Questions

1. Note how the author of the essay uses biblical texts, external literature (such as Philo), and archaeological evidence to develop a history of the ritual of Torah reading. Why do Deuteronomy, Ezra, and Nehemiah loom so large in understanding the development of this tradition? How does this history compare with the tradition that Moses originated this practice?

2. How do you understand the statement that Ezra read "a prototype of the five books that we know today"?

3. Do you find the lack of uniform traditions in the Palestinian Jewish community to be significant? Why do religious communities sometimes crave uniformity?

4. Lionel Moses notes that the Mishnah originally prohibited women from reading from the Torah because of "*k'vod ha-tzibbur*—the

dignity of the community." What do you think bothered the rabbis of the Mishnah? Does the idea of *k'vod ha-tzibbur* still have a place in contemporary Jewish life?

5. Do you think that the development of an expert Torah reader (to replace the classical model of reading one's own aliyah) was beneficial or detrimental? Some congregations today have a policy that a person may not read his or her own aliyah, since it could embarrass those who do not possess this skill. What do you think?

6. What might be the reason that the Babylonian/Ashkenazi traditions organize the Torah reading so that it begins and concludes at the end of the autumn festival season? Would it be preferable to structure the reading so that the Exodus narrative is always read in the spring?

7. What have been reasons for the contemporary adoption of a triennial cycle? What arguments exist for retaining the annual pattern?

8. What are some reasons in support of Rabbi Yohanan's suggestion that the Bible be studied with a melody? Does it add to your appreciation during a public reading, or is it a barrier to participation?

Study materials by *Baruch Frydman-Kohl*

HAFTARAH

Michael Fishbane

Summary

This essay gives us a backstage glimpse at the instructional intentions of Rabbinic Judaism. Communal reading of the Torah seems to have obscure origins in the public recitation of the Torah in Deuteronomy 31 and Ezra's revival of the practice as depicted in Nehemiah 8. The Mishnah (*Megillah*) has a more developed description of a defined cycle for these readings. What eventually developed was a three-part ritual of reading from the Torah, the prophets, and a homiletic sermon. While the actual readings varied over time and from one community to another, this structure became an established feature of Jewish communal worship. Fishbane traces the significance of this format and demonstrates that it is meant to present a seamless set of revelations from the Torah to the prophets and then to the lessons of the sages. This provided institutional legitimacy to the *beit midrash* (rabbinic schools) and the *beit knesset* (synagogues). Even today it guarantees an ongoing renewal of our relationship to God through a weekly in-depth encounter with the Bible. If prayer is the medium for communicating with God, study is the medium in which God continues "to speak" to us.

The *haftarah* (plural: *haftarot*) is the selection from *N'vi·im* (Prophets) recited publicly after the designated portion from the Torah (Five Books of Moses) has been read on *Shabbat,* on festivals, and on other specified days. These communal readings are an integral part of classical Judaism, in both form and function.

The primary feature of the ancient institution of the synagogue is the recitation of the Torah. The Torah is chanted on *Shabbat* in a continuous sequence throughout the year, from beginning to end in a fixed cycle, interrupted only when a holiday (or an intermediate day of a festival) coincides with *Shabbat*. Next in importance for the synagogue is the recitation from a book of the prophets, selected to complement the Torah reading or to highlight the theme of a specific ritual occasion. These prophetic readings are selective, topical, and not read in sequence. These two recitations from Scripture (Torah and prophets) are enhanced by a homily (*d'rashah*) that interprets the readings in the light of tradition, theology, or historical circumstance.

This triad of Torah, prophets, and homily represents three levels of authority in Judaism, as well as three modes of religious instruction. The Torah is the most important of these, for it is the revelation to Moses and the teaching received from him—the foremost prophet, with whom God spoke directly (Num. 12:6–8). According to later (Rabbinic) tradition, the difference between the divine revelations to Moses and those granted to other prophets is the difference between two modes of envisioning or experiencing the divine. Moses was allowed to see God clearly, through a shining mirror, whereas all other prophets had to perceive God through a glass darkly, as in an unclear and unpolished mirror (BT Yev. 49b).

Even though God's revelation to the prophets is less direct, the truth of their message is not diminished, because it too flowed from divine inspiration. Nevertheless, by making such a formal distinction, the ancient Sages differentiated between the primary teachings of Moses and the secondary teachings of the prophets. Their goal was to exhort the people to return to faithfulness to the Covenant and to announce the consequences of their behavior and the future fate of the people. The synagogue preacher could see his task as explicating the teachings of Moses, of the other prophets, or of both, on those occasions when he renewed God's message in the hearing of an assembled congregation.

The preacher thus added his words of interpretation to the divine words, to make their eternal relevance and significance clear and immediate to his contemporaries. However, even though he spoke on behalf of Moses and the prophets, the preacher's authority came from the Sages in their role as transmitters of the divine word. Their self-appointed task, in the synagogue as in the study hall, was to make Scripture come alive for the people. For these reasons, the Sages saw themselves as heirs to the prophets. "Since the day when the Temple was destroyed, prophecy has been taken from the prophets and given to the Sages" (BT BB 12a). The

Sages, as teachers, thus gave institutional stability to the ancient words of Moses and consoled their community with the prophets' hopes and promises for the future.

When was the Torah first recited at communal gatherings? Evidence is scanty and often obscure. Two biblical passages are of note in this regard. In Deuteronomy (31:10–13), Moses instructs the priests into whose keeping he has given a written copy of "this teaching" (*ha-torah ha-zot*), namely, Deuteronomy. He tells them to "read" it "aloud in the presence of all Israel," "every seventh year" when they come before the LORD during the pilgrimage feast of *Sukkot*. The purpose of this septennial recitation was to instill both reverence for and observance of the precepts of the Torah in the entire community (Deut. 31:12–13). We may assume that the event was something of a covenant renewal ceremony, reproducing the event outlined in Deut. 29:9–14. On the basis of Moses' injunction to "gather [*hak·hel*] the people" together to hear the law (Deut. 31:12), this occasion traditionally has been known as the *mitzvah* of *hak·hel*. The other occasion of public Torah reading in the Bible is found in Neh. 8. There, it is reported that Ezra the Scribe, having returned recently to the land of Israel from Babylonian exile, gathered the people on the first day of the seventh month (*Rosh ha-Shanah*) to present to them the "book of the *torah* of Moses." This event is of interest for several reasons. First, it records a public reading that lasted from dawn to midday, with Ezra standing on a wooden platform surrounded by Levites. Second, when the scroll was opened, Ezra first blessed "the LORD, the great God," and the people responded "Amen, Amen" with upraised hands, after which they bowed down. Third, the Levites added meaning from the scroll with various clarifications and interpretations of the text (Neh. 8:8).

The practice of reading from the Torah each week on *Shabbat* is ascribed to Moses by ancient traditions (including the Mishnah). The recitation of a Torah portion on Monday and Thursday mornings and on *Shabbat* afternoon is considered one of the 10 legal innovations (*takkanot*) instituted by Ezra.

Our earliest evidence for reading the Torah in a continuous cycle is found in the Mishnah. There it states explicitly that on the four special

Sabbaths between the first of *Adar* (the month of *Purim*) and the first of *Nisan* (the month of *Pesaḥ*), the regular *Shabbat* reading is interrupted. "On the fifth [*Shabbat*] one returns to the [regular] sequence" (M Meg. 3:4). Interruptions also occurred when a festival or other special day coincided with *Shabbat*. On all of these occasions, other readings (out of sequence) were prescribed (M Meg. 4:2).

A continuous cycle of Torah readings was followed in the land of Israel near the beginning of our era, possibly as early as the 1st century c. e., although customs varied. Some authorities held that continuity implies reading portions from the Torah progressively each *Shabbat* morning, with the intervening readings on *Shabbat* afternoons; and brief readings on the market days of Monday and Thursday should be merely anticipations of the next *Shabbat* morning portion. Others held the opinion that a continuous reading implies an incremental reading of the Torah portion at the four public readings each week, with each reading continuing where the last stopped.

Far more complicated was the matter of how the continuous recitation should be subdivided, thereby determining when the cycle of readings from the entire Torah would be completed. There is a Babylonian tradition that "Westerners [Jews in the land of Israel] finish the Torah in three years" (BT Meg. 29b). This is confirmed in the later Gaonic statement about one of the differences in religious practice between the communities of Babylon and of the land of Israel: The "Easterners [Jews in Babylon] celebrate *Simḥat Torah* at the end of their reading cycle every year, whereas the residents of the land of Israel do so every three and a half years." Evidently, practices varied widely within the land of Israel itself depending on the way the special readings (e. g., for *Shabbat T'shuvah* or New Moon) affected the continuous recitations; and it is also possible that the number of readings were adjusted so that two triennial cycles could be completed every seven years. Most scholars regard the one-year cycle of 53 or 54 portions (*parashiyyot*) as a derivative Babylonian practice; it became dominant after the authority of the Babylonian academy was transferred to Spain in the 11th and 12th centuries c. e., especially because of the backing of Maimonides.

Determining specific portions of each *Shabbat* also was a prerequisite for the selection of readings from the prophets as *haftarot*, as they were correlated with the Torah portion by words, by theme, or by place in the liturgical cycle.

The origin of the *haftarah* is obscured both by the paucity of ancient evidence and by medieval legend. According to the latter, the custom of reciting several verses from the prophets in the synagogue service is said to go back to the 2nd century B.C.E. in the reign of Antiochus Epiphanes IV. When the king issued an edict prohibiting the reading of the Torah, the Jews were said to have evaded it by reading a passage from the prophets instead. This custom continued after the persecutions ceased. This theory still enjoys popular currency, although there is no corroborating evidence for it.

In antiquity, the selection of the *haftarah* varied greatly from community to community. This is clear from the diverse lists of prophetic readings for the so-called triennial cycle found in the Cairo Geniza and in many other collections of customs, including the references or allusions to *haftarot* found in the Midrash.

The correlation between the Torah and the *haftarah* readings could be established on the verbal or on the thematic level, on the basis of verbal similarities and thematic relationships. The triennial and annual cycles exhibit both features, although the element of verbal similarities occurs primarily on regular Sabbaths, when the main concern is the lesson of the Torah portion. The element of thematic relationships appears primarily on special Sabbaths, when the main concern is the religious topic of the day.

Thematic links between the Torah and the prophets in the early rabbinical sources in the land of Israel appear, as noted earlier, when *Shabbat* or another day commemorates a special ritual or religious occasion. The Mishnah mentions several days when a special selection from the Torah is recited. These include the four Sabbaths between the 1st of *Adar* and the 1st of *Nisan* (M Meg. 3:4); the three pilgrimage festivals of *Pesah, Shavu·ot* (Pentecost), and *Sukkot* (Booths); and the holidays of *Rosh ha-Shanah* and *Yom Kippur* (M Meg. 3:5). They also include *Hanukkah, Purim,* and the New Moon (M Meg. 3:6).

The annual cycle also conforms to old Palestinian traditions in its overall liturgical structure. As noted earlier, the weekly core of regular *Shabbat* readings, constituting a perpetual recitation of "God's word" in sequence, is sometimes interrupted by the substitution of other passages from the Torah. All of these sacred days had special Torah readings assigned to them. And pertinent *haftarot* were recited on the special Sabbaths, on holidays, and festivals (and the *Shabbat* of the festival week of *Pesah* and of *Sukkot*), the *Shabbat* of *Hanukkah,* and when the New Moon coincided with *Shabbat* or occurred on the day after *Shabbat.* In addition, special *haftarot* were recited on 10 successive Sabbaths during the summer, beginning with the *Shabbat* after the 17th of *Tammuz,* which commemorates the first breach in the walls of Jerusalem during the Romans' final siege of the First Temple. The first three weeks of this period, which commemorates the destruction of the Temple and the exile of the people, are known as Sabbaths of Admonition. Warnings and exhortations are read from the first two chapters of Jeremiah and from the first chapter of Isaiah. The subsequent seven weeks, beginning with the *Shabbat* after *Tish·ah b'Av,* are known as Sabbaths of Consolation. During this period, words of comfort and hope are recited from Isa. 40 ff.

Any year can have almost half as many special *haftarot* (21 or more) as *haftarot* for regular Sabbaths (54 or less). This ratio changes in favor of the special *haftarot* when holidays and festivals coincide with *Shabbat* or when there are two Sabbaths during the feast of *Hanukkah.* All such occasions interrupt the regular cycle of Torah readings and require an adjustment that results in the combination of two Torah portions on one *Shabbat.* This, in turn, leads to a reduction of regular *haftarot,* for when two Torah portions are joined, only the *haftarah* assigned to the second one is recited. The combined total ensures that the teachings and topics preserved in the prophetic literature have a dominant place in the public instruction of the community. This intrusion was aided and furthered by the homiletic use of these passages in the synagogue as well as by the Aramaic translation and paraphrasing (*targum*) that accompanied them.

The annual cycle has roots in the older multiyear cycles. Its choice of prophetic readings may be in part a selection from all the available *haftarot* in those cycles. This is particularly evident when the link between the Torah portion and the *haftarah* in the annual cycle occurs somewhere in the middle of the weekly *parashah* and not at the beginning. This striking phenomenon is explainable only by the fact that the length of any given section (*parashah*) for the annual cycle could embrace about three sections from the Palestinian triennial cycle. Thus each *haftarah* could have been chosen from a number of possibilities.

The broad base of instruction through the prophetic literature is also clear from the distribution of the books from which the *haftarot* are derived in the annual cycle. Of the 54 selections, the largest cluster is from the book of Isaiah (14), with fewer from Jeremiah (8), Ezekiel (6), and the minor prophets (9). This cluster makes up two thirds of the Torah readings and constitutes a contrast with the *haftarot* in the triennial cycle. In that cycle, two thirds of the *haftarot* were from Isa. 40–66 (dealing with redemption and ingathering) and fully four fifths of them had a messianic or eschatologic dimension. In the *haftarot* of the annual cycle, by contrast, the smaller percentage of material from the later chapters of Isaiah is notable, as is the lesser emphasis on messianic features. The *haftarot* of the annual cycle emphasize the national future and the restoration of the people to the Land and reflect a strong interest in historical parallels or symmetries between the Torah portion and its *haftarah*.

Parallels between events, persons, or institutions also highlight many types of continuities and correlations within Scripture.

One cannot speak of any consistent literary feature or style among the *haftarot*. Each individual reading sculpts its discourse out of a larger context and establishes its own rhetorical emphasis and features. In several cases, the *haftarot* overlap separate units of Scripture, thus underscoring the fact that the prophetic readings are a rabbinical creation and institution. The diverse forms are discussed in the commentary to the *haftarot* in this volume. Also because of the great variety of texts and topics, there is no consistent theme or emphasis among the *haftarot*. Nevertheless, religious instruction and national hope are frequent features. The individual types are also considered in the commentary.

For the synagogue, the *haftarah* marks the "leaving off" (*aftarta*) or "completion" (*ashlamata*) of the official Torah service and is formally set off from it in several ways. The *haftarah* service, so to speak, begins after the reading from the Torah portion has been completed and a half *Kaddish* has been recited to mark a break between it and what follows. Then a brief passage (of at least three verses) at the end of the Torah portion is repeated. After the Torah scroll is rolled up and set aside, the *haftarah* is chanted. Blessings before and after the recitation of the *haftarah* enhance the authority of the lesson from the Prophets and present it within a sacred liturgical framework.

Study Questions

1. How does the legend of the origin of the haftarah express the unique concerns of the Jewish community in the Middle Ages who contended with public disputations, Talmud burnings, and theological assaults from the Church? Notice that the evil king is the infamous Antiochus of Hanukkah. What moral message about Torah study and the ingenuity of Jewish survival is implied by these stories?

2. For some, a formative experience—bar or bat mitzvah—centers around a particular part of the Torah. Do you remember your Torah or haftarah portion? Do you feel some ongoing personal connection to these small sections of the Bible?

3. The selections of *haftarot* differ, according to Fishbane, in the annual and triennial cycles. The annual cycles, which seem to be the Babylonian practice, tend to have as their theme "the national future and restoration of the people to the Land of Israel." The triennial cycle, reflective of the community in *Eretz Yisra'el*, emphasizes messianic themes. What might have influenced these selections?

4. The Torah reading cycle is an interesting example of how different Jewish communities could maintain diverse ritual practices while staying unified. At some point, one community comes to dominate

and decide on a "norm" for all communities. Can you think of ways in which Jewish practice differs among various communities? Can you think of any examples in Jewish life today where practice is modified for all communities by the sphere of influence of one or another?

Study materials by *Jane Sherwin Shapiro*

The Challenge to Continue Study

ḤAZAK ḤAZAK V'NITḤAZZEK

Jeffrey H. Tigay

Summary

This essay is a fitting conclusion to the *Etz Hayim* original series of essays. Just as you are completing study and discussion on the subject of Torah study, so may you learn the Jewish ritual for completing study of the Torah itself. Just as Joshua needed reassurance from God *"hazzak v'amatz"* (Josh. 1: 6–7) when he assumed leadership of the Israelites and began entry into the Promised Land, so may you take strength from your studies with an eye toward continuing your investigations.

It is the custom in the synagogues of *Ashk'nazim* that when each book of the Torah is completed, the congregation rises and exclaims, *"Ḥazak ḥazak v'nitḥazzek!"* (Be strong, be strong, and let us summon up our strength!). The phrase is an expansion of the exhortation of King David's general Joab before battle, "Be strong and let us summon up our strength [*ḥazak v'nitḥazzak*] for the sake of our people and the towns of our God" (2 Sam. 10:12).

Recitation of this phrase on completing a book of the Torah reflects the transformation of an exhortation to physical, military prowess into a wish for spiritual strength. This custom is first clearly seen in 19th-century Germany, where the briefer form *"Ḥazak v'nitḥazzak!"* (vocalized exactly as in the Bible) was addressed to the person who had the final *aliyah* of each book. Earlier, congregations would simply exclaim, *"Ḥazak!"* (Be strong!). *S'fardim* also used to follow the latter custom; but nowadays they say, *"Ḥazak u-varukh!"* (Be strong and blessed!) to each person who returns to sit after having an *aliyah*, just as *Ashk'nazim* exclaim, *"Yishar koḥakha!"* (to a male) or *"Yishar koḥekh!"* (to a female)—that is, "May your strength be firm!" (Contrary to popular opinion, this exclamation does not mean "May your strength be straight!" *Yishar* is not derived from יָשָׁר "straight," but from שָׁרַר "strong.")

Originally, whether after each *aliyah* or on the completion of a book, the exclamation *"Ḥazak!"* was addressed to the person who had read the Torah. It meant essentially, "More power to you!" Various explanations have been suggested for the practice. Because reading the Torah is a form of learning, some interpret the exclamation as encouragement to persist in learning the Torah. Others understand it as encouraging and wishing strength for the Torah reader because serious learning of the Torah—including accurately preparing the public reading with all of its vocalization, punctuation, and cantillation—can be exhausting. The phrase *"v'nitḥazzak,"* "let us summon our strength" or "let us be strengthened," was subsequently added (on the basis of 2 Sam. 10:12) because the entire congregation had completed the book along with the reader and wished to include itself in these wishes.

Other uses of these exclamations are instructive. Authors of *piyyutim* (liturgical poems) sometimes wrote their names and the word *"ḥazak"* at the end of their poems, and some writers of *zmirot* (table songs) spelled out their names acrostically, followed by *"ḥazak."* Medieval scribes sometimes wrote *"ḥazak"* or *"ḥazak v'nitḥazzak"* at the end of manuscripts of books of the Bible and other Jewish texts. These poets and scribes intended the words as self-encouragement and self-blessing on the completion of a difficult and painstaking task. Scribes often shed light on the intended meaning by adding other phrases, such as: "Blessed is He who gives strength to the weary and renews the vigor of the exhausted" (based on Isa. 40:29), "Be strong and let us exert ourselves in Torah and commandments," "May God ... grant His servant strength to complete the entire Bible," and "We have been privileged to complete [this manuscript] in peace; may we be privileged to begin and complete [another] in peace." The last example is reminiscent of a custom once practiced in Italy when the Torah was completed on *Simḥat Torah:* The cantor and the congregation would say, *"Ḥazak!* We have been privileged to begin and complete [it again] in peace."

In light of the meanings that have been found in all of these practices, we may understand *"Ḥazak ḥazak v'nitḥazzek!"* as follows:

Ḥazak—More power to you, Torah reader, who has worked so hard to read the Torah accurately and pleasantly! *Ḥazak*—Congratulations to you, the person who has had the final *aliyah* of the book! *V'nitḥazzek*—May you and we (the entire congregation) persist, study, read, and complete all the other books, drawing strength from the Torah!

Study Questions

1. The original source of the expression *ḥazak ḥazak v'nitḥazzak* is found in a military context. What is it like to consider Torah study in some way as a battle? How have you wrestled or contended with these *Etz Hayim* essays?

2. The second half of the quotation from 2 Sam. 10:12, "For the sake of the people and the towns of our God," is also revealing. What is at stake in Torah study? How would you articulate the relationship between Torah study for the sake of the people and for the sake of God?

3. In what ways have your own studies (of this volume or Jewish study in general) enabled you to experience a stronger connection to God or to the Jewish people?

Study materials by *Jane Sherwin Shapiro*

BOOKS OF THE HEBREW BIBLE

TORAH: THE FIVE BOOKS OF MOSES

Genesis

Exodus

Leviticus

Numbers

Deuteronomy

NEVI'IM: THE PROPHETS

Joshua

Judges

1 Samuel

2 Samuel

1 Kings

2 Kings

Isaiah

Jeremiah

Ezekiel

Hosea

Joel

Amos

Obadiah

Jonah

Micah

Nahum

Habakkuk

Zephaniah

Haggai

Zechariah

Malachi

KETHUVIM: THE WRITINGS

Psalms

Proverbs

Job

The Song of Songs

Ruth

Lamentations

Ecclesiastes

Esther

Daniel

Ezra

Nehemiah

1 Chronicles

2 Chronicles

TIME LINE FOR THE HEBREW BIBLE

Please note that all dates are B.C.E.
and that those before the 9th century are only approximate.

18th to 14th centuries	Patriarchal Period
14th to 13th centuries	The Sojourn in Egypt
13th century	Exodus from Egypt
12th to 11th centuries	Settlement in the Promised Land
	The United Kingdom:
ca. 1020	Saul
ca. 1004	David
ca. 965	Solomon
954	First Temple Completed
928	The Kingdom Divided
722	Fall of Samaria
597	Capture of Jerusalem
586	Babylonian Exile (First Temple Destroyed)
538	Edict of Cyrus and Return to Land
515	Second Temple Completed
458(?), 398(?)	Ezra and Second Return
167	Desecration of Temple by Antiochus IV
164	Rededication of Temple

BLESSINGS FOR TORAH STUDY

Blessing Before Study

בָּרוּךְ אַתָּה יְיָ אֱלֹהֵינוּ מֶלֶךְ הָעוֹלָם, אֲשֶׁר קִדְּשָׁנוּ בְּמִצְוֹתָיו, וְצִוָּנוּ לַעֲסוֹק בְּדִבְרֵי תוֹרָה.

וְהַעֲרֶב נָא יְיָ אֱלֹהֵינוּ אֶת דִּבְרֵי תוֹרָתְךָ בְּפִינוּ וּבְפִי עַמְּךָ בֵּית יִשְׂרָאֵל, וְנִהְיֶה אֲנַחְנוּ וְצֶאֱצָאֵינוּ וְצֶאֱצָאֵי עַמְּךָ בֵּית יִשְׂרָאֵל כֻּלָּנוּ יוֹדְעֵי שְׁמֶךָ וְלוֹמְדֵי תוֹרָתֶךָ לִשְׁמָהּ. בָּרוּךְ אַתָּה יְיָ, הַמְלַמֵּד תּוֹרָה לְעַמּוֹ יִשְׂרָאֵל.

Praised are You, Adonai our God, who rules the universe,
instilling in us the holiness of mitzvot
by commanding us to study words of Torah.

May the words of Torah, Adonai our God, be sweet in our mouths and in the mouths of all Your people, so that we, our children, and all the children of the House of Israel may come to love You and to study Your Torah for its own sake. Praised are You, Adonai, who teaches Torah to His people, Israel.

(Adapted from *Siddur Sim Shalom for Shabbat and Festivals*)

Meditation After Study

Before reciting this meditation, take a moment to consider new ideas you have encountered through your study. What has brought you closer to the text? To Judaism? To God? What still challenges you?

Thank you, Adonai, for the gift of Your Torah, for its mysteries and its inspiration. May the knowledge we have gained, and the ideas we have shared, bring meaning and holiness to our lives. May we be privileged to continue to study your Torah, to grow in knowledge, and to have the opportunity to carry out Your teachings.

בָּרוּךְ אַתָּה, הַמְלַמֵּד תּוֹרָה לְעַמּוֹ יִשְׂרָאֵל.

Praised are You, who teaches Torah to His people, Israel.

CONTRIBUTORS

HOWARD AVRUHM ADDISION, Assistant Professor, Intellectual Heritage Program, Temple University, Philadelphia, Pennsylvania.

HANAN A. ALEXANDER, Head of Center for Jewish Education and Professor of Education, University of Haifa, Haifa, Israel.

BEN ZION BERGMAN, Sonny and Isadore Familian Emeritus Professor of Rabbinic Literature, University of Judaism, Los Angeles, California.

JACOB BLUMENTHAL, Founding Rabbi of Congregation Shaare Torah, Gaithersburg, Maryland.

MARTIN S. COHEN, Rabbi of the Shelter Rock Jewish Center, Roslyn, New York.

ELLIOT N. DORFF, Rector and Sol and Anne Dorff Distinguished Service Professor in Philosophy, University of Judaism, Los Angeles, California.

SHELDON DORPH, Consultant for educational and religious planning and curriculum; past Director of National Ramah.

MICHAEL FISHBANE, Nathan Cummings Professor of Jewish Studies, University of Chicago, Chicago, Illinois.

GORDON FREEMAN, Rabbi of Congregation B'nai Shalom, Walnut Creek, California.

BARUCH FRYDMAN-KOHL, Anne and Max Tanenbaum Senior Rabbi of Beth Tzedec Congregation, Toronto, Ontario; Senior Rabbinic Fellow of the Shalom Hartman Institute, Jerusalem, Israel.

STEPHEN P. GARFINKEL, Assistant Professor of Bible, Dean of Graduate School, and Dean of Academic Affairs, Jewish Theological Seminary, New York, New York.

NEIL GILLMAN, Aaron Rabinowitz and Simon H. Rifkin Professor of Jewish Philosophy, Jewish Theological Seminary, New York, New York.

DANIEL GORDIS, Vice President, Mandel Foundation-Israel; Director, Mandel Leadership Institute, Jerusalem, Israel.

DAVID M. GORDIS, President and Professor of Rabbinics, Hebrew College, Brookline, Massachusetts; Director of Wilstein Institute of Jewish Policy Studies, Brookline, Massachusetts.

MICHAEL GRAETZ, Rabbi of Congregation Magen Avraham, Omer, Israel; Spiritual Director of Mercaz Shiluv Educational Institute in the Negev, Israel.

EDWARD L. GREENSTEIN, Past Professor of Bible, Jewish Theological Seminary, New York; Chair of Biblical Studies, Tel Aviv University, Tel Aviv, Israel.

REUVEN HAMMER, Former President of the Rabbinical Assembly and Head of the Rabbinical Court of the Masorti Movement.

JUDITH HAUPTMAN, Philip R. Alstat Professor of Talmud, Jewish Theological Seminary, New York, New York.

STUART KELMAN, Trained *Sofer*; Rabbi of Congregation Netivot Shalom, Berkley, California.

SHOSHANA JEDWAB, Middle School Jewish Studies coordinator, Abraham Joshua Heschel School, New York, New York.

DOV LEREA, Dean of Judaic Studies, Abraham Joshua Heschel School, New York, New York.

BARUCH A. LEVINE, Skirball Emeritus Professor of Bible and Ancient Near Eastern Studies, New York University, New York, New York.

LEE I. LEVINE, Professor of Jewish History and Rev. Moses Bernard Lauterman Family Chair Professor in Classical Archaeology, Hebrew University, Jerusalem, Israel; Past President, Seminary of Judaic Studies (Schechter Institute of Jewish Studies), Jerusalem, Israel.

DAVID L. LIEBER, President Emeritus and Flora and Arnold Skovron Distinguished Service Professor of Biblical Literature and Thought, University of Judaism, Los Angeles, California.

HARVEY MEIROVICH, Dean, Schechter Rabbinical Assembly, Jerusalem, Israel.

JACOB MILGROM, Professor Emeritus of Biblical Studies, University of California at Berkeley, Berkeley, California.

LIONEL MOSES, Rabbi of Shaare Zion Congregation, Montreal, Quebec.

DEBRA R. ORENSTEIN, Rabbi of Congregation Makor Ohr Shalom, Westwood and Tarzana, California.

SHALOM M. PAUL, Past Professor of Bible, Jewish Theological Seminary, New York, New York; Professor Emeritus of Bible and Past Chair of Bible, Hebrew University, Jerusalem, Israel.

JACOB PINNOLIS, Judaics educator, Solomon Schechter High School, New York, New York.

JOSEPH H. PROUSER, Rabbi of Little Neck Jewish Center, Little Neck, New York.

JOEL REMBAUM, Senior Rabbi of Temple Beth Am, Los Angeles, California.

GILBERT S. ROSENTHAL, Director of the National Council of Synagogues.

JOEL ROTH, Louis Finkelstein Professor of Talmud and Jewish Law, Jewish Theological Seminary, New York, New York; Rosh Yeshiva of the Conservative Yeshiva, Jerusalem, Israel.

NAHUM M. SARNA, Gimelstob Eminent Scholar and Emeritus Professor of Judaica, Florida Atlantic University, Boca Raton, Florida; Dora Golding Emeritus Professor of Biblical Studies, Brandeis University, Waltham, Massachusetts.

BENJAMIN EDIDIN SCOLNIC, Rabbi of Temple Beth Shalom, Hamden, Connecticut; Past Instructor of Bible, Jewish Theological Seminary, New York, New York, and Yale University, New Haven, Connecticut.

BENJAMIN J. SEGAL, President of Melitz, the Centers for Jewish Zionist Education, and Past President, Schechter Institute of Jewish Studies, Jerusalem, Israel.

DANIEL YECHIEL SEPTIMUS, Assistant Director of The Skirball Center for Adult Jewish Learning, Temple Emanu-El, New York, New York.

JANE SHERWIN SHAPIRO, Adult Jewish education specialist and faculty member, Florence Melton Adult Mini-School, Chicago, Illinois.

JEFFREY H. TIGAY, Ellis Professor of Hebrew and Semitic Languages and Literatures, University of Pennsylvania, Philadelphia, Pennsylvania.

GORDON TUCKER, Rabbi of Temple Israel Center, White Plains, New York; Adjunct Assistant Professor of Jewish Philosophy, Jewish Theological Seminary, New York, New York.

ROBERT WEXLER, President and Irma and Lou Colen Distinguished Lecturer in Bible, University of Judaism, Los Angeles, California.

DAVID WOLPE, Senior Rabbi of Sinai Temple, Los Angeles, California.